Business Marketing Face to Face

The Theory and Practice of B2B Marketing

Chris Fill & Scot McKee

 (G) blishers Ltd

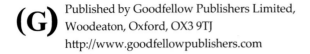 Published by Goodfellow Publishers Limited,
Woodeaton, Oxford, OX3 9TJ
http://www.goodfellowpublishers.com

British Library Cataloguing in Publication Data: a catalogue record for this title is available from the British Library.

Library of Congress Catalog Card Number: on file.

ISBN: 978-1-906884-55-0

 Design and typesetting by P.K. McBride, www.macbride.org.uk

Printed by Marston Book Services, www.marston.co.uk

Cover design by Cylinder, www.cylindermedia.com

Photographs by Chris Knox

Contents

Acknowledgements   x

1   An Introduction to Business Marketing   1
A Slice of Life – Bare Essentials   2
The Characteristics of Business Markets   6
Types of Organisational Customers   9
Types of Business Goods and Services   16
The Characteristics of B2B Marketing   18
B2B Marketing Mix   18
Introducing Perceived Value   21
The Importance of B2B Relationships   25

2   Business Products and Services   31
A Slice of Life – The Battle between Products and Services   32
Product Characteristics   34
Business Product Strategy   36
Business services   38
Service Processes   41
The Product–Service Spectrum   43
Product Life Cycle   44
Technological Applications and the PLC   46
Strategic Implications Arising from the PLC   47
New Product Development (NPD)   47
New Service Development   52
Stages of Product/Service Innovation Development   53
The Technology Adoption Life Cycle   54

3   Organisational Buying Behaviour   60
A Slice of Life – Consulting with Consultancies   61
Comparing Organisational and Consumer Buyer Behaviour   64
Decision Making Units – Characteristics   66
The Decision Making Process   68
Influences Shaping Organisational Buying Behaviour   75
Uncertainty, Risk and Relationships in OBB   80
eProcurement   83

4   Relationship Marketing   88
A Slice of Life – The Devil You Know   89
Business Relationships – Background   93
Relationship Marketing – Theoretical Foundations   98

The Customer Relationship Life Cycle	101
Differing Types of Relationships	104
Partnerships and Alliances	106
Trust, Commitment and Customer Satisfaction	108

5 Strategy: Segmentation, Positioning and Pricing **117**
A Slice of Life – A Little Ray of Sunshine	118
Segmentation	120
Bases for Segmenting Business Markets	125
Target Market Selection	130
Barriers to Segmentation	133
Positioning	135
Pricing	139
Leasing	143

6 Marketing Channels **149**
A Slice of Life – User Journeys	150
Function and Purpose of Marketing Channels	154
Service Outputs	159
Channel Flows	160
Types of Distribution Channel	162
Channel Roles and Membership	167

7 Supply Chains, Channel Structures and Networks **178**
A Slice of Life – The Chain of Events	179
Supply Chains	182
Key elements in Supply Chain Management	183
Principles of Supply Chain Management	188
Marketing Channel Design	190
Channel Configuration	191
Channel Structure	193
A Spectrum of Influence in Channel Structures	193
Networks	198
Electronic Channels	202

8 Managing B2B Relationships **208**
A Slice of Life – Believing in the Relationship	209
The Concept of Power	211
Channel Conflict	215
The Nature of Conflict	216
Reasons for Conflict	218
Managing Interorganisational Conflict	221
Building Relationships	226

The Impact of Technology on Business Relationships 228
eCommerce and Conflict 229
Customer Relationship Management Systems 231

9 Principles of Business Marketing Communications 238
A Slice of Life – Evolution or Revolution? 239
Defining Marketing Communications 242
The Role of Marketing Communications 243
The Tasks of Marketing Communication 246
Strategy and Planning MCs 248
Is it about Campaigns or Activities? 251
B2B Branding 252
Integrated Marketing Communications 256
Channel-based Marketing Communications 261
Relationship Marketing and Communications 265

10 The Business Marketing Communications Mix 272
A Slice of Life – The Importance of Pants 273
Advertising and B2B communications 276
Trade Promotions and B2B communications 277
Public Relations and B2B communications 279
Direct Marketing and B2B Communications 281
Personal Selling and B2B Communications 283
Business-to-Business Media 285
Digital Media and B2B Marketing Communications 287
Content or Messages 293
User-Generated Content 296
Demand Generation 297

11 Personal Selling and Key Account Management 302
A Slice of Life – The Origin of Business 303
The Role and Tasks of Personal Selling 306
Characteristics of Personal Selling 308
Personal Selling and the Communication Mix 309
Personal Selling and Managing Relationships 313
Multichannel Selling 315
Key Account Management 319

Index 329

Preface

■ Overview

Business Marketing is an academic textbook written from a marketing management perspective. It is about the marketing methods, issues and principles associated with the relationships and interactions between organisations. However, unlike most other textbooks this one is injected with a marketing practitioner's view on business-to-business marketing matters.

■ The nature and theme of the book

The once predictable world of business marketing is changing. It is now a complex and challenging environment populated by an increasing number of channels, fast developing technology, the expectation that everything and everyone is accountable, and characterised by changing buyer behaviours and an emphasis on conversations and connectedness.

Despite these complexities and challenges, at the root of business marketing remains the need to find, develop and maintain relationships. Accordingly, this book is anchored to two main principles, namely, generating demand and building fruitful marketing-based relationships.

To drive demand, establish relationships that are of mutual value, and to weave a route through the various complexities, it is important to understand the nature and changing perspectives of B2B buyers. From this knowledge, organisations are better placed to create more buyer-centric demand generation strategies. This book is underpinned and shaped by these ideas. Demand generation issues are recognised throughout the book and a chapter is dedicated to understanding relationship marketing principles.

This is an applied book, in the sense that the theory and concepts of business marketing are interpreted in the light of business practice. This is an important structural feature of the book with each chapter containing a number of brief examples of business practice that demonstrate marketing theory in action. Each contains a question, designed to encourage readers to consider the issues at hand. A range of organisations are used to illustrate practice, from the large multinational blue chip organisations to small and medium-sized companies with relatively scarce resources, and from the commercial and private companies to the not-for-profit and public sector organisations.

Each chapter opens with a 'Slice of Life.' These are commentaries written by Scot McKee, recalling his experiences of customers, events and issues over the last 20 years when running his own B2B marketing agency, *Birddog*. Sometimes serious, sometimes humorous, sometimes reflective, his contributions are always insightful, and they add perspective, vitality and realism.

■ Target market

A high proportion of graduates enter organisations which operate within the B2B sector. This book is intended to help students and lecturers explore this aspect of marketing and to provide an important counterbalance to the mainly North American consumerist perspective adopted by the majority of marketing educators, their courses and the available resources.

In particular, this book is aimed at both final year undergraduate and post-graduate students. Final year undergraduates will find the book useful if study-ing Marketing, Business Studies, Business Information Systems, eCommerce and degree programmes with business-related units such as those increasingly found in Engineering and Social Studies-based programmes. In my experience postgraduate students studying on programmes such as Marketing, Marketing with eCommerce, Media and Multimedia Marketing, eBusiness and MBA programmes in particular, find this material interesting, helpful and a useful counterbalance to the mainstream consumer orientation that is often present on these types of programme.

Students following the Chartered Institute of Marketing's Professional Diploma will also benefit from this textbook. There are a number of stand-alone professional B2B marketing programmes that will find the book supportive. In addition to students, many of those working in the business marketing sector are encouraged to read this book.

■ Book structure and organisation

This book consists of 11 chapters and is designed to support a taught unit or module, delivered over a term or a semester. This structure enables tutors to deliver in sequence particular chapter topics in class. They can also set any neces-sary further reading and exercises, such as coursework assessments or independ-ent learning vehicles, based on material from across the book.

The book is intended to be a single primary source for tutors, although other resources, for example, newspapers, websites, journal papers and edited readers, will be required to supplement and enhance student learning. Each chapter has a complete set of aims and learning objectives, examples, discussion questions, and navigation aids. Each chapter opens with a overview and closes with a sum-mary based on each of the learning objectives. This is designed to help readers develop their understanding in a structured and logical manner. There is a full set of references at the end of each chapter.

Chapter 1 introduces the fundamental characteristics of B2B markets and considers the nature, size and dynamics of the sector. Reference to the consumer market is made to highlight both the differences and similarities between the two fields and approaches. The main objective of this chapter is to set out the essential characteristics and importance of business marketing, the pivotal aspects of value creation and interorganisational relationships. This enables readers unfamiliar with the B2B sector to become conversant with topics that are developed and explored in subsequent chapters.

Chapter 2 considers the various issues associated with managing products and services in business markets. It is important to understand how business products can be classified and to appreciate the characteristics associated with both the new product and service development processes. Attention is given to the product life cycle before concluding with a consideration of the technology adoption life cycle, appropriate in high technology markets.

Chapter 3 focuses on organisational buyer behaviour and the various issues concerning the way organisations determine which products and services to buy. Attention is given to some of the classic ideas and frameworks about decision making units, processes and the influences that shape decision making. The chapter closes with a brief consideration of eProcurement.

Chapter 4 is about relationship marketing, a pivotal topic in this book. Readers can explore its evolution and examine the conceptual underpinning associated with relationship marketing practices. The chapter examines the customer relationship life cycle and finishes by looking at trust and commitment.

Chapter 5 considers some of the elements that have strategic significance in business marketing: segmentation, positioning and pricing. The opening part of considers issues concerning different approaches to segmenting B2B markets. It develops conventional approaches and explores the implementation and practicalities of B2B segmentation. It then discusses ways in which organisations can use different positioning, once segments and target markets are agreed. The chapter concludes with a consideration of pricing issues in business markets.

Chapter 6 seeks to develop an understanding of the principles and core concepts associated with marketing channels. In particular, consideration is given to their purpose, basic structure and key intermediaries, their characteristics and contribution to the way in which channels work. These include service output theory and channel flows.

Chapter 7 builds on the previous chapter and explores two main elements. The first concerns the management of the logistical and physical flow of goods from producers to end user customers. This is referred to as 'supply chain management'. The second element concerns the management of the marketing channels. These are structural configurations organisations use to add value and which enable end users to access finished goods (and services) in the most convenient way. Attention is given to conventional marketing channel structures, vertical marketing systems, and network approaches to interorganisational channel structures. The chapter closes with some ideas concerning the use of electronic channels in B2B trading contexts.

Chapter 8 considers some of the managerial issues, processes and systems associated with maintaining and developing collaborative business relationships. First, the nature, dispersion and use of power in relationships is examined, then time is spent looking at channel conflict and ways in which it can be minimised, recognising that some conflict can be constructive. A foundation of most successful B2B relationships is the presence of trust and commitment. These concepts are examined before the chapter concludes with a brief overview of the role of technology in managing relationships with a focus on CRM systems.

Chapter 9 examines some of the roles and strategic issues associated with business marketing communications. Their core characteristics and roles are examined before considering the key strategies that can be pursued by organisations. Ideas concerning B2B branding and integrated marketing communications are also explored before examining marketing channel-based communications. The chapter concludes with an examination of relationship-based marketing communication, and in particular, client/agency based relationships.

Chapter 10 introduces the marketing communications mix and its three constituent elements; tools, media and messages. Consideration is given first to the key characteristics and effectiveness of each of the primary tools. The chapter then examines each of the main media from a communication perspective, and includes ideas about the use of social media. It considers the type of messages used to reach business audiences, including user generated content. This leads to the closing section which introduces ideas about demand generation.

In **Chapter 11** consideration is given to the role and characteristics of personal selling. The main thrust is centred on the impact of personal selling on interorganisational relationships and how the other communication tools can be blended to provide cost and communication effectiveness. In addition, issues concerning the management and organisation of the sales force are explored before concluding with an examination of key account management.

■ Teaching support and learning resources

This book is supported by a range of teaching and learning resources. An instructor's manual is available for those who decide to adopt the text. This contains PowerPoint overheads of figures and diagrams from the book, plus teaching notes together with ideas for assessment and in-class study.

A website designed to support the book is available at .... for both tutors and students. It has instructor teaching-support facilities, including all the materials outlined above, as well as other cases studies, examples and a range of hyperlinks to sites of interest and value to help students develop their knowledge and understanding of this exciting and important subject.

Chris Fill
Author
chris@fillassociates.co.uk
www.fillassociates.co.uk
uk.linkedin.com/in/chrisfill

Scot McKee
Author – *Creative B2B Branding (no, really)*
scotmckee@gmail.com
www.scotmckee.com
uk.linkedin.com/in/scotmckee
www.twitter.com/scotmckee

■ Acknowledgements

This book would not have been possible without the contributions of a large number of researchers, academics, authors and practitioners whose work has advanced our understanding of business marketing. Some of their ideas have been incorporated in this book and hopefully fully referenced and acknowledged and to them all I offer my thanks.

I would also like to say a special thank you to Scot McKee for the richness and flavour that his original contribution brings to the book. I would like to thank the editorial team at Goodfellow Publishers, and in particular Tim Goodfellow, P.K. McBride and Catherine McGregor, who between them have supported and steered the production of this book.

In addition it is important to acknowledge the photographic skills of Chris Knox, especially when you consider the nature of the two subjects with whom he was dealing. As always, Graham Hughes provided some extremely valuable insights and Peter Williams who provided clarity and wisdom.

I should also like to acknowledge Karen Fill, who contributed much to an earlier version of this book, and provided support while this edition was configured.

And now for a 'Slice of Life' from Scot McKee

If I've learnt anything in the last 25 years as a business to business (B2B) marketing professional, it is to 'assume nothing'. I still use that mantra as one of the single most useful pieces of advice I can offer new employees – assume nothing. It has been, and will doubtless continue to be, almost impossible to predict the market. It's even harder to predict the responses of the individuals within the market. We are all individuals with our own personalities, our own characteristics and our own set of values. Our individual make-up guides and often determines how we will act and respond. That being the case, there should be an infinite capacity for change, for experimentation – for creativity within B2B marketing. Unfortunately not.

The B2B market has its own characteristics that suppress the predictive responses of the individual in favour of the greater corporate good. We don't make decisions as individuals within business, we make business decisions for the business. It's different. We are accountable to the business for our decisions, we require finance and support from the business and we have to wait while the business undertakes elaborate decision making processes before being allowed to progress. Individual creativity, particularly within a B2B marketing context, is more often than not replaced by the mitigation of corporate risk. Protecting the company, the team even the product becomes more important than taking a chance in the market. And then there's personal protection. The job, the career, the promotion, the next holiday, the wife, the kids… they all influence how we make business decisions within a corporate environment, and they all make predictability of the outcomes almost impossible.

Within this variable landscape, as B2B marketing professionals, we are expected to build brands – corporate brands, product brands, service brands, even personal brands. Mmmm… well, ok, yes, we can do that, but it's unlikely ever to take the path that you might predict or expect from the outset. You will be told the project is 'urgent' but the decision to proceed is delayed for months. You will be told that the product is 'unique' when the market is saturated with similar competitive offerings. You will be expected to take instruction from people who have no understanding or experience of marketing and you will be seen as a 'cost' instead of a source of revenue… The challenges of delivery within this environment are significant. It's therefore important, if not critical, that you arm yourself with as deep an understanding of the processes and practicalities of the B2B marketing space as possible.

My role within this book is to provide the latter in order to offer context and relevance to the former. If we are to truly learn from and appreciate the value of the theory that forms the body of this work, we should do so with one eye on the real world. How better can we understand the businesses in which we hope to apply our theory? How can we learn to adopt and adapt the theory to suit the challenges that lurk just around the corner? Well, perhaps we can learn from experiences gained not in the textbook or classroom, but at the coalface. At the very least we can review some practical, real life examples and seek improvements and solutions for the future based on our deeper understanding of the text.

My role then, is to bare my soul from the school of hard knocks. I'll be doing it in small stages admittedly, and mainly with my clothes on, but don't let that put you off. I will draw on my experience of the last 25 years delivering against the kind of challenges that you will face for the next 25 years. At the start of each chapter to this book, you will find my anecdotal insights from specific client engagements that I have worked on. The client names have been removed to protect the guilty (mainly me...) but rest assured the stories are true to the very best of my recollection. And they're not always pretty. That's the thing about real life – sometimes, despite your best efforts, real life just sucks.

The 'Slice of Life' sections that preface each chapter are therefore intended as practical interludes to the chapter content. Treat them as stepping stones for learning and for discussion, or just as a pause for thought – how would you have handled the situations differently? How might the theory have been applied to the cases thereby improving some of the outcomes?

I wish you well with your studies and learning, and, most of all, I wish I had read this book 25 years ago...

Scot McKee

1 An Introduction to Business Marketing

Overview

This chapter explores some of the principal characteristics used to define business markets and marketing. It establishes the key elements of business-to-business (B2B) marketing and makes comparisons with the better-known business-to-consumer (B2C) sector. This leads to a consideration of appropriate definitions, parameters and direction for the book.

After setting out the main types of organisations that operate in the B2B sector and categorising the goods and services that they buy or sell, the chapter introduces ideas about the business marketing mix, perceived value, supply chains, interorganisational relationships and relationship marketing.

This opening chapter lays down the vital foundations and key principles which are subsequently developed in the book.

Aims and objectives

The aim of this chapter is to introduce and explore the characteristics and dimensions of business-to-business marketing.

The objectives of this chapter are to enable readers to:

1   Consider the nature, scope and characteristics of business markets.

2   Identify the different types of organisational customers

3   Categorise the goods and services that are sold and bought in the sector.

4   Explore the characteristics of B2B marketing.

5   Describe the perceived value and supply chain concepts.

6   Explain the importance of relationships in B2B marketing.

A Slice of Life – Bare Essentials

Finance companies lend money to businesses. This particular company lent money to small businesses and large corporates and every business in-between. Sometimes the money was lent directly to the business, but the primary lending channel was via an intermediary – a broker or financial advisor. So the market was broad and the channels were multiple. In every single case, the company was competing with larger, more visible high street banks. If your business needed to borrow money, you would likely make the initial decision of which lender to use based on the answer to the question: 'what's the interest rate?' Why would you pay more than you had to for your borrowing? But my client couldn't compete against the banks based on price alone – it would lose – so when the company approached me to assist with their channel marketing programme, I advised them that they had no choice but to compete on personality, in other words, using the company brand.

Unfortunately, there was no compelling reason to select this particular company and no indication that the customer experience would be anything other than… ordinary.

So the objective was to get noticed. To make the brand stand out from the crowd, to develop awareness and differentiation thereby creating the alternative to high street lenders for internal and external channels. The brand existed, but it was time to reposition it and reintroduce it to three very distinct audience types:

➤ Introducers – professional finance advisors (predominantly accountants and brokers) providing independent business advice and solutions to support the cashflow and financial stability of clients.

➤ Clients and prospects – Over 600 clients predominantly within the SME category. Growth companies were the preferred targets and managing directors/financial directors and owners/managers were the targeted audiences.

➤ Internal staff – C level, managers, and staff – the people who lived, breathed and needed to feel proud and engaged with the brand every day.

Through a combination of discussion, research and workshops, we refined the proposition. Those seeking finance would always have the option of the high street lenders, but, there were many prospective clients who would not readily embrace the one size fits all generic approach of the banks. Those potential clients had to be told that there was an alternative. They had the choice of the banks, or something different.

To achieve the agreed objective of 'get noticed', communications featuring images of corporate handshakes and pinstriped suits were clearly not going to cut much ice. It was therefore agreed that creative development would be built around the message that 'Not all finance companies are the same'. For the communications to be effective however, it was the channel – the financial advisors and brokers who would recommend the company's services – that the brand really had to reach.

It turned out that the accountants who everyone assumed were dull and grey and boring maintained a much higher opinion of themselves. A little research revealed tales of wild celebrations, late night parties and general breaking-free of the 'corporate suit' label. They actively objected to the stereotype their industry had been given and confirmed that they would respond more favourably to communications that better reflected their 'true' personalities. To date, this had meant communications from banks featuring suited professional advisors shaking hands with business customers. Well, that was about to change…

The creative work I presented to the board featured a night-time image of a man at a party, looking slightly the worse for wear and stark bollock naked – apart from a tie covering his core assets. Next to the image was the word 'Exposed?' The supporting message explained that, 'Not all finance companies are the same'.

'That, gentlemen, is how you engage the channel,' I said. As you might imagine, it was very quiet in the boardroom that day. I was about to pack my bags and leave when the managing director started laughing. Then they were all laughing.

In the following year, that single campaign doubled the number of referrals made to the company by its channel. It reactivated more than half of the inactive brokers within the channel network. It attracted more new channel partners than had ever been achieved in a single year. And it generated a few million pounds of revenue.

Having established the communication strategy for the brand and assisted in delivering almost every conceivable tactical campaign material online and offline, I encouraged the company not to overlook one of its most important channels of business – its own staff. Internal communications are often overlooked by marketing departments under pressure to deliver external ROI. The reality however, is that without the understanding and support from internal staff, external communications can never achieve their full potential. This was particularly true because the company was perfectly positioned to secure business from staff referrals. Almost every member of staff would meet prospective clients in and out of working hours who they could influence – if only they knew what to say (and were incentivised to do so…). The launch of the internal marketing scheme placed a formal structure around an existing policy of encouraging and rewarding prospect referrals from staff. Style and tone of communications to the internal audience were similar to the external communications in order to both keep the process of referral uppermost in staff minds and to strengthen the links between the internal team and the external advisor channel. The initial success led to the extension of the scheme to include combined sources of referral – an extended introducer channel, brokers and other partners now successfully participate in the referral process secure in the knowledge that their efforts will not go unrewarded.

I have been working with the brand for over 10 years now. Our work together has spanned all online and offline communication channels to deliver award-winning, market beating performance. The Creative Platform® on which the brand message has been built has evolved almost annually from initial awareness generation to consistent, reliable communications as the alternative provider of business finance – still under the single focused concept of 'Not all finance companies are the same'. My relationship with the company has transcended three changes of marketing director, three changes of marketing manager and two corporate acquisitions. The one constant throughout has been the growing ability of the brand to drive revenue for the business.

Scot McKee

■ Introduction

The market for goods and services bought and sold between businesses is huge. Far larger than the consumer market, the business market comprises many types and sizes of organisations that interact selectively and form relationships of varying significance and duration with one another. Although these organisations are often structurally and legally independent entities, a key characteristic is that they are also interdependent. That is, they have to work with other organisations to varying degrees in order to achieve their goals.

Imagine the complicated, multi-player chain of buying and selling for all the component parts that Airbus Industries needs in order to build an aeroplane. The operational complexity is enormous and the value of the total materials, components, labour and energy involved far exceeds consumer spending in either the confectionery or clothing markets. Regardless of whether they sell their products and services to consumers or to other organisations, all businesses buy and sell items in order to create their own offerings. In recognition of their added value, other businesses may then buy these products to use, to create other products or to sell as finished items to consumers.

ViewPoint 1.1: Enormity, complexity and the Olympics

When it was announced that London had won the bid to host the summer Olympic Games in 2012, a huge wave of excitement was released. For individuals in London, the UK and internationally this represented a significant spectator event. For many businesses there were many opportunities resulting from the many infrastructure and other business projects. Not least of these was the building of stadia where the various activities would take place.

The Olympic Delivery Authority was the body set up to manage such projects including the construction of the focal point athletics stadium. Work commenced on the site in the east end of London in May 2008, some four years in advance of the start of the Games.

Initial clearing of the site involved the removal of 800,000 tonnes of soil to be used elsewhere in the Olympic site area. 6,500 cubic metres were recycled from other site areas to create a platform to support construction works. At the height of construction works around 1000 staff were based on-site including engineers, architects and general construction workers.

A consortium of businesses was responsible for the main elements of the overall project.

- Sir Robert McApline Ltd were the main Construction Contractor
- HOK Sport Ltd were the Architect and Sports Venue Designer
- Buro Happold Ltd were the Structural and Building Services Engineers
- HED were the Landscape Architects and
- Savills Hepher Dixon the Planning Consultants.

The overall cost of the stadium construction was a little under £500 million. It was completed ahead of target date, and on budget.

Source: www. London2012.com; www.e-architect.com (accessed 23/02/2011)

Question: What might be the marketing implications for the businesses involved in such complex projects?

B2B marketing is fundamentally different from consumer goods or services marketing because buyers do not consume the products or services themselves. Unlike consumer markets, where goods and services are consumed personally by the people who buy them, the essence of business markets is that individual organisations undertake the act of consumption. This text is developed around this important principle which has critical implications for the marketing strategies and associated programmes that are used to satisfy organisational buyers.

Before looking at the characteristics of business markets and B2B marketing, it is important to note that, although there are several vital differences to consumer marketing, organisations which have a market orientation, regardless of the sector in which they operate, share at least two key similarities:

1 Both have a customer orientation and work backwards from an understanding of customer needs.

2 Both need the ability to gather, process, and use information about customers and competitors in order to achieve their objectives.

This market orientation is an essential foundation upon which to begin exploring the exciting and dynamic world of business markets and the contribution of B2B marketing.

This chapter introduces various fundamental aspects of B2B marketing. It is designed to provide an overview and to set out the parameters for exploring the subject. It is not intended to provide an in-depth analysis or understanding, but to outline issues and concepts that are covered in detail in later chapters.

■ The Characteristics of Business Markets

Business markets are characterised by a number of factors, the main ones being the nature of demand, the buying processes, international dimensions and, perhaps most importantly, the relationships that develop between organisations in the process of buying and selling. These are now considered from an introductory point of view.

■ The nature of demand

One of the key factors is the nature of demand in business markets. Three aspects of demand are considered: derivation, variance and elasticity.

- **Demand is derived** in business markets. It is derived from consumers (Gummesson and Polese, 2009). With respect to the Airbus example, consumers (and business travellers) determine, through the number of flights they make and what they are prepared to pay, the number of aircraft that airlines make available. However, each aircraft is the product of hundreds of organisations interacting with one another. Air passengers stimulate demand.

- **Demand is variable** in business markets. Simply because it is derived, fluctuations develop according to changes in consumer preferences and behaviour. This means that organisations should monitor and anticipate demand as cycles emerge. Note the decline in the demand for air travel following the events of 9/11 and the subsequent impact on airlines, support services, aircraft manufacturers and the whole array of suppliers and subcontractors in the commercial aviation market.

- **Demand has limited elasticity** in business markets. Once a manufacturer has incorporated a differentiated product into its processes, unforeseen and uncontrollable supplier price increases have to be absorbed until a revised or redesigned product can be developed, eliminating the original materials or part. On the basis that manufacturers are generally reluctant to let their customers down by a delayed or failed delivery while searching for new suppliers, these price increases have to be incorporated, at least over the short to medium term, hence the inelasticity or low price sensitivity.

It should not be a surprise therefore to understand that demand generation is a key activity within business marketing. This topic is explored further in Chapter 10.

Buying processes

Another major aspect of B2B marketing concerns the buying processes used to purchase goods and services. In consumer markets, decisions are made relatively quickly, the level of risk is low, at least for everyday items, and the focus is primarily on the emotional aspects attaching to a purchase.

In B2B markets the potential risk is often quite large so decisions take much longer and involve considerably more people. Consequently, the nature and form of interaction between organisations is based on an understanding of individual business customers' needs and a willingness to provide and share information.

In consumer markets, purchases are generally made, and often consumed, individually. Purchasing in B2B markets is essentially a group activity, with the composition and size of the group changing according to the significance of the item being purchased. The group is referred to as the decision making unit (DMU) or buying centre. Consumption, or product usage, is an organisational activity. However, the basis on which each member of the unit makes their decision can vary considerably. For example, the decision making unit for an engineering company considering the purchase of solar energy may consist of the following, all of whom will have different criteria when selecting suitable suppliers.

- Senior management — Reduce costs, use and be seen using latest technology
- Financial director — Achieve best value solution and financial propriety
- Purchasing manager — Get value for money, increase own credibility and colleague satisfaction
- Plant engineer — Use modern equipment and provide cover for power breakdown
- Production manager — Reduce operating costs and improve reliability
- Consultants — Improve plant efficiency, improve staff working conditions

■ International aspects

Increasingly B2B organisations are engaging in international markets. Advances in technology, most notably the Internet, have enabled organisations to do business more or less anywhere. In comparison to consumer markets, international business is easier. In B2C markets there are a wide range of issues concerning the culture and values that consumers hold, and how products and promotional activities need to be adapted to accommodate colour, ingredient, style, buying processes, packaging and language requirements to ensure success. By contrast, B2B organisations benefit from a lower diversity in product functionality and performance. This is partly because of the inherent nature of the products and materials but also due to various trading associations across the world agreeing standards relating to content and performance. For example, the steel, plastic, chemicals and paper industries all have common agreed standards which facilitate the interorganisational exchange process. Thus, B2B organisations are able to work together to help shape their trading environment.

■ Relationships

A fundamentally key characteristic of business marketing concerns the significance of relationships. In B2C markets, relationships between manufacturer and consumer, or reseller and consumer have been regarded, at least in the past, as relatively weak and unimportant. Although many organisations have now recognised the importance of developing these relationships, the nature of the products, their perceived value to consumers, and competitive factors, particularly in the fast-moving consumer goods (FMCG) markets, suggests that such relationships will remain difficult and costly to establish and maintain.

In B2B markets, by contrast, the development and maintenance of positive relationships between buying and selling organisations is pivotal to success. Collaboration and partnership over the development, supply and support of products and services is considered a core element of B2B marketing. Indeed, Morgan and Hunt (1994) recognise this when they refer to relationship marketing and the importance of marketing activities that seek to establish, develop and maintain successful exchanges with customers. Unlike consumer markets, where relationships are often considered to revolve around an active seller and a passive buyer, understanding of relationships in B2B markets now encompasses networks of relationships in which participants are regarded as interactive. This means that both buyers and sellers are actively involved in initiating and maintaining relationships. All parties to a network have the capability to influence a wide range of relationships, either directly or indirectly.

The importance of this aspect of B2B marketing cannot be underestimated nor should it be understated. This book adopts a relationship-based marketing perspective.

■ Types of Organisational Customers

Business-to-business marketing was previously referred to as industrial market-ing, but this phrase failed to recognise the involvement of a range of other, non-industrial enterprises. For example, governments and the not-for-profit sector also contribute a significant amount of commercial activity. Think about the economic transactions necessary to support the prison and military services. The sheer volume and value of pharmaceutical and medical supplies necessary to provide adequate health services, alone represent a major slice of the B2B sector. In addition, charities and institutions generate a substantial level of economic transactions. Therefore, the term organisational marketing has been adopted for this book and encompasses all these activities and types of organisation.

One way of characterising organisations is by size, to differentiate between the very large and the very small. For example, there are a number of differ-ences between global and national organisations, the public sector, small and medium-sized enterprises (SMEs) and small office/home office (SOHOs) not least in the ways they specify products and services (Macfarlane, 2002). Although this approach based on size and structure may be suitable for market research purposes, it is not entirely appropriate for understanding different purchasing procedures and buyer needs.

The approach presented here considers three broad types of organisation yet encompasses a number of sub-sections all based on their roles within marketing channels. These are commercial, government and institutional organisations (see Figure 1.1).

Institutional Organisations

- Not- for-profit

- Community based organisations

Government Organisations

- Health
- Environmental protection
- Education
- Policing
- Transport
- National defence and security

Commercial Organisations

- Distributors
- Original Equipment Manufacturers
- Users
- Retailers.

Figure 1.1: Types of B2B organisations

■ Commercial organisations

There are four main sectors in commercial B2B, all characterised by the different ways in which they use products and services. They share common buyer behaviour characteristics and associated communication needs. These four commercial organisational types are:

- distributors
- original equipment manufacturers
- users
- retailers.

Distributors

These organisations are sometimes referred to as intermediaries. The most common types are wholesalers, distributors/dealers and value added resellers. Their role is to facilitate the transfer of products through the marketing channel and to add value-creation opportunities, perhaps by providing credit facilities, storage or service support.

Ownership and physical possession of the goods often pass from one distributor to another, but there are occasions when this might not always be true. For example, the involvement of an agent in negotiations may mean that ownership passes over, rather than through, it to the next intermediary or customer.

Distributors fulfil a vital service. As middlemen they enable manufacturers to reach customers who do not require sufficient quantities to buy directly from them. Breaking bulk is an important concept and is examined further in Chapter 6. It allows manufacturers to concentrate on their core activities and leave the skills associated with distribution to others, namely the dealers and distributors.

- *Distributors/Dealers* supply both end-user business customers and original equipment manufacturers. They take full title to the industrial goods they purchase for resale and fulfil the important role of providing a wide range of products from a number of different manufacturers, offering easy access to them for their customers. In addition dealers and distributors provide advice, repair and credit facilities where necessary.

- *Value added resellers* are a relatively recent type of intermediary. Their role is to bring together a variety of software and hardware products to design customised systems solutions for their business customers. They provide integrated systems by drawing on a network of providers and in doing so create a value network, at the business customer level.

Original Equipment Manufacturers

Original equipment manufacturers (OEMs) purchase materials that are subsequently built into the products that they market to their customers. These materials may take many forms, such as parts, finished and partly finished goods, and even sub-assemblies which have been outsourced.

For example, a number of car manufacturers buy in radio components and assemble their own branded car radios. They source light bulbs directly from a range of authorised manufacturers and tyres from a variety of suppliers all of whom meet specific quality and performance standards. A finished Ford car, for example, might have Michelin tyres, a radio branded as Ford, and other equipment such as headlight bulbs where it is not possible to identify the manufacturer(s).

Users

Users are organisations that purchase goods and services to support their production and manufacturing processes. Users consume these materials, they do not appear in the final offering but contribute to its production.

Ford will purchase many support materials; for example, machine tools, electrical manufacturing equipment, vending machines, office furniture and stationery. None of these can be identified within the cars they manufacture.

Retailers

Technically, retailers are intermediaries, but their role is different. A retailer's customer is an end-user, the consumer. Retailers need to purchase goods in order to offer them to consumers but the buying processes, although similar, are not always as complex or as intricate as those in the DMU.

Recognition of the role and significance of retailers is an important aspect of B2B marketing. Organisations need to sell into retailers and understand the needs of this market and accommodate them accordingly. Retailing is a specialist activity and, although the roles and tasks of retailers are considered in Chapter 6, it does not form a major part of this book.

In all of the situations described above, organisations are involved in the buying of products and only in the last are consumers at all involved. The nature and form of cooperation, and the interorganisational relationships that develop from the various exchange transactions, influence the type of marketing activities used. The degree of cooperation between organisations will vary, and part of the role of marketing is to develop and support the relationships between partner organisations.

■ Government

Governments, and related institutions, are responsible for a huge volume and enormous value of business purchases. Health, environmental protection, education, policing, transport, national defence and security are just some of the areas that attract funding and sellers.

The procedures and guidelines relating to buying behaviour in a government context are in many ways radically different from those encountered in commercial organisations. However, despite many of the differences outlined below, the principle remains that a continual focus on customer needs is paramount. Suppliers that fail on a regular basis to win government business might well be too product-orientated. Many of the larger projects that concern governments, ministries and regional and local councils are not only massive, but also complex and involve a huge number of stakeholders. It is unsurprising that many encounter problems, delays and run way over their original budgets and planned timescales. For an example of these types of challenges see ViewPoint 1.2.

Of the many differences between government and private commercial purchasing, van Weele (2002) cites the following as the more prominent: political objectives, budget policies, accountability and EC directives.

ViewPoint 1.2: Political turbulence in the Shetlands

The development of a 150-turbine wind farm in the Shetlands caused considerable difficulties for all the key stakeholders. It was estimated that the 540-megawatt wind farm could supply approximately 20% of Scotland's domestic electricity needs. At a local level the scheme would generate a return of about £37 million a year to the local Shetland community. This would include about 230 construction and 50 maintenance jobs, plus rental payments.

For the application process to receive the go-ahead from the Scottish Government, the application must first be approved by the local council. However, each of the 22 councillors is a trustee of a local funding body, the Shetland Charitable Trust. The Trust has a substantial stake in Viking Energy, which is one of the companies behind the wind farm application, and set up by the local community.

Individual trustees have a statutory requirement to act in the charity's best interest. However, there was strong opposition to the proposal and the people fighting the application felt it was difficult for the councillors to hold an objective debate about the application. How could the trustees reconcile their position as trustees? It was even suggested it was a breakdown of local democracy and proper representation in Shetland.

Whilst this problem had been known about for a long time it was the sheer scale of the project that brought the trustee issue to the surface. Apart from the conflict of interest, objections to the scheme were based on fears that the number of tourists visiting the Shetlands would be hit and that there would be a considerable loss of revenue at a local level.

Source: Based on Haworth (2009) and Forrest, (2010)

Question: Make a list of the key issues the construction company Viking Energy, might have to deal with once permission had been granted.

Political objectives

The balance between meeting different goals can be difficult in the public sector. The drive to meet efficiency targets might not accord with the need to satisfy political or social goals. For example, in ViewPoint 1.2, Viking Energy, a partnership with the Scottish and Southern Energy, experienced considerable political hurdles trying to get permission to build a large wind farm in the Shetland Islands.

Budget policies

All government spending is bounded and constrained by central government policy and, in that sense priorities are predetermined and generally immovable. For example, budgets associated with projects to build or extend the road network may be modified on a change of government (and road transport policy) or subject to serious downgrading, even withdrawal, should the overall economy move into recession such that spending has to be reduced or switched into other areas.

Government budgeting techniques and policies are very different from those in the private commercial sector. Government budgets are subject to public scrutiny and, as a result, some decisions regarding major projects are deliberated for a considerable time. Procedures are normally detailed and protracted, involving a large number of people. The Department of Health in the United Kingdom publicises its purchasing policy, as required by EC regulations. Interested readers can review it at the website www.doh.gov.uk/purchasing/policy.htm.

If the allocated funding is not spent within the prescribed budget period, any under spend (or saving) may not be retained. Indeed, the budgeting process might have to be started again, causing delay, frustration and possibly a decrease in the amount of money made available.

Accountability

The hierarchical nature of government institutions means that purchasing procedures are invariably slow as each manager is required to give authorisation. The root cause is that these managers are spending public money and they are accountable for the money they authorise. As a result the whole system becomes bureaucratic, with an emphasis placed on procedure rather than the quality of the purchase itself.

Associated with the notion of accountability is the practice of contract management, quite common in many countries. Under this approach, contracts are awarded to contractors when both parties are fully aware that the actual cost will be far in excess of that originally agreed. This process leads to a failure to implement significant and consistent purchasing procedures, resulting in inefficiency and inappropriate spending of public money.

Partly in response to these failings the UK government introduced the Office of Government Commerce (OGC) in order to improve the purchasing procedures. Readers particularly interested in this aspect of business-to-business purchasing should visit the OGC website at www.ogc.gov.uk.

One of the more recent initiatives by the UK government has been the Private Finance Initiative (PFI). This involves partnership between the public and private sectors to access the skills and expertise of the private sector in providing public services and facilities. It is about the financing of capital investments and exploiting the full range of private sector management, commercial and creative skills.

These schemes promote the development of new partnerships and relationships and, of course, new ways of purchasing products and services for the public sector. There is debate about whether these schemes are in the best interests of the public and, in particular, public sector employees. However, this new approach is expected to be the model for government financing of major capital projects.

EC directives

The European Commission has tried to regularise purchasing and contract procedures throughout member countries. The detail concerning procedures is beyond the scope of this book. Interested readers could start by visiting the portal at www.ojec.com. However, the EC directives that have evolved attempt to achieve two main aspects. One is to specify who and what is covered by any directive, and the second is to regularise or standardise the procedures by which public expenditure on contracts worth over €200,000 are communicated, tendered, suppliers selected and contracts, including the technical specifications, are prepared, awarded and managed.

Just as individual countries have purchasing procedures, policies and guidelines, so the European Commission also has a set of purchasing directives and procedures. Table 1.1 sets out the three types of procedure that are available for the award of public supply contracts.

Table 1.1: Three types of procedure for the award of public supply contracts

Procedure	Explanation
The open procedure	This involves the submission of tenders from a huge variety of suppliers, most of who will not be known to the government.
The restricted procedure	This involves only those suppliers previously invited (and vetted) by the contracting organisation to tender for the work.
Negotiated procedure	Subject to special conditions, specified by the EC, the contracting authority may choose five suppliers and enter into negotiations with them, as long as, among other things, all parties are treated fairly.

Source: Based on van Weele (2002).

■ Institutions

There are a range of other organisations, which are neither entirely governmental nor private and commercial in nature. For example, there are not-for-profit organisations such as churches and charities, there are government-related organisations such as hospitals, schools, museums, libraries and universities and there are community-based organisations such as housing associations. This brief list serves to demonstrate the breadth and variety of institutional markets and the impact that these types of organisations can have on the overall B2B market. All these organisations need to buy a range of goods, materials and services as part of their drive to satisfy their customers' needs.

In many respects, these organisations adopt some of the characteristics associated with both commercial and government markets. Purchasing in some institutional markets can be significantly constrained by political influences (for example, schools under the direct control of local education authorities), while in others the drive for corporate efficiency is an overriding influence.

One of the main characteristics of this market is the willingness of organisations to unite to form large buying groups. The primary advantage of group purchasing is the ability to command increased discounts based upon volume purchases. For example, local health services combine and agree a list of drugs and medicines from which all doctors must prescribe. This enables discounts and hence lower costs and better value for the public they serve. This 'formulary list' both constrains the range of suppliers and items purchased and also provides improved efficiencies. Supplier organisations must adapt their marketing approaches, as the processes and personnel associated with group purchasing can be very different to individual institutional buying procedures. With group purchasing, members of the purchasing team may be motivated by needs that differ from those of personnel responsible for purchasing at individual institutions.

Therefore, relationships will need to be determined and developed, communications adapted, and price will inevitably be paramount while delivery and support is required at individual group member level.

Finally, the impact of multiple buying influences in institutional markets can be strong. In service-based institutions, for example schools, universities and hospitals, the primary provision is delivered by professionals such as teachers, lecturers and doctors. It has been known for their purchasing departments to impose restrictions on certain supplies or materials or to deny access to particular products or suppliers. This can lead to resentment and conflict between those in 'administration' and the professional staff. From a marketing perspective, supplier organisations need to be aware of this potential conflict and communicate with all parties.

Types of Business Goods and Services

Following the above examination of market characteristics and customers in the B2B sector, this section highlights the variety and complexity of the goods and services that are bought and sold.

If the production process is adopted as the template it is possible to discern three main categories of goods. These are input goods, equipment goods and supply goods (see Table 1.2).

Table 1.2: A categorisation of business market goods

Type of goods	Explanation
Input goods	Raw materials and semi-manufactured parts, which become part of the finished item
Equipment goods	Capital items that are not part of the finished item but necessary to enable production process to take place (e.g. land and buildings)
Supply goods	Materials necessary to keep the production process running (e.g. electricity and oil)

Input goods

Input goods become part of the finished item. There are two main types, raw materials and semi-manufactured parts.

- *Raw materials* have been subject to minimal processing and enter the production process in their natural state, e.g. copper, iron ore, coffee and oranges.

- *Semi-manufactured parts* have undergone some processing before entering the main manufacturing process. For example, car manufacturers buy in sheet metal and cloth for the interior, previously prepared by other organisations. Components such as pistons, headlights and radios are bought in and physically unchanged. They are assembled into the finished product.

In addition to this there are finished goods. Retailers and resellers buy finished products and physically add very little, if anything to them. For example, mobile phone manufacturers, such as Nokia and Motorola, may offer carry cases and hands-free attachments as additional items but these are made by specialist suppliers and bought in as required.

Equipment goods

Items that are purchased to enable the production of finished goods, yet are not part of the finished product, are referred to as equipment, capital or investment goods. They are depreciated in value over time because they are not consumed immediately. For example, land and buildings, computer systems and machine tools are all necessary to support the production process, but are not an integral part of the finished product.

■ Supply goods

Each production process requires consumable materials to keep it running. These are not assets and are not depreciated. They appear as an expense item. Sometimes these are referred to as **maintenance, repair and operating materials** (or MRO items). For example, lubricants, paint, screws and cleaning materials may all be necessary to maintain a firm's operations.

In addition to MROs are **services**. Normally managed on a contract basis with a third-party organisation, services are necessary for the smooth running of the organisation. For example, computer servicing is necessary to maintain operations and to avoid down time, while accounting audits are a legal requirement.

Developments in technology have led to an increase in IT and related services, for example, website design and hosting eCommerce/eBusiness facilities. These services have to be outsourced when organisations do not have sufficient internal skills or expertise. They often do not want to hire and develop these skills internally because they prefer to concentrate on their core business activities.

ViewPoint 1.3: Procurement targets for Unilever

Unilever, the global supplier of home, personal care and food products, has claimed that procurement improvements have saved them £1.2 billion in 2010. This has largely resulted from supply chain savings. Systems and processes have been improved allowing faster and higher quality information to assist in procurement decision making.

The group sources raw materials and packaging from over 10,000 suppliers and non-production goods and services from almost 100,000. In October 2010, Unilever introduced a revised Supplier Code which provides a framework which details the group's approach and responsible sourcing requirements. All suppliers must demonstrate adherence to the Code including the need for management systems to ensure compliance.

In North America the group has two major divisions, Unilever Bestfoods and Unilever Home and Personal Care. These two divisions utilise an extensive enterprise resource planning (ERP) system, supported by a number of vast databases.

Supplying 400 brands in 14 product categories across both divisions, presents a major logistical challenge and a need to ensure the highest level of control of sourcing, manufacturing and distribution.

Source: Based on www.logisticit.com; www.supplymanagement.com /news; www. unilever.com

Question: What do you believe are the three most important indicators that procurement strategies are working?

The Characteristics of B2B Marketing

So far in this chapter, the characteristics of the business market, the different types of products and services, the variety of customers and different approaches to pricing have been considered. What do these factors contribute to an understanding of B2B marketing?

Overall, the marketing of goods and services between organisations is not the same as consumer goods marketing and, because there are a number of fundamentally different characteristics, diverse marketing strategies and operations need to be implemented to meet the needs of business customers.

However, many products and services are targeted at both consumers and organisations. Products such as office furniture, software and cellular phones can be sold into consumer and business markets. Business marketing is distinguished from consumer marketing by two main ideas: first, the intended customer, which is an organisation; second, the intended use of the product to support organisational objectives. As a result, different marketing programmes are required to reach and influence organisational buyers as opposed to consumers.

In the business sector, organisations buy a range of products and services either to make new products or to enable the production or added value process to operate successfully. Defined processes and procedures are used to buy products and services, and the decisions attached to securing the necessary materials very often involve a large number of people. Fuller details about these characteristics can be found in Chapter 3. However, central to an understanding of organisational purchasing is the decision making unit and the complexities associated with a variety of people and processes. There are pivotal implications for suppliers in terms of timescales and the communication mix and messages necessary to reduce the levels of risk inherent in these buying situations. These issues are examined in the next section and throughout the rest of this book.

B2B Marketing Mix

The first main approach to marketing was based on the marketing mix concept, popularly known as the 4Ps. McCarthy (1960) identified the elements of the original mix and Borden (1964) popularised the concept as the 4Ps. Sometimes referred to as the *Marketing Management* approach, the mix has been applied equally in B2B and B2C markets. The main differences concern the nature of the individual variables and the way the mix is deployed. The traditional 4Ps interpretation of the marketing mix was subsequently challenged with the rise of services marketing and the increasing complexity of industrial marketing, as business marketing was then known. As a result the marketing mix incorporated people, physical evidence and processes, 4 had become 7Ps.

■ Products

In consumer markets products are traditionally made available with limited opportunities for adaption or customisation. Increasingly, manufacturers are seeking ways in which customers feel they can customise a product. For example, some cars can be ordered via a dealer showroom directly from the production unit. This enables customers to specify the interior and exterior finishes, grade of in-car entertainment and perhaps a range of other cosmetic touches. However, the norm is to provide relatively little flexibility within different product ranges.

In the B2B market the entire offering (product and service components) can often be reconfigured to meet a customer's particular requirements. It is quite usual for more technical products to be developed and specified through joint negotiations and partnership arrangements. The result is an offering that is unique to the buying organisation.

■ Pricing

Price is a measure of the value that both parties assign to their contribution to an exchange. In consumer markets, list prices are usually the norm and limited discounts applied to them, especially for more expensive items. Hire purchase and credit-based schemes are designed to spread the financial risk, make purchase more accessible for a greater number of consumers and so increase the perceived value to a consumer. Negotiation is not usually a feature of pricing in consumer markets, the exceptions being cars and houses.

In business markets the designated value is likely to increase as a relationship becomes more collaborative and partnership-orientated. Therefore, prices associated with transaction exchanges will be based largely on list prices, quantity discounts and competitive bidding. As exchanges become more relational, so price becomes an integral part of the design, specification, development, trial and finishing processes. Discounts and allowances become more varied and complicated and reflect the risks and opportunities faced by the two parties. Negotiation becomes an important aspect of pricing in B2B markets. Large projects and intricate technical offerings often require complex financing arrangements, while pricing for international markets introduces new risks and financial uncertainties.

■ Place

In consumer markets, intermediaries provide utility in terms of reducing the complexity of the range of goods consumers are offered, by providing a level of specialisation and support (advice) and enabling consumer expectations to be met. Consumer preferences in terms of location, the quantity of items that need to be purchased and the ease with which they can be acquired are deemed to be of value to consumers and so effort is concentrated in satisfying consumer needs in these areas and enhancing the level of perceived value. However, these services still need to be aggregated and provided on a group basis.

In B2B markets, the utility principles are similar but the main difference lies in the length of the channels and the number of intermediaries deemed necessary to deliver the level of functionality required. Individual attention and customisation of product offerings, plus the need to deliver in the quantities and at the time required by the buyer, result in a shortening of the marketing channel. This leads to direct relationships and new dimensions in terms of the way in which offerings are made available.

■ Promotion

In consumer markets, advertising has long been regarded as the focal point of the marketing communications mix. Some of the reasons for this concern the need to reach large, widely dispersed audiences, with relatively simple messages relating to awareness, interest and beliefs. Feedback is minimal and relationships between reseller and consumer are more commonly temporary and not very close. In recent years increased use of the other tools in the mix has reduced the high reliance on advertising, but it remains the focal part of a consumer organisation's promotional strategy.

Advertising is a relatively impotent marketing communications tool in B2B markets because of the need to provide more detailed, often technical information. Audiences are small in number and can be more closely defined and easily targeted with less wastage. Messages need to provide means of differentiation, reinforcement and persuasion. Feedback is important in B2B and so the emphasis is traditionally placed on personal selling. This helps the development of both a dialogue and also a relationship. Relationships between organisations in business markets are expected to be close and their duration much longer than in consumer markets.

Direct marketing is also important in B2B markets and, in some situations, can be used effectively to support the personal selling effort. Technology can be used to support all aspects of an organisation's marketing communications strategy and some applications are considered in this book.

■ People

In business marketing, and service industries in particular, people who represent the manufacturer or service provider, are extremely important. This is because they have a direct impact on the way customers, and other stakeholders, make judgements about the quality of the overall service.

Staff representing the service should deliver their element of the service process consistently. The appropriate recruitment, training, and rewarding of staff is an imperative if the required standards and expectations associated with customer interaction are to be achieved.

Ensuring that the right physical and electronic environments are in place, can also be significant in business/service marketing. For example, enabling business customers to electronically access pertinent information, or ensuring a suitable tone of voice is used throughout all communications can improve business performance, for both buyer and seller.

■ Physical evidence

The intangibility of a service means that it is important to provide tangible cues for potential customers. This is to enable them to understand the product quality. One of the more common approaches is to use sales literature and brochures to give signs about the quality and positioning. Staff deportment and dress also provide clues about a service provider's attitude and attention to tidiness, routines, safety, and customer orientation.

Physical evidence can be considered as essential evidence or peripheral evidence. (Shostack, 1977). Essential evidence refers to those few, key elements that are important criteria when customers make purchasing decisions. For example the quality of cars used by a car rental company, the newness of planes, or the location and architecture of cinemas provide essential information.

Of lower importance when evaluating the overall quality of the service provision, is peripheral evidence. Downloadable white papers, repeat showings of webinars, and sales literature which can be taken away by customers and used as a reminder of the product/service offering are examples of peripheral evidence.

■ Processes

Processes include all the activities, tasks, schedules, systems and routines that enable a product/service to be delivered to a customer. Overall success requires that the processes customers use when interacting with a supplying organisation, work effectively and appropriately.

Processes vary in their complexity. These can be simple, as in ordering stationery, or complicated, for example, when ordering a fleet of new aircraft, or a satellite. However complex it may be, marketers need to understand the process so that they can integrate benefits into key steps. This helps to provide differentiation, assist any repositioning and at an individual level, avoid boredom and enhance the brand experience.

■ Introducing Perceived Value

The Marketing Management approach based on the 7Ps has been superseded by ideas relating to relationship marketing. This is explored in detail in Chapter 4 and forms the basis for many of the ideas and approaches adopted in this book. However, in order to better appreciate the relationship marketing concept it is helpful to first have an understanding of perceived value and related concepts.

The concept of value and the importance of providing it for customers has become an increasingly significant aspect of business and marketing strategy. It has long been understood that customers buy benefits not features. Business customers buy solutions to business problems not just stand-alone products. They buy products and services because they have the potential to add value to the offerings they make available. These benefits and solutions constitute a potential added value opportunity for customers, and represent the reason why one offering is selected in preference to another. For both consumers and business customers, value is determined by the net satisfaction derived from a transaction, not the costs to obtain it.

Another way of viewing these solutions and benefits is to consider them as customer needs. Customers seek to satisfy their needs through their purchase of products and services. The satisfaction of needs therefore is a way for suppliers to offer value generation opportunities. Kothandaraman and Wilson (2001) argue that the creation of value is dependent upon an organisation's ability to deliver high performance on the benefits that are important to the customer and this in turn is rooted in their competency in technology and business processes, or core competences. Doyle (2000) regards the creation of customer value to be based on three principles. These are:

1 Customers will choose between alternative offerings and select the one that (they perceive) will offer them the best value.

2 Customers do not want product or service features, they want their needs met.

3 It is more profitable to have a long-term relationship between a customer and a company rather than a one-off transaction.

Value is a customer's estimate of the extent to which a product or service can satisfy their needs. Customers determine a product/service's value potential by considering alternative solutions and the costs associated with satisfying their need. Therefore, value is relative to a customer's needs, expectations, and experience of competitive offerings.

Value can be derived from sources other than products and prices. For example, it can be generated through the provision of additional services, such as:

■ Training or support facilities, for example those normally provided by Carphone Warehouse for their customers;

■ Association with a highly regarded brand, for example the co-branding arrangement between Adidas and Porche and between Disney and Mattel;

■ Legal or insurance provision, for example the financial support provided by government and some regional councils for start-up entrepreneurs and small businesses;

■ Joint working relationships between government and building/finance schemes such as those associated with the Private Finance Initiative.

Menon *et al.* (2005) refer to these as add-on benefits and suggest these may be more important than the core benefit arising from product and price attributes.

Lindgreen *et al.* (2009) refer to value creation through financial value (Anderson and Narus, 1998), emotional bonds (Butz and Goodstein, 1996), subjective interpretations of the product or service (Neap and Celik, 1999) and feelings about the amount of resources sacrificed in making these decisions (Zeithaml, 1988).

Perhaps the most potent representations of value can be observed in the relationships between buyers and sellers (Simpson *et al.*, 2001). Indeed, the creation and the sharing of value is a critical aspect of buyer–seller relationships (Anderson, 1995), if only because they are longer lasting and difficult for competitors to copy or destroy. This is important when considering marketing channel relationships which are an integral and critical aspect of B2B marketing.

The customer value concept should be considered from two complementary perspectives according to Lefaix-Durand *et al.* (2009). These are *value-to-customers* and *value-of-customers*. *Value-to-customers* focuses on the net-value customers realise from using the products/services provided by suppliers. *Value-of-customers* assumes a supplier's perspective of the net value they derive from their customers (Ulaga and Eggert, 2005). These ideas are explored in Chapter 4.

The Value Chain

Customers choose among competitive offerings on the basis of their perceptions of the relative value they can derive from each supplier. Each selling organisation competes for business by offering enhanced value creation opportunities. These are developed internally, through a coordinated chain of activities. These activities include product design, production, marketing, delivery and support. Porter (1985) referred to these activities as the *value chain*, which is depicted at Figure 1.2.

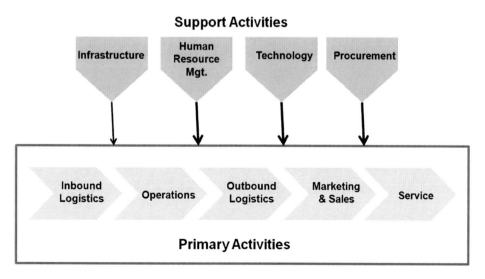

Figure 1.2: Porter's value chain

The value chain was devised as a tool to appraise an organisation's ability to create what Porter terms differential advantage. It consists of nine activities, five primary and four support, all of which incur costs but together can (and should) lead to the creation of value.

The primary activities are those direct actions necessary to bring materials into an organisation, to convert them into final products or services, to ship them out to customers and to provide marketing and servicing facilities. Support activities facilitate the primary activities. For example, the purchase of parts and materials, the recruitment of suitably trained personnel and the provision and maintenance of suitable technology are important support activities. Management should attempt to create value by reducing costs or improving the performance of each of the activities. However, real value is generated by linking together these activities through processes and in such a way that customers perceive they are getting superior value.

The value generation processes used by an organisation become a critical part of the way in which they can add value. Customers, however, lie at the heart of the value chain. Only by understanding particular customer needs and focusing value chain activities on satisfying them, can superior value creation opportunities be generated. This has implications for B2B segmentation strategies and is explored further in Chapter 5.

ViewPoint 1.4: Xerox adds value in more ways than one

Xerox's association with paper copying had led to the brand becoming synonymous with the process. People made Xeroxes rather than copies. Significant product competition from such firms as Hewlett Packard, Toshiba, Canon and others was led from a technology perspective. The printing facilities offered via desktop computing led to further market challenges. The company had to readdress what value they were offering customers. This led to a shift from being positioned as a copier machine manufacturer to a business solutions provider.

In order to provide differentiation from the competition and to overcome customer perceptions of the brand as just a machine supplier, an advertising campaign was devised to promote an emotional connection between Xerox and the users of their equipment. This focused on the creative applications of their machines and the positive feelings of those users resulting from having produced high quality documents.

In order to continue adding value to customers, further developments of this concept have led to the creation of a number of business partnerships. The Xerox Premier Partners Global Network Community provides customers with opportunity to share ideas, find out about latest technologies and access product information.

Source: Based on Precourt (2009); www.xerox.co.uk

Question: How else might Xerox have differentiated themselves?

■ Supply chains

So far the value chain has been considered within an internal context. However, organisations do not exist in isolation but combine with others in order to provide a consistent stream of resources. Therefore, organisations join their value chains together and form supply chains. The operation of the overall supply chain helps generate sustainable value for each business. Issues concerning supply chains and marketing channels are explored in more detail in Chapter 7.

The concepts of value and the value chain are important because they provide a reminder of basic principles. First, customers buy superior value-enhancing opportunities, which means that the creation of profits can only be achieved through value propositions that customers want. Trimming costs to save money and to improve the bottom line may result in removing the element that constitutes a customer's reason to buy. Many organisations cut back on aspects of their offerings in times of recession or economic difficulty. The objective is to save costs and improve profits but this short-term approach can damage the long-term prospects if it dispenses with a crucial part of the value that customers perceive to be important.

Second, value can be perceived in many ways, for example by providing associations with prestige (exclusivity or membership), reliability, modular formats, ease and speed of servicing, stock and delivery flexibility, ease of customisation and access to new markets, to name a few. Therefore, the whole of an organisation's activities must be considered and their contribution to the generation of superior value creation appraised. Among other things, this means looking at pre- and post-purchase customer support, pricing, communications, distribution and logistics and positioning.

The development of new technology and the increasing breadth and depth of business applications has provided new value creation opportunities for organisations. Consistent advances in information systems and technology (IST) can lead to new forms of value opportunities being created. Apart from the obvious impact on speed and accuracy of information transfer between organisations, value can be enhanced through product development and customisation, production and manufacturing, supply chain management, marketing communications and, of course, closer interorganisational understanding and relationships (Sharma *et al.*, 2001).

■ The Importance of B2B Relationships

Following on from the introduction to value and value chains, the supply chain concept raises interesting points about the nature and scope of the relationships that exist between sellers and buyers. Organisations interact with other organisations to provide superior value-creation opportunities for their customers.

However, it should come as no surprise to read that the quality, duration and level of interdependence between organisations in the supply chain can and does vary considerably. The reasons for this variance are many and wide-ranging but at the core are perceptions of value shared by both parties. The value that organisations offer each other can be visualised as a continuum, as set out at Figure 1.3.

At one end of the continuum are transactional or market exchanges, characterised by short-term, commodity or price-orientated exchanges, between buyers and sellers coming together for one-off exchanges independent of any other or subsequent exchanges. Both parties are motivated mainly by self-interest.

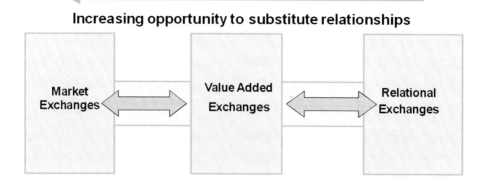

Figure 1.3: Continuum of exchange relationships, adapted from Day (2000)

Movement along the continuum represents increasingly valued relationships. Interactions between parties are become closer and stronger. The focus moves from initial attraction to retention, cooperation and a mutual understanding of each other's needs.

At the other end of the continuum are relational exchanges or what Day (2000) refers to as collaborative exchanges. These are characterised by a long-term orientation, where there is complete integration of systems and processes and the relationship is motivated by partnership and mutual support. Trust and commitment underpin these relationships and these variables become increasingly important as relational exchanges become established.

B2B marketing is characterised by a portfolio of relationships that all need managing. Some relationships are price-orientated and some are fully collaborative, while the large majority fall somewhere between the two. This book seeks to explore B2B marketing by taking into account the rich variety of interdependent activities that occur between organisations.

It is important to put these ideas in the context of organisational practice. Pels *et al.* (2009: 323) report a series of independent research studies that 'provide clear evidence' that 30% of B2B companies practise transactional marketing, as advocated by the Marketing Management school of thought. A further 30% practise a combination of transactional and collaborative marketing. The numbers practising pure collaborative marketing are not itemised but it would clearly be a minority.

Summary

The following material is intended to help readers consolidate their understanding of the key points introduced in this chapter and the learning objectives.

1 Consider the nature, scope and characteristics of business markets.

The market for goods and services bought and sold between businesses is far larger than the consumer market. It comprises many types and sizes of organisations that interact selectively and form relationships of varying significance and duration with one another.

Business markets are characterised by a number of factors, the main ones being the nature of demand, the buying processes, international dimensions and, perhaps most importantly, the relationships that develop between organisations in the process of buying and selling.

2 Identify the different types of organisational customers

It is possible to classify business customers by their size but in order to understand purchasing needs and processes a categorisation based on commercial, government and institutional organisations is helpful.

3 Categorise the goods and services that are bought and sold in the sector.

These organisations consume a variety of goods and services all of which can be considered as input goods, equipment goods and supply goods.

4 Explore the characteristics of B2B marketing.

Business marketing is distinguished from consumer marketing by two main ideas: first, the intended customer, which is an organisation; second, the intended use of the product to support organisational objectives. As a result, different marketing programmes are required to reach and influence organisational buyers as opposed to consumers. The way products and services are bought, the numbers of people involved, the length of time for decision making, the size of orders, the configuration of the communications used to reach and interact with customers are just some of the differences between consumer and business markets.

5 Describe the perceived value and supply chain concepts.

Value is a customer's estimate of the extent to which a product or service can satisfy their needs. Customers choose among competitive offerings on the basis of their perceptions of the relative value they can derive from each supplier.

Each selling organisation competes for business by trying to offer enhanced value creation opportunities. These are developed internally, through a coordinated chain of activities, known as the 'Value chain'. These activities include product design, production, marketing, delivery and customer support and constitute a critical part of the way in which they can add value. Organisations join their value chains together to form supply chains. The operation of the overall supply chain helps generate sustainable value for each business.

6 Explain the importance of relationships in B2B marketing.

Organisations interact with other organisations to provide superior value-creation opportunities for their customers. B2B marketing is characterised by the variety of relationships that all need managing. Some relationships are price-orientated and some are fully collaborative, while the large majority fall somewhere between the two. Organisations manage a portfolio of relationships.

■ Discussion Questions

1 Identify the key characteristics associated with B2B markets and suggest how they might impact on B2B marketing activities.

2 Explain why demand is said to be derived from consumers.

3 Commercial organisations can be considered as distributors, original equipment manufacturers, users, or retailers. Describe the core characteristics associated with each of these.

4 Discuss the key differences between B2B and B2C marketing. What are their similarities?

5 Draw the value chain as depicted by Porter (1985) and include the nine constituent elements.

6 Examine the contention that the traditional concept of the marketing mix (4Ps) is now redundant and should be replaced by a relationship-centred approach to marketing activities.

References

Anderson, J. (1995) Relationships in business markets: exchange episodes, value creation and their empirical assessment, *Journal of the Academy of Marketing Science*, **23** (4), 346–50.

Anderson, J.C. and Narus, J.A. (1998) Business marketing: understand what customers value, *Harvard Business Review*, **76** (June), 53–65.

Borden, N. (1964) The concept of the marketing mix, *Journal of Advertising Research*, June, 2–7

Butz, H.E. and Goodstein, L.D. (1996) Measuring customer value: gaining the strategic advantage, *Organisational Dynamics*, **24** (3), 63–77

Day, G.S. (2000) Managing market relationships, *Journal of Academy of Marketing Science*, **28** (1) (Winter), 24–31

Doyle, P (2000) *Value Based Marketing*, John Wiley

Forrest, D. (2010) Divided Islands: The Pros and Cons of a Wind Farm, *Engineering* by Suite 101, 18 December, retrieved 26 May 2011 from www.suite101.com/content/divided-islands-the-pros-and-cons-of-a-wind-farm-a322588

Gummesson, E. and Polese, F. (2009) B2B is not an Island, *Journal of Business and Industrial Marketing*, 24, 5/6, 337–350

Haworth. J. (2009) Conflict of interest clouds council's position on wind farm project vote, *The Scotsman*, 15 July, retrieved 26 May 2011 from http://thescotsman.scotsman.com/alternativeenergysources/39Conflict-of-interest39-clouds-council39s.5458860.jp

Kothandaraman, P. & Wilson, K. (2001) The Future of Competition – Value Creating Networks, *Industrial Marketing Management* **30**, 379–389.

Lefaix-Durand, A., Kozak, R., Beauregard, R. and Poulin, D. (2009) Extending relationship value: observations from a case study of the Canadian structural wood products industry, *Journal of Business & Industrial Marketing*, **24** (5/6), 389–407

Lindgreen, A., Antioco, M., Palmer, R. and van Heech, T. (2009) High tech innovative products: identifying and meeting customers' value needs, *Journal of Business and Industrial Marketing*, **24** (3/4), 182–197

Macfarlane, P. (2002). Structuring and measuring the size of business markets, *International Journal of Market Research*, **44** (1) (Winter), 7–31

McCarthy, E.J. (1960). *Basic Marketing: A Managerial Approach*, Homewood, IL: Irwin.

A. Menon, Ch. Homburg, N. Beutin (2005), Understanding Customer Value in Business-to Business Relationships, *Journal of Business-to-Business Marketing*, **12** (2).

Morgan, R M and, and S D Hunt (1994), The commitment-trust theory of relationship marketing, *Journal of Marketing*, July, 20–38

Neap, H.S. and Celik, T. (1999), Value of a product: a definition, *International Journal of Value-based Management*, **12** (2), 181-91

Pels, J., Möller, K. and Saren, M. (2009) Do we really understand business marketing? Getting beyond the RM and BM matrimony, *Journal of Business and Industrial Marketing*, **24** (5/6), 322–336

Porter, M.E. (1985). *Competitive Advantage: Creating and Sustaining Superior Performance*, New York, NY: The Free Press.

Precourt, G. (2009) *Warc Exclusive*, September, retrieved 15 March 2011 from www.warc.com

An Introduction to Business Marketing

Sharma, A., Krishman, R. and Grewal, D. (2001) Value creation in markets: a critical area of focus for business-to-business markets, *Industrial Marketing Management*, **30** (4) (May), 341–402.

Shostack, G. L. (1977), Breaking free from product marketing, *Journal of Marketing*, **41** (April), 73–80.

Simpson, P.M., Sigauw, J.A. and Baker, T.L. (2001) A model of value creation: supplier behaviors and their impact on reseller-perceived value, *Industrial Marketing Management*, **30** (2) (February), 119–34

Ulaga, W. and Eggert, A. (2005), Relationship value in business markets: the construct and its dimensions, *Journal of Business-to-Business Marketing*, **12** (1), 73-99.

van Weele , A.J. (2002). *Purchasing and Supply Chain Management: Analysis, Planning and Practice*, 3rd edn, London: Thomson Learning.

Zeithaml, V. (1988) Consumer perceptions of price, quality, and value: a means-end model and synthesis of evidence, *Journal of Marketing*, **52** (4), 2-22

2 Business Products and Services

Overview

This chapter considers the various issues associated with managing products and services in business markets.

Business products can be classified according to the degree of standardisation and customisation that the organisation decides to offer. It is important to establish this view before considering how organisations might develop strategies to manage their product/service offerings, both established and new. Attention is given to the product life cycle before examining issues concerning the new product and new service development processes. This section concludes with a consideration of the technology adoption life cycle, appropriate in high technology markets.

Aims and objectives

The aims of this chapter are to consider some of the key managerial issues and characteristics associated with business products and services.

The objectives of this chapter are to enable readers to:

1 Examine the characteristics of business products.

2 Appreciate the nature and significance of product strategies.

3 Understand the significance of services in business markets and marketing.

4 Evaluate the new product and new service development processes.

5 Examine the product life cycles and determine how these might impact on business marketing.

6 Explain the technology life cycle model

A Slice of Life – The Battle between Products and Services

Most B2B enterprises have grown from a product base. I think that's a fair, albeit sweeping, generalisation. It's particularly true of the technology space in my experience. Technology is notorious for conceiving the latest widget that will revolutionize your life, or the latest 'killer-app' (application) that you need to download, "like, now, dude..." Some widgets are ultimately more successful than others – often by luck more than judgement. That success is manifest in the growth of the business – they become small businesses, mid-size companies and sometimes even large corporates – but always with the 'product' at the heart of operations.

Product focus only really becomes a problem when the business can no longer simply 'sell more products'. Sales people are expensive and competitors are quick to replicate any successful product. It may be that associated services to the product become a more valuable revenue stream than the product itself. Suddenly the brand, which up until that point was only ever a single entity, becomes confused about whether it is a product, a service or a company. It suffers a loss of identity amongst the growing diversity of audiences and, frustratingly, (and slightly ironically) the technology can't help.

That was very much the case with a technology client of mine that provided data security technology for the banking and public sectors. The company had been built by the CEO, helping banks secure the integrity of card transactions through any 'device'. After several years of painful brand development, the company had most recently changed its name at the time of my involvement and was now struggling to both create a meaningful identity and understand it. Within the corporate structure there were multiple software brands, none of which had a clear or obvious link to the corporate parent. That, in isolation, wouldn't have been a problem were it not for the associated services that the company had started to offer customers across the multiple product brands. The services were broadly the same across all products, but the actual products were very different – performing different tasks in different vertical markets for different clients. The rising star of the business – 'services' – was confused. What to say, how to say it, the style and tone it should adopt, how to respond to variable audiences... all became too difficult.

I was asked by the Group Marketing Director to fix it – to unify the corporate, product and service brands. The CEO had moved to the USA to oversee North American activities and the global management team was given the responsibility of reviewing the company's market positioning. The objective was to deliver a clear brand strategy (what to say) a Creative Platform® (a concept for communications) and a corporate identity (the badge).

Working closely with the team responsible for communications was quite revealing. We established, for the first time, a clear view of the customer's needs across all products and services. Customers (banks and governments) required greater 'control' of remote devices – they needed to know that the millions of transactions they were processing daily were both genuine and secure. We established that my client's role (and value) was its ability to extend the 'trusted environment'. Banks and governments were only prepared to transact within highly secure environments and the company was able to provide software products and supporting services that enabled trusted transactions to take place using 'remote devices'. The technology enabled secure mobile banking transactions, for example, and it provided the secure data contained within passports and identity cards.

Being able to agree what the company actually 'did' (extending trusted environments) was a significant step forward. Whether the company was talking to bank issuers, product vendors or systems integrators – there was common ground on which to base the brand proposition. While audience needs included, at different times, cost-efficiency, safety/security, functionality, control and reach from their security solutions, ultimately they required one thing that the company could provide: greater control of remote devices. It was demonstrated and, importantly, agreed that at a corporate level, the company's products and services were able to tame hostile transaction environments for its customers. The products transformed those risky environments from unpredictable and threatening places into quantifiable, understood and manageable spaces in which to operate. The services offered by the company in addition to the software supported and maintained the ongoing delivery of trust within those high risk transactional markets. Splendid.

It should have been a downhill run from that point. But no. Even with the full endorsement of all international stakeholders, the CEO blocked the execution of the strategy. Positioning and messaging had been agreed. Creative work had been developed and agreed. Media had been planned and agreed. After a difficult conversation with the now very embarrassed Marketing Director, the entire rollout plan was cancelled because Sir wasn't ready to acknowledge the business shift from selling a product, to selling a broader corporate 'platform' or enterprise solution.

It was a painful end to the client engagement. Without completely reworking the entire brand delivery process (this time with Sir involved from the outset...) there would have been no way to redirect the business communications or the brand. To do so would have doubled the budget and timings for delivery and any attempt would likely have ended with internal dispute. So nothing changed. Except the logo. For all the effort, the company received a new badge. Which was nice, but hardly world-stopping.

Five years later, desk research shows that no further advances have been made to the brand architecture. The company has adopted the name of the dominant product which has become the sole product of note. Services are offered based around that single product. It's certainly a viable business, but the possibilities were so much greater. It could have been a contender...

Scot McKee

■ Product Characteristics

The development of superior value is based on a number of elements. These may vary across sectors and markets. One of these is price, but others include products and services, which are the focus of this chapter and relationships, which are considered in Chapter 4.

Business products and services contribute significantly to customers' perception and evaluation of a supplier's competitive stance. However, products are more than just the pure physical form and utility they outwardly present. Products have two main types of attribute – tangible and intangible, whose characteristics are set out in Table 2.1.

Table 2.1: Attributes and properties of business products

Attribute or property		Explanation
Tangible	Core	These are the basic features which describe the simple capabilities of the product. These are generic to all product offerings in the market.
	Augmented	These are features added to the core attributes, which either provide extra facilities and performance opportunities or provide marks to distinguish and differentiate the basic product from competitive offerings. For example, packaging, brand names and logos, quality achievements and fittings and attachments.
Intangible		Additional elements that are provided to improve the atmosphere that surrounds a product. Technical service and support, financial services, warranties and delivery serve to embellish products and assist differentiation.

The **tangible** (or physical) attributes, consist of two elements, core and augmented. Core attributes represent the functional capability of a product, its primary features. For example, the core features of earth-moving equipment from JCB are strength, capability and reliability. In addition to core features there are also augmented or advanced properties providing various additional customer benefits and helping to differentiate products. Styling, performance capabilities, packaging, size or weight are features that help distinguish a product or enable it to perform better than competitive products. For example, JCB's wheeled excavators have stabilisers that can be operated independently.

The **intangible** attributes are all the other aspects that customers perceive to surround a product. These concern the psychological aspects associated with service and support, the warranties and guarantees, the financial services, the training and, very importantly, the reputation of the company and its perceived status. These intangible elements are increasingly recognised as important discriminators and can help customers understand the relative value of market offerings. As products can be copied faster and as basic levels of operational performance become standardised, so differentiation has to be achieved primarily through superior service and reputation. For example, JCB provide a 24-hour global support service helping to ensure that their clients are able to meet their customers' deadlines.

Product attributes also assume varying levels of importance for buyers at particular organisations and for those operating in a particular category or market sector. As a result, organisational buyers perceive business products as a bundle of attributes and therefore it is important to understand which bundle different buyers prefer. Hutt, *et al.* (2009) suggest that some attributes can be regarded as determinant, which means that they are perceived by buyers as both important and differentiating. Other attributes may be non-determinant, that is, either important or differentiating but not both.

Determinant attributes   = **important and differentiating**

Non-determinant attributes = **either important or differentiating**

ViewPoint 2.1: Broadstock set out their attributes

The office furniture market consists of four sectors; desking, seating, storage and other miscellaneous products. The overall percentage shares held by each sector have remained reasonably stable in recent years although the overall market value has declined following the recession and the surplus capacity that remains. Broadstock Office Furniture Ltd is a leading player in the supply of furniture for commercial organisations operating in a number of sectors. Products include desks, work stations, tables, chairs, partitions and storage equipment. Over 50% of products are manufactured by Broadstock themselves, with the remainder sourced from suppliers around the UK and Europe.

This is a highly competitive market. In order to maintain a position in the premium sector of the market, Broadstock rely on a range of intangible attributes to supplement their product offerings. They provide a custom/bespoke design service which involves space planning surveys and the use of 2D/3D visualisations. Their use of eco-friendly raw materials is featured in their communications. A full delivery and installation service is provided.

Broadstock have won a number of industry accreditations which not only provide credibility for Broadstock themselves, but they also reduce uncertainty for customers and deliver a stronger level of reassuarance. The Broadstock brand also has a strong market reputation.

Source: Based on Hubbard (2011); www.broadstock.co.uk; www.fira.co.uk

Question: Identify the tangible and intangible attributes that can be used by organisations such as Broadstock.

Consideration should be given to the perception buyers have of a firm's key attributes relative to those of the competition. What might be considered as a differentiating attribute may be perceived by buyers as a standard requirement in the market. In this situation a new form of differentiation would need to be developed such as a superior service support dimension.

■ Business Product Strategy

Normally, organisations offer a range of products and services to their target markets. These products vary in many ways but management must devise and implement strategies that enable the organisation to achieve its marketing and, ultimately, business objectives.

Product strategy should consider the organisation's portfolio of products. Within the portfolio, two elements should be examined. One concerns the individual products, and plans should be developed for them accordingly. The second element concerns the whole product range and how products contribute to the overall, strategic framework of goods and services that make up the portfolio. Strategically, the management of the product portfolio is crucial.

Portfolios are made up of individual product items, lines of products, product mixes and the depth within each line, as follows:

- Product item: each individual product.
- Product line: clusters of products and services that are offered, in combination, to a designated market segment(s).
- Product mix: the number of product lines.
- Depth of line: the number of products offered within each line.

Within the portfolio approach, the goal is to make decisions that enhance the long-term profitability of the total set of products. This involves trading off one product line against another. For example, one product line might not be as technologically advanced as that offered by some competitors, but because one particularly strategically important customer is satisfied with this line, it has to be continued.

Another issue might concern the development of new products. Innovation requires reallocating some resources away from current product lines. Decisions need to be made about the potential contribution of new products and the opportunity costs this involves.

■ Product Lines

Organisations develop product strategies and policies. These concern the decisions that impact on the mix of products and product lines that an organisation chooses to offer its customers. Product lines are clusters of products and services that are offered together to a market segment(s). These lines should represent a coherent product mix so that when business customers move across segments, they perceive a consistency of value and hence competitive advantage. This has implications for positioning and marketing communications, which are considered later in the book.

Therefore, it is through the company's line of products that superior value and competitive advantage can be developed. The policies and strategies adopted by a company should be designed to sustain any advantage that might have been gained or be part of the process that seeks out new advantages.

One way in which product lines can be classified is based on the degree to which the content of product lines is standardised and mass produced, or customised to meet the individual, personal needs of each business customer. Using this approach, Shapiro (1977) suggested four main product line categories, each based on the level of customisation or the level of 'content specificity'. These are catalogue products, custom-built products, custom-designed products and business services.

Proprietary or catalogue products

These products are produced in anticipation of orders. Sellers speculate that there will be sufficient demand and stock is produced in a standard format. Although each type of proprietary good can have a number of different applications, the level of overall content specificity is limited and there is no opportunity to change the specification to meet the needs of different markets.

Product line decisions in this category, concern levels of stock to be made and held, the type of stock to be carried (adding and deleting lines) and the repositioning of products within the line.

Custom-built products

Not to be confused with custom-designed, these are products which are assembled for customers using preformed parts, subassemblies and components. They are then configured in particular ways so that they meet a specific customer's needs. For example, a computer network is a system assembled by using, among other things, particular hardware, such as cables, servers and modulators and software applications to meet the requirements of a particular customer. Some of these same parts, perhaps in different quantities and using different software, could be used for a different customer.

The approach is similar to the Lego building-block system, so apart from ensuring that the mix of 'blocks' is correct, product-line decisions revolve mainly around presenting different solutions to customer problems based upon a reconfiguration of the 'blocks'.

Custom-designed products

These products are custom-designed and built to meet the specific needs of a particular customer or very small group of customers. These products are often of high capital value. For example, a military tank or jet fighter, power generation plant or a type of machine to be used by astronauts working on a space station.

Product-line decisions are based around identifying and understanding the very specific needs of customers and then being able to present proposals that provide a tight fit with those needs.

■ Business services

Almost all B2B organisations provide a service. The main offering may be a product but there are services attached such as order processing, invoicing, delivery and warranty-based support. Some organisations provide a specific service package to support their products (for example, computer support packages) while for some organisations service is their core business activity (for example, management consultants). Whatever the level of services provided they are, by definition, unique. As suggested earlier in this chapter, the very intangibility of a service means that each time it is delivered there will be a slight variance or difference in quality.

■ Levels of Service

The interrelationship between products and services has become more entwined and complex. This is because organisations search for new ways to add value and differentiate themselves in markets characterised by rapid growth and shortening life cycles.

If all organisations provide a level of service then it follows that there is a spectrum across which products and services intertwine. At one end there will be completely 'tangible' products, and at the other end, completely 'intangible' services.

Support services are provided to augment product offerings. They are best characterised by high technology organisations such as IBM, Cisco or Sun Microsystems who offer products such as servers, cabling and disk drives but support these with installation, downloadable updates, training and consultancy services. Distributors also offer their channel partners a variety of added value services such as transportation, fulfilment and storage. The range and quality of services used to support the product offering will inevitably vary but they provide organisations with a means of sustainable differentiation. In addition, the provision of support services can be very profitable, often with margins higher than those generated through the sale of products alone.

Primary service providers do not have a tangible product and the service stands alone. Business insurance, management consultancy, professional services such as accountancy and financial audit services, security and advertising and marketing research agencies reflect some of the core activities in this area. In these situations, where there is an absence of a tangible product, the added value offered by service providers has to be concentrated on the quality and consistency of the service alone, as it cannot be bundled and dissipated across products.

■ Service Characteristics

As Gronroos (2000) argues, above all else, services are essentially processes. These processes are made up of a number of activities which in turn use resources. Customers interact directly with these activities so that at the point of production there is simultaneous consumption.

A large number of authors have turned their attention to issues concerning the marketing of services and most agree that services can be distinguished by five main characteristics (Wilson et.al. 2008; Gronroos, 2000; Lovelock *et al.*, 1999; Heskett *et al.*, 1997). These are intangibility, perishability, lack of ownership, inseparability and heterogeneity. See Table 2.2.

The idea that services can be distinguished by their intangibility has been questioned (Gronroos, 2000; Zeithaml and Bitner, 2000). The argument is that products are not always considered purely in terms of their tangible aspects and many services are themselves sometimes augmented by the presence of a tangible element. For example, consultancy services are perceived in terms of trust, feelings and overall confidence but part of the manifestation of a consultancy exercise is the tangible report submitted as evidence at the end of the consultancy process.

Gronroos (2000) highlights two main classifications namely, high-touch/ high-tech services and discretely/continuously rendered services. High-touch services are those which are very dependent on people for their delivery. In contrast high-tech services are dependent upon physical resources such as IS&T for their delivery. Gronroos recognises that there is often an overlap between these two, for example when people need to recover from a high-tech systems failure, but in the main these two approaches drive different approaches and service strategies.

Providers of continuously rendered services are typified by office cleaning, out-sourced contract delivery companies, facilities management and financial services. These represent a regularised flow of interaction through which it is possible to develop relationships. By definition, providers of discretely rendered services, such as brand or systems consultancy, printing, decoration or electrical testing services fail to present sufficient opportunity for relationships to be developed.

Table 2.2: Key characteristics of services

Characteristic	Explanation
Intangibility	Services are difficult to evaluate prior to purchase, they are perceived subjectively and are experienced at the point of consumption. Services deny people the opportunity to touch, feel, see or hear, prior to, during or after the consumption of a product, unlike products.
Perishability	Services are not capable of being stored, simply because they are created and consumed simultaneously.
Lack of ownership	Services are used but there is no transfer of ownership prior to consumption.
Inseparability	Services are produced and consumed simultaneously which means that the service providers and the customer are in contact with each other at the point of consumption.
Heterogeneity	Services involve the interaction of many people in their production and consumption. This means that each service encounter is likely to be different, making it difficult to deliver a consistent service experience for all customers.

ViewPoint 2.2: DHL deliver physical evidence

The service sector now accounts for some two thirds of economic activity in developed economies. From a marketing perspective, services present challenges associated with intangibility, perishability, ownership, inseparability and heterogeneity.

DHL are a global delivery service business. In addition to package and document collection and delivery for business and consumer markets, they offer a range of support services for businesses including address management, direct marketing, letter shop printing and fulfilment.

In terms of the extended service mix, the **process** involves door to door delivery and collection on a global scale using a range of mechanisms including vans, lorries and aeroplanes. These transport facilities provide **physical evidence** with livery painting in the DHL corporate colours of red and yellow incorporating the DHL logo. Call centres and delivery depots provide the base for those **people** involved in organising the delivery processes. Delivery personnel wear corporate uniforms supporting the physical evidence role.

These kinds of activities combine to provide what is more usually termed customer service, the effectiveness of which helps service organisations differentiate themselves competitively and establish ongoing customer relationships.

Source: Based on www.dhl.com; www.warc.com

Question: Why is it important for product manufacturers to add the elements associated with customer service to their business proposition?

■ Service Processes

Services are considered to be processes and indeed a substantial part of the academic literature on services is based on a process perspective. A process is a series of sequential actions that lead to predetermined outcomes. So, a simple process might be the steps necessary to visit a, whereas a complex process might be the actions necessary to manage company directors on a fact-finding trip to India or China.

If processes are an integral part of the operations performed by service organisations, in the general sense, what are they processing? Lovelock *et al.* (1999) argue that these processes are directly related to the equipment/people dimension referred to above. On the one hand, a haircut is people intensive but the failure of a network server is intensely equipment oriented. Lovelock *et al.* (1999) present a four-cell categorization of services based on tangible and intangible actions on people's bodies, minds, and physical assets. The categories involve four different processes: people processing, possession processing, mental stimulus processing, and information processing.

■ People Processing

In this type of processing, people have to physically present themselves so that they become immersed within the service process. This involves them spending varying amounts of time actively cooperating with the service operation. So, people taking a train have to physically go to the station and get on a train and spend time getting to their destination. People undergoing dentistry work will have made an appointment prior to attending the dentist's surgery, sit in the chair and open their mouths and cooperate with the dentist's various requests. They have physically become involved in the service process offered by their dentist.

From a marketing perspective, consideration of the process and the outcomes arising from participation in the service process can lead to ideas about what benefits are being created and what non-financial costs are incurred as a result of the service operation. For the dentistry example, a comfortable chair, background music, a non-threatening or neutral to warm décor, and a pleasant manner can be of help.

■ Possession Processing

Just as people have to go to the service operation for people processing, so objects have to become involved in possession processing. Possessions such as kitchen gadgets, gardens, cars, and computers are liable to breakdown or need maintenance. Cleaning, storing, repairing, plus couriering, installation, and removal services are typical possession-processing activities.

In these situations people will either take an item to the service provider, or invite someone in to undertake the necessary work. In possession processing the level of customer involvement is limited compared to people processing. In most cases the sequence of activities is as follows. In order that the object will be attended to, a telephone call is often required to fix an appointment. Then the item either needs to be taken to the service provider or you must wait for an attendant to visit. A brief to explain the problem/task/solution is given before returning at an agreed time/location to pay and take away the renewed item. This detachment from the service process enables people to focus on other tasks. The key difference here is that the quality of the service is not dependent on the owner or representative of the possession being present whilst the service operation takes place.

■ Mental Stimulus Processing

These types of services try to shape attitudes or behaviour. In order to achieve this, these services have to be oriented to people's minds, hence the expression 'mental stimulus processing'. Examples of these types of services include education, entertainment, professional advice, and news. In all of them, people have to become involved mentally in the service interaction and give time in order that they experience the benefits of this type of service.

Service delivery can be through one of two locations. First, services can be created in a location that is distant to the receiver. In this case, media channels are used to deliver the service. Alternatively, they can be delivered and consumed at the point where they originate, that is, in a studio, theatre, or hall. One of the key differences here is the form and nature of the audience experience. The theatre experience is likely to be much richer than the distant format. Digital technology has enabled opportunities for increased amounts of interactive communication, even though the experience will be different from the original. In the same way, online or e-learning in its purest form, has not yet become an established format, due perhaps to learners' needs to spend some of their learning time in interaction with their co-learners and in the presence of a tutor, for example, the use of summer schools operated by the Open University, and the increasing success of blended learning programmes.

■ Information Processing

The final type of service concerns the huge arena of information processing, the most intangible of all the services. Transformed by advances in technology, and computers in particular, information processing has become quicker, more accurate, and more frequent. The use of technology is important but we should not exclude people as individuals have a huge capacity to process information.

One key question that arises concerns the degree to which people should become involved in information processing. Some organisations deliberately route customers away from people processing and into information processing. EasyJet makes it difficult for customers to telephone the company and seek advice from expensive staff. Their approach is to drive people to their website and use the FAQs to answer customer queries.

■ The Product–Service Spectrum

Having considered products and services separately, it is necessary to bring them together as a product–service spectrum. This considers a range of services, from some that are attached directly to a product and some which consists of a pure stand-alone service. This enables the development of a services mix.

- *Pure product* – the offering is purely a product and devoid of any services. Examples include floor cleaning liquid, salt, and machine oil.

- *Product with some services* – here the product is supported with a range of one or more services. The more technologically sophisticated the product the more likely that it needs to be supported by services (Levitt, 1972). For example, conveyor belts require delivery, installation, warranties, and repair facilities.

- *Combination* – here products and services are used in equal proportion in order that customers' expectations are met. So, training and support services are expected to accompany enterprise and manufacturing software products.

- *Service with some products* – here the emphasis is on the service but some products are a necessary part of the mix. For example, business travellers book seats but in order that these are consumed, some products, such as food, drink, and internet facilities, are necessary to complete the travel experience.

- *Pure service* – here no products are involved in the service experience. Examples include financial/tax advice, consulting and training.

This interpretation should not of the service mix has been developed from Kotler (1997) and is useful because it demonstrates the wide range of services that are available, their complexity in terms of their variability, and the difficulty of defining and categorising them.

Services can also be appreciated in terms of other variables. For example, the degree to which customers need to be present at the time a service is delivered (training), or remote (the repair of a lorry). Another important variable concerns the significance and intensity of the equipment that is required to provide the service, as opposed to the intensity of people's contribution to the delivery of a service. So, at one extreme, use of automatic ordering system, is an example of an equipment-intensive service whilst office window cleaning an example of people-intensive services.

■ Product Life Cycle

The product life cycle (PLC) model follows the development of products from inception to decline. Despite not using the term 'product life cycle', Dean (1950) is accredited with being the pioneer of the PLC model (Tibben-Lembke, 2002). Since then the PLC concept has become established within the marketing litera-ture. Indeed, most readers are probably aware of the basic dynamics associated with this simple interpretation of the way a product is thought to evolve. The product life cycle suggests that, like human beings, products have a life. They are born, they grow, they become mature and they eventually decline and die (Meenaghan and Turnbull, 1981; Rickard and Jackson, 2000). The theory describes the progress of products, in terms of sales volume, over time. In other words, it depicts the functional relationship between sales, the dependent variable and time, the independent variable (Brockhoff, 1967). See Figure 2.1.

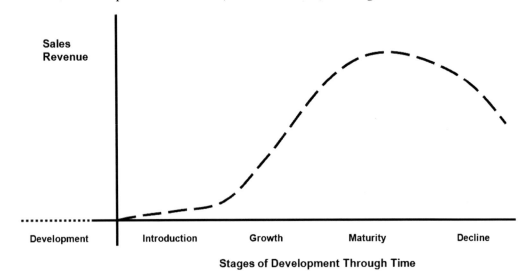

Figure 2.1: The product life cycle

There has been some confusion about what the PLC represents and this has lead to a debate about how useful the concept really is. As a result of this, three main PLC formats have emerged. These are an industry or class interpretation (for example telephone communications), a product-based interpretation (for exam-ple wireless or mobile telephones) and a brand-based perspective (the Motorola V50). Each of these has particular characteristics, different shaped curves and different managerial implications. This book refers to the product category level of the product life cycle.

Many authors and commentators, when referring to the PLC, discuss the model in terms of four main stages or phases. However, this view ignores the development activities, investments and effort required by organisations to bring new products and services to the marketplace. In the light of this important phase, a five-stage model is considered more appropriate.

Table 2.3 : Stages in the product life cycle

Stage in the PLC	Brief explanation
Development	Resources are allocated to testing and analysing materials and prototypes. Investment of resources is high as is collaboration with partners.
Introduction	Sales build slowly as customers are attracted to and want to try the product. Organisations in the supply chain adapt to the new processes and procedures and profits remain low or even negative, reflecting the heavy development costs and initial promotional investment. Customers learn how to adapt their own systems and to incorporate or use the product within their own operations to their best advantage.
Growth	Increased demand boosts sales, which together with profits start to increase quickly and the overall market expands rapidly. Competitors enter the market because demand is proven and their risk is lowered. The impact is to increase supply and the rate of market growth starts to subside. Organisations attempt to differentiate their products. Growth results from the product being specified by B2B customers as an integral or significant part of their own product offerings.
Maturity	Most potential buyers have adopted the product and soon sales reach their highest point before starting to slow. Very often competitors resort to discounting and price-based strategies. Due to increased competition, an increasingly stagnant market and suppliers who have achieved high volumes of production, some even experiencing economies of scale, strategy becomes orientated to protecting the volume of production.
Decline	The product eventually loses customer appeal as new products and new technologies enter the market. As a result the market consolidates as products (or organisations) are withdrawn. The focus of those that remain reverts to maintaining an efficient production capacity.

Overall commentary in the wealth of literature about the PLC, suggests the following as the main points of agreement:

■ Products have a limited life and their sales history follows an S-shaped path, at industry and product levels;

■ Products move through the different stages, within an overall cycle at different speeds (development, introduction, growth, maturity and decline);

■ The life of the product can be extended by many ways, such as introducing new ways of using the product, finding new users, developing new attributes (for example, service enhancements);

■ The average profitability per unit rises and then falls as products move through the later stages.

In the 1950s and 1960s, when markets focused on consumer goods, simple segmentation and unsophisticated communications, the product life cycle model was an acceptable interpretation of market dynamics (Wood, 1990). However, Dhalla and Yuspeh (1976) and then Wood began to cast doubt on the validity of the PLC concept. The former suggested that the sequential nature of the concept was the actual cause of its failure to be of any real assistance. They argued that the theory induces executives to neglect existing brands and place undue emphasis on new products. In this way, the company may not only lose an opportunity to prolong the life of a profitable offering, but also risk developing an ambitiously new product, one which requires a bigger budget than would be required to sustain an established product. Wood drew attention to the different levels of market stability that existed over the decades.

The PLC is a simple and intuitively appealing concept. Wood, Dhalla and Yuspeh and others have challenged its validity and practicality as a planning tool.

■ Technological Applications and the PLC

Product lifecycle management or PLM can be considered to be a strategic approach that organisations develop to manage product information in order to optimise the returns of a product. Product lifecycle management solutions have evolved to provide a way for all parties involved with different phases of the life cycle to collaborate with one another in order to reduce cycle costs and to reach their markets more quickly. Sometimes referred to as collaborative PLM, these systems seek to improve operational performance across the supply chain, from new product design through to decline and retirement.

The material requirements, logistics and complex array of people, technologies and organisations involved with the cycle of product development and delivery mean that there has always been scope for inefficiency, communication breakdown and lengthy and expensive time delays. PLM applications are designed to foster collaboration among all those involved in managing the product life cycle, in particular the new product development process.

PLM solutions are a collection of integrated software tools and operations that are used to manage the whole process, single stages of the lifecycle or to connect different tasks. Some software providers cover the whole PLM range while others a single niche application. These systems use web-enabled technologies in order to blend all or some of the following applications: CAD/CAM (Computer Aided Design/Computer Aided Manufacturing), PDM, visualisation technologies, collaboration capabilities and integration with existing enterprise applications. See, for example, offerings at www.appliedgroup.co.uk, the PLM pages on the IBM website www.ibm.com and articles at www.technologyevaluation.com. See also ViewPoint 2.3.

Strategic Implications Arising from the PLC

In order for a product to be successful, marketing activities need to be varied throughout its life. No one strategy is sufficient for a product to achieve its potential. Chattopadhyay (2001) believes that the way a product is managed, at each stage, is key to its survival. Each stage of the product life cycle requires different strategies. Each stage has particular characteristics and thus requires different strategies relating to promotion, pricing, distribution and competition, to achieve its objectives and to maximise profitability (Barksdale and Harris, 1982; Onkvisit and Shaw, 1983; Grantham, 1997).

One strategy, referred to by Levitt (1965) is the 'used apple policy'. Here a company does not attempt to be first into a market, but chooses to wait while other companies do the pioneering and take the 'first bite of the apple'. If it is a 'juicy apple' these waiting organisations will then enter the market with a much reduced risk. The penalty for this approach is that they are unlikely to achieve market leadership and the best possible return on their investment. However, the second bite of a juicy apple is judged to be good enough. Shankar *et al.* (1999) support the 'used apple policy' as their research found that products which enter a market in the growth stage reach a high level of sales faster than the pioneer products. However, market strategies have already been shaped so there is reduced flexibility for radically changing elements of the marketing mix in order to improve their return.

Product differentiation is an important aspect of both the growth and maturity stages. Products that are able to find a strong position and which provide superior customer value are more likely to generate higher margins and help build relationships.

When a product reaches the latter end of its productive life, there are two main alternative ways to ending it. The first involves no managerial intervention and product sales decline steadily to the point where the product eventually dies. The second, which does require intervention, is referred to as 'euthanasia' and entails voluntary withdrawal of the product from the market. There is a possible third approach, which involves the rejuvenation of a product that was in decline, perhaps by proposing new uses or radically different target groups. This may require repositioning but, if physical changes are made, it is questionable whether it is the same product or a new one.

New Product Development (NPD)

An important part of the management of portfolios and product life cycles is to be able to control the development of new products. The reasons for this are many but the main ones include a need to balance the demise of older products, to provide new ways of providing superior customer value and to reduce the risks inherent when developing new products.

Business Products and Services

There are many approaches to new product development and the process and it would be wrong to suggest that there should be uniformity (Ozer, 2003). The procedures adopted by an organisation reflect its attitude to risk, its culture, strategy, the product and market and, above all else, its approach to customer relationships. This ranges along a spectrum from an engineering approach at one end to a customer relationship perspective at the other. Those who exhibit an engineering approach tend to be product-orientated and prefer market or transactional exchanges. Some organisations try to generate new products either in response to gaps identified in markets or as a direct result of working with customers and developing products to meet their particular needs. These exhibit a preference for relational exchanges.

The term 'new products' can be misleading, because organisations do not just develop genuine new products. They also develop and extend products and services and they adapt and mould the processes associated with products. For example, in high-technology markets various project formats have been identified. Some projects centre on improving products but others focus on the associated manufacturing processes. Some projects look at both elements. Wheelwright and Clark (1992) suggest four types of development project (see Table 2.4).

Table 2.4: Four types of development project

Type of project	Explanation
Derivative projects	The incremental development of product and/or process improvements (e.g. new product features).
Platform projects	The creation of components that are shared by a mix of products and/or processes (e.g. a new battery to fit a range of products).
Breakthrough projects	The creation of genuine new products and/or processes (e.g. computer disks).
Research and development	The creation of new materials and technologies that lead to commercial development.

Source: Based on Wheelwright and Clark (1992).

Due to the complexity and risks associated with the development of new products, organisations usually adopt a procedural approach. These phases enable organisations to monitor progress, test-trial and consult before committing themselves to the market. The most common general new product development (NPD) process is set out at Figure 2.2. This sequence should be considered not only as a generalisation, but that the various NPD episodes do not necessarily occur in the linear sequence that this depiction suggests. However, the one major difference concerns the level of end-user involvement. In consumer markets the level of customer involvement is restricted and distant. In business markets customer involvement, especially where collaborative relationship conditions exist, is actively encouraged and is an important driver in the overall process.

■ Idea generation

Ideas for new products should not be expected to emerge just from the marketing department. Responsibility for the generation of great ideas that lead to great new products should rest with everyone. That means a corporate culture which fosters creativity and supports people when they bring forward new ideas for product processes, enhancements and other improvements. Ideally, new ideas should be driven by customers and so reflect a sharing and collaborative relationship. In many cases this happens but ideas can emerge from many other sources. The origin of these ideas can be classified as either internal or external sources.

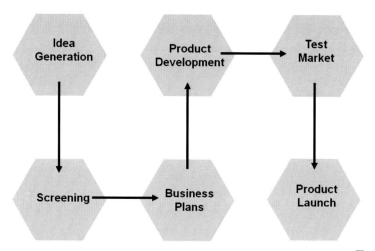

Figure 2.2: The new product development process

- ■ *Internal* sources include R&D departments, customer service employees, the sales force, project development teams and secondary data sources such as sales records. This list should emphasise the breadth of the internal sources available to organisations when seeking to develop their portfolios.

- ■ *External* sources include market research data, competitors, website and sales literature analysis, and customers themselves who draw attention to specific problems or their own market opportunities.

In some business markets there are a few customers who dominate the volume of purchases made in that sector (for example, capital equipment markets). These small number of customers are referred to as lead users and are the equivalent to early adopters in consumer markets (von Hippel, 1982). Working with these lead users to identify opportunities can be beneficial, as it is probable that if their needs can be met then the rest of the market will subsequently follow on.

■ Screening

All ideas need to be evaluated in order that only those that meet predetermined criteria are taken forward. This screening process must be separate to the idea generation stage otherwise creativity might be hampered. Concept testing allows for a small representative sample of customers to review the product idea in order to gauge their attitudes before any substantial investment is made to develop the idea further.

Screening needs to ensure that the proposed new product meets strategic criteria and fits with organisational objectives. Following the earlier consideration of core competences, all new ideas should be evaluated in the light of the future competences that are determined as necessary to provide customer value. The other screening process involves considering the ideas in the light of how it is believed the market will react and the effort that the organisation will need to make to bring the product to the market.

Business plans and market analysis

Drucker (1985) determined that there were three main reasons why new products fail:

1 There is no market for the product.

2 There is a market need but the product does not meet customer requirements.

3 The product's ability to meet the market need, although satisfactory, is not adequately communicated to the target market.

It is crucial that, as well as a thorough analysis of the size, shape and dynamics of the market, a business plan is prepared. From this information the potential profitability can be established early on. Weak profit forecasts, problematic manufacturing requirements, market need already being met by stronger competitive products or the market simply not being strong enough, are all indicators that the product proposal may not be in the best interests of the organisation and should be dropped.

Product Development and Selection

Management must decide, in the light of all the information at their disposal, which of the ideas that have reached this stage in the process are selected for further development. Those ideas that are selected and progress from this point are now clearly deemed to have commercial potential.

It is at this stage that prototypes and test versions are developed and subjected to functional performance tests, design revisions, manufacturing requirements analysis, distribution investigations and a multitude of other testing procedures. The objective is to minimise risk and maximise potential. Consequently there is a trade-off between the need to test and reduce risk and the need to go to market and drive income.

Test Market

The urge to go to market is tempered by the penultimate stage of taking the product, in its finished format, to a test market. This piloting procedure is designed to launch and test the product under controlled, real market conditions. Using a particular geographical region or specific number of customer locations the intention is to evaluate the product and the whole marketing programme under real working conditions. Test marketing, or field trials, enable the product and marketing plan to be refined or adapted in the light of market reaction, before release to the whole market. Again the overriding goal is to reduce risk.

Test marketing in terms of regional or limited customer conditions does not apply to new products that have been developed through collaborative customer–seller relationships. Under these relational conditions the product is first tested by the customer, with the intention of fine-tuning the final product.

ViewPoint 2.3 Bombardier develop new aircraft with PLM

Based in Montreal, Bombardier Aerospace is a world leader in the design and manufacture of innovative aviation products and services for the regional and amphibious markets. Demand for regional aircraft has increased and so has the competition.

Much of Bombardier's success is due to high levels of efficiency within its design and manufacturing processes. Bombardier's primary point of differentiation is its innovative capacity and that means staying ahead of the competition.

Bombardier's regional jet, the CRJ1000 NextGen, was designed to achieve two main goals: provide significant operating cost advantages for clients and improve the passenger experience. Yet to attain these goals and stay ahead of the competition Bombardier needed to cut two years from its design-to-manufacture cycle. The company already used product lifecycle management (PLM) tools to streamline its design processes it needed to use these faster and without disrupting its core business activities.

The solution was to outsource all aspects of its PLM systems to a specialist PLM provider (IBM), enabling Bombardier to operate even more effectively and competitively. Some of the benefits included:

- A 40% increase in the efficiency of complex machining processes associated with a new wing design
- An estimated $30 million reduction in costs associated with deploying and maintaining PLM over 5 years
- A faster time to market
- The elimination of the time, effort and cost of acquiring highly specialized PLM technicians over the multiple phases of a new aircraft programme.

Source: Based on IBM Case Study retrieved 9 January 2011 from www-1.ibm.com/software/success/cssdb.nsf/CS/JSTS7C6LYM?OpenDocument&Site=default&cty=en_us

Question: Identify three PLM issues associated with building a new distribution warehouse.

■ Product launch

The launch of a final product into a target market represents the culmination of the preceding tests, analysis and development work. To launch a new product organisations normally prepare a launch plan. This considers the needs of distributors, end-user customers, marketing communication agencies and other relevant stakeholders, many of them internal. The objective is to schedule all those activities that are required to make the launch successful.

In addition to promotional work such as the preparation of articles and features to appear in trade and technical journals, customers and/or dealers need to be advised. First, they need to be informed and educated in terms of product capabilities; later, they need to be trained to use the product. In addition to the obvious need to train and instruct the sales force, internal customer support services, such as finance, distribution, order processing and the communications team should be included in the launch plan. The purpose is to enable them to provide product support based on appropriate knowledge and training so that they understand how customers are expected to use the product and what to do to enable them to derive its full benefits.

■ New Service Development

For many years researchers have focused on the processes associated with developing new products, rather than services. This is partly because researchers have perceived the development of new services as either problematic or very similar to that of products. This has begun to change as many western economies have become increasingly service orientated.

Three service innovation strategies have been identified (Moller et al. 2008). These are established services within competitive markets; incremental service innovation targeting value-added offerings; and radical service innovation, which aim to produce completely novel offerings. These are based on the view that developing value creation is key to the development of innovative service offerings and concepts.

Established services with a relatively stable value creation process are often generated under intense competitive behaviour in order to improve operational efficiency. Dell is cited as a business based on a simple concept, namely selling computer systems direct to customers. Dell's market leadership is the result of a constant focus on delivering positive product and service experiences to customers.

Incremental service innovation is a value creation strategy in which services are developed to provide additional value. Through collaboration, the service provider and client can produce more effective solutions. For example, Google provides search services for corporate clients, including advertisers, content publishers, and site managers. Google continually develops new service applications based on its back-end technology, and the use of linked PCs which respond immediately to each query. Google's innovation has resulted in faster response times, greater scalability, and lower costs.

Radical service innovation is about the generation of value creation through novel or unusual service concepts. This requires new technologies, offerings, or business concepts and involves radical system-wide changes in existing value systems. MySQL is regarded as the world's leading open-source database software producer. By making the source code of the software freely available to everybody, the software is available to everyone to use and/or modify. However, all derivative works must be made available to the original developers. As a result MySQL have been able to increase the number of users and developers, and subsequently offer their clients improved levels of service. This has led to increased financial performance.

■ Stages of Product/Service Innovation Development

As established earlier, services are not always just an add-on to a product offering. They can also be a way of creating value opportunities for clients. The degree to which the service element contributes to an offering can vary. For example, the initial stages of innovation maturity can be characterised by a product-focus with a relatively small amount of services used only to augment and complement the products. Later stages, such as maturity, are characterised by increased levels of service, some integrated with the products to provide solutions for customer problems. Shelton (2009) extends this two-stage approach and considers service innovation in the context of four stages.

Stage 1 – Services are used as after-sale product support, for example, parts and repair. Service innovation is framed around maintaining the product, and ensuring that customers are satisfied with their product purchase. As a result, customers typically view the service and product businesses as distinct entities.

Stage 2 – After-sale services are designed to complement the core product. Services should attempt to improve customer satisfaction with existing products, increase loyalty and may generate additional purchases. Sheldon refers to Hewlett-Packard's 'PC Tune-Up', which for a fee, provides a set of diagnostics to assess and manage customers.

Stage 3 – A full set of services and products are designed to provide a clearly differentiated offering aimed at solving clients' life cycle problems. Again, Sheldon refers to Motorola's 'Total Network Care' (TNC) which provides end-to-end support services for wireless networks. Although the service organisation is often consolidated in one identifiable business, products are still core to the company. End-user customers see no major perceived boundaries between products and services.

Stage 4 – Firms seek to integrate the services dimension as part of their total offer. Referred to as 'servitisation', this stage involves the provision of an integrated bundle of product/service solutions for the entire life cycle of their customers, 'from cradle to grave'. Firms work collaboratively to construct innovative solutions that are of mutual value. For example, Rolls Royce will contract with an airline to service an engine throughout its life.

■ The Technology Adoption Life Cycle

Further to discussions about life cycles and the development of new products and services is the technology adoption life cycle, proposed by Moore (1991). This model was developed to explain the way in which high-technology products are adopted by customers. Of particular interest are breakthrough or discontinuous innovations. These are new products/services that require users to break away from established behaviours, to behave differently and derive other benefits. Moore refers to dramatic changes in behaviour and spectacular benefits to be gained.

The idea builds on the innovation diffusion model, offered by Rogers (1983), but identifies different types of buyer. See Table 2.5.

From technophiles, through visionaries, pragmatists, conservatives to sceptics or laggards, these customer groups all use these discontinuous products but adopt them at different times, for different reasons. Business-to-business marketing should account for these different customer segments and develop appropriate strategies.

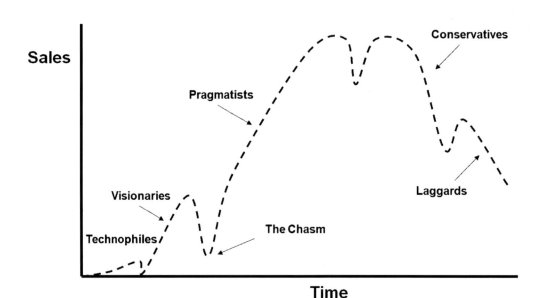

Figure 2.3: The technology adoption life cycle (Moore, 1991)

Sales of these high-technology products follow a cycle similar to that in Figure 2.3. Technophiles are influential in that they will provide credibility and endorsement for a new technical product. Visionaries on the other hand have the resources necessary to adopt these products. However, they will invariably demand changes and adaptions to the product which pose problems for the supplying organisation. Technophiles and visionaries provide early growth and visibility for these innovative products but, as Moore observed, sales often begin to fall after a bright start and a chasm develops between the visionaries and the pragmatists. Pragmatists are analytical and provide a route to the mass markets. The trick is to be able to cross the chasm and sell into the high-volume purchasers and then sell on to the conservatives, who although reluctant to buy high-technology products do so because they do not want to be left behind in the market.

Table 2.5: Different types of buyer in high-technology markets

Type of customer		Key characteristics
Moore	**Rogers**	
Technophiles	Innovators	Customers who enjoy using and mastering new technological products. They like to be at the forefront of developments and to be seen to be involved in developing and shaping how products are perceived. They do not always have sufficient influence over resources to impact on organisation-wide adoption. However, they do have a big influence over visionaries.
Visionaries	Early adopters	Customers who can see the competitive advantage to be gained from being first to use new technology products in their industry. However, they often demand customised solutions which are often difficult to deliver. As in consumer markets, this group is characterised by their willingness to accept high levels of risk (for high reward).
Pragmatists	Early majority	Evolution rather than revolution characterises the views of this group. Rather than be passionately involved they see technology as a necessity. They will buy once the products have been tested by others and even then are dependent upon third-party recommendation. Despite their slightly cautious approach the majority of mainstream high-technology sales are made to this group.
Conservatives	Late majority	This group are reluctant to involve themselves with new technological solutions and doubt the value they bring to an organisation. Purchases are made because of a fear of being left behind the competition but even then price is a sensitive issue and they demand a great deal in negotiations.
Sceptics	Laggards	This is not a viable customer group as they are critical of technology and do not believe technology can improve productivity. They often strive to block new technological initiatives.

Source: Based on Moore (1991) and Rogers (1993).

To get across the chasm the seller needs to find a niche market of pragmatists who are willing to risk purchase without the support of other pragmatists. A very customer-focused strategy is required to target buyers who have a real need for the innovation. Moore asserts that once the chasm is breached a tornado strategy often develops as sales rise rapidly. This is because these buyers prefer to buy from a market leader, which in turn leads to the development of new industry-wide standards and the rush of new peripheral products and software that support the product.

It should be noted that there is little empirical research to support Moore's ideas. However, there is a great deal of observational research that endorses this interpretation and the strategies that explain the initial break in sales development (the 'chasm') and the rush of sales (the 'tornado') that often occurs later.

Summary

In order to consolidate your understanding of the principles of business products and services, here is a summary of the main points set against the learning objectives.

1 Examine the characteristics of business products.

Products are more than just the pure physical form and utility they outwardly present. Products have two main attributes: tangible and intangible. Organisational buyers perceive business products as a bundle of attributes and therefore it is important to understand which bundle different buyers prefer.

2 Appreciate the nature and significance of product strategies.

Organisations offer a range of products and services and management must devise and implement strategies that enable the organisation to achieve its marketing and, ultimately, business objectives.

Product strategy should consider an organisation's portfolio of products. Within the portfolio, two elements should be examined. One concerns the individual products, and plans should be developed for them accordingly. The second element concerns the whole product range and how products contribute to the overall, strategic framework of goods and services that make up the portfolio. Strategically, the management of the product portfolio is crucial.

3 Understand the significance of services in business markets and marketing.

In a search to add value and provide a point of differentiation, organisations often incorporate a level of service into their portfolios. The level of service offering varies to the extent that a spectrum of product/service combinations can be determined.

Services should be considered to be a process and four process types can be identified. These are: people processing, possession processing, mental stimulus processing, and information processing.

4 Evaluate the new product and new service development processes.

An important part of the management of product portfolios and life cycles is to be able to control the development of new products and services. The reasons for this are to balance the demise of older products, to provide new ways of providing superior customer value and to reduce the risks inherent when developing new products.

The new product development process identifies distinct stages in the development of products. Each stage is designed to reduce risk and improve the chances of success. Although New Service development can also be considered in terms of stages or phases, their role also needs to be evaluated in terms of their integration with any products offered.

5 Examine the product life cycles and determine how these might impact on business marketing.

The product lifec yle theory describes the functional relationship between sales and time. Five distinct yet difficult to anticipate or predict stages can be identified: development, introduction, growth, maturity and decline.

A variety of strategies and technological applications have been developed to help manage products in order to optimise performance and return on investment.

6 Explain the technology life cycle model

The technology adoption life cycle was developed to explain the way in which high-technology products are adopted by customers. Of particular interest are, breakthrough or discontinuous innovations. These are new products/services that require users to break away from established behaviours, to behave differently and derive other benefits.

■ Discussion Questions

1 Identify and explain the four main product line categories which are based upon the level of customisation, as suggested by Shapiro (1977).

2 To what extent should B2B marketers use the product life cycle concept?

3 Discuss some of the key issues associated with the new product development process.

4 Explain the ideas associated with servitisation.

5 Consider the issues associated with using digital technologies to develop value creation.

6 Identify the key characteristics and evaluate the different types of buyer said by Moore (1991) to typify high-technology markets.

References

Barksdale, H.C. and Harris, C.E. Jr (1982) Portfolio analysis and the product life cycle, *Long Range Planning*, **15** (December), 74–83

Brockhoff, K. (1967). A test for the product life cycle, *Econometrica*, **35** (3–4), 472–484

Chattopadhyay, S.P. (2001). Relationship marketing in an enterprise resource planning environment, *Marketing Intelligence and Planning*, **19** (2), 136–139

Dean, J. (1950). Pricing policies for new products, *Harvard Business Review*, **28** (6), 45–53

Dhalla, N.K. and Yuspeth, S. (1976). Forget the product life cycle, *Harvard Business Review*, **54** (January/February), 102–104.

Drucker, P. (1985). The discipline of innovation, *Harvard Business Review*, **63** (May–June), 167–72

Grantham, L.M. (1997). The validity of the product life cycle in the high-tech industry, *Marketing Intelligence and Planning*, **15** (1), 4–10

Gronroos, C. (2000). *Service Management and Marketing*, 2nd edn, Chichester: Wiley.

Heskett, J.L., Sasser, Jr., W.E. and Schlesinger, L.A. (1997) *The Service Profit Chain: How Leading Companies Link Profit and Growth to Loyalty, Satisfaction and Value*, New York: Free Press.

Hubbard, R. (2011) Office furniture market sees further decline, *ID News*, retrieved 7 April 2011 from www.idnews.co.uk/office-furniture-market-sees-further-decline-cms-1392

Hutt, M., Hutt, M.D. and Speh, T.W. (2009) *Business Marketing Management*, 10 edn, Fort Worth, TX: Harcourt

Kotler, P. (1997), *Marketing Management*, 9th (international) edn., Upper Saddle River, NJ: Pearson Education.

Levitt, T. (1965) Exploit the product life cycle, *Harvard Business Review*, **43**, (November/December), 81–94.

Levitt, T. (1972), Production-line approach to service, *Harvard Business Review*, **50** (5), 20–31.

Lovelock, C., Vandermerwe, S. and Lewis, B. (1999) *Services Marketing*, Hemel Hempstead: Financial Times/Prentice Hall

Meenaghan, A., and Turnbull, P.W. (1981) The application of product life cycle theory to popular record marketing, *European Journal of Marketing*, **15** (5), 1–50

Möller, K., Rajala, R. and Westerlund, M. (2008) Service innovation myopia? A new recipe for client/provider value creation, *California Management Review*, **50** (3) (Spring), 31-48

Moore, G.A. (1991). *Crossing the Chasm: Marketing and Selling Technology Products to Mainstream Customers*, New York: HarperCollins.

Onkvist, S. and Shaw, J.F. (1983) Examination of the product life cycle and its applications within marketing, *Columbia Journal of Word Business*, **18** (Fall), 73–99

Ozer, M. (2003) Process implications of the use of the Internet in new product development: a conceptual analysis, *Industrial Marketing Management*, **32** (6) (August), 517–30

Rickard, L. and Jackson, K. (2000) *The Financial Times Marketing Casebook*, 2nd edn, London: Prentice Hall, pp. 52–59.

Rogers, E.M. (1983). *Diffusion of Innovations*, 3rd edn, New York, NY: Free Press.

Shankar, V., Carpenter, G.S. and Krishnamurthi, L. (1999) The advantages of entry in the growth stage of the product life cycle: an empirical analysis, *Journal of Marketing Research*, 36, 2, 269–277.

Shapiro, B.P. (1977). *Industrial Product Policy: Managing the Existing Product Line*, Cambridge, MA: Marketing Science Institute, pp. 37–39.

Shelton, R (2009) Integrating product and service innovation, *Research Technology Management*, **52** (3), (May/June) 38-44,

Tibben-Lembke, R.S. (2002). Life after death: reverse logistics and the product life cycle, *International Journal of Physical Distribution and Logistics Management*, **32** (3), pp. 223–244

von Hippel, E. (1982) Get new products from customers, *Harvard Business Review*, **60**, (March/April), 117–122.

Wheelwright, S.C. and Clark, K.B. (1992)Creating product plans to focus product development, *Harvard Business Review*, **70** (March/April), 70–82.

Wilson, A., Zeithaml, V.A., Bitner, M.J. and Gremler, D.D. (2008) *Services Marketing*, Maidenhead: McGraw-Hill

Wood, L. (1990) The end of the product life cycle? Education says goodbye to an old friend, *Journal of Marketing Management*, 6 (2), 145–155.

Zeithaml, V.A. and Bitner, M.J. (2000) *Services Marketing*, New York, NY: McGraw-Hill

3 Organisational Buying Behaviour

Overview

This chapter introduces traditional views about organisational buying behaviour, before progressing to consider the importance of relationships and the contribution that systems and technology have made to this aspect of business marketing.

The chapter starts with a comparison of the main characteristics associated with both consumer and organisational purchasing behaviour. Then, following an examination of the decision making unit and the decision making processes generally assumed to be adopted by organisations, the focus moves to reflect upon the different influences that can impact on an organisation's purchasing activities.

The last section looks at the nature of uncertainty and the way in which organisations attempt to reduce buyer-perceived risk. It ends by examining how relationships between buyers and sellers can evolve and affect the purchasing behaviour of organisations.

Aims and objectives

The aim of the chapter is to examine the behaviour, characteristics and processes that organisations use to purchase products and services.

The objectives of this chapter are to:

1 Compare the characteristics of organisational and consumer buying behaviour.

2 Explore the membership and main characteristics of the decision making unit.

3 Explain organisational decision making processes.

4 Consider the influences on organisational buyer behaviour.

5 Determine and reflect upon the nature of risk and uncertainty in B2B markets.

6 Consider some of the issues concerning the use of technology within eProcurement.

A Slice of Life – Consulting with Consultancies

The trap that many internal marketing departments fall into is that of 'familiarity'. They have a 'proven' list of to-dos based on last year's list of to-dos and unless there is some form of intervention, that's what they're going to deliver. Again. They repeat the same mistakes from the previous year(s) either because they are incapable of learning from their mistakes, or, more likely, because they have no alternative benchmark from which to learn and no available resource with which to explore new opportunities. At that point the enterprise will buy-in external expertise to provide the required products and services. The process for engaging those external services, however, varies considerably – from, "I need help with my brand strategy, I'll call Scot…" to, "I need help with my brand strategy, Scot will be one of a dozen agencies that will be asked to respond to a 300-page Request for Proposal developed, issued and evaluated by the Enterprise Procurement Team."

Sellers always want to sell fast. The spectrum of buying behaviour is therefore limited only by the capacity for procrastination of the buying organisation. We can call it something else if you like – best practice, due diligence, risk mitigation, creative appetite – but if you really want to buy something, there is a product (and/or service) and a price. That's it. And yet for every successful 'trade', there are any number of trade failures for both buyer and seller.

I was somewhat surprised to receive a phone call from the marketing department of a very large, global, management consultancy one day. The caller's Marketing Director had heard me speak at a conference and had been sufficiently impressed to have 'his people talk to my people…' We arranged a meeting to explore how I might provide creative services to the company.

In conversation, the client explained that the management consultancy had an internal marketing team of over 350 people – in the UK alone. I nearly fell off my chair. "Three HUNDRED and fifty? What on earth do you need me for then?"

It transpired that while there was any number of 'worker ants' delivering the various components of marketing services, no one within the organisation really thought about the creative development of the brand. Or rather, such strategic thinking was reserved for the senior partners within the consultancy – and they had better things to do. So they wanted some creative help. They didn't call it that of course, because this organisation could never be seen to need 'help'. But that's what they were looking for and they'd asked me to challenge their thinking creatively and deliver concepts that would excite their market place.

So that's what we did – challenge. Not without due consideration for the brand or its audiences of course, but there seemed little point in submitting traditional corporate communications of the type that over 300 of their staff might equally conceive. One example of the work that I presented was a picture of a clearly aggressive and very old lady sticking two fingers up at the camera. The accompanying headline for the concept read, "Two things that your grandma never told you about the mid-tier market…" It was controversial no doubt, but it played directly to the younger 'Y-Generation' audience whose attention the client was seeking. And the client liked it.

The consultative nature of the client business had made it unable to make an instinctive decision however. So the client took the concept to focus group research. Unsurprisingly, the younger groups loved the 'in your face' approach and confirmed that they would respond favourably to any such communication from the client. The older generation of business leaders were appalled, shocked and more than a little outraged. Faced with a potential backlash of opinion and in order to protect the brand's reputation the client ultimately decided to do what it seemingly always decided to do when creatively challenged – it did nothing. The project was considered a success – "We've established how far not to step over the line…" The work was paid for, assimilated and quietly consigned to the too-scary shelf.

This was a process to be repeated several times with the consultancy on a variety of projects that were all paid for, considered successes, but with no output. They liked being scared, they liked the challenge. They liked being taken to the precipice and peering over, but were unable to take the plunge. As the internal decision making process escalated, the exuberance and initial approval of junior management was being countermanded by the safety-conscious senior management.

In every instance of the projects delivered, there was a clearly viable business case for creative communications. It started with the brief and the initial requirement demanding a creative response and it ended with market research confirming that the target audience would respond positively. But they still never left the parking lot. In the example of the 'two fingers granny' given, there was a clear and compelling strategy to segment the audience into the 'old' and the 'new' and simply deliver the new communications to the new audience. But no.

The result of indecision is inertia and that's what transpired with this consulting firm. In the end, I declined to accept any further projects from the client. There didn't seem much point. It's hard to continue to deliver creative services when the creative component is slowly and painfully eroded. It would have been considerably more efficient to eliminate creativity as a mandate and simply select a tried and tested headline to accompany any one of the many corporate handshake or blue sky photographs that were abundant within the brand guidelines carefully compiled by over 300 staff…

We had a meeting about my declining the work and my client was clearly surprised. They wanted to continue giving me work that would never see the light of day and they weren't used to hearing the word "no". But it's not just the clients who make decisions – the decision making process cuts both ways. As well as companies making decisions about how they spend their money, it's worth remembering that as individuals within companies, we also make decisions about how we earn it.

Scot McKee

■ Introduction

Organisational buying, according to Webster and Wind (1972), is 'the decision making process by which formal organisations establish the need for purchased products and services and identify, evaluate and choose among alternative brands and suppliers'. One of the important aspects of this definition is that organisational buying behaviour is a process rather than a static, one-off event. There are a number of stages, or phases, associated with product and service procurement, each one often requiring a key decision to be made. Organisations buy products and services on a regular basis and professional purchasing is a requirement in most businesses. Thus organisational buying behaviour is an integral part of the external relationships that an enterprise develops, either as a part of market-based exchanges or as fully developed relational exchanges.

The purchase of products and services by organisations presents a risk which varies according to many factors. For example, the complexity of the product or the frequency of purchase decisions may impact on the risk factor. The formalisation of buying behaviour in organisations symbolises the potential risk as well as being a means to reduce it. Perceived risk in this context will be examined later in the chapter.

Organisational buying behaviour is not just about the purchase of goods and services. In addition to this fundamental task, it is concerned with the development and management of interorganisational relationships. The placement of orders and contracts between organisations can confirm a current trading relationship, initiate a new set of relationships, or may even signal the demise of a relationship. Clearly this aspect of organisational buying behaviour is important where there are relational exchanges. However, even in market exchanges, organisations should be alert to the relationship potential.

In order to explore organisational buying behaviour (OBB), attention will first be given to comparing organisational with consumer buying behaviour. This is followed by an exploration of the characteristics of the decision making unit, the different types of buying situations, the process stages that are often involved. In conclusion, the impact of the use of technology within eProcurement is considered.

■ Comparing Organisational and Consumer Buyer Behaviour

There is a natural inclination, when exploring organisational buyer behaviour, to refer to consumer buyer behaviour and to highlight the differences. However, this only serves to differentiate and fails to reveal areas of overlap and similarity. The intention here is to consider the main characteristics and evaluate both the differences and the similarities that exist between the two. The differences are presented in Table 3.1.

Table 3.1: A comparison of buying characteristics in organisational and consumer markets

	Consumer buying	Organisational buying
Number of buyers	Many	Few
Purchase initiation	Self	Others
Evaluative criteria	Social, ego and level of utility	Price, value and level of utility
Information search	Normally short	Normally long
Range of suppliers used	Small number of suppliers considered	Can be extensive
Importance of supplier choice	Normally limited	Can be critical
Size of orders	Small	Large
Frequency of orders	High	Low
Value of orders placed	Low	High
Complexity of decision making	Low to medium	Medium
Range of information inputs	Limited	Moderate to extensive

One of the main characteristics is that there are far fewer buyers in organisational markets than in consumer markets. Even though there may be several people associated with a buying decision in an organisation, the overall number of people involved in buying, say, packaging products or road construction equipment is very small compared with the millions of people who might potentially buy a chocolate bar. The financial value of organisational purchase orders is invariably larger and the frequency with which they are placed is much lower. It is quite common for agreements to be made between organisations for the supply of materials over a number of years. Similarly, depending upon the complexity of the product (for example, photocopying paper or a one-off satellite), the negotiation process may also take a long time.

Although there are differences, many of the characteristics associated with consumer decision making processes can still be observed in the organisational

context. However, organisational buyers make decisions which ultimately contribute to the achievement of corporate objectives. To make the necessary decisions, a high volume of pertinent information is often required. This information
needs to be relatively detailed and is normally presented in a rational and logical
style. The needs of the buyers are many and complex and some may be personal.
Goals, such as promotion and career advancement within the organisation, cou-
pled with ego and employee satisfaction combine to make organisational buying
an important task, one that requires professional training and the development
of expertise if the role is to be performed optimally.

Similarities

It was mentioned earlier that, as well as the major differences between the two
types of purchasing contexts, an increasing number of similarities are now being
recognised. For example, the implied rationality of decision making in organisational contexts and the assumption that consumer decision making is more
unstructured and emotionally driven is questionable. Many personal purchases
are of such technical complexity (for example financial services) that consumers
need to adopt a more rational, fact-based approach to their buying.

Wilson (2000) explores the issues related to rationality and the implied differences. For example, consumers make product-related purchase decisions based
on a wide array of inputs from other people and not just those in the immediate
family environment. This is akin to group buying dynamics associated with the
DMU. He argues that the rationality normally associated with organisational
decision making is misplaced, suggesting that in some circumstances the protracted nature of the process is more a reflection of organisational culture and the
need to follow bureaucratic procedures and to show due diligence.

In addition, issues concerning established behaviour patterns, difficulties and
reluctance to break with traditional purchasing practices, intra- and interorganisational politics and relationships, and the costs associated with supplier switching all contribute to a more interpretive understanding of organisational decision
making. Further support for this view is given by Mason and Gray (1999) who
refer to the characteristics of decision making in the air travel market and note
some strong similarities between consumers and business passengers.

It is interesting to observe the similarity between the extended problem
solving, limited problem solving and routinised response behaviour phases of
consumer buying and the new task, modified rebuy and rebuy states associated
with organisational buying. There is a close match between the two sets in terms
of the purpose, approach and content. Risk and involvement are relevant to both
categories and, although the background to both may vary, the principles used to
manage the various phases and conditions are essentially the same, just deployed
in different ways.

It is important to recognise that many of the characteristics of both consumer and organisational decision making show a greater number of similarities than is normally assumed (or taught).

Decision Making Units – Characteristics

Reference has been made on a number of occasions to organisational buyers, as if such people are the only representatives of an organisation to be involved with the purchase decision process. This is not the case, as very often a large number of people are involved in a purchase decision. This group is referred to as either the decision making unit (DMU) or the buying centre.

DMUs vary in size and composition in accordance with the nature of each individual task. Webster and Wind (1972) identified a number of roles within the buying centre.

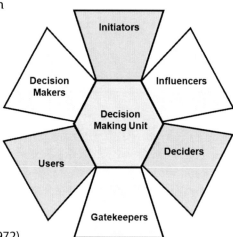

Figure 3.1: Membership of the decision making unit. Based on Webster and Wind (1972).

- *Initiators* request the purchase of an item and propel the purchase decision process. They may be other members of the DMU or others in the organisation.

- *Users* may not only initiate the purchase process but are sometimes involved in the specification process. They will use the product once it has been acquired and subsequently evaluate its performance. Their role is continuous, although it may vary from the peripheral to highly involved.

- *Influencers* very often help set the technical specifications for the proposed purchase and assist the evaluation of alternative offerings by potential suppliers. These may be consultants hired to complete a particular project. This is quite common in high-technology purchases where the customer has little relevant expertise.

- *Deciders* are those who make purchasing decisions and they are the most difficult to identify. This is because they may not have formal authority to make a purchase decision yet are sufficiently influential internally that their decision carries most weight. In repeat buying activities the buyer may well also be the decider. However, it is normal practice to require that expenditure decisions involving sums over a certain financial limit be authorised by other, often senior, managers.

- *Buyers* (purchasing managers) select suppliers and manage the process whereby the required products are procured. As suggested previously, buyers may not decide which product is to be purchased but they influence the framework within which the decision is made.

- *Gatekeepers* have the potential to control the type and flow of information to the organisation and the members of the DMU. These gatekeepers may be assistants, technical personnel, secretaries or telephone switchboard operators.

The size and form of the buying centre is not static. It can vary according to the complexity of the product being considered and the degree of risk each decision is perceived to carry for the organisation. However, one element that each member of the DMU considers is the value in the product or service being considered. The value perceived will reflect the context and the frame of reference each member brings to the decision process (Lindgreen et al., 2009).

Different roles are required and adopted as the nature of the buying task changes with each new purchase situation (Bonoma, 1982). All of these roles might be subsumed within one individual for certain decisions. It is vital for seller organisations to identify members of the buying centre and to target and refine their messages to meet the needs of each member of the centre.

ViewPoint 3.1 SAP target their DMUs

Traditional communications with DMU members are usually around personal selling and various types of trade promotions and direct marketing. Databases and CRM programs have been utilised for storage and analysis of relevant customer data. More recently, firms have been identifying and using technology in a more creative way for communicating with their target audiences.

SAP Business Objects wanted to develop a method to enhance the visualisation of Excel presentation for their customers. A new software system package was created called 'Crystal Xcelsius' which allows users to produce colourful charts and graphs for raw spreadsheet data.

In order to communicate this system to the small and medium business sector, individuals in different disciplines within such businesses, accountants, marketing HR, finance, analysts and sales professionals were identified. A digital campaign using emails and online banners was launched. The promotion used a combination of digital illustration, photography and animation as well as the product itself. Responders were allowed to download a free trial version. Personalisation was enhanced with a link to an interactive Career Projector.

Source: Based on www.dnxmarketing.com; www.sap.com

Question: How might a key account sales manager make use of technology in communicating with their customers?

3

Organisational Buying Behaviour

Ronchetto *et al.* (1989) provide some insight into how influential members of a DMU might be recognised. Their research suggests that there are several criteria that indicate those members who have above average influence. In addition to those members who occupy particularly significant hierarchical positions, they cite people who:

- Work close to the organisational boundary
- Are near the centre in terms of work flow
- Play an active and positive role in communication across customer departments
- Are linked directly to senior managers.

It can be instructive to visit purchasing sections of organisational websites and try to determine both the emotional character and likely membership of a DMU.

Membership of the DMU is far from fixed, and this sheer fluidity poses problems for selling organisations simply because it is not always possible to identify key members or shifts in policy or requirements. As Spekman and Gronhaug (1986) point out, the DMU is a 'vague construct that can reach across a number of different functional roles with any number of individuals participating or exerting influence at any one time'. It is worth noting therefore, that within this context the behaviour of DMU members is also largely determined by the interpersonal relationships of the members of the centre.

■ The Decision Making Process

Organisational buying decisions vary in terms of the nature of the product or service, the frequency and the relative value of purchases, their strategic impact (if any) and the type of relationship with suppliers. These, and many other factors, are potentially significant to individual buying organisations. However, there are some broad criteria that can be characterised within three main types of buying situations. Referred to by Robinson *et al.* (1967) as buyclasses these are: new task, modified rebuy and straight rebuy (see Table 3.2).

Robinson *et al.* also determined that OBB consists of a series of sequential activities through which organisations proceed when making purchasing decisions. These they referred to as buying stages or buyphases. These are shown in Table 3.3 where the buyclasses are brought together with the buyphases.

This buygrid serves to illustrate the relationship between these two main elements and highlights the need to focus on buying situations rather than on products. At the time of its publication this was regarded as a major advance in our understanding of OBB. It is still an important foundation for this topic. The next few sections work first through the characteristics of the buyclasses and then proceed to examine the key aspects of each of the buyphases.

Table 3.2: Main characteristics of the buyclasses

Buyclass	Degree of familiarity with the problem	Information requirements	Alternative solutions
New task	The problem is fresh to the decision makers	A great deal of information is required	Alternative solutions are unknown, all are considered new
Modified rebuy	The requirement is not new but is different from previous situations	More information is required but past experience is of use	Buying decision needs new solutions
Rebuy	The problem is identical to previous experience	Little or no information is required	Alternative solutions not sought or required

Source: Based on Robinson *et al.* (1967).

Table 3.3 : The buygrid framework

Buyphases	New task	Modified rebuy	Straight rebuy
Problem recognition	Yes	Possibly	No
General need description	Yes	Possibly	No
Product specification	Yes	Yes	Yes
Supplier search	Yes	Possibly	No
Supplier selection	Yes	Possibly	No
Order process specification	Yes	Possibly	No
Performance review	Yes	Yes	Yes

Source: Based on Robinson *et al.* (1967).

■ Buyclasses

New task

As the name implies, the organisation is faced with a first-time buying situation. Risk is inevitably large at this point as there is little collective experience of the product/service or of the relevant suppliers. As a result of these factors there are normally a large number of decision participants. Each participant requires a lot of information and a relatively long period of time is needed for the information to be assimilated and a decision to be made.

In terms of decision making stages this is referred to as extensive problem solving (Howard and Sheth, 1969) and the main characteristic is the high risk that is derived from the uncertainty involved in the decision. The uncertainty might be containable because of the nature of the product or if the contribution it makes to the organisation's value system is negligible. However, the uncertainty might be high because of the potential to disrupt production or perhaps lead to customer dissatisfaction (for example, missed delivery dates).

Modified rebuy

Having purchased a product, uncertainty is reduced but not eliminated, so the organisation may request through their buyer(s) that certain modifications be made to future purchases. For example, adjustments to the specification of the product, further negotiation on price levels or perhaps the arrangement for alternative delivery patterns. Fewer people are involved in the decision process than in the new task situation.

In terms of decision making stages this is referred to as limited problem solving (Howard and Sheth, 1969) and the main characteristic is that buying organisations only perceive moderate risks involved in the decision, due to previous purchasing experience. While the decision criteria is understood there is uncertainty about which suppliers might be best suited to satisfy the revised specifications.

Straight rebuy

In this situation, the purchasing department reorders on a routine basis, very often working from an approved list of suppliers. These may be products that an organisation consumes in order to keep operating (for example, office stationery), or may be low-value materials used within the operational, value added part of the organisation (for example, manufacturing processes). No other people are involved with the exercise until different suppliers attempt to change the environment in which the decision is made. For example, a new supplier may interrupt the procedure with a potentially better offer. This may stimulate the emergence of a modified rebuy situation.

In terms of decision making stages, the straight rebuy situation is referred to as routine problem solving. Uncertainty is low and risk minimal because the buying criteria are established and there is little reason to find improved supplies and/or suppliers.

Straight rebuy presents classic conditions for the use of automatic reordering systems. Costs can be reduced, managerial time redirected to other projects and the relationship between buyer and seller embedded within a stronger framework. One possible difficulty is that both parties perceive the system to be a significant exit barrier should conditions change, and this may deter flexibility or restrict opportunities to develop the same or other relationships.

The use of electronic purchasing systems at the straight rebuy stage has enabled organisations to empower employees to make purchases although control still resides with purchasing managers. Employees can buy direct, through their PCs, from a catalogue list of authorised suppliers. The benefits are that employees are more involved, purchasing process is speeded up, costs are reduced and purchasing managers can spend more time with other higher priority activities.

■ Buyphases

Just as there are buyclasses so there are buyphases, or stages through which a buying decision moves before a conclusion is reached (Robinson *et al.*, 1967).

The following sequence of buyphases, developed from Robinson *et al.*'s (1967) original list, is peculiar to the new task situation. Many of these buyphases are often ignored or compressed according to the complexity of the product and when either a modified rebuy or a straight rebuy situation is encountered.

ViewPoint 3.2: The complexity of public contracts

Regulations covering procurement by governments and public sector bodies are rigorous and often complex, depending of the value and scope of the products and services being purchased. In Europe, all public sector contracts over set values or 'thresholds', are detailed in the European Union's (EU) Procurement Thresholds. These vary depending on what is being procured and are detailed on the Office of Government Commerce (OGC) website. The regulations set out the required procedures and standards for inviting and choosing those wishing to tender for contracts, and for the awarding of contracts.

The first stage of the process involves all contacts which are above the threshold limits being advertised in the *Official Journal of the European Union* (OJEU). Four procurement procedures are laid down to cover differing procurement situations:

- Open procedure – this requires tenders to be submitted by a specified date which are then evaluated and contracts awarded.

- Restricted procedure – a two stage process involving pre-qualification and short listing followed by an Invitation to Tender.

- Competitive Dialogue procedure – used for more complex contract situations. The purchasing authority will negotiate with potential suppliers to develop suitable solutions prior to tenders being submitted.

- Negotiated procedure – the public sector body enters into contract negotiations with one of more suppliers.

In addition to the above, Framework agreements can be arranged by one or more public sector bodies to provide for the purchase of goods, works and services based on agreed price, quality and quantity. Such Framework agreements usually cover a fixed time period.

Source: Based on www.businesslink.gov.uk; www.ogc.gov.uk

Question: Discuss the value of implementing a structured approach to business purchasing making use of examples.

3

Organisational Buying Behaviour

■ Need/problem recognition

Organisations buy products or services because of two main events (Cravens and Woodruff, 1986). Difficulties may be encountered, first as a result of a need to solve problems, such as a stock-out or new government regulations, and second, as a response to opportunities to improve performance or enter new markets. Essentially, the need/recognition phase is the identification of a gap – the gap between the benefits an organisation has now and the benefits it would like to have. For example, when a new product is to be produced there is an obvious gap between having the necessary materials and components and being out of stock and unable to build. The first decision therefore is about how to close this gap and there are two broad options: outsource the whole, or parts, of the production process or build/make the objects oneself. The need has been recognised and the gap identified. The rest of this section is based on a build decision being made.

■ Product specification

As a result of identifying a problem and the size of the gap, influencers and users can determine the desired characteristics of the product needed to resolve the problem. This may take the form of a functional or general description or a much more detailed analysis and the creation of a detailed technical specification for a particular product. For example, what sort of photocopier is required? What is it expected to achieve? How many documents should it copy per minute? Is a collator or tray required? This is an important part of the process, because if it is executed properly it will narrow the supplier search and save on the costs associated with evaluation prior to a final decision. The results of the functional and detailed specifications are often combined within a purchase order specification which, according to van Weele (2002), consists of five main components. These are set out in Table 3.4.

Table 3.4: Dimensions of a purchase order specification

Dimension	Explanation
Quality specifications	Statement concerning the technical standards the product meets and whether there should be a quality certificate.
Logistics specifications	Statement concerning the quantity of products required and delivery details.
Maintenance specifications	Statement about how the supplier will service and maintain the product.
Legal and environmental	Statement detailing how the product and associated requirements processes should meet health, safety and environmental legislation.
Target budget	Statement about the financial constraints within which the product is to be produced, delivered and supported.

Source: based on van Weele (2002).

■ Supplier and product search

At this stage the buyer actively seeks organisations which can supply the necessary product(s). There are two main issues at this point. First, will the product reach the required performance standards and match the specification? Second, will the potential supplier meet the other organisational requirements? In most circumstances organisations review the market and their internal sources of information and arrive at a decision that is based on rational criteria.

Organisations work, wherever possible, to reduce uncertainty and risk. By working with others who are known, of whom the organisation has direct experience and who can be trusted, risk and uncertainty can be substantially reduced. This highlights another reason why many organisations seek relational exchanges and operate within established networks and seek to support each other.

The quest for suppliers and products may be a short task for the buyer; however, if the established network cannot provide a solution, the buying organisation has to seek new suppliers, and hence new networks, to be able to identify and short-list appropriate supplier organisations.

■ Evaluation of proposals

Depending upon the complexity and value of the potential order(s), the proposal is a vital part of the process and should be prepared professionally. The proposals of the short-listed organisations are reviewed in the context of two main criteria: the purchase order specification and the evaluation of the supplying organisation. If the organisation is already a part of the network, little search and review time need be allocated. If the proposed supplier is new to the organisation, a review may be necessary to establish whether it will be appropriate (in terms of price, delivery and service) and whether there is the potential for a long-term relationship or whether this is a single purchase that is unlikely to be repeated.

Once again, therefore, is the relationship going to be based on a market exchange or a relational exchange? The actions of both organisations, and of some of the other organisations in the network to the new entrant, will be critical in determining the form and nature of future relationships.

■ Supplier selection

The DMU will undertake a supplier analysis and use a variety of criteria depending upon the particular type of item sought. This selection process takes place in the light of the comments made in the previous section. A further useful perspective is to view supplier organisations as a continuum, from reliance on a single source to the use of a wide variety of suppliers of the same product.

Jackson (1985) proposed that organisations might buy a product from a range of different suppliers, in other words maintaining a range of (a practice of many government departments). She labelled this approach 'always a share', as several suppliers are given the opportunity to share the business available to the buying centre. The major disadvantage is that this approach fails to drive cost as low as possible, as the discounts derived from volume sales are not achieved. The advantage to the buying centre is that a relatively small investment is required and little risk is entailed in following such a strategy.

At the other end of the continuum are organisations which only use a single source supplier. All purchases are made from the single source until circumstances change to such a degree that the buyer's needs are no longer being satisfied. Jackson referred to these organisations as 'lost for good', because once a relationship with a new organisation has been developed they are lost for good to the original supplier. An increasing number of organisations are choosing to enter alliances with a limited number, or even a single source of suppliers. The objective is to build a long-term relationship, to work together to build quality and help each other achieve their goals. Out-sourcing manufacturing activities for non-core activities has increased, and this has moved the focus of communications from an internal to an external perspective.

■ Evaluation

The order is written against the selected supplier which is then monitored and evaluated against such diverse criteria as responsiveness to enquiries, modifications to the specification and timing of delivery. When the product is delivered it may reach the stated specification but fail to satisfy the original need. In this case, the specification needs to be rewritten before any future orders are placed.

Developments in the environment can impact on organisational buyers and change both the nature of decisions and the way they are made. For example, the decision to purchase new plant and machinery requires consideration of the future cash flows generated by the capital item. Many people will be involved in the decision, and the time necessary for consultation may mean that other parts of the decision making process are completed simultaneously.

Understanding ideas about buyclasses and buyphases informs us that buyers adopt broadly similar behaviours when buying particular products/services in certain categories. This suggests that understanding these patterns of behaviour will assist the suppliers in their quest for orders and contracts. What we do know is that buyers are becoming more self-driven, evidenced by two factors. These are their use of a broader channel mix, mainly online, and through this, their greater propensity to interact, that is converse and listen to their peers (Wells, 2010). If we accept the concept of buying cycles, which is reasonable for rebuy goods and services, then it make sense to develop a marketing communication mix with content that reflects the needs of buyers at different stages of the cycle. The content should reflect the desired form of engagement, delivered through channels which are content-compatible and then enabled so that the content can be shared easily or used to provoke conversations. As an example, Wells suggests the following content patterns.

- Thought leadership to build interest
- Educational content to build lead generation
- Cases studies to support sales
- Social media content to develop relationships and brand awareness
- How-to guides to add value.

Influences Shaping Organisational Buying Behaviour

Not surprisingly, there are a number of forces that shape the way in which organisations purchase products. Organisational buying behaviour takes place in an environment which can change quickly and dynamically. Sellers need to understand the nature of the changes and either anticipate or react in appropriate ways. Four main areas of influence can be identified namely, internal, external, individual and relationship forces (see Figure 3.2).

Internal influences

One of the main issues internally is the way in which purchasing is structured. The policy may be that the organisation prefers to manage its buying from a central point. This enables tighter control and greater consistency. It allows for improved integration and costs can be reduced by buying on behalf of all operating units.

The alternative is to decentralise purchasing to divisions or geographically dispersed operating departments. This facilitates purchasing to meet local needs, enables flexibility and promotes a sense of empowerment. However, because management do not have as much control or influence, there tends to be a pressure to move towards a centralised approach and often this move is undertaken in the name of cost saving. Very often organisations will move towards a centralised structure when trading performance declines over several periods or when they are under attack from the stock market or competitors.

Other internal pressures emanate from purchasing policy (for example a move towards lean manufacturing), changes to the levels of authority and responsibility for purchasing activities, enhancements to purchasing systems and technology and, of course, organisational changes arising from restructuring, a change in ownership (or merger and acquisition activities) or any politicising.

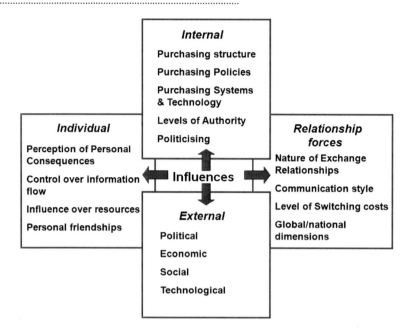

Figure 3.2: Major influences on organisational buying behaviour

■ External influences

The main source of external influence can be traced back through the political, economic, social and technological (PEST) framework.

- ■ *Political* and regulatory influence has the potential to radically change the nature of products and services that organisations purchase. Changes to packaging and labelling, adjustments to the safety requirements concerning the use of products and even changes to the taxation regulations can all influence the choice of supplier and the frequency of purchase.

- ■ *Economy.* Changes in the overall economy and confidence in the stock market can impact on the purchase behaviour. Because B2B markets are based primarily on derived demand, organisations need to be sensitive to expectations concerning the buoyancy of the end-user consumer market. Movements in interest rates can impact on particular sectors in the economy. For example, higher rates will tend to raise the cost of mortgages and suppress the housing market and all related activities, such as building materials, financial services and labour market employment, whereas printing, soft drinks and medicines will be unaffected. This suggests that changes in the economy are not necessarily always spread evenly.

- ■ *Social* changes can also affect organisational buying behaviour. Part of the aftermath of 9/11 in the United States was the huge downturn in air travel. This led to some airlines going out of business and aircraft manufacturers and associated supply chains having to retrench as airlines deferred or cancelled orders. Saturation in the mobile phone market caused cellphone manufacturers to reconfigure their production plans and make large numbers of staff redundant.

- *Technological* changes have had a dramatic impact on organisational buying behaviour. The Internet has changed the ways organisations communicate, do business and interact with one another. Some of these systems, technology and communications facilities are exemplified throughout this book but the net effect has been to change the way organisations buy and sell to each other. Technical and engineering employees are enjoying greater participation in the DMU as the rate of technological change increases and the influence of the purchasing manager declines. Weiss and Hyde (1993) found that buyers tend to undertake more intense search efforts but spend less time on the overall search process when they detect that the pace of technological change is increasing. Technological changes have given rise to new types of intermediaries and suppliers in the marketing channels, both up and down stream. This means that the nature and form of the supply chain has also changed and required organisations to appraise and review their purchasing procedures.

Individual influences

Participation in the buying centre has been shown to be highly influenced by individuals' perceptions of the personal consequences of their contribution to each of the stages in the buying process. The more that individuals think they will be blamed for a bad decision or praised for a good one, the greater their participation, influence and visible DMU-related activity (McQuiston and Dickson, 1991). The nature and dispersal of power within the unit can influence the decisions that are made. Certain individuals are able to control the flow of information and/or the deployment of resources (Spekman and Gronhaug, 1986). This assertiveness can enable individuals to have undue influence within a DMU.

Individuals may develop personal friendships with suppliers and buyers. Such personal relationships overlie interorganisational relationships and work perfectly smoothly but they can also give rise to conflict, for example when interorganisational relationships change.

Relationship influences

Relationships develop between the focus organisation and other stakeholders in the network. The nature of the exchange relationship and the style of communications will influence buying decisions. If the relationship between organisations is trusting, mutually supportive and based upon a longer-term perspective (a relational structure) then the behaviour of the buying centre may be seen to be cooperative and constructive. If the relationship is formal, regular, unsupportive and based upon short-term convenience (a market structure-based relationship) then the purchase behaviour may be observed as courteous yet distant. It has been suggested that the major determinant of the organisational environment is the cost associated with switching from one supplier to another (Bowersox and Cooper, 1992).

When one organisation chooses to enter into a buying relationship with another, an investment is made in time, people, assets and systems. Should the relationship fail to work satisfactorily then a cost is incurred in switching to another supplier. These switching costs can heavily influence buying decisions. This means that the higher the potential switching costs, so the greater the loss in perceived flexibility, and the stronger the need to make the relationship appropriate at the outset.

Buyers and sellers that have a predominantly market exchange relationship can be hit hard by these forces, especially in comparison to those organisations that operate on a more relational exchange basis. Because they work together and anticipate changes that might disrupt their relationship, organisations within a relational exchange seek solutions to reduce the impact of some of these forces. The ability to be flexible, innovative and yet sufficiently enduring enables organisations to develop relationships and their purchasing systems in the face of the forces acting upon them.

Organisational buying has shifted from a one-to-one dyadic encounter, salesperson to buyer, to a position where a buying team meets a selling team. The skills associated with this process are different and are becoming much more sophisticated while the demands on both buyers and sellers are more pronounced.

However, organisational buyer behaviour is changing as evidenced in the 'Buyersphere' report (Bottom, 2010). This report highlighted that there are a variety of reasons for these changes, and the primary one concerns the development of digital technology, and social media in particular. Some of the key points arising from the report include:

- Marketers underestimate the influence of more recent information channels, in essence, social media.

- The proportion using these channels is low but growing. The majority use traditional channels.

- Those that do use social media consider them to be more influential than marketers believe.

- 45% of users rated blogs as very influential at the early stages of the buying process. Only 9% of marketers agreed.

- Supplier websites are also considered to be very important at the early stages of the buying process.

There is clearly an imbalance between what marketers on the supply side believe and the practices undertaken by buyers. The processes of buying and selling should not be underestimated as they are complex and interactive.

ViewPoint 3.3: O_2 influences HR directors

O_2, the mobile phone network service provider, developed an innovative way of promoting increased call volumes amongst business customers by targeting HR directors. A more traditional approach to achieve this kind of objective would have been to influence IT directors who normally have control and responsibility for mobile phone and network provider purchasing.

The campaign was launched in 2009 at the height of the economic recession. The creative idea was based around attempting to make employees feel happier and more productive despite the economic gloom. It was felt that this kind of message would be more appropriate for HR directors to improve the spirits and morale of their staff. This would hopefully stimulate internal demand for the initiatives suggested in the promotion and subsequently influence IT directors to make purchases from O_2.

A book was created, *The Happiness Book for Businesses*, containing ideas to make staff happy, including business tips as well as O_2 related benefits such as O_2 Arena priority tickets. The campaign led to a 45% uplift in calls amongst targeted businesses and many visits by customer employees to the campaign microsite which contained additional related content and benefits.

Source: Based on www.o2.com; www.warc.com

Question: How might a business marketer use communications to influence decision making at each stage of the purchasing process?

For a long time B2B buyer behaviour was relatively uncomplicated and predictable. This gave suppliers opportunities to develop and implement campaigns and sales behaviours that were not particularly inventive but which achieved the necessary goals. However, in recent years, there has been a shift in the source of power to buyers, mainly due to digital technology. For example, B2B buyers now use online sources much earlier in their buying process. Much of their research process is undertaken independently of external providers, then contact is often made with other users, via Twitter, blogs and email to advise on possible solutions, and only then is contact made with a supplier's sales team. So, the trend appears to be that many B2B buyers start with a search, proceed to consider industry news/information sites, and only then consider supplier websites.

Research indicates that the 'single buyer' is a thing of the past and that the role of a buying unit is much more in evidence. Evans (2010) reports on data from MarketingSherpa 'which indicates that even for purchases in the £16.5k–£66k range, more than four decision-makers are engaged 64 per cent of the time. And for purchases in the £66k–£660k range, more than four decision-makers are engaged 92 per cent of the time.'

■ Uncertainty, Risk and Relationships in OBB

As asserted previously, organisations encounter risk when purchasing products and services. The way organisations organise and manage purchasing activities is recognition of the existence of risk and a broad means by which they attempt to reduce their perceived risks.

The risk concept consists of three main elements, namely the potential loss, the significance of those losses and the uncertainty attached to the losses (Yates and Stone, 1992). Therefore perceived risk incorporates uncertainty but uncertainty itself is not the same as risk. Mitchell (1999) refers to Haakansson and Wootz (1979) who identified three types of uncertainty: need, transaction and market-related uncertainties. Valla (1982) suggested that there are five categories of organisational risk which must be addressed by buyers and suppliers. From these it is possible to identify seven types of risks that are relevant to organisational buyers, as set out at Table 3.5.

Table 3.5: Seven types of organisational decision-making risk

Risk type	Explanation
Technical	Will the parts, equipment or product/service perform as expected?
Financial	Does this represent value for money, could we have bought cheaper?
Delivery	Will delivery be on time, complete and in good order? Will our production schedule be disrupted?
Service	Will the equipment be supported properly and within agreed time parameters?
Personal	Am I comfortable dealing with this organisation, are my own social and ego needs threatened?
Relationship	To what extent is the long-term relationship with this organisation likely to be jeopardised by this decision?
Professional	How will this decision affect my professional standing in the eyes of others and how might my career and personal development be impacted?

A variety of factors might contribute to the level of perceived risk. Mitchell (1995) identifies 11 risk enhancing factors, as presented in Figure 3.3. In order to reduce these risks organisations adopt a number of different approaches. By far the most common method is the search for information. This concerns the nature, the amount and the reliability of the information that is sought.

From a selling perspective, organisations should seek to provide marketing communications messages that provide the information that buyers need and value. The use and development of websites, portals and extranets provides rich information, necessary to reduce risk. The use of the sales force, sales literature and direct marketing materials, once the primary form of information, is now a complementary source of information. What is not entirely clear is how information should be used by buying organisations to reduce their risks, nor is there much research on how cost-effective these information search activities are in reducing organisational perceived risk.

Risk Perception Factors

Buyer Demographics - Job Function - DMU - Buyer's Personality - Buy Type - Product/Service Characteristics - Degree of Buyer/Seller Interaction - Market Characteristics - Company Size - Organisational Performance - Country/Region

Information Gathering - Approved Supplier Lists - Deliberation - Structured Buying Procedures - Quantitative techniques - Multiple Sourcing - Partnering and Alliances - Consider more Suppliers - A Leading company in the field - Branding - Performance guarantees - Multiple Incentive Contracts - User Participation - Social Media

Risk Reduction Methods

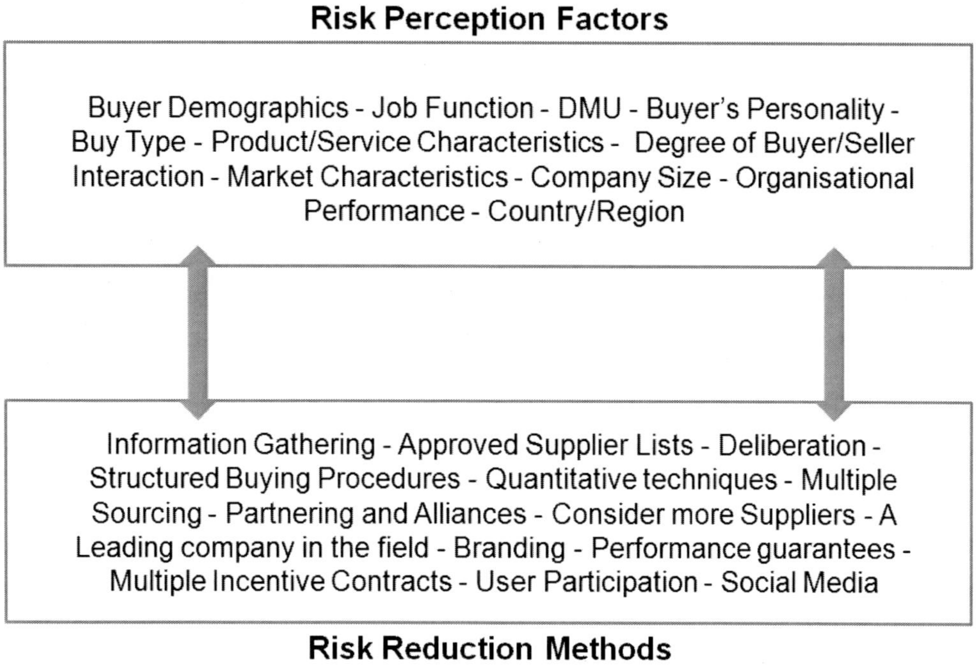

Figure 3.3: Factors that enhance organisational buyers' perceived risk (based on Mitchell 1995)

Research suggests that organisations configure their DMUs in the light of the level of perceived risk and the type of purchase under consideration (Wilson *et al.*, 1991). DMU size is likely to grow proportionally to the size of the risk and as modified rebuys and new task situations develop. Therefore, individual purchase actions give way to group DMUs as risk increases. Johnston and Lewin (1996) found that increases in risk are countered by:

■ An increase in the size of the DMU and populated with members with higher authority and status

■ An intensifying information search

■ DMU participants becoming more involved throughout the whole process

■ Organisations who are known to and preferred by the DMU becoming more likely to win the contract.

This last point suggests that the development of interorganisational relationships is important to both supplying and buying participants, particularly where new task situations are identified. Some of the more common approaches used by organisations to reduce risk are set out in Figure 3.4. Organisational perceived risk should be reduced by both prospective suppliers and buying organisations. Through the development of suitable relationships uncertainty and risk can be moderated to acceptable levels.

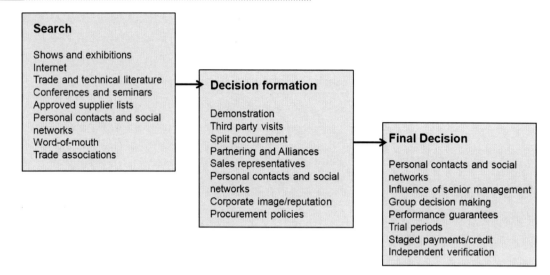

Figure 3.4: Risk reduction approaches for organisational purchase decisions

Purchasing risk is also observed in electronic trading formats. For example, in online reverse auctions, Smeltzer and Carr (2003) identified different types of risk experienced by suppliers and buyers. One of the key risks experienced by buyers is that they might be destroying the trust that had developed with suppliers (in offline purchasing). A key risk for suppliers was that price becomes the only significant factor for the first and subsequent transactions. Therefore there is little motivation to invest in resources and support mechanisms because there is little incentive to develop a long-term relationship with the buyer.

Readers may recall the movement towards lean manufacturing and lean supply. This involves reducing the number of suppliers to a number that enables buyers to develop relationships with sellers that have a long(er)-term orientation and which may result in significant added value and competitive advantage. Knox (2000) suggests that there are three reasons why competitive advantage might be improved through stronger relationships.

1 Systems cost reduction – cost savings from improved working practices (e.g. improved order cycle times, reduced stock and working capital).

2 Increased effectiveness through innovation – as a relationship develops more information is exchanged and suppliers become more willing to invest in the relationship.

3 Enabling technologies – electronic systems and communications help suppliers to anticipate and understand the needs of their customers. Suppliers become better able to evaluate the cost-effectiveness of their customer portfolios and to determine where to invest.

Relationships, however, are far from similar and they add value in different ways. Knox offers the idea that supplier/buyer relationships should be regarded as a continuum.

- *Level 1.* The relationship is based on market structure principles and the supplier provides specified products on the basis of price, service and quality.
- *Level 2.* The supplier actively attempts to help the customer by reducing their costs and improving their competitiveness.
- *Level 3.* The supplier takes responsibility for a major part of the customer's value adding capabilities and is in partnership with the customer. Outsourcing and subassembly arrangements typify this level of cooperation.
- *Level 4.* Here there is a relational exchange and the supplier becomes a major source of strategic added value for the customer. For example, Aviva provide the financial expertise for Virgin's Financial Services. This co-branding arrangement enables the value within the technical expertise of the supplier to be partnered with the strong highly visible Virgin brand.

Knox suggests four levels but there could be more depending upon the required level of sophistication. Implicit within this approach is that DMU perceived purchase risk is associated with the actions of suppliers and that the relationship incorporates levels of trust. Gao *et al.* (2003) determine that a buyer's trust in a supplier is crucial to reducing their risk. Suppliers should therefore seek to build trust by allocating resources (for example, time, expertise, flexibility) to buyers in order to demonstrate commitment to the relationship and to be seen to be looking to the longer rather than the shorter term. Issues concerning trust and commitment are developed further in Chapter 8.

■ eProcurement

There are several benefits for sellers who use information sharing technologies such as web-based EDI, electronic portals, interconnected ERP systems, and online order processing systems (Smart, 2008). These include building closer links with various stakeholders (customers, suppliers and third parties), reduced printing and distribution costs and delays; an improved ability to market new products, quickly reduce prices on older ones, reduce the number of incoming telephone calls; improve efficiency, more accurate ordering; and improve customer satisfaction. The benefits for buyers include access to up-to-date product and price data; have fewer outgoing telephone calls; and, when online order processing is also available, faster ordering.

The disadvantages of eProcurement are largely felt by suppliers and include IST costs; downward pressure on prices; and the ease with which customers can compare and switch suppliers. Both suppliers and buyers may welcome or regret the decreased personal contact of sales visits, telephone calls and face-to-face competitive tendering.

Research by Smart (2008: 228) shows that real integration between firms in the supply chain has often been thwarted by issues concerning 'rival cultures, information technology deficiencies, lack of process alignment and other organisational legacies (Barratt and Oliveira, 2001; Akkermans *et al.*, 1999).'

Online auctions are one such technology which are becoming increasingly popular in two specific areas of B2B commerce: sourcing supplies and disposing of surplus stock or other assets. Unlike traditional auctions, online auctions tend to be longer and end at pre-set times. Buyers (or sellers) do not have to attend face-to-face, indeed participation is in real time, can be global and transaction costs drastically reduced (Sashi and O'Leary, 2002).

Particularly of interest in B2B procurement, is the 'reverse auction'. Instead of searching online auction sites for the supplies it needs and bidding for them, an organisation posts its requirements and invites potential suppliers to bid to fulfil them. The buying unit staff can do this themselves or use an intermediary such as FreeMarkets. Interestingly Smart found no evidence of supply chain considerations in the implementation of reverse auctions technology.

A portal is an interface to other relevant content. There is no single type of portal or strategy for developing one. Internet-based trading communities can be either vertically or horizontally focused, bringing together buyers, suppliers and ecommerce service companies. Although there are issues about how seamlessly systems can create true communities, there are notable benefits including cost savings, wider exposure within the marketplace, and virtually round-the-clock trading.

Summary

In order to consolidate your understanding of the principles of organisational buyer behaviour here is a summary of the main points.

1 Compare the characteristics of organisational and consumer buying behaviour.

Many of the characteristics associated with consumer decision making processes can be observed in the organisational context. However, organisational buyers make decisions which ultimately contribute to the achievement of corporate, not personal objectives. The value and number of purchases differ considerably, the amount and type of information required, plus the length of the decision making process and the number of people involved, also serve to differentiate organisational from consumer buying behaviour.

2 Explore the membership and main characteristics of the decision making unit.

Very often a large number of people are involved in a purchase decision. This group of people is referred to as either the decision making unit. DMUs vary in size and composition in accordance with the nature of each individual task. Six main roles have been identified within a standard DMU: *initiators, users, influencers, deciders, buyers,* and *gatekeepers.*

3 Explain organisational decision making processes.

Organisational buying can be considered in terms of some broad criteria that can be characterised within three main types of buying situations. Referred to by Robinson *et al.* (1967) as 'buyclasses' these are: new task, modified rebuy and straight rebuy.

Organisational buying behaviour consists of a series of sequential activities through which organisations proceed when making purchasing decisions. These are referred to as buying stages or buyphases, the main ones being; need/problem recognition, product specification, supplier and product search, evaluation of proposals, supplier selection, and evaluation.

4 Consider the influences that impact on organisational buyer behaviour.

Organisational buying behaviour takes place in dynamic environments. This dynamism is actuated by several macro forces which shape the way in which organisations purchase products and services. Four main forces can be identified namely, internal, external, individual and relational.

5 Determine and reflect upon the nature of risk and uncertainty in B2B markets.

Organisations encounter risk when purchasing products and services. The way organisations organise and manage their purchasing activities is recognition of the uncertainty they face

The risk concept consists of three main elements, namely the potential loss, the significance of those losses and the uncertainty attached to the losses.

One of the key ways to reduce risk and uncertainty is the provision and use of information. The use and development of websites, portals and extranets provides rich information, necessary to reduce risk. The use of the sales force, sales literature and direct marketing materials, once the primary form of information, is now a complementary source of information.

6 Consider some of the issues concerning the use of technology within eProcurement.

The benefits for buyers and sellers from the use of web-based EDI, electronic portals, interconnected ERP systems, and online order processing systems are not always realised yet the speed There are several benefits for sellers and buyers who use eProcurement technologies and processes. Apart from the efficiency and effectiveness gains associated with buying and selling, there are opportunities to build closer links with various stakeholders (customers, suppliers and third-parties), improve the marketing and information associated with new products and services, adjust pricing quickly, and improve customer satisfaction.

The main disadvantages of eProcurement experienced by suppliers include technology costs, a downward pressure on prices; and the ease with which customers can compare and switch suppliers.

■ Discussion Questions

1 Evaluate the key differences and similarities associated with both organisational and consumer buyer behaviour.

2 Write brief notes explaining the main characteristics and membership of the decision making unit.

3 Discuss the likely buying processes associated with the purchase of a suite of photocopiers.

4 Name four different types of influences that impact on organisational decision making.

5 Identify the different types of risk and uncertainty that organisations face when purchasing critical components. How might these risks be reduced, or even minimised?

6 List Knox's different relationship levels and find examples to illustrate each level. Is this framework of value?

References

Akkermans, H., Bogerd, P. and Vos, B. (1999) Virtuous and vicious cycles on the road to international supply chain management, *International Journal of Operations & Production Management*, **19**, 565-81

Barratt, M. and Oliveira, A. (2001) Exploring the experiences of collaborative planning initiatives, *International Journal of Physical Distribution and Logistics Management*, **31**, 266-89

Bonoma, T.V. (1982). Major sales: who really does the buying?, *Harvard Business Review* (May/June), p. 113

Bottom, J. (2010) In tune or out of touch? *B2B Marketing*, **7** (10) (November/December), 40

Bowersox, D. and Cooper, M. (1992) *Strategic Marketing Channel Management*, New York: McGraw-Hill

Cravens, D.W. and Woodruff, R.B. (1986) *Marketing*, Reading, MA: Addison Wesley.

Evans, R. (2010) *Demand Generation: The 'new' B2B buyer*, retrieved 21 January 2011 from www.b2bm.biz/default.asp?ProductGroupId=&docId=37226&articleId=38736

Gao, T., Sirgy, M.J. and Bird, M.M. (2003). Reducing buyer decision making uncertainty in organisational purchasing: can supplier trust commitment and dependence help?, *Journal of Business Research*, www.sciencedirect.com/science (accessed 11 Sept 2003).

Howard, J. and Sheth, J.N. (1969) *The Theory of Buyer Behavior*, New York: Wiley.

Jackson, B. (1985), Build customer relationships that last, *Harvard Business Review*, 63 (6), 120–8.

Johnston, W.J. and Lewin, J.E. (1996) Organisational buyer behavior: towards an integrative framework, *Journal of Business Research*, 35 (1) (January), pp. 1–15

Knox, S. (2000). Organisational buyer behaviour, in Cranfield School of Management (eds), *Marketing Management: A Relationship Marketing Perspective*, Basingstoke: Macmillan, 62–76

Lindgreen, A., Antioco, M., Palmer, R. and van Heech, T. (2009) High tech innovative products: identifying and meeting customers' value needs, *Journal of Business and Industrial Marketing*, **24** (3/4), 182-197

Mason, K.J. and Gray, R. (1999) Stakeholders in a hybrid market: the example of air business passenger travel, *European Journal of Marketing*, **33** (9/10), 844–858

McQuiston, D.H. and Dickson, P.R. (1991) The effect of perceived personal consequences on participation and influence in organisational buying, *Journal of Business*, **23**, 159–177

Mitchell, V-M. (1995). Organisational risk perception and reduction: A literature review, *British Journal of Management*, **6**, 115–133.

Mitchell, V-M. (1999). Consumer perceived risk: conceptualisations and models, *European Journal of Marketing*, **33** (1/2), 163–95.

Robinson, P.J., Faris, C.W. and Wind, Y. (1967). *Industrial Buying and Creative Marketing*, Boston, MA: Allyn & Bacon

Ronchetto, J.R., Hutt, M.D. and Reingen, P.H. (1989). Embedded patterns in organisational buying systems, *Journal of Marketing*, **53** (October), 51–62

Smart, A. (2008) eBusiness and supply chain Integration, *Journal of Enterprise Information Management*, **21** (3), 227-246

Sashi, C.M. and O'Leary, B. (2002). The role of Internet auctions in the expansion of B2B markets, *Industrial Marketing Management*, **31** (2) (February), 103–10

Smeltzer, L.R. and Carr, A.S. (2003) Electronic reverse auctions: promises, risks and conditions for success, *Industrial Marketing Management*, **32** (6) (August), 481–8

Spekman, R.E. and Gronhaug, K. (1986) Conceptual and methodological issues in buying centre research, *European Journal of Marketing*, **20** (7), 50–63

Valla, J-P. (1982). The concept of risk in industrial buying behaviour, Workshop on Organisational Buying Behaviour, European Institute for Advanced Studies in Management, Brussels, December, 9–10

van Weele, A.J. (2002). *Purchasing and Supply Chain Management*, 3rd edn, London: Thomson Learning

Webster, F.E. and Wind, Y. (1972) *Organisational Buying Behaviour*, Englewood Cliffs, NJ: Prentice Hall

Weiss, Allen M., and Jan B. Heide (1993), The nature of organizational search in high technology markets, *Journal of Marketing Research*, **30** (May), 220–33

Wells, G. (2010) How to …develop an effective content marketing programme, *B2B Marketing*, **7** (10), (November/December) 36

Wilson, D.F. (2000). Why divide consumer and organisational buyer behaviour?, *European Journal of Marketing*, **34** (7), 780–796

Wilson, E.J., Lilien, G.L. and Wilson, D.T. (1991) Developing and testing a contingency paradigm of group choice in organisational buying, *Journal of Marketing Research*, **28** (November), 452–466

4 Relationship Marketing

Overview

The relationship marketing approach is presented here as a contemporary basis upon which to consider business marketing. It is regarded as a successor to the 4Ps approach, which is considered by many to be irrelevant and outdated.

The development of collaborative and mutually rewarding relationships between buyers and sellers is considered to be fundamentally more appealing and an intuitively appropriate interpretation of business-to-business marketing. This view also sees the development of partnerships with other organisations as more suitable than former adversarial ideas based on competition and where the sole focus is on customers.

Organisations are shown to have a portfolio of relationships with a range of stakeholders, most notably suppliers, employees, customers and shareholders. This chapter considers the nature, development and characteristics of interorganisational relationships and examines the potential of technology to enhance relationships with customers and suppliers based on trust and commitment.

Aims and objectives

The aims of this chapter are to consider the scope and nature of interorganisational relationships and to explore how this impacts on the contemporary view of business-to-business marketing.

The objectives of this chapter are to:

1 Explore the development and evolution of relationship marketing.

2 Examine the conceptual underpinning associated with relationship marketing practices.

3 Introduce ideas concerning the customer relationship life cycle.

4 Examine the nature and characteristics of partnerships and alliances with suppliers and other stakeholders.

5 Consider trust and commitment as key elements of business relationships.

A Slice of Life – The Devil You Know

I have burnt my fair share of bridges over the years. We work in a creative services industry and with creativity comes artistic differences, philosophical differences and even differences in procedural administration that places a strain on a business relationship. It's inevitable that there will be breakdowns in client agency relationships – some involving door slamming and shouting and doorsteps that are never to be darkened again and others that simply reach natural conclusions. The latter is preferable, although not always achievable. It's my experience that even when a project reaches a natural conclusion, if it carries with it any degree of success, the business relationship is never really 'over'. It'll probably come back, sporadically, or years later when you least expect it. Stakeholders move jobs and take their little black book of relationships with them, or the need arises (again) and the phone rings. So it's important to nurture the relationship and not just the database.

I delivered a brand project for a technology solutions provider a few years ago that never really fulfilled my expectations, but the relationship didn't crash and burn either. What actually crashed was the stock market. The 'dot com' bubble that burst in 1999 was formative for many business relationships – I lost about 85% of my client base in under two weeks. They all cut-back, many of them went bust and we all had the joy of figuring out how we would survive in the new millennium.

In the subsequent years this solutions company certainly survived, but the market for their partner-based technology changed significantly – as did their marketing activity. During that period of reconstruction, I received a call from the CEO asking me to pick up the brand and fix it. Again. The company had done what it could in the post-dot com years, but the marketing and brand strategy was functional rather than exceptional. Development work had been undertaken internally and with another agency, but the CEO wasn't satisfied with the outcome.

I worked with the CEO for the next year or so to build the brand strategy in line with his business goals which was to attract the attention of a prospective buyer for the company. The plan worked, but not quite as expected. The company was duly bought as part of a multiple IT/Telecoms acquisition by an investment company and my client's company was recognised as the group brand holding the most brand equity.

The CEO was appointed as the Group CEO of what had become four disparate technology companies with very different audience profiles and his task was to unify the whole. His task became my task, because as he wrestled with the integration at the organisational level, he asked me to fix the brand(s).

Bringing four acquired companies together is not easy. Ever. The relationships between the companies and their customers were all very different. The relationships between the companies themselves were complex and strained and the relationships between the various companies' staff and the new business owners were fraught. In a memorable brand workshop, I was addressing the senior executive stakeholder group in an attempt to broker a working relationship and find the common ground between them all when the CEO's mobile phone rang. "Sorry," he said, "I've got to take this. We're losing 130 staff across the group today and they've just found out…"

We covered a lot of ground that day. We identified and agreed the relative importance of every relationship within the group. The low-cost, low-value transactional customers handled online or with tele-sales support were of little strategic importance, but provided a quick and easy income in the short-term transitionary period. The key customer relationships that held future long-term value were almost non-existent within the organisation and needed to be built. And I leant a little bit about my relationship with the CEO that day. As the maelstrom of HR upset swirled around us, the Group CEO had insisted that his entire senior management team take a day out to attend a workshop to fix the brand. As he furiously punched his Blackberry during the course of the day he assumed I would take care of it. And so I did.

We constructed a brand that was built not on the relationships that the various companies had had with their customers, but on the values that they should have. It was a forward thinking and far-reaching strategy. In the present, the brands, the businesses and the relationships they maintained with their customers were combative and factionalised. In the future however, things could be different – they could be improved for the benefit of the company and its customers.

The brand strategy allowed the company to clear out the old, inappropriate customers that held (and would hold) no significant future value and concentrate its efforts on building more profitable long-term relationships with a new and evolving audience. In order to understand where the future success of the brand lay, the company first had to understand and then build the appropriate relationships with its customers.

My own relationship with that particular client has spanned over 15 years. That's a long time. We have encountered business growth, collapse, re-build, consolidation, acquisition, integration and projection. But that's not all. We've also encountered the birth of six kids, two house moves, 15 cars, four office relocations and a legendary 50th birthday party. I'm not even going to think about the bottles of wine. There's a difference between business, brands and personal relationships – but it's not much of a difference. Treat them with respect and they pay dividends emotionally and financially.

Scot McKee

■ Introduction

In the mid-1990s, relationship marketing was proclaimed as a new marketing paradigm (Gronroos, 1994). Today it is more established, and persistently challenges past interpretations of interorganisational marketing activity. While these may be sound observations and comments, relationship marketing does represent a totally new perspective. Marketing is, and always has been, about customers. Gronroos (2009) even refers to marketing as an organisation-wide customer management activity. The principles of looking after customers have not changed, although they might have been overlooked at times in the past. There has always been a relationship between buyers and sellers, even if the depth of understanding about the significance and character of different types is emergent. Ideas concerning the development of relationship marketing have evolved from extensive research based initially on exchange transactions and, in particular, buyer–seller interaction.

One of the broad characteristics of consumer marketing is that interaction and exchanges generally take place between anonymous individuals. By contrast, according to Easton and Araujo (1993), exchanges in interorganisational marketing contexts occur between individuals who are, in general, known to each other. The more frequent and intense these exchanges become, so the strength of the relationships between buyers and sellers improves. It is this that provided the infrastructure for a new perspective of marketing, one based on relationships between organisations (Spekman, 1988; Rowe and Barnes, 1998), rather than the objects of a transaction, namely products and services. It should be noted that the development of electronic trading formats may reduce the level and frequency of interpersonal contact for some types of transaction.

At the end of Chapter 1, following an introduction to value chain principles, reference was made to a range of different types of exchanges in which organisations engage. The continuum of value-orientated exchanges (Figure 1.3) illustrated the diversity of exchanges with which organisations are involved; from one-off, short-term exchanges to those based upon collaboration and partnership.

Founding ideas about industrial marketing were based on market exchanges between organisations, where there was no prior history of exchange and no future exchanges expected. These paired organisations were considered to enter into transactions where products were the main focus and price was the key mechanism to exchange completion. Organisations were perceived to be adversarial and competition was paramount. These undertakings are referred to as market (or discrete) exchanges and often termed 'transactional marketing'.

In contrast, relationship marketing is based on the principles that there is a history of exchanges and an expectation that there will be exchanges in the future. Furthermore, the perspective is on the long term, envisioning a form of continued attachment by the buyer to the seller. Price as the key controlling mechanism is replaced by customer service and quality of interaction between the two organisations. The exchange is termed collaborative because the focus is on both organisations seeking to achieve their goals in a mutually rewarding way and not at the expense of one another. Table 4.1 provides a comprehensive list of the fundamental differences between transactional and collaborative exchange-based marketing.

ViewPoint 4.1: Market and collaborative exchanges for cars

Car manufacturers do not normally sell cars direct to individual consumers. This is because consumers are relatively infrequent buyers of new cars and when they do buy (from a dealer), it is normally a one-off or discrete exchange.

Car manufacturers normally develop relational exchanges with their fleet customers. These organisations tend to buy large quantities of cars on a regular basis. Communications and interaction between the parties tends to be continuous and designed to support the relationship over the longer term.

Car manufacturers sell batches of cars to their appointed dealers at pre-agreed dates. These exchanges cannot always be regarded as relational, as the goal of the manufacturer is stock turnover and their decisions are not always based on the financial or marketing situation facing each dealer. The element of collaboration and mutual self-help characteristic of relational exchanges is often missing within these relationships.

Source: Various

Question: How might dealers help car manufacturers develop more relational exchanges?

Table 4.1: Characteristics of market and collaborative exchanges

Attribute	Market exchange	Collaborative exchange
Length of exchange	Short-term	Long-term
Relationship history	No history	Relationship history and future
Basis of relationship	Products and prices	Relationships and mutual value
Relationship strength	Weak	Strong
Communication	Non-personal	Personal
	Predominantly formal	Predominantly informal
Propensity to share information	Little and infrequent	High and regular
Conflict	Domain and goals	Interests
Cooperation	None	Many
Activities	Clearly defined roles and tasks	Roles and tasks likely to vary

The suggestion, implied in the terms 'market' and 'collaborative exchanges', is that the former is devoid of a relational component. However, although market exchanges focus on products and prices, there is not a complete absence of a relationship. Indeed, Cousins (2002) refers to the relationship marketing literature in terms of two broad perspectives. One of these is based on a behavioural dimension and the other is based on economic power. The former considers relationships as the prime determinant of interorganisational relations, while the latter considers market exchanges based on power and competition as the prevalent mechanism.

Payne (2000) and Bruhn (2003) make the point that relationship marketing is not a new marketing paradigm, merely an extension of the marketing concept. The approach adopted in this book recognises the importance of both economic and behavioural dimensions and accepts that there is a relational dimension in all exchange activity. Rather, it is the case that the strength of focus varies between the two dimensions according to the contextual conditions facing organisations. Relationship marketing is therefore not necessarily a new marketing paradigm, but a fresh approach to marketing, one which puts relationships, not products, at the centre of marketing activities.

With this in mind, Dwyer *et al.* (1987) refer to B2B relationship marketing as an approach which encompasses a wide range of relationships, not just with customers, but also those that organisations develop with suppliers, regulators, government, competitors, employees and others. From this, relationship marketing might be regarded as all marketing activities associated with the management of successful relational exchanges. Christopher *et al.* (2002) refer to a six-markets model of relationship marketing, where, in addition to customer markets, relationships should be developed with recruitment, supplier, influence, internal and referral markets, on the grounds that these represent groups that contribute to an organisation's performance and marketplace contribution.

This chapter explores some of the characteristics associated with market and collaborative exchanges, it considers the development of relationship marketing, explores aspects of network interpretations and the impact on partnerships and alliances, not only with customers but suppliers and key stakeholders. The chapter closes with an examination of customer relationship management (CRM) systems and marketing automation issues.

■ Business Relationships – Background

In the commercial world, managers have long recognised the importance of relationships with their counterparts in other organisations. Both individual and inter-organisational perspectives have been of interest. Academic research progressed in the 1990s with recognition of the varying, observable forms of relationships. Organisations were deemed to be capable of close collaborative relationships as well as remote, discrete (or market) relationships with other organisations. In addition, the dyadic approach, although still useful when considering market exchange-based relationships, appeared to provide a limited perspective on organisational conduct. Attention has moved on to consider triads and networks of interacting organisations. Presence and position in a network are considered to influence the actions of parties to a degree not previously considered.

Originally, marketing, especially B2B marketing theory, focused on the actions of individual organisations. This evolved into the recognition of interorganisational interaction with varying degrees of cooperation and interdependency. Initially, attention concentrated on dyads that is, pairs of organisations interacting with market exchange principles guiding their relationship. At first, consideration was given to pairings of individual people, but this changed to a group orientation with the 'introduction of buying centre and selling centre concepts' (Borders *et al.*, 2001, p. 201).

Business marketing in the 1960s, 1970s and early 1980s focused on the units of exchange, namely the products that were transacted between two organisations. The 4Ps approach to the marketing mix variables was used to guide and construct transaction behaviour. These transactions represented market exchanges between a single buying and a single selling organisation. The centre of attention was on the transaction between these two parties. Buyers were considered to be passive and sellers active in these short-term exchanges. According to Johanson and Mattsson (1994), cited by McLoughlin and Horan (2000), this early work was rooted in the stimulus-organism-response model, which assumes that passive buyers react to the offers of sellers in a more or less subservient and unquestioning manner. Consequently researchers, assuming a purchasing manager's perspective, sought to understand the processes that buyers used when making buying decisions. Work by Webster and Wind (1972) and Sheth (1973) typified this period. The goal was to develop marketing plans that made better use of resources and that targeted appropriate members of the buying centre. Business marketing was based on the premise that marketing and purchasing are separate activities and that the purchase activity involved just a single, one-off purchase event.

However, the assumption that buyers are passive was soon challenged by the notion that in reality, business customers (organisations) are active problem solvers and seek solutions that are both efficient and effective. It was then accepted that buyers actually practised cooperative behaviours in order to find suitable suppliers. For the first time, the study of interorganisational behaviour became prevalent and focused on the relationship between the pair of organisations, rather than the products traded. Thus, research moved to encompass buying centre and selling centre characteristics, with one of the goals being to better align both parties to achieve greater efficiencies through improved cooperation. For example, the high profile given to just-in-time systems was a manifestation of the prevailing orientation. So, although research remained fixed on the buyer–seller dyad, interaction had now replaced reaction.

ViewPoint 4.2: Pressing together in the world of print

In February 2011 two major printing companies, Ricoh Company Ltd and Heidelberger Drucksman AG (Heidelberg) agreed to work cooperatively on a global scale. The two companies are global leaders in printing technology for the office, production printing and print media industries. Ricoh's sales were around $21 billion in the year ended March 2010, and Heidelberg had sales of €2.3 billion in the year ended December 2010.

Initially the collaboration will involve a global distribution contract for Ricoh's Production Printing Product Portfolio. The first phase will cover the UK and Germany followed by a complete geographic rollout by 2012. The partnership allows for customers to combine the best features of digital and offset printing.

Future plans for cooperation include integration with Heidelberg's industry standard workflow solution in the graphic arts industry. Taking effect in April 2011, the first public exhibition of the partnership involved a live demonstration of the production portfolio at the digi:media tradeshow in Dusseldorf, Germany.

The President and CEO of Ricoh, Shiro Kondo, described Heidelberg as the 'ideal strategic partner who shares our values of customer focus, environmental sustainability, innovation, quality and customer service."

The cooperation will allow both companies to lead the way in short run and variable data colour printing for the graphic arts industry.

Source: Based on www.heidelberg.com; www.ricoh.com

Question: What are the potential pitfalls associated with inter-company collaborations?

4

Relationship Marketing

In essence, this was a move away from regarding purchasing as a single discrete event, to considering it as a stream of activities between two organisations. These activities are sometimes referred to as episodes. Typically these may be price negotiations, meetings at exhibitions or a buying decision but these all take place within the overall context of a relationship. Any one episode may be crucial to the relationship but analysing individual episodes is usually insufficient if the context, that is the overall relationship, is not understood.

However, understanding the relationship alone does not produce a complete picture either, so as Ford (1980: 340) argues, 'it is important to analyse both individual episodes and the overall relationship, as well as to understand the interaction between the two'. Therefore, buyers and sellers were considered to behave (or interact) within the context of their own dyadic relationship. The unit of attention was no longer the product, or even the individual buying or selling unit, but the relationship, the stream of associated episodes and its attendant characteristics.

Around the same time, attention moved away from vertical integration as the preferred structural business model, to recognition of the significance and relevance of networks and loose alliances among organisations. In terms of understanding business interaction, this brought into consideration the potential influence of the indirect relationships that organisations have with one another. Relationship research (and marketing) needed to focus not just on buyers and sellers but on a wide range of other organisations each interacting with one another in a network of relationships.

Understanding about what value means has also developed. An emerging view, encouraged by the service-dominant logic (SDL) group is to consider relationships as a function of value, or what is known as, value-in-use, rather than as a function of exchange. Conventional ideas refer to sellers 'delivering value' through product and services to customers. However, as Grönroos (2009) points out, value can only be realized by buyers when utilized through consumption, through the use of their own processes, resources and capabilities. Value cannot be created by sellers, but it can be proposed.

The implication of this is that value should be considered in terms of two fundamental elements; value propositions and value creation. Sellers develop *value propositions* or promises of value creation opportunities embedded in their offerings. Buyers achieve *value creation* when they incorporate a seller's offering (products and services) into their processes. For example, the benefits or value arising from the use of a conveyor belt only occur once the belt is installed and used by a customer. So, a conveyor belt manufacturer might offer (the value proposition) to tailor the mechanisms or flexibility of their belts to meet the needs of a particular buyer, install it for them and train their employees. This means that the conveyor belt can be installed faster, more accurately and be of great(er) benefit to the buyer, than a belt system that is not tailored to their needs. The manufacturer only derives value when the conveyor belt system is running and actually supporting their manufacturing processes.

What this does is refocus the way value is understood and the roles sellers and buyers play in the value creation process. As Gronroos (2009) suggests, sellers make value creation propositions (promises) and buyers enable value fulfilment. Sellers can assist buyers by creating opportunities for them to create value. This depends on the degree to which the seller can engage with the buyer's value generating processes. Therefore, as there are varying levels of engagement with these processes, so an alternative to the spectrum of exchange relationships can be identified. Now it is possible to envisage a continuum of different value propositions, leading to various forms of value actualisation.

To better understand this approach, the continuum expressed at Figure 4.1 reflects four primary value strategies, as developed by Ribeiro et al. (2009). These are exchange (or commodity) value, added value, performance value and value co-creation strategies. Table 4.2 provides an explanation of each of these value based strategies.

Figure 4.1: A spectrum of value creation strategies. Based on Ribeiro *et al.* 2009.

Table 4.2: Value creation strategies

Value strategy	Explanation
Commodity value	These are market exchange based relationships, where sellers offer a core product/service but it is buyers who assume full responsibility and resources, to create the value they require out of the resources transacted.
Added value	Sellers choose to provide buyers with the resources they need to help them create value. By providing training, financial assistance or installation support, the interaction between parties becomes closer and stronger. The original value perceived in the exchange of products (for a price) becomes more orientated to the relationship, which itself is of value.
Performance value	Value is created by the activities of buyers and sellers working together for mutual benefit. However, value is still passed from one to another. Also known as value-in-use, examples include joint product development and projects to enhance a buyer's software systems and processes and initiatives designed to improve manufacturing efficiencies.
Co-creation value	Collaborative relationships are characterised by value that is created by both parties. Value emerges from co-production or 'value co-creation' (Sheth and Uslay, 2007). This occurs where both organisations work together for mutual benefit, and value is generated together, not traded by a supplier to a buyer, as in performance value.

Source: Based on Ribeiro *et al.* (2009).

Understanding about the role and nature of relationships, within an interorganisational context, has therefore evolved over several decades. Relationships, whether expressed as degrees of collaboration or value creation, provide a platform for understanding contemporary business marketing theory and practice.

■ Relationship Marketing – Theoretical Foundations

The development and underpinning of relationship marketing can be traced through a variety of theoretical perspectives. These are reviewed extensively by others (Varey, 2002; Bruhn, 2003). Three concepts are considered here: social exchange theory, social penetration theory and interaction theory. These are considered in organisational terms but it should be remembered that many of these theories have their origins in individual relationships.

■ Social Exchange Theory

The central premise associated with social exchange theory (Blau, 1964) is that relationships are based upon the exchange of values between two or more parties. Whatever constitutes the nature of an exchange between the participants, equality or satisfaction must be felt as a result. An absence of equality means that an advantage might have been gained by one party and this will automatically result in negative consequences for another. Therefore, organisations seeking to maintain marketing channel relationships should not raise prices past threshold levels or allow levels of service output (see Chapter 7) to fall below those of competitors. If channel partners perceive a lack of added value from these exchanges they are more likely to compare performance with other potential suppliers and even withdraw from the relationship by establishing alternative sources of supply.

Exchanges can occur between two parties, three parties in sequence or between at least three parties within a wider network and not necessarily sequentially. Relationships evolve from exchange behaviour which serves to provide the rules of engagement. They are socially constructed and have been interpreted in terms of marriage and social relationships (Tynan, 1997). Social norms drive exchange reciprocity within relationships and serve to guide behaviour expectations.

Whether in personal or interorganisational relationships, exchanges are considered to consist of two main elements. First, there are value exchanges which are based on the exchange of resources (goods for money) and second, there are symbolic exchanges where, in an interorganisational context, goods are purchased for their utility plus the feelings and associations that are bestowed on the user.

Social exchange theory serves to explain customer retention on the basis that the rewards derived through exchanges exceed the associated costs. Should expectations about future satisfaction fall short of the levels established through past exchanges, or alternative possibilities with other organisations suggest potentially improved levels of satisfaction, then the current partner may be discarded and a new relationship encouraged.

■ Social Penetration Theory

This theory is based on the premise that, as relationships develop, individuals begin to reveal more about themselves. Every encounter between a buyer and seller will allow each party to discover more about the other and make judgements about assigning suitable levels of relationship confidence. Consequently, the behaviour and communications exhibited between organisations may well change from a very formal and awkward introduction to something more knowledgeable, relaxed and self-assured.

Altman and Taylor (1973) refer to personality depth and personality breadth as two key aspects of the social penetration approach. Personality breadth is concerned with the range of topics (or categories) discussed by the parties and the frequency with which organisations discuss each topic. Unsurprisingly, products and customer needs are two main categories that are discussed by organisations. The analogy of an onion is often used to describe the various layers that make up the depth of a personality. The outer layers are generally superficial, contain a number of elements (of personality) and are relatively easy to determine. However, the key personality characteristics, those which influence the structure of the outer levels, are embedded within the inner core. The term' personality' depth refers to the difficulties associated with penetrating these inner layers, often because of the risks associated with such revelations.

From an organisational perspective, personality depth can be interpreted in terms of the degree to which a seller understands each of its customers. This client knowledge will vary but may include the way they use the products, their strategies, resources, culture and ethos, difficulties, challenges, successes and other elements that characterise buying organisations. Through successive interactions each organisation develops more knowledge of the other, as more information is gradually exposed, revealed or made known. At the outset of relationships, organisations tend to restrict the amount of information they reveal about themselves, but as confidence and trust in the other party develops so the level of openness increases. Likewise, as relationships develop so the degree of formality between the parties decreases, becoming more informal. This relationship intensity impacts on the quality of the relationship between two, or more, organisations.

Deconstructing a relationship reveals that it is composed of a series, or layers, of interactions. Each interaction results in judgements about whether to terminate or proceed with the relationship. The judgement is based on the accumulation of interactions, the history of the relationship and the level of customer knowledge that has been revealed.

4

Relationship Marketing

■ Interactional Theory

The development of relationship marketing appears to coincide with the emergence of network approaches to interorganisational analysis. This is referred to as industrial network analysis, and has evolved from the original focus on dyadic relationships (Araujo and Easton, 1996). A significantly strong and influential body of research, focusing on the interaction between members of a network, has been developed by the International Marketing and Purchasing Group (IMP).

The IMP Group analyses relationships, rather than transactions between buyers and sellers but, unlike relationship marketing theorists, they believe that both parties are active participants. Relationships between buyers and sellers are regarded as long-term, close and complex and through episodes of exchange, the links between organisations become institutionalised. Processes and roles become established, ingrained and expected of one another. It is particularly significant in this interactional approach that other organisations are considered to influence the relationship between a buyer and a seller. This incorporates ideas concerning network interpretations of business-to-business and channel configuration, considered in Chapter 7.

Table 4.3: Elements of exchange episodes

McLoughlin and Horan (2000)	IMP Group
Financial and economic exchange	Product/service exchange
Technological exchange	Information exchange
Information exchange	Financial exchange
Knowledge exchange	Social exchange
Legal exchange	

The interactional approach is based on relational exchanges with a variety of organisations within interlocking networks. An important aspect of network operation is the high degree of cooperation and reciprocity necessary between participants. This cooperation is manifest through the various exchanges that organisations undertake. McLoughlin and Horan (2000) identify five main exchange elements, while the IMP Group consider four, as set out in Table 4.3. These two lists are largely similar and both encompass formal and informal exchanges. These occur over time with varying levels of intensity between two or more organisations.

Relationships are developed through the different exchange episodes and are largely influenced by four main factors: technology, organisational determinants (size, structure and strategy), organisational experience and individuals. The result of this is an atmosphere in which a relationship exists and reflects issues of power-dependence, the degree of conflict or cooperation and the overall closeness or distance of the relationship.

■ The Customer Relationship Life Cycle

As already suggested, customer relationships move through a variety of phases and are therefore dynamic in nature and structure. By utilising the life cycle concept it is possible to chart these different phases over the natural course of a relationship. Just as different strategies can be applied to different phases of the product life cycle, it is possible to observe that customers have different requirements as a relationship evolves.

This particular life cycle tracks the evolution of relationships through time against the intensity of relationship at any one moment. The variables that constitute the intensity of relationship dimension are subject to various interpretations. Bruhn (2003) draws on psychological, behavioural and economic indicators, as depicted in Figure 4.2.

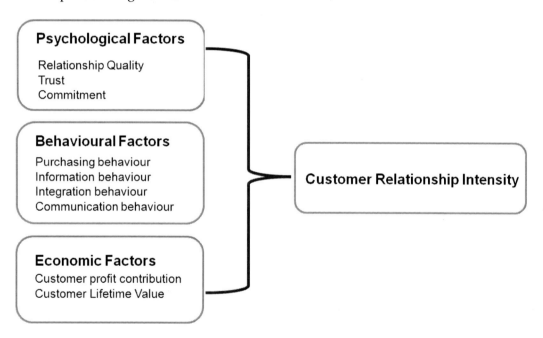

Figure 4.2: Dimensions of relationship intensity

Paramount to the psychological indicators are the concepts of trust and commitment. These are examined in greater detail later in this chapter but, for now, they should be regarded as foundations for establishing and maintaining ongoing, mutually rewarding two-way relationships. Behavioural indicators refer not just to purchasing but also to communication and information (search) behaviours.

It is possible to break down customer relationships into a number of different phases but at the aggregate level there are four, namely customer acquisition, development, retention and decline. The duration and intensity of each relationship phase will inevitably vary and it should be remembered that this representation is idealistic. A customer relationship life cycle is represented at Figure 4.3.

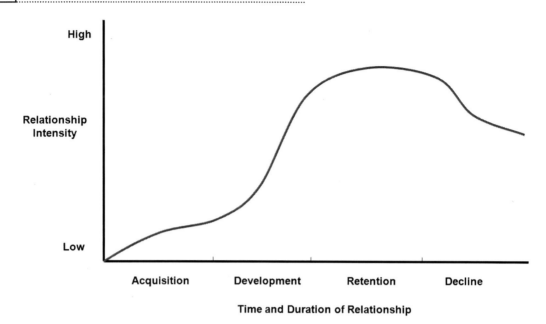

Figure 4.3: Customer relationship life cycle

■ Customer acquisition

During the acquisition phase three main events occur. First, there is a buyer–seller search for a suitable pairing. Second, once a suitable partner has been found there is a period of initiation during which both organisations seek out information about the other before any transaction occurs. The duration of this initiation period will depend partly on the strategic importance and complexity of the products and partly upon the nature of the introduction. If introduced to each other by an established and trusted organisation certain initiation rites will be shortened. Once a transaction occurs the socialisation period commences during which the buyer and seller start to become more familiar with each other and gradually begin to reveal more information about themselves. The seller is able to collect payment, delivery and handling information about the buyer and as a result is able to prepare customised outputs. The buyer is able to review the seller's products and experience the seller's service quality.

■ Customer development

During the development phase the seller encourages the buyer to try other products, to increase the volume of purchases, to engage with other added value services and to vary delivery times and quantities. The buyer will acquiesce according to specific needs and the level of drive to become more involved with the supplier. It is during this phase that the buyer is able to determine whether or not it is worth developing deeper relationships with the seller.

ViewPoint 4.3 Redeeming business customers

Nectar Business is the UK's largest business-to-business loyalty scheme. Aimed at the SME sector, the scheme has over 500,000 members. Despite having a significant membership, they were concerned that lower redemption levels might lead to higher levels of customer churn with resultant affects on customer retention.

It was Nectar's experience from their consumer programme that reward redemption had a positive impact on engagement and loyalty. Research identified that business members felt that the redemption process was over complex and not user-friendly. They offered high value collectors a personalised reward selection and delivery service 'Silver Service' and re-categorised the awards sections to make them easier to understand and navigate. One of the reward offerings allowed members to collect points when hiring vehicles from Hertz online. In addition, rewards suppliers were asked to make their offerings more exciting.

An initial mailing/emailing of 5,000 members produced significant responses in terms of engagement and redemption levels. Further campaigns were developed along similar lines aimed at strengthening relationships and establishing retention levels. Redemption preferences are continuously monitored to update the rewards portfolio.

Source: Based on Carter (2011); www.nectar.com/business

Question: In what ways might strategies aimed at customer retention differ between business and consumer markets?

■ Customer retention

The retention phase will last as long as both the buyer and seller are able to meet their individual and joint goals. If the relationship has become more involved greater levels of trust and commitment between the partners will allow for increased cross-buying and product experimentation, joint projects and product development. However, the very essence of relationship marketing is for organisations to identify a portfolio of organisations with whom they wish to develop a range of relationships. This requires means to measure levels of retention and also determine when resources are moved from acquisition to retention and back to acquisition.

■ Customer decline

This period is concerned with the demise of the relationship. Termination may occur suddenly as a result of a serious problem or episode between the parties. The more likely process is that the buying organisation decides to reduce their reliance on the seller and either notifies them formally or begins to reduce the frequency and duration of contact and moves business to other, competitive organisations.

■ Customer Loyalty

Implicit within this customer relationship cycle is the notion that retained customers are loyal. However, this may be deceptive as 'loyalty' may actually be camouflage for convenience or extended utility. Loyalty, however presented, takes different forms, just as there are customers who are more valued than others. A prospect becomes a purchaser, completed through a market exchange. Clients emerge from several completed transactions but remain ambivalent towards the seller organisation. Supporters, despite being passive about an organisation, are willing and able to enter into regular transactions. Advocates represent the next and penultimate step. They not only support an organisation and its products but actively recommend it to others by positive, word-of-mouth communications. Partners, who represent the top rung of the ladder, trust and support an organisation just as it trusts and supports them. Partnership status, discussed in greater detail later in this chapter, is the embodiment of relational exchanges and interorganisational collaboration.

This cycle of customer attraction (acquisition), customer retention and customer development represents a major difference to the 4Ps approach. It is, above all else, customer-focused and more appropriate to marketing values. However, even this approach is questionable as, although the focus of analysis is no longer the product but the relationship, the focus tends to be orientated towards the 'customer relationship' rather than the relationship *per se*. In other words there is a degree of asymmetry inherent in the relationship marketing concept.

■ Differing Types of Relationships

The simplicity of the loyalty ladder concept illustrates the important point that customers represent different values to other organisations. That perceived value (or worth) may or may not be reciprocated, thus establishing the basis for a variety and complexity of different relationships.

The theoretical development of relationship marketing encompasses a number of different concepts. These involve a greater emphasis on cooperation rather than competition and the identification of different development phases within customer relationships, namely acquisition, development and retention.

According to Wagner and Boutellier (2002), the degree to which buyer–seller relationships are developed can depend on the configuration of internal and external factors. Internal factors involve the nature of the product, the degree of technological sophistication and the core competences of the organisation. The external factors involve the industry environment, the market, the competitive situation and the condition of the overall economy. Bringing these elements together and making relationship development decisions involves a level of management judgement but two guiding principles can be of assistance. These concern the strategic influence of the supplier's input goods and the degree to which supplying organisations can be substituted.

Organisations which supply goods and materials that are not strategic, that is, they do not provide added value or enable a degree of differentiation, do not warrant an investment in close relationship development. It is better that relationships should be remote, enabling buying flexibility and the exertion of downward pressures on price, quality and delivery. However, suppliers of goods and materials that are central to the buying organisation's strategic thrust, such as those that supply customised goods or critical systems architecture services are important. This is because they contribute to the development of customer value through differentiation. This requires the formation of close relationships, even partnerships and collaborative arrangements, to facilitate intensive negotiations and provide continuity of personal supply and continued customer value.

The second principle concerns the state of the market environment. In markets where the products are relatively standardised or simple, then a remote relationship is preferable due to the ease with which buyers can switch suppliers and substitute the source of their input goods. Where products are complex and or highly customised, then partnerships are preferable in order to provide continuity of supply. As a general rule therefore, when product supply is easy and there is active competition between suppliers for business, then a remote relationship may be advisable. When supply is tight, especially in growth markets, close collaboration and the development of partnerships with key suppliers is the best course of action.

Wagner and Boutellier (2002) cite DaimlerChrysler and their global procurement and supply strategy process as an example of an organisation that segments its suppliers and commodities based on the type of relationship it seeks. Using the following seven criteria, the organisation allocates commodities and input suppliers to one of four extended enterprise (EE) relationship types.

- Share in value adding costs
- Dependency on suppliers' technical know-how
- buyer's own knowledge about specifications and design
- Number of possible suppliers
- Switching costs and strength of exit barriers
- Supplier's negotiating power
- Importance to and contribution towards DC's own customers perceptions.

DaimlerChrysler identify transaction, coordination, co-operation and alliance types of relationship. The first two are regarded as essentially operational and the second two as strategic types of relationship.

Bensaou (1999) reported similar work with automobile manufacturers in Japan and the United States and identified four types of relationships, namely market exchange, captive supplier, captive buyer and strategic partnerships.

Allocation to one of these categories is based on customer, supplier and product characteristics and each type of relationship requires particular strategies if the relationship is to be successful.

The development of suitable segmentation strategies is critical to understanding customers and their individual potential value to the seller, in order that they develop appropriate relationships (Tinsley, 2002). Decisions concerning segmentation require that database management and associated systems generate appropriate information. However, as Tinsley also points out, reliance on simplistic information systems to determine the potential of a customer who is currently of low value status is problematic and insufficiently strategic.

The development and implementation of a relationship marketing strategy can impact on a wide range of organisational activities. One of these concerns implementation and the range of resources required to be successful (Tinsley, 2002). Not all relationships are the same, indeed each may require different approaches and resources. An organisation has finite resources so must decide, among its portfolio of buyers, which warrant developing relationships and the type of relationships to nurture. Resources can then be allocated accordingly.

■ Partnerships and Alliances

The development of strategic alliances is a step that some organisations undertake, very often with organisations with whom they already work closely, in order to gain competitive advantage through their complementary resources or core competences. An alliance in this sense implies a commitment to another organisation(s) in which partners invest resources to achieve particular goals. It is strategic because the relationship is long-term, all partners are committed and the relationship is mutually supportive.

The term 'alliance' is just one of many used to describe the way some organisations have tried to gain advantage and reduce uncertainty through the development of committed working partnerships. According to Teece (1992), such organisations can obtain complementary resources in a fast, flexible and cost-efficient way. Terms such as 'channel partners', 'distribution partners' and 'partnerships' are also used in this context. Unlike vertical integration, where ownership dominance and control are the prime structural factors, strategic distribution-based alliances rely on trust and commitment to achieve the agreed outcomes.

The main advantages of forming such alliances is that they enable organisations to reduce the uncertainties associated with developing channel operations and relationships and, through cooperation, the partners are able to strengthen their market positions. Lerner and Merges (1997) refer to small biotechnology firms who partner large and established pharmaceutical firms in order to gain access to large markets and distribution and marketing resources while the pharmaceutical firm develops knowledge in new products and leading-edge research. Airlines such as British Airways and Qantas form alliances so that their flights can be connected to each other. Passengers prefer the continuity, and the airlines generate increased traffic flows (Bamberger *et al.*, 2001).

For manufacturers, long lead times and high extended costs, associated with building both distributor relationships and the core skills necessary to operate in a variety of markets, can be reduced through a single partner. The ideal partner organisation, possessing the experience and core competences required by the manufacturer, can implement market solutions more or less immediately.

Distribution alliances require all parties to work together and be flexible in their approach to the inevitable problems that arise through such activities. Kanter (1994) suggests that there are five levels of integration necessary if strategic alliances are to be successful (see Table 4.4).

Table 4.4: Five levels of alliance integration

Type of integration	Explanation
Strategic	Post-contract dialogue between senior managers to maintain and enhance the relationship.
Tactical	Middle managers to develop systems to facilitate the transfer of knowledge and to cement interorganisational infrastructures.
Operational	The information necessary to complete the day-to-day activities associated with the alliance.
Interpersonal	The development of personal knowledge of other people in the partnership.
Cultural	All managers to develop awareness and communication skills to bridge the cultural gaps that arise between the organisations.

Source: Based on Kanter (1994).

The reasons for forming alliances vary according to the position occupied in the marketing channel. Distributors and retailers seek alliances upstream to ensure a flow of desirable products and in doing so differentiate themselves from other distributors and retailers. Although manufacturers look for better market coverage and lower costs, some of the increasingly important reasons for alliances with downstream channel members concern the logistical advantages of lower order cycle times, lower stock-related costs and higher service output levels.

In order for a supplier to achieve partnership status, Lemke *et al.* (2003) determined five key constructs:

■ That the business relationship is developed at a personal rather than organisational level

■ That the supplier is capable of supplying bespoke products

■ That the supplier contributes to the new product development process of the manufacturer

■ That there is regular, active relationship management

■ That the supplier is located near to the manufacturer for both interaction and delivery purposes.

Contemporary supplier–manufacturer partnerships are therefore less orientated, around product quality, on-time delivery and competitive pricing, as these are now commonly expected factors and are no longer critical discriminators.

There are numerous examples of distribution alliances such as those between Pepsi Cola and Cadbury Schweppes, Yahoo with Compaq Europe, Gateway, Hewlett-Packard, IBM, Micron Electronics, and alliances between Hitachi Data Systems and Network Appliances and Sun Microsystems.

The success factors associated with external collaboration and partnerships are goal congruence, trust at all levels of interaction and intensive positive communication. Additionally, for partnerships to be successful, attention must be given to internal factors. As with a change management project, senior management must provide their support and the use of cross-functional teams appears to be an integral aspect of successful alliances (Wagner and Boutellier, 2002).

B2B eCommerce alliances have been categorised by Dai and Kauffman (2002) into four functional types, which are set out in Table 4.5.

Table 4.5: Functional types of eMarket alliances

Type of alliance	Explanation
Marketing	To facilitate improved promotion and distribution of online services.
Participation	To improve levels of cooperation and involvement in online exchanges.
Functionality	To improve the utility offered by a marketplace so that it works more efficiently and more effectively.
Connection	To encourage linkages into an electronic marketplace.

Source: Based on Dai and Kauffman (2002).

The first two types, marketing and participation alliances, seek to develop the number of organisations involved in an exchange. In doing so they are essentially relationally orientated. The other two try to improve the technical services offered to participants of the marketplace and hence have a functional orientation.

■ Trust, Commitment and Customer Satisfaction

Many writers contend that one of the crucial factors associated with the development and maintenance of interorganisational relationships is trust (Morgan and Hunt, 1994; Doney and Cannon, 1997). However, Cousins and Stanwix (2001) believe that the concepts, although important, are difficult to define and suggest that many authors fail to specify clearly what they mean when using them. A review of the literature indicates that trust is an element of personal, intra-organisational and inter-organisational relationships, being both necessary for and resulting from their perpetuation. As Gambetta (1988) argues, trust is a means of reducing uncertainty in order that effective relationships can develop.

Cousins and Stanwix also suggest that, although trust is a term used to explain how B2B relationships work, often it actually refers to ideas concerning risk, power and dependency and these propositions are used interchangeably. From their research of vehicle manufacturers, it emerges that B2B relationships are about the creation of mutual business advantage and the degree of confidence that one organisation has in another.

Interorganisational trust is based on two main dimensions; credibility and benevolence. Credibility concerns the extent to which one organisation believes (is confident) that another organisation will undertake and complete its agreed roles and tasks. Benevolence is concerned with goodwill, that the other organisation will not act opportunistically, even if the conditions for exploitation should arise (Pavlou, 2002). In other words, interorganisational trust involves judgements about another organisation's reliability and integrity.

It has been suggested that interorganisational trust consists of three main elements (Zucker, 1986; Luo, 2002). Characteristic trust, based on the similarities between parties, process trust, developed through familiarity and typically fostered by successive exchange transactions and institutional trust, see below. This third category might be considered to be the most important, especially at the outset of a relationship when familiarity and similarity factors are non-existent or hard to discern respectively.

Table 4.6: Elements of institutional trust

Element	Key aspect
Perceived monitoring	Refers to the supervision of transactions by, for example, regulatory authorities or owners of B2B market exchanges. This can mitigate uncertainty through a perception that sellers or buyers who fail to conform with established rules and regulations will be penalised.
Perceived accreditation	Refers to badges or symbols that denote membership of externally recognised bodies that bestow credibility, authority, security and privacy on a selling organisation.
Perceived legal bonds	Refers to contracts between buyers, sellers and independent third parties, so that the costs of breaking a contract are perceived to be greater than the benefits of such an action. Trust in the selling organisation is therefore enhanced when bonds are present.
Perceived feedback	Refers to signals about the quality of an organisation's reputation and such feedback from other buyers about sellers, perhaps through word-of-mouth communication can deter sellers from undertaking opportunistic behaviour.
Perceived cooperative norms	Refers to the values, standards and principles adopted by those party to a series of exchanges. Cooperative norms and values signal good faith and behavioural intent, through which trust is developed.

Source: Based on Pavlou (2002).

Relationship Marketing

4

Pavlou (2002) argues that there are five means by which institutional trust can be encouraged (see Table 4.6). Institutional trust is clearly vital in B2C markets where perceived risk is present and known to prevent many people from purchasing online. In the B2B market, institutional trust is also important but more in terms of the overall reputation of the organisation. The development and establishment of trust is valuable because of the outcomes that can be anticipated. These have been identified by Pavlou (2002) as satisfaction, perceived risk and continuity.

Trust reduces conflict and the threat of opportunism and that in turn enhances the probability of buyer satisfaction, an important positive outcome of institutional trust. Perceived risk is concerned with the expectation of loss and is therefore tied closely with organisational performance. Trust that a seller will not take advantage of the imbalance of information between buyer and seller effectively reduces risk. Continuity is related to business volumes, necessary in online B2B marketplaces, and the development of both on- and offline enduring relationships. Trust is associated with continuity and when present is therefore indicative of long-term relationships.

According to Young and Wilkinson (1989) the presence of trust within a relationship is influenced by four main factors. These are the duration of the relationship, the relative power of the participants, the presence of cooperation and various environmental factors that may be present at any one moment. Extending these ideas into what is now regarded by many as a seminal paper in the relationship marketing literature, Morgan and Hunt (1994) argued, and supported with empirical evidence, that the presence of both commitment and trust leads to cooperative behaviour and this in turn is conducive to successful relationship marketing.

Morgan and Hunt regard commitment as the desire that a relationship continue (endure) in order that a valued relationship be maintained or strengthened. They postulated that commitment and trust are key mediating variables (KMV) between various antecedents and outcomes. The impact is that trust affects commitment that in turn strengthens cooperation between partners (see Figure 4.4).

According to the KMV model the greater the losses anticipated through the termination of a relationship the greater the commitment will be expressed by the exchange partners. Likewise, when these partners share the same values commitment increases. Trust is enhanced when communication is perceived to be of high quality but decreases when one organisation knowingly takes action that will be to the detriment of the other to seek to benefit from the relationship.

Kumar *et al.* (1994) distinguish between affective and calculative commitment. The former is rooted in positive feelings towards the other party and a desire to maintain the relationship. The latter is negatively orientated and is determined by the extent to which one party perceives it is (not) possible to replace the other party, advantageously.

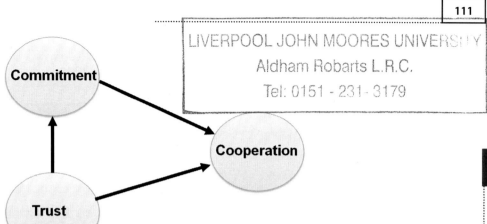

4

Figure 4.4: The KMV model of trust, commitment and collaboration (Morgan and Hunt, 1994)

The centrality of the trust and commitment concepts to relationship marketing has thus been established and they are as central to marketing channel relationships as to other B2B relationships (Achrol, 1991; Goodman and Dion, 2001).

Summary

Here are the key points about relationship marketing, set out against the learning objectives.

1 Explore the development and evolution of relationship marketing.

B2B relationship marketing as an approach which encompasses a wide range of relationships, not just with customers, but also those that organisations develop with suppliers, regulators, government, competitors, employees and others. From this, relationship marketing might be regarded as all marketing activities associated with the management of successful relational exchanges.

Relationship marketing is based on the principle that there is a history of exchanges between a buyer and seller, and an expectation that there will be exchanges in the future. Furthermore, the perspective is on the long term, envisioning a form of continued collaboration between the buyer and the seller.

2 Examine the conceptual underpinning associated with relationship marketing practices.

Originally B2B marketing theory focused on the actions of individual organisations as they exchanged products, from a seller's perspective. This view evolved into the recognition that organisations were active participants in the buying process and a group orientation emerged with a focus on buying centres. Soon it was accepted that there were varying degrees of cooperation and interdependency between buyers and sellers.

Rather than consider the exchange of products, interorganisational behaviour became focused on the relationship between the pair of organisations. In essence, this was a move away from regarding purchasing as a single discrete event, to considering it as a stream of activities between two organisations. This view was extended to encompass groups of interacting organisations (networks) rather than a simple pair.

One of the more recent ideas concerns the perception of value. The current view is that there are two fundamental elements; value propositions and value creation. Sellers develop *value propositions* or promises of value creation opportunities embedded in their offerings. Buyers achieve *value creation* when they incorporate a seller's offering (products and services) into their processes.

3 Introduce ideas concerning the customer relationship life cycle.

Customer relationships move through a variety of phases, namely customer acquisition, development, retention and decline. These are dynamic in nature and structure and it is possible to observe that customers have different requirements as a relationship evolves.

The duration and intensity of each relationship phase will inevitably vary and it should be remembered that this representation is idealistic.

4 Examine the nature and characteristics of partnerships and alliances with suppliers and other stakeholders.

An alliance implies a commitment to another organisation(s) in which the partners invest resources to achieve particular goals. It is strategic because the relationship is long-term, all partners are committed and the relationship is mutually supportive.

The reasons for forming alliances vary according to the position occupied in the marketing channel. Distributors and retailers seek alliances upstream in order to ensure a flow of desirable products and services, and in doing so differentiate themselves from other distributors and retailers. Although manufacturers look for better market coverage and lower costs, some of the increasingly important reasons for alliances with downstream channel members concern the logistical advantages of lower order cycle times, lower stock-related costs and higher service output levels.

5 Consider trust and commitment as key elements of business relationships.

Trust refers to ideas concerning risk, power and dependency and is a means of reducing uncertainty in order that effective relationships can develop. B2B relationships are about the creation of mutual business advantage and the degree of confidence that one organisation has in another. The centrality of the trust and commitment concepts to relationship marketing is agreed and they are as central to marketing channel relationships as to other B2B relationships.

■ Discussion Questions

1 Find examples of three distribution alliances and consider the benefits the new arrangement might have brought to the constituent organisations.

2 Write brief notes outlining the differences between market exchanges and collaborative exchanges.

3 Prepare notes for a presentation to be given to colleagues in which you seek to explain the differences between social, exchange, penetration and interaction theories.

4 Discuss the extent to which customer-driven relationship marketing concepts can be applied to suppliers and members of an organisation's supply chain.

5 Identify the main elements that are used to characterise interorganisational trust.

6 How might Social CRM help overcome some of the problems incurred to date with CRM systems?

References

Achrol, R.S. (1991). Evolution of the marketing organisation: new forms for turbulent environments, *Journal of Marketing*, **55** (4), 77–93

Ahlert, D., Kenning P. von and Petermann, F. (2001) Die Bedeutung von Vertrauen fur die Interaktionsbeziehungen zwischen Dienstleistungsanbietern und Nachfragern, in M. Bruhn and B. Strauss (eds) *Dienstleistungsmanagement, Jahrbuch 2001. Interaktionen im Dienstleistungsbereich*, Wiesbaden: Gaber, 239–318

Altman, I. and Taylor, D.A. (1973) *Social Penetration: The Development of Interpersonal Relationships*, New York: Holt, Reinhart and Winston

Araujo, L. and Easton, G. (1996) Networks in socioeconomic systems: a critical review, in D. Iacobucci (ed.), *Networks in Marketing*, Thousand Oaks, CA: Sage.

Bamberger, G.E., Carlton, D.W. and Neumann, L.R. (2001) An empirical investigation of the competitive effects of domestic airline alliances, working paper, Graduate School of Business, University of Chicago, Chicago, IL.

Bensaou, B.M. (1999). Portfolios of buyer–seller relationships, *Sloan Management Review*, **40** (4), (Summer), 35–44.

Bergen, U., Dutta, S. and Walker, Jr. O.C. (1992) Agency relationships in marketing: a review of implications and applications of agency and related theories, *Journal of Marketing*, **56** (2), 1–24.

Blattberg, R.C. and Deighton, A.R. (1996) Manage marketing by the customer equity test, *Harvard Business Review*, **74** (4), 136–144

Blau, P. (1964). *Exchange and Power in Social Life*, New York: John Wiley & Sons.

Borden, N.H. (1964) The concept of the marketing mix, *Journal of Advertising Research*, **4** (June), 2–7.

Borders, A.L., Jonston, W.J., and Rigdon, E.E., 2001, Beyond the Dyad: Electronic Commerce and Network Perspectives in Industrial Marketing Management, *Industrial Marketing Management*, **30** (2), pp199-205.

Bruhn, M. (2003) *Relationship Marketing: Management of Customer Relationships*, Harlow: Financial Times/Prentice Hall

Carter, M. (2011) Silver service, *themarketer*, March, 20-22

Chen, S. (2003). The real value of "e-business models", *Business Horizons* (November–December), 27–33

Christopher, M., Payne, A. and Ballantyne, D. (2002) *Relationship Marketing: Creating Stakeholder Value*, Oxford: Butterworth-Heinemann.

Cousins, P.D. (2002) A conceptual model for managing long term inter-organisational relationships, *European Journal of Purchasing and Supply Management*, **8** (2) (June) 71–82

Cousins, P. and Stanwix, E. (2001) It's only a matter of confidence! A comparison of relationship management between Japanese and UK non-owned vehicle manufacturers, *International Journal of Operations and Production Management*, **21** (9) (October) 1160–1180

Dai, Q. and Kauffman, R.J. (2002). Understanding B2B e-Market alliance strategies, paper presented at the 2002 Workshop on Information Systems and Economics, Barcelona, Spain, December 2002. Current working paper version available at the MIS Research Center website, www.misrc.csom.umn.edu

Day, G. (2000). Managing market relationships, *Journal of the Academy of Marketing Science*, **28** (1) (Winter) 24–30.

Doney, P.M. and Cannon, J.P. (1997) An examination of the nature of trust in buyer–seller relationships, *Journal of Marketing*, **62** (2), 1–13

Dowling, G.R. and Uncles, M. (1997) Do customer loyalty programs work?, *Sloan Management Review*, eLibrary.com, 22 June, www.static.elibrary.com/s/sloanmanagementreview/ june221997/docustomerloyaltyprogramsreallywork.

Dwyer, R.F., Schurr, P.H. and Oh, S. (1987) Developing buyer–seller relationships, *Journal of Marketing*, **51** (April), 11–27

Easton, G. and Araujo, L. (1993) A resource-based view of industrial networks, in *Proceedings of the Ninth IMP International Conference on International Marketing*, (Bath: University of Bath, School of Management)

Ericson, J. (2001). The 'Failure' of CRM, *Line 56*, August, www.line56.com/articles/default.asp?News10 = 2802 (Accessed 1 January 2004.)

Feeny, D.F., Earl, M.J. and Edwards, B. (1997) Information systems organisation: the roles of users and specialists, in L. Willcocks, D. Feeny and G. Islei (eds), *Managing IT as a Strategic Resource*. London: McGraw-Hill, 151–168.

Fischer, T. and Tewes, M. (2001) Vertrauen und Commitment in der Dienstleistungs-interaktion, in M. Bruhn and B. Strauss (eds), *Dienstleistungsmanagement, Jahrbuch 2001. Interaktionen in Dienstleistungsbereich*, Weisbaden: Gaber, 299–318.

Ford, D. (1980). The development of buyer–seller relationships in industrial markets, *European Journal of Marketing*, **14** (5/6), 339–354

Gambetta, D. (1988). *Trust: Making and breaking Co-operative Relations*, New York: Blackwell.

Goodman, L.E. and Dion, P.A. (2001) The determinants of commitment in the distributor–manufacturer relationship, *Industrial Marketing Management*, **30** (3) (April), 287–300

Grion, R.S. (2003). Rethinking customer acquisition before talking retention, *Journal of Integrated Communications*, 2002–03 issue, 29–33, www.medill.northwestern.edu/imc/studentwork/pubs/jic/journal/2002/grion.pdf (Accessed 5 December 2003.)

Gronroos, C. (1994) From marketing mix to relationship marketing, *Management Decision*, **32** (2), 4–20

Grönroos, C., 2009. Marketing as promise management: regaining customer management for marketing. *Journal of Business & Industrial Marketing*, **24** (5/6), 351-359.

Houston, F.S. and Gassenheimer, J.B. (1987) Market and exchange, *Journal of Marketing*, **51** (4), 3–18

IMP Group (1982). *International Marketing and Purchasing of Industrial Goods*, H.Hakansoon, (ed.), Chichester: Wiley.

Jensen, M.C. and Meckling, W. (1976) The theory of the firm: managerial behavior–agency costs and capital structure, *Journal of Financial Economics*, **3**, 305–360

Johanson, J. and Mattsson, L-G. (1994) The markets as networks tradition in Sweden, in G. Laurent, G.L. Lilien, and B. Pras (eds), *Research Traditions in Marketing*, Boston MA: Kluwer Academic Publishing, 321–342.

Kanter, R.M. (1994). Collaborative advantage: the art of alliances, *Harvard Business Review*, July–August, 96–108

Klee, A. (2000). *Strategisches Berziehungsmanagement: ein integrativer Ansatz zur strategischen Planning und Implementierung des Beziehungsmanagement*, Aachen: Shaker.

Kumar, N., Hibbard, J.D. and Stern, L.W. (1994) *The Nature and Consequences of Marketing Channel Intermediary Commitment, Marketing Science Institute Report No. 94–115*, Cambridge, MA: Marketing Science Institute.

Lemke, F., Goffin, K. and Szwejczewski, M. (2003) Investigating the meaning of supplier–manufacturer partnerships, *International Journal of Physical Distribution and Logistics Management*, **33** (1), 12–35

Lerner, J. and Merges, R.P. (1997) The control of strategic alliances: an empirical analysis of biotechnology collaborations, Working Paper 6014, National Bureau of Economic Research, Cambridge, MA.

Luo, X. (2002). A framework based on relationship marketing and social exchange theory, *Industrial Marketing Management*, **31** (2) (February) 111–118.

McCarthy, E.J. (1960). *Basic Marketing: A Managerial Approach*, Homewood, IL: Irwin.

McLoughlin, D. and Horan, C. (2000) Perspectives from the Markets-as-Networks Approach, *Industrial Marketing Management*, **29** (4), 285–292

Morgan, B. (2001). How does your call centre grow?, *Operations and Fulfillment*, 1 July 2001, www.opsandfulfillment.com/ar/fulfillment_call_center_grow/ (accessed 1 January 2004)

Morgan, R.M. and Hunt, S.D. (1994) The commitment-trust theory of relationship marketing, *Journal of Marketing*, **58** (July), 20–38

O'Malley, L. and Mitussis, D. (2002) Relationships and technology: strategic implications, *Journal of Strategic Marketing*, **10** (3) (September), 225–38

Payne, A. (2000), *A strategic framework for customer relationship management*, BT CRM White Paper.

Pavlou, P.A. (2002). Institution-based trust in interorganisational exchange relationships: the role of online B2B marketplaces on trust formation, *Journal of Strategic Information Systems*, **11** (3–4), (December), 215–243

Reichheld, F.F. and Sasser, E.W. (1990) Zero defections: quality comes to services, *Harvard Business Review*, (September), 105–111

Reinartz, W.J. and Kumar, V. (2002) The mismanagement of customer loyalty, *Harvard Business Review* (July), 86–94

Rowe, W.G. and Barnes, J.G. (1998) Relationship marketing and sustained competitive advantage, *Journal of Market-Focused Management*, **2** (3), pp. 281–97

Sheth, J. (1973) A model of industrial buyer behaviour, *Journal of Marketing*, **37** (October), 50–56

Sheth, J.N. and Parvatiyar, A. (1995) Relationship marketing in consumer markets: antecedents and consequences, *Journal of the Academy of Marketing Science*, **23** (4), 255–271.

Spekman, R. (1988). Perceptions of strategic vulnerability among industrial buyers and its effect on information search and supplier evaluation, *Journal of Business Research*, **17**, 313–326.

Steinfield, C., Kraut, R. and Plummer, A. (1995) The impact of interorganisational networks, on buyer–seller relationships, *Journal of Computer Mediated Communication*, **1** (3), www.ascusc.org/jcmc/vol1/issue3/steinfld.html

Teece, D.J. (1992). Competition, cooperation and innovation: arrangements for regimes of rapid technological progress, *Journal of Economic Behaviour and Organisation*, **18**, 1–25.

Thomas, D. (2003). Sainsbury's boosts supplier collaboration, *Computer Weekly*, 12 October; www.computerweekly.com/articles/ (accessed 29 November 2003)

Tinsley, D.B. (2002). Relationship marketing's strategic array, *Business Horizons*, **45** (1) (January/February), 70–6

Tynan, C. (1997). A review of the marriage analogy in relationship marketing, *Journal of Marketing Management*, **13**, 695–703

Varey, R.J. (2002). *Relationship Marketing: Dialogue and Networks in the e-Commerce Era*, Chichester: Wiley.

Wagner, S. and Boutellier, R. (2002) Capabilities for managing a portfolio of supplier relationships, *Business Horizons* **46** (6), (November–December), 79–88

Webster, F.E. and Wind, Y. (1972) A general model for understanding organisational buying behaviour, *Journal of Marketing*, **36** (April), 12–14

Weill, P. and Vitale, M.R. (2001) *Place to Space: Migrating to eBusiness Models*, Boston, MA: Harvard Business School Press.

Williamson, O.E. (1975). *Markets and Hierarchies*, New York: The Free Press.

Young, L.C. and Wilkinson, I.F. (1989) The role of trust and co-operation in marketing channels: a preliminary study, *European Journal of Marketing*, **23** (2), 109–122

Zucker, L. (1986). Production of trust: institutional sources of economic structure 1840–1920, *Research in Organisation Behaviour*, **8** (1), 53–111

5 Strategy: Segmentation, Positioning and Pricing

Overview

This chapter considers some of the elements that have strategic significance, namely segmentation, positioning and pricing.

Segmentation is presented as a less than perfect form of marketing management, as consideration is given to some of the problems associated with choosing between segments and implementing the whole segmentation, targeting and positioning process successfully. In particular, the barriers to segmentation are examined.

The following section examines how businesses should determine particular positioning strategies. Just as optimal target markets should be derived in the light of customer needs and seller resources and strategies, so positioning needs to take into account the requirements of all parties to a marketing relationship.

The chapter concludes with a consideration of pricing issues in business markets.

Aims and objectives

The aim of the chapter is to examine current issues concerning segmentation, positioning and pricing issues in B2B markets.

The objectives of this chapter are to:

1 Examine the bases for segmenting business markets.

2 Consider the breakdown and build-up approaches to market segmentation in B2B markets.

3 Explore some of the processes used to select target markets.

4 Evaluate the practice of segmentation in business markets.

5 Consider the role of positioning (and strategies) in the segmentation, targeting and positioning (STP) process.

6 Consider the role and characteristics of pricing issues in B2B marketing

A Slice of Life – A Little Ray of Sunshine

By the time I'm asked to consider the positioning and creative delivery of a brand, there are usually a few assets already in place. The most important of these assets is the marketing strategy. I can't really deliver much without one – the vision, the objectives, the business imperatives, the overall understanding of and direction for the brand comes from the marketing strategy (and the audience). There is a significant overlap between the marketing and brand strategies, but nevertheless, the brand doesn't fix everything – the marketing plan at least provides something to aim at. I've seen my share of 'marketing plans' and they can be... variable. The good ones shine and the bad ones can be laughable. The plans can be delivered in a multitude of ways – written, verbal and (my favourite) telepathic. The importance of the marketing plan, however, is best illustrated by way of an occasion where the marketing plan was just, well, wrong.

I was engaged by a Japanese company that called me out of the blue. I've learnt to be sceptical of the random phone calls – "Hello, do you do marketing...?" "Err, yes, shall I wrap a couple up and send them over? What colour would you like your marketings?" – but the call was interesting and I was sufficiently intrigued to have the initial meeting. So I met with a Japanese woman who was the General Manager for the company in the UK. She was accompanied by a Japanese executive who had been brought out of retirement by the company to oversee the initial launch of the UK operation.

The company's billion-dollar operation comprised the manufacture of a single product – happy pills made from seaweed. I know. That's what I thought. But the billion dollar part meant I had to take the conversation seriously. The company grew the seaweed, harvested it and processed it into elephant-sized pills. The seaweed was almost impossible for the human body to ingest and obtain any material benefit from, so because most of the goodness just passed through the human body, the pills had had to be BIG. Not only that, but you were expected to take between 10 and 20 of these mothers every day. As a natural product, you could take more if you wanted, but why would you? I laughed so hard I let out a little wee. The miracle pills claimed to prolong life-expectancy, reduce the signs of ageing, provide energy, prevent cancer and generally promote all kinds of inner wellbeing. The medical studies (of which there were many – all paid for by the company...) seemed to me to focus on the message that the pills didn't do any harm rather than conclusively prove any real efficacy as a miracle cure, but there were two very serious looking Japanese executives and a billion dollars telling me not to wee at the table.

The company had expanded in recent years into North America and were now seeking a foothold in Europe. The marketing plan was very simple – to take the working model from the USA and apply it to the UK market. Everyone would then buy millions of horse pills and chew them fervently every day. Job done. Everything sounded good until I enquired what the strategy in the USA was.

This company was applying the 'Chinese' marketing strategy – following the principle that if the population is big enough, you just need a small percentage of the market to buy your product for the volume of sales to be (potentially) very significant. In Japan, a large percentage of the population with a very broad demographic profile took the pills daily. In the US the profile was very different. The company had had to segment the market aggressively and had ended up with a single viable segment of prospects.

The segment, tactfully put, was 'women of a certain age'. They were 45–65 years old, single, female, cat owners. There was considerably more detail to the profile, but sometimes the top line is enough. They were concerned about their appearance and keen to extend their youthfulness. They also had significant disposable income. So, of the 300 million population in the USA, there were 10s of millions of women who fitted nicely into the 'Witches of Eastwick' segment that the brand was targeting. The marketing strategy then, was to produce direct mail materials and continue mailing the segment, repeatedly and relentlessly, until the target conceded and purchased the product – at which point the direct mail became more frequent and more relentless to ensure repeat purchase.

Every week, the company mailed 100,000 women with printed direct mail the scale of which was broadly comparable to a large mail order catalogue. These 'white papers' and 'medical studies' were produced as text-only medical/legal style documents of over 100 pages each. There might be additional supporting 'evidence' combined with order forms and envelops to constitute a significant package. Every week the mailings went out and every week, 0.2% of the segmented audience purchased pills. It wasn't much, but it was enough. The price, volume and repeat purchase opportunity from the pills made the operation viable – very profitable actually. This was the model that was to be repeated in the UK.

I explained that it wouldn't work. I explained that the UK was not the US and that the segmentation strategy was non-viable on any matrices that I could think of – scale, disposable income, lifestyle, health aspiration… you name it. After applying the USA segmentation criteria to the UK market, there would be roughly three women in the whole of the UK that might be classified as the target audience. There certainly wouldn't be 100,000 people in the target, so what were we going to do after the first week of mailings? I explained that they would have to reposition the brand for the UK market. If we could appeal to a wider (larger) audience – younger, male and female – that might help. If we could use considerably shorter, sharper, creative communications instead of the dry text from the USA, there may be a chance that the UK market would read it. The budget was available – they just needed to apply it in different areas. I gave the smiling Japanese visitors a long list of what not to do, why to not do it and a viable alternative – a solution to their problem.

They listened politely. They explained the potential riches that would be bestowed upon me for the successful execution of their strategy and suggested that their way was the agreed strategy. We were to segment, send out 100,000 mailers per week and the ladies of a certain age would buy pills. They asked me to confirm that I could implement their plan. Naturally, I told them to shove it up their ass.

I may have been wrong. Certainly, the company is still very much alive and well and healthy and detoxified. Their happy pills are available by mail order in the UK. But it has never become the 'Coca-Cola' brand of the natural supplements world. A missed opportunity or a focused segmentation strategy? You decide.

Scot McKee

■ Introduction

A key strategic issue for all organisations concerns the way their products and services are perceived. Although corporate and marketing communications have a prime responsibility for informing, differentiating and positioning business offerings, there are several strategic activities that need to be accomplished first.

These strategic issues concern segmenting markets, then selecting appropriate target markets and then positioning products and services in the minds of members of the target audience. This chapter follows this order before concluding with an exploration of pricing issues. This is a topic which despite its apparent importance, has been shown to receive scant attention in many organisations.

■ Segmentation

The principles of market segmentation have been established since Wendell Smith (1956) first proposed market segmentation as an alternative to product differentiation. It was Wind (1978) who then suggested that segmentation should be at the heart of marketing strategy and since then there has been widespread agreement that it is an important foundation for successful marketing strategies and activities (Hooley and Saunders, 1993; Powers and Sterling, 2008).

Generally, segmentation is a technique for dividing a mass market into identifiable subunits, in order that the individual needs of buyers and potential buyers can be more easily satisfied. Traditionally it is about the division of a mass market into distinct groups that have common characteristics, needs and display similar responses to marketing stimuli.

Wind and Cardozo (1974) referred to market segmentation in B2B markets as the identification of 'a group of present or potential customers with some common characteristic which is relevant in explaining (and predicting) their response to a supplier's marketing stimuli'.

However, for a long time B2B market segmentation had not been as well researched and documented as that in consumer markets (Bonoma and Shapiro, 1983). Abratt (1993) and Weinstein (1994) sought to extend our understanding, the latter making comparisons of both markets' characteristics. Recalling the simple principle that 80% of profits are usually delivered by just 20% of customers, there is a significant need to segment markets and create precisely targeted marketing programmes.

The intricacies involved in business market segmentation are said to make it a more exacting activity than in consumer markets. Griffith and Pol (1994) argue this point on the basis of multiple product applications, greater customer variability and problems associated with the identification of the key differences between groups of customers. However, there have been numerous attempts to define and describe business segmentation, using a variety of variables ranging from product-specific to customer-specific attributes. See for example Mitchell and Wilson (1998).

The overall process associated with target marketing is referred to as the Segmentation, Targeting and Positioning process (STP), as set out at Figure 5.1.

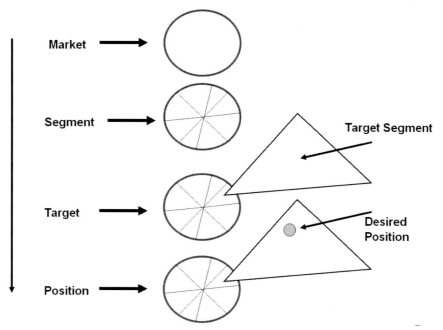

Figure 5.1: The STP process

The first task is to identify the mass market and then identify the various segments within the overall market using a variety of criteria. The second task is for organisations to select and target the particular segments which appear to represent the strongest marketing opportunities and match most closely the resources available to the organisation.

Having selected particular target markets, the final activity is to position products and/or services in such a way that buyers can clearly differentiate what is being offered from the prevailing competition. Distinct marketing programmes can be developed for each market selected. For example, Albert (2003) shows how segmentation analysis can be used for developing targeted communication strategies within marketing channels.

Segmentation is a critical activity for buyers as well as sellers, as it serves to link a buyer's and a seller's operational supply side capabilities, in order to create mutual value (Day *et al.* 2010). However, Bailey *et al.* (2009) review much of the segmentation literature and conclude that segmentation research tends to focus around the choice of segmentation bases, rather than investigate how a segmentation programme is used once generated. Indeed, the implementation of market segmentation plans is regarded as problematic, and that 'segmentation is particularly challenging in industrial markets' (Boejgaard and Ellegaard, 2010: 1291).

This brief overview is both a simplified and understated summary of what is a complex and hard-to-implement marketing management activity.

■ The Process of Segmenting B2B Markets

The justification for segmentation is that groups of customers, or potential buyers, who share similar needs and buying characteristics are more likely to respond to an organisation's marketing programmes in similar ways. As Beane and Ennis (1987) suggest, this enables organisations to focus resources more efficiently and deliver more targeted marketing programmes in order better to meet customer needs. Instead of reaching out to a mass audience, the selection of particular submarkets concentrates activities and leads, in theory, to improved profitability. Dibb and Simkin (2001) also point out additional benefits in terms of improving market intelligence, being customer-orientated and competitor aware, which leads to improved targeting and positioning programmes.

However, whilst the merits of segmentation are agreed among practitioners and academics, the practice of market segmentation can be vague. Simkin (2008: 466) reports that most business-to-business marketers use the term mistakenly. He reports that in practice their 'segments' are often little more than "product group classifications, a geographical location of customers, and/or the business sector activity of the client or customer. For example, IT services business Fujitsu has management teams separately handling clients in local government, utilities, health, financial services, retailing, manufacturing, and so forth".

There are two main approaches to segmenting B2B markets. The first adopts the view that the market is considered to consist of businesses (and buyers) that are essentially the same, so the task is to identify groups that share particular *differences*. This is referred to as the breakdown method. The second approach considers a market to consist of businesses that are all different, so here the task is to find *similarities*. This is known as the build-up method.

ViewPoint 5.1: Cisco segments in many ways

Many companies such as Cisco have segmented markets by geography and size of company. However, Cisco has started using new approaches, segmenting by technology lifecycle, by purchasing method and customer life cycle.

The technology life cycle segmentation model divides small and medium-sized businesses (SMB) into three tiers, each of directs Cisco's approach.

- Tier 1 companies are referred to as Experimenters, who are relative risk takers but require Cisco to provide heavy levels of service to support them. Here the goal is to sell service contracts.

- Tier 2 are referred to as the Early Majority using Rogers's (1962) terminology. This is the most profitable group, and hence a prime target.

- Tier 3 prefer to purchase from a service provider. Here one of the main goals is to ensure service providers carry sufficient stock to meet demand.

The purchasing method segmentation acknowledges that customers can buy products in a number of ways. They can purchase products and install them on their own premises, or they can have the service provided through a third-party distributor such as BT. Either of these models can be applied with a lease plan as opposed to paying for the product outright.

The customer life cycle segmentation approach, requires Cisco managers to identify "events and triggers". These are events that drive technology purchases and are categorised as follows:

- *Inherent and known* events occur within the business itself, for example, an office move or new strategic direction. As several Cisco solutions apply to companies that are starting up or moving premises, so it purchases lists of office-movers and targets them with telemarketing.

- *Inherent but unknown* events are those that may be known to Cisco, but are not necessarily known to the customer. For example, if a service contract on a product has or is about to expire, Cisco could call the customer with a view to renewing the contract.

- *Created and unknown* events occur where Cisco anticipates and communicates a technological and commercial benefit which the customer was not previously aware.

Source: Bailey *et al.* (2009)

Question: What might be the reasons to explain Cisco's move away from geographic and company size as segmentation variables?

The breakdown approach is perhaps the most established and well recognised. Some of the first advocates were Wind and Cardozo (1974) with their Macro-Micro method and Bonoma and Shapiro (1983) who promoted a Nested method. Both methods try to establish the general case and then seek individual clusters of businesses that share common differences.

According to Freytag and Clarke (2001) the build-up approach seeks to move from the individual level where all businesses are different, to a more general level of analysis based on the identification of similarities. The build-up method is customer-orientated as it seeks to determine common customer needs.

The debate however, should not be about the direction but the content of the segmentation approach. Many of these ideas about segmentation were developed at a time when transactional marketing was the overriding marketing orientation and the allocation of resources to achieve the designated marketing mix goals was paramount.

Contemporary B2B market segmentation should not be solely about the allocation of resources, but concerned with buyer needs and relationship requirements. Even back in 1985, Plank believed that B2B segmentation should involve an analysis of buyers' attitudes towards relationships, attitudes towards each seller and a greater understanding of the reasons and ways in which organisations use products and services. In plain terms this calls for B2B psychographic segmentation. Barry and Weinstein (2009) trace some of the developments associated with largely consumer segmentation approach and define B2B Psychographic segmentation as:

> "The segmentation of organisational buyers into homogenous clusters of mindsets and behaviours that are distinguished by motives, risk perceptions and social interaction styles, in order to identify prospects as well as predict the predispositions of the firm's decision makers for the sake of adopting products, marketing messages and relational selling behaviours" (319).

Freytag and Clarke (2001) quite rightly identify that market segmentation is not a static concept and that the process should reflect current market conditions. Some organisational exchanges are purely transactional, while others are rooted within complex relationships. Indeed, it could be argued that the development of electronic data interchange (EDI) and eCommerce processes sought to routinise a large part of organisational commercial activities. In that sense, transactional marketing is encouraged when eCommerce is implemented. Indeed, Whitely (2000: 6) defines eCommerce in solely transactional terms as 'formulating commercial transactions at a site remote from the trading partner and then using electronic communications to execute that transaction'. This relatively early view has since been supplanted as technology is now used to encourage, foster and actively engage collaboration. In other words increased relational exchanges are supported.

To be fully successful, the process and development of market segmentation activities should reflect a continuum between those organisations that only seek purely transactional marketing activities and those for whom the management and development of complex relationships is essential. All customers' needs are important; some are very different, even unique to the particular context in which the stakeholders operate.

When considering purely transactional situations, the breakdown method would appear to be most appropriate. If relationship marketing issues dominate a business, or businesses, then the build-up approach seems more appropriate, simply because of the customer focus and the detailed information that is required when managing relationships.

Thus, the segmentation process will vary according to the prevailing conditions and needs of the parties involved, not just the needs of the selling organisation. Relationships concern the interaction of stakeholders, very often multiple stakeholders, and it is the needs of the interrelationship(s) that should dominate any segmentation activity. For example, an analysis of the relationship potential and buyer attitudes towards the supplier and other related stakeholders might provide a useful means of segmenting a market to the advantage of all relevant stakeholders.

As indicated above, target marketing is the process whereby specific segments are selected and marketing programmes are then developed to satisfy the needs of the potential buyers and other stakeholders, including the selling organisation, in the chosen segments. The development, or rather identification, of segments can be perceived as opportunities – as Beane and Ennis (1987: 20) suggest, 'a company with limited resources needs to pick only the best opportunities to pursue' – but can also be seen as a means of recognising and determining the nature and form of relationships between stakeholders (Freytag and Clarke, 2001).

For any segmentation approach to work, a basis by which markets are to be analysed has to be appreciated and applied before any meaningful analysis can commence.

■ Bases for Segmenting Business Markets

Ideas concerning the segmentation of consumer markets are well documented (Dibb and Simkin, 2001), increasingly in industrial markets (Powers and Sterling, 2008) and not very much in supplier markets (Day *et al.*, 2010). Although similar principles apply, the bases used to segment business and consumer markets are different. Indeed, there is no fixed way of simply identifying business segments, mainly because the needs of business markets vary considerably.

There are two main groups of variables used to segment B2B markets, and they are interrelated. The first set of variables involves market characteristics, such as organisational size and location. Those seeking to segment markets where transactional marketing and the breakdown approach dominates would be expected to start with these variables.

The second group is based upon the characteristics surrounding the decision making process employed within each of the organisational segments, and this is referred to as the buyer characteristics. Those organisations seeking to establish and develop particular relationships would normally be expected to start with these variables, and build-up their knowledge of their market and customer base. Table 5.1 sets out these two main groups.

Table 5.1: Bases for segmenting B2B markets

Main segment variables	Explanation
Market characteristics	Based on organisational size and location variables.
	Used primarily where there is transactional marketing and the breakdown approach predominates.
Buyer characteristics	Based on the decision making process and associated variables.
	Used primarily where collaborative relationships and the build-up approach predominates.

■ Segmenting by Market Characteristics

These factors concern the buying organisations that make up a business market. There are a number of criteria that can be used to cluster organisations but size, market served, value, location, usage rate and purchase situation characteristics are some of the more common methods used.

Size

By segmenting organisations by size it is possible to identify particular buying requirements. Large organisations may have particular delivery or design needs, while purchasing activities in smaller organisations may be heavily influenced by key individuals, such as owners or managing directors.

Market served

Very often, organisations buy a particular part of a supplier's range of products. This may reflect their business activity. For example, a road construction company may only purchase particular size diggers and rollers. Opportunities exist to determine new users in the same business area, develop new products and services for the sector, or communicate the whole of the current range more effectively to existing road construction companies.

Value

Similar to the usage rate factor, this aims to divide markets according to the value they represent to the selling organisation. This value (high, medium or low) may be based on sales revenue or, more appropriately, on profit contribution or to some softer factors – such as strategic access to new markets – or on terms of production efficiencies.

Location

Targeting by geographic location is one of the more common methods used to segment B2B markets, and is often used by new or small organisations attempting to establish themselves. However, the use of the Internet and websites means that location need not always be an important factor.

Usage rates

By grading existing customers and category users according to their rate of product and/or service consumption, it may be possible to isolate low, light, medium and heavy user segments. The goal would then be to encourage some medium users to become heavy users by changing some aspect of the marketing mix variables.

Purchase situation

There are three factors associated with the purchase situation. First, the structure of the buying organisation's purchasing procedures; is it centralised, decentralised, flexible or inflexible? Second, what type of buying situation is present; new task, modified rebuy or straight rebuy? Third, what stage in the purchase decision process have target organisations reached; are buyers in early or late stages and are they experienced or new? The marketing programme will need to consider, and attempt to answer, these questions in order to be successful.

SIC codes

Standard Industrial Classification (SIC) codes are often used to get an initial feel for the size of various markets. Although they are easily available and standardised, Walker's criticisms of SIC codes, namely that they suffer from being highly aggregated, often superficial and not based on customer need (cited by Mitchell and Wilson, 1998) has constrained their use. Indeed, SIC codes have limited application and are far from being a complete solution to business segmentation, although they do provide, as Naudé and Cheng (2003) suggest, 'some preliminary indication of the industrial segments in [a] market'.

■ Segmenting by Buyer Characteristics

Segmenting by market characteristics alone, both product and buyer alone is considered by many to be less than effective. Christensen *et al.* (2007) argue that target market strategies should be more aligned to the behaviours and attitudes of targeted customers.

This set of criteria can be considered at two levels. The first level concerns the approach and requirements of the decision making unit (DMU). The second level focuses on the personal characteristics of key decision makers or members of the DMU.

■ Decision Making Unit

An organisation's decision making unit may have specific requirements that influence their purchase decisions in a particular market. There may be policy factors, purchasing strategies, a level of importance attached to these types of purchases, attitudes towards vendors and toward risk, all or some of which may help segregate groups of organisations for whom particular marketing programmes can be developed/refined and delivered.

Policy factors

Organisations may establish certain policies that govern purchasing decisions. A business may require specific delivery cycles to support manufacturing plans. Increasingly organisations require certain quality standards to be met by their suppliers, and membership of particular quality standards organisations (for example ISO 9002) is required as evidence of these thresholds having been reached. Policy may dictate that the reputation of all their suppliers is critical and that contracts can only be signed with organisations that meet certain internally determined criteria. For example, if a proposed supplier is currently contracted to a significant competitor it may be a sufficient signal to open negotiations.

Purchasing strategies

Cardozo (1980) determined that organisations tend towards one of two main purchasing strategies or profiles. These are referred to as optimisers and satisficers. Optimisers prefer to consider a wide range of potential suppliers and are prepared to evaluate a range of proposals before selecting a supplier. On the other hand, satisficers tend to prefer dealing with familiar suppliers and award contracts to the first supplying organisation to meet purchase requirements.

It is important for suppliers to appreciate the purchasing profile of buying organisations as it may help to allocate resources. A new entrant is likely to have more success becoming established by approaching optimisers rather than satisficers.

Level of importance

The importance of a purchase may be related to the value it represents to the purchasing organisation. However, the importance may also be perceived in terms of the opportunities it enables an organisation to exploit, such as its own new product development, entry to new markets or even the significance of the purchase in terms of the size and nature of the purchasing organisation. For example, buying a fork-lift truck may be fairly routine for an organisation such as Perkins Engines or Rolls-Royce, but for a printer working on a small industrial estate, the fork-lift truck represents a major purchase, both financially and in terms of its work contribution.

ViewPoint 5.2: Segmenting print buyers

The characteristics of those involved in a purchasing DMU often identify different buyer types. A number of studies have identified differing buyer types and why it is important for sales and marketers to understand their differing needs. Devine (2011) who has worked in the print industry offers four major buyer types which he claims enables increased sales performance.

- **Economic Buyer** – often has significant power and influence in terms of decision making including financial control. This might include the Managing Director or Finance Director.

- **Technical Buyer** – for the purchase of products and services such as IT equipment, the person who understands the detailed product specifications. This could be the Engineering Director or IT Director.

- **User Buyer** – there potentially a number of user buyers who are dependent on the number of functions or departments in the business where the products or services will have application. For IT equipment this might include production, personnel, marketing, finance etc.

- **Coach Buyer** – the person who might co-ordinate the internal activities during the buying cycle and liaise with the selling organisation. This might be the actual company Buyer.

Devine states that it is important to know who all the buyers are and what their information needs are in order to sell effectively to all the types identified.

Source: Devine, (2011); www.theprintcoach.com

Question: What kind of information should each buyer type look for to aid their decision making?

Relationships

The relationship between organisations is obviously a critical factor. While this is considered in greater depth elsewhere in the book, the attitudes and relationships between the people who represent organisations can be used as a means of segmentation. Segmentation might be based on the closeness and level of interdependence that may already exist between organisations. This could be measured in terms of a continuum from partners to unknowns. The attitude of DMUs may also be a determining factor.

Attitude to risk

Organisational attitude towards risk and the degree to which an organisation is willing to experiment through the acquisition of new industrial products can vary a great deal. This variance is partly a reflection of the prevailing culture and philosophy, leadership and managerial style. The extent to which the buying organisation resists or embraces change is in turn reflected in the speed with which new product decisions are made, as well as the nature of the products selected and choice of suppliers.

■ Personal Characteristics

Individuals are normally considered to have a greater decision making impact in consumer rather than in business markets. However, the personal characteristics of some decision makers have been used in B2B segmentation.

Demographic variables such as age and education are often too simplistic to provide any significant bases for segmentation. However, personality, decision style, risk and lifestyle can provide interesting ways of segmenting B2B markets. These dimensions are wrapped up in psychographic segmentation approaches which are becoming of increasing interest to organisations (Barry and Weinstein, 2009).

Barry and Weinstein (2009) use the inner ring of the Nested approach developed by Bonoma and Shapiro (1983) to argue that there are three dimensions associated with the personal characteristics of B2B buyers. These are their rational and non-rational motivations, their attitude towards risk and their relationship styles and preferred forms of social interaction. These are represented at Figure 5.2.

Figure 5.2: Influences on buyer personal characteristics. (Based on Barry and Weinstein, 2009)

The key is to appreciate that beyond the strategy and planning stages in B2B segmentation work, it is important to use B2B psychographics as this enables more precise positioning and associated communications.

■ Target Market Selection

The next step in the STP process is to select appropriate target segments that represent the best opportunities for the organisation, given their resources, strategy and the prevailing internal and external conditions. The selection of target segments should be based on a systematic analysis of the market. This involves first considering the market characteristics and then moving through to the buyer characteristics. The cost of this activity increases as buyer characteristics are considered. This is because the market characteristics can usually be drawn from secondary sources. Invariably the information necessary for the analysis of buyer characteristics has to be gained through primary research and this is where the required investment can rise substantially.

The role of market and marketing research in the segmentation process cannot be underestimated. Indeed, one of the reasons often cited for not analysing and identifying precise market segments is the research cost involved. Many organisations, particularly small and medium-sized organisations, do not have the time, expertise or financial resources to assign to this important foundation work. However, preliminary research need not be too expensive or time consuming, and can use third-party services/tools. Commercially available databases and prospect-finding services, based on market characteristics, are becoming increasingly inexpensive.

The goal is to identify segments that in the medium to long term will provide suitable returns. This is not an easy task. Care needs to be taken to ensure that all the costs and benefits are understood. This entails considering the necessary changes to the products and services, pricing requirements, alterations and investments in distribution channels and the consequent knock-on impact on the promotional plans.

It is now generally accepted that use of the following criteria helps to identify valid and reliable segments:

- All segments should be **measurable** – is the segment easy to identify and measure?
- All segments should be **accessible** – can the buyers be reached effectively with marketing programmes?
- All segments should be **substantial** – is the segment sufficiently large to warrant a separate marketing programme and will it provide sufficient return on investment?
- All segments should be **actionable** – has the organisation the capability to reach the segment?
- All segments should be **compatible** – with current business strategy and expected market conditions.

These criteria, the basis for which was originally proposed by Kotler (1984), are only intended to be used as guidelines and are of greater use when segmenting consumer rather than B2B markets. Managerial discretion and judgement will determine which markets are selected and exploited and which are ignored. To that extent the segmentation process should not be regarded as a perfect marketing management activity. Much of what is passed off as segmentation is merely an *ad hoc* market adjustment to reflect product amendments and principal buyer requirements. Dibb and Wensley (200: 1) argue that the method of segmentation analysis is often inappropriate and the implementation is seriously blemished to the extent that the whole segmentation process is of 'limited practical value'.

The STP process used earlier in this chapter looks at segmentation in a narrow way. Goller *et al.* (2002) present what they refer to as an integrative framework for business segmentation (see Figure 5.3).

This framework is useful because it draws together the various factors that constitute business segmentation and provides an overview of the whole process.

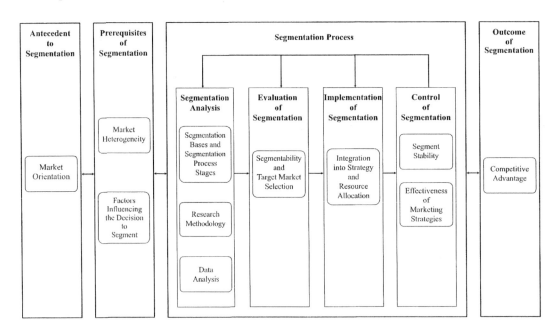

Figure 5.3: The process stages for segmenting business markets. Based on Goller *et al.* (2002), Used with permission.

The Goller framework assumes a more encompassing perspective and depicts four linked components. These are driven initially by the overall market orientation of the organisation. These authors argue that behaviour is manifest in the level of orientation that exists towards customers, competitors and inter-functional coordination. These impact on the subsequent components of the framework and the success of business segmentation is influenced largely by the degree to which the organisation is market-orientated.

One final comment regarding the Goller framework concerns the last component, the outcomes of the segmentation process. This aspect is often lost or neglected as attention can be focused on the nature of the segment bases and the size of the segments established. The purpose of business segmentation should be to develop a commercial advantage in order to improve efficiency and market effectiveness. Goller *et al.* suggest that the most advantageous outcome of business segmentation is gaining competitive advantage. This may be rather too broad, and difficult to measure easily, but the point that segmentation for segmentation's sake is worthless, is well made.

■ Barriers to Segmentation

The processes involved in the evaluation and determination of suitable target markets is not as precise or clear-cut as many authors suggest or imply. Dibb and Simkin (2001) point out that one of the major problems associated with segmentation in B2B markets is a failure of businesses to implement segmentation plans. They suggest that there are three main reasons for this failure. These are set out in Table 5.2.

Table 5.2: Barriers to segmentation

Barriers	Explanation
Infrastructure	These concern the culture, structure and resources which can prevent the segmentation process starting or being completed successfully.
Process	These reflect a lack of experience, guidance and expertise concerning the way in which segmentation is undertaken and managed.
Implementation	Practical barriers concerning a move to a new segmentation model.

Source: Based on Dibb and Simkin (2001).

Dibb and Simkin argue that these three segmentation barriers serve to prevent businesses from either starting the segmentation process or from implementing their chosen course of action.

- *Infrastructure* barriers are common and lie at the root of the problems facing many organisations. These concern the culture, structure and resources which prevent the segmentation process starting. For example, there may be a lack of financial resources to collect market data or a culture that is rigidly product-orientated. An organisation that has a strong product orientation will find it problematic to move to a new segmentation approach, especially one that follows the build-up method.

- *Process* issues concern the lack of experience, guidance and expertise concerning the way in which segmentation is undertaken and managed. There is little information at both academic and practical levels to help managers with the processes involved with segmentation.

  Increasingly, however, there are websites describing the processes and giving examples, which may help the less experienced with segmentation modelling, or offering consultancy or software tools; for example, www.marketsegmentation.co.uk and www.market-modelling.co.uk.

Many of the websites and consultants recommend using factor analysis when determining market segments. This is a statistical method for identifying a small number of variables or attributes that explain correlations in buyers' attitudes and behaviour. Examples might be age, gender or postcode. In consumer markets, factor analysis is performed on vast data sets collated from surveys, or point of sale systems. In B2B markets, the challenge is to acquire data in the first place and in sufficient numbers for the results to be statistically significant. It is quite easy to perform factor analysis using a statistical package such as SPSS, but care must be taken in deciding which factors to investigate and especially in interpreting the results.

- *Implementation* barriers concern the way in which an organisation can move towards a new segmentation model. This may be due to a move away from a business model based on products (for example, engine sizes for fleet buyers), to one based on customer needs. Goller *et al*. (2002) suggest that there is insufficient information and practical guidance for managers in order that segmentation strategies be implemented successfully. It may be that the established ways of doing business become a barrier to moving over to a new approach. The practical issues involved in moving a business from one type of segmentation are often overlooked yet these invariably impede organisations from developing their segmentation policies.

Segmentation in business markets should reflect the relationship needs of the parties involved and should not be based solely on the traditional consumer market approach, which is primarily the breakdown method. Through use of both the breakdown and the build-up approaches, a more accurate, in depth and potentially more profitable view of industrial markets can be achieved (Crittenden *et al*., 2002). However, problems remain concerning the practical application and implementation of B2B segmentation. Managers report that the analysis processes are reasonably clear, but it is not clear how they should 'choose and evaluate between the market segments' which have been determined (Naudé and Cheng, 2003).

■ Positioning

Market segmentation and target marketing are prerequisites to successful positioning. Following the analysis, determination and final selection of market segments and target markets, the next task is to position the organisation, brand or product/service through the development and implementation of targeted marketing communication programmes. Positioning is the natural conclusion to the sequence of activities at the core of business marketing strategy.

Positioning takes place in the minds of the buyers in the target market. According to Ries and Trout (1972) it is not what you do to a product that matters, it is what you do to the mind of the prospect that is important. This is an important aspect of the positioning concept. Positioning is not about the product but what the buyer thinks about the product or organisation. It is not the physical nature of the product that is important for positioning, but how the product is perceived that matters.

Traditionally, and more commonly, this idea is applied to consumer markets but the principle is the same in business marketing. The difference between the two lies in the types of messages conveyed and the balance of the promotional mix used to deliver the positioning messages. Messages in B2B markets are traditionally rational and product-orientated, with the emphasis on personal selling and increasingly on direct marketing. This is changing as more organisations are using social media and B2B branding is becoming more widespread.

The aim of positioning, therefore, is to enable buyers and potential buyers to view a supplier or group of suppliers as different from other suppliers and as a source of added value. It is important that the supplier is regarded not only as different from other suppliers but also that they offer a set of values that will enable them to achieve their own goals more effectively and more efficiently.

All products and all organisations have a position. The position held by each organisation can be managed or it can be allowed to drift. Interest in business-to-business positioning has developed for two main reasons. The first is concerned with the increasingly competitive market conditions, where there is now little compositional, material or even structural difference between the products offered by many organisations. This has, in many cases, led to an increase in the provision of pre- and post-sales services, which have the potential to generate higher margins. Additionally, in markets where mobility barriers (ease of entry and exit to a market, for example, plant and production costs) are relatively low, the need to position is also important.

The second reason is related to the seemingly incessant pressure to reduce costs and improve margins over the short term. By switching the emphasis of marketing communications from individual products (or categories) to development of the corporate brand, large savings in promotional activities can be achieved. The development and implementation of electronic-based marketing communications has also helped to reduce costs. For example, the provision of product information through a corporate website has enabled salespeople to spend a greater proportion of their time in front of buyers and potential buyers, rather than servicing small, low-value and low-potential buyers. The switch to corporate branding and the development of web-based communications focuses marketing management attention on what the organisation stands for and how it should be presented to the target market.

5

Strategy: Segmentation, Positioning and Pricing

■ Positioning Strategies

As in consumer markets, there are two main approaches to positioning a brand, these are functional and expressive (or symbolic). Functionally positioned brands stress the features and benefits, while expressive positioning emphasises the ego, social and hedonic satisfactions that a brand can bring. Both approaches make a pledge, for example to deliver on time, every time (functional) or just to do business with nice people (symbolic). The first delivers a rational message, the second one is largely emotional.

As mentioned earlier, traditionally B2B marketers have used the former, rationally based approach which emphasises product features, attributes and benefit claims. A tried and trusted sales training aid is based around the concept of telling customers features and then drawing out the benefits. Some organisations have moved to a more expressive approach drawing on softer messages that attempt to develop associations.

The development of positions which buyers can relate to and understand is an important, even vital, part of the marketing communications plan. In essence, the position adopted is a statement about what the organisation (brand) is, what it stands for, and the values and beliefs that customers, hopefully, will come to associate with, and appreciate in, the particular brand.

Positioning approaches should also reflect the type of target market that has been selected. Positioning with regard to mainly transactional-based segments should be more rational and product-orientated, as the needs of buyers there are invariably purposeful and product-orientated. Positioning in target markets where relationship issues are significant and important should be more expressive, with a focus on support, participation, interaction between parties and a knowledge of and interest in the customer's business.

■ Developing a Position

To develop a position it is recommended that a series of steps or process stages are followed. The following represents a composite from the literature (Boyd *et al.*, 1998; Fill, 2009).

1 Which positions are held by which competitors?

2 Identify the key or determinant attributes perceived by buyers as important. This will almost certainly require marketing research to determine attitudes and perceptions.

3 Sample the target segment and assess how they rate each product/service.

4 From the above, determine the current positions held by relevant products and organisations.

5 From the information gathered so far, is it possible to determine the desired position for the brand?

6 Is the strategy feasible in view of the competitors and any budgetary constraints? A long-term perspective is required, as the selected position has to be sustained.

7 Implement a programme to establish the desired position.

8 Monitor the perception held by customers and their changing tastes and requirements on a regular basis.

■ Positioning Tactics

To implement the broad approaches a number of tactics have been developed. The list that follows is not intended to be comprehensive, nor to suggest that these approaches are discrete. They are outlined here to illustrate the tactical style. In reality, a number of hybrid approaches are often used.

Product features

Traditionally this is one of the easier concepts and one that is quite commonly adopted. The brand is set apart from the competition on the basis of key attributes or features that the brand has relative to the competition. For example, a product's superior durability, strength or design features are often used to provide customers with a means of differentiating various product offerings.

Price/quality

This strategy is more effectively managed than others because price itself can be a strong communicator of quality. This approach is particularly effective in segments where discrete exchanges predominate. A high price denotes high quality, just as a low price can deceive buyers into thinking a product to be of low quality and poor value.

User

Some organisations attempt to differentiate themselves and their products on the basis that they are of specific benefit to a particular type of user organisation or even individual buyers. IBM once claimed that no one ever got sacked for buying IBM, and Canon UK who used to segment the business market by using customer size as the main base: SoHos (Small office, Home office), small and medium-sized enterprises, large corporate players and government.

Benefit

Positions can also be established by proclaiming the benefits that usage confers on the customer. This is an extension of the features position. By turning the feature into a benefit, the focus moves from the product to the customer and their needs. For example, many high technology companies and software vendors position themselves in terms of the benefits provided by their solutions to customer problems. These might be lower costs, quicker order processing, less wastage, more satisfied customers, higher levels of service or improved profitability.

ViewPoint 5.3: Making adjustments at Fujitsu

Fujitsu Siemens Computers was renamed as simply Fujitsu in April 2009. This led to a relaunch of the business and subsequent repositioning of the business proposition.

Fujitsu's aim was to demonstrate their understanding of the issues facing their customers. This entailed positioning the company as a 'thought leader or trusted advisor', not just a supplier of IT equipment and associated services. More specific objectives were to create awareness and generate business sales leads.

A new campaign microsite was developed and aimed at a target audience of existing customer accounts and potential new business targets. Further segmentation was in two tiers, IT decision makers (IT Directors) and IT influencers (IT Managers). Access to the microsite was via a personalised URL for each member of the contact database. This personalisation led to higher response rates and meant that each visit could be tracked by Fujitsu to profile the viewer and allow further communications to be tailor-made including telemarketing activity.

The campaign led to potential sales estimated to be £35 million and established Fujitsu as a leading player in the UK IT market.

Source: www.btbmarketing.net; www.fujitsu.com

Question: Find another company that has repositioned itself. What was the reason for repositioning and was it successful?

Experience, depth of knowledge and corporate reputation

Many organisations attempt to position themselves on the grounds of their expertise, leading technical capabilities and, in some cases, the length of their corporate history. Hewlett-Packard position themselves on their ability to be innovative and to bring their customers leading-edge technologies. These types of positions are used by organisations to convey quality, experience and depth of knowledge, to reduce risk and increase trust and credibility.

Whatever the position adopted by a brand or organisation, both the marketing and promotional mixes must endorse and support the position so that there is consistency throughout all communications. For example, if a leading high-technology position is taken, such as that of Cisco or Sun Microsystems, then product quality must be superior to the competition, price correspondingly high and distribution synonymous with quality and exclusivity. Sales promotion activity will be minimal, so as not to dilute these cues, and all other marketing communication messages should be visually affluent, rich in tone and copy, with complementary public relations and personal selling approaches.

The dimensions used to position brands must be relevant and important to the target audience and the image cues used must be believable and consistently credible. Positioning strategies should be developed over the long term if they are to prove effective, although minor adaptions can be made in order to reflect changing environmental conditions.

Pricing

Pricing is one of the more complex and critical decisions that managers must make. It is critical because price impacts not only on the volume of products sold, but also the contribution that the product makes to the organisation's overall profit performance. As Brennan *et al.* (2007) indicate, price has a direct and substantial effect on profitability.

In addition, the price of one product can influence other products in the mix or line, while price is often used by customers as short-hand for quality, value and market position.

Price in business markets differs from consumer markets in many ways. Two of the more important differences concern the perception and flexibility of price. Although perceived value is an important determinant of a product's worth to both consumers and business customers, consumers consider price in relation to similar, competitive products. Their evaluation of price can be strongly influenced by horizontal comparison. In business markets price can be evaluated in the context of the relative value the product represents within the customer's supply chain. For example, the more crucial a part or assembly is to the manufacturing process and the lower the opportunity for the customer to substitute one product with that of a rival, the higher the price (and margins) are likely to be.

Prices in retail markets are generally fixed (list prices) and these constitute a major part of a consumer's decision making process. In business markets price is subject to discounting, negotiation, tendering and competitive bidding approaches. Pricing is a strategic marketing management activity, yet there is evidence that relatively few companies undertake systematic research on pricing (Brennan *et al.*, 2007) and there is substantial anecdotal comment to suggest that pricing does not always receive sufficient focus or consideration as it should merit.

Strategically prices can be set in two main ways. One is an inside-out approach and the other is outside-in.

Inside-out pricing

This approach to pricing assumes that price is a reflection of the costs incurred in developing, manufacturing and bringing the product to market. This inside-out approach, or cost-based pricing, is used a great deal in B2B marketing but it is problematic. One of the main problems concerns the identification and accurate allocation of the real costs involved in this process. Another problem is its lack of market orientation. By accumulating the costs and adding a margin, the resultant price may be higher than the market is willing or able to pay. As Christopher (2000) suggests, this approach assumes that customers are actually interested in the supplier's costs, whereas their principal concern rests with managing their own costs.

■ Outside-in pricing

This approach starts by considering the customer's perception of the price and the value they attribute to the product. This value is determined by the perceived benefits product ownership will bring. These benefits are assessed in terms of what the product will enable the customer to do, and/or how it will solve particular problems.

Products can be considered in terms of their tangible and intangible attributes. It is these intangible attributes, for example, the guarantees, support and servicing, that provide the enhanced value and the price that customers are willing to pay. Therefore, the pricing decision should be based on disaggregating the intangible attributes to determine the benefits customers perceive (value) in each of the individual elements that constitute the whole.

Inside-out approaches are intuitively more appealing and easier to determine through an organisation's financial management information systems. There are implementation difficulties associated with the outside-in approach, which impede its overall adoption. However, if pricing decisions are linked to segmentation strategy based on customers' perceived value, then it is easier to identify individual customer benefits. The use of customer questionnaires to isolate key attributes that deliver different value together with conjoint analysis to determine the trade-off customers are prepared to make between attributes at different price levels, enables suppliers to establish the perceived value of the different attributes. It is from this point that it becomes possible to build a price relative to customer value. See Christopher (2000) for more information.

■ Strategic and tactical pricing

As with any management task the setting of objectives informs and frames the decisions that follow. Pricing objectives are no different and several overall goals should be considered when developing pricing strategy. The first concerns the level of desired profitability as price influences volume and margins. Second, price needs to be set in the context of the relationships the organisation has or hopes to develop. Setting what might be perceived as a maximum price within a category may be regarded as exploitative. This could lower trust and, in effect, raise barriers to a mutually beneficial long-term relationship. Therefore, price needs to be set such that the perceived value is deemed fair, relative to the benefits derived.

There are other strategic objectives which may have a direct impact on price. For example, an organisation may wish to maximise profits prior to selling a product (or an organisation). Price might be used to discourage competitors from entering a market, or to enter a new market and become established. There are a few pricing strategies and a number of methods.

ViewPoint 5.4: BT's B2B packaged pricing

BT is one of the globe's leading communications services companies, offering fixed line telephone services, broadband, mobile phone and TV products. These products and services cover both business and consumer markets.

In the BTB sectors pricing methods are based on differential models with service packages and prices dependent on the specific needs and size of the business. Most telephone services include fixed charges for line rentals and then variable amounts depending on use levels. Specific packages are available combining services options including telephone, broadband and web hosting. Complete telephone systems are offered on a fixed price basis depending on the number of users. Prices using line leasing options provide business users with guaranteed internet access 24/7. Prices can also vary dependent on the length of contact entered into.

As the former monopoly supplier of telecommunications services and products in the UK, BT still has a dominant position in the market. They control wholesale prices charged to other telecommunications suppliers. Given the competitive nature of the market this can lead to tensions. In December 2010, two competitors reported BT to the Government watchdog Ofcom, accusing them of setting prices for business users which were below cost, aimed at weakening or eliminating competition.

Source: www.bt.com; www.computing.co.uk

Question: Are there any other pricing models that might be appropriate for companies of this type?

Strategy: Segmentation, Positioning and Pricing

■ Pricing strategies

- *Price skimming* occurs when there are few competitors and customers are willing to pay higher prices in order be associated with the values and benefits of the new product. Skimming also occurs as a positioning tool, to convey prestige and high status.

- *Penetration pricing* is the opposite to skimming. The goal is to sell at a low price during the introductory and growth stage of a new product. This approach, common in low-technology markets, can generate high relative market shares and can be effective in deterring competitors from entering the market.

- *Price leadership* opportunities arise when an organisation has high market share and there are many ways in the category to develop customer value.

- *Follow the leader* strategies are advisable when there few ways to reduce costs, relative to competitors, and the product category has few ways to increase value. This strategy can often be seen in commodity markets

■ Pricing methods

Many of the methods used by organisations to price business products are based on the inside-out costing approach. These include:

- *Mark-up* pricing involves applying a set percentage of the cost of production or purchase price.

- *Break-even* pricing is similar to mark-up pricing except that both direct and variable costs are incorporated. The method requires the calculation of the number of units that need to be sold in order to cover all costs associated with the production of those units.

- *Peak-load* pricing, unlike the previously mentioned methods, takes into account customer demand. By understanding levels of demand and system capacities it is possible to use price to smooth demand to manageable levels. Telephone companies will price off-peak calls at a lower rate, thereby encouraging some users to use the system at different times. The same principles apply to those supplying gas, electricity and water. The main advantage is that the overall system does not have to be built (capacity) to meet 100% demand. This saves on investment, return and the overall cost base. Road-haulage and container-shipping companies use peak-load pricing concepts in order to smooth demand.

- *Marginal cost* pricing is often used by organisations such as airlines and hotels, who have high fixed costs. By trying to cover just the variable costs the organisation, especially in times of recession and economic downturn, is able to generate a contribution rather than no revenue at all.

- *Product line* pricing moves away from an individual product, cost-based approach to one which takes into account the relationship between all the products in a particular line. The objective is to allow customers to choose lines according to their price (value) range and to allow the organisation to maximise their profits across the lines. Although this method is preferred more by retailers than by manufacturers, there are instances of manufacturers selling the same line to different markets, taking advantage of the different levels of price elasticity, to maximise profits.

- *Competitive bidding* is undertaken by a significant number of organisations and forms the basis for a large number of transactions in both private and public sector organisations. For example, in the UK construction industry, the development and formulation of bids is thought to cost approximately 5% of the total value of contracts awarded in any single year (Wykes, 2003). Therefore bidding not only consumes a large amount of resources but also represents an area in which significant efficiency gains can be made. Partly as a response to these issues, online resources have been used to provide effective and more efficient solutions. For example, Freight Traders is an online intermediary, which uses web-based applications, many of them founded on game theory. Their aim is to bring shippers (with cargo to send) together with carriers (with transport capacity to fill). It uses tendering and quick quotes as the primary ways of broking parties' requirements.

Competitive bidding occurs when buyers ask suppliers to tender to supply particular goods or services. There are two main types of bidding, closed and open. In closed bids only the customer knows the value of all the bids and normally selects the lowest offer, although on occasions the best overall value bid is elected. In open bids, suppliers are able to see each other's offers and make adjustments accordingly. The buyer uses this approach to drive up the value of the offers in order to maximise the potential of the work. The natural progression from closed and open bidding is an auction. New technology has given auctions a new dimension and enabled both buyers and suppliers to reduce their costs.

The Internet allows for dynamic pricing, which can often be observed through reverse auctions (Smeltzer and Carr, 2002). This means that the market price for an item alters instantaneously when auctioned electronically. An assumption is made by sellers that as prices change in real time so prices will continue to decline until the market price is reached, a point at which demand is equal to supply. Sellers can see the actual price levels required to obtain the sell.

■ Leasing

An important variant to the outright purchase of products is leasing. The use of leasing in business markets has grown especially in markets where there are substantial fixed costs or where technology changes quickly. For example, in the aircraft industry, leasing gives an airline an opportunity to manage its overall seat capacity, but they pay a risk premium to leasing companies for taking the risks (Hsu *et al*, 2011).

Three types of leases can be identified: sales/leaseback leases, operating leases and capital leases (Wengartner, 1987). These are set out at Table 5.3.

Leasing enables organisations to reduce their exposure to debt and to concentrate their use of debt on areas where it is strategically more imperative. It frees up resources to enter markets or acquire the latest technology or capital equipment. Unfortunately, leasing can tie an organisation into particular equipment or a specific technology for a long period of time. This can prevent the organisation from making changes when the environment or internal conditions change.

In an attempt to improve the way in which organisations manage the pricing process, Shipley and Jobber (2001) suggest an integrative pricing technique.

This multistage process, or 'wheel' seeks to incorporate a range of influences and issues into the pricing process. However, although this is admirable in terms of the process and range of issues covered, it perpetuates a costing orientation. Organisations need to develop a more relational approach to their pricing by understanding the value customers derive from the products and services and then work this information into their pricing procedures.

Finally, although the pricing of services is very similar to that of products, particular issues arise from the perishability characteristic. In an attempt to manage demand pricing must take into account the capacity of the service system and the likely or known patterns of demand that occur. Peak-load and off-peak pricing strategies can help smooth demand and in conjunction with a variety of price incentive programmes demand and capacity can be brought into a reasonable balance.

Table 5.3: Types of leasing arrangements

Type of lease	Explanation
Sales/leaseback	Assets are sold to a leasing company and then leased back to the original owners for a fee over a fixed period of time. The advantage of this approach is the cash receipt resulting from the initial sale.
Operating leases	Maintenance of the asset is often included in these financial arrangements. There is no transfer of ownership (of the asset) when the payment schedule is complete.
Capital leases	Having agreed a purchase price with the supplier, customers then arrange a capital lease with a leasing company. There is no maintenance facility within these leases nor can they be cancelled.

Source: Based on Wengartner (1987).

Readers who are interested in pricing issues and wish to know more about the pricing process, objectives and more detailed methodologies are referred to *Marketing* (2nd edn) by Baines *et al.* (2011).

Summary

Here are the key points about segmentation and pricing issues, set out against the learning objectives.

1 Examine the bases for segmenting business markets.

Segmentation is a technique for dividing a mass market into identifiable subunits, in order that the individual needs of buyers and potential buyers can be more easily satisfied. Traditionally it is about the division of a mass market into distinct groups that have common characteristics, needs and display similar responses to marketing stimuli.

2 Consider the breakdown and build-up approaches to market segmentation in B2B markets.

The breakdown method assumes that a market consists of businesses (and buyers) that are essentially the same, so the task is to identify groups that share particular *differences*. The breakdown approach is perhaps the most established and well recognised.

The build-up method considers a market to consist of businesses that are all different, so here the task is to find *similarities*. The build-up method is customer-orientated as it seeks to determine common customer needs.

3 Explore some of the processes used to select target markets.

The goal is to identify segments that in the medium to long term will provide suitable returns. The selection of target segments should be based on a systematic analysis of the market. This involves first considering the market characteristics and then moving through to the buyer characteristics.

4 Evaluate the practice of segmentation in business markets.

Segmentation is a theoretically neat concept, but a practically challenging idea to utilise. As a result one of the major problems associated with segmentation in B2B markets is a failure by businesses to implement segmentation plans. There are three main barriers preventing or hindering the way in which organisations practice segmentation activities. These are *infrastructure* barriers, *process* issues *and implementation* difficulties.

5 Consider the role of positioning (and strategies) in the segmentation, targeting and positioning (STP) process.

The aim of positioning is to enable (potential) buyers to view a supplier as different from other suppliers and that they represent a source of added value. It is important that a supplier is regarded not only as different from other suppliers but also that they offer a set of values that will enable them to achieve their own goals more effectively and more efficiently.

Positioning is not about the product but what the buyer thinks about the product or organisation. Functionally positioned brands stress the features and benefits, while expressive positioning emphasises the ego, social and hedonic satisfactions that a brand can bring.

6 Consider the role and characteristics of pricing issues in B2B marketing

Strategically prices can be set in two main ways. Inside-out pricing assumes that price is a reflection of the costs incurred in developing, manufacturing and bringing the product to market. This cost-based pricing, is used a great deal in B2B marketing but it is problematic. Outside-in pricing considers a customer's perception of the price and the value they attribute to the product. This value is determined by the perceived benefits product ownership will bring.

Four key pricing strategies can be determined. These are price skimming, penetration pricing, price leadership, and follow the leader.

■ Discussion Questions

1 Make notes describing the principles that underpin the build-up and breakdown approaches to market segmentation. What are their main disadvantages?

2 Evaluate the bases used to segment B2B markets.

3 Identify five variables that might influence the nature of the decision making unit and its utility within the segmentation process.

4 Describe the three main barriers to successful B2B segmentation. Consider ways in which these might be overcome.

5 Identify four organisations operating in the business market and determine their positioning strategies. Consider how these strategies differ and make proposals how each might be developed.

6 What are the key issues that need to be considered when advising organisations about adopting a strategic approach to pricing?

References

Abratt, R.R. (1993) Market segmentation practices of industrial marketers, *Industrial Marketing Management*, **22**, 79–84

Albert, T. (2003) Need based segmentation and customised communication strategies in a complex-commodity industry, *Industrial Marketing Management*, **32** (4), 281–290.

Bailey, C., Baines, P., Wilson, H. and Clark, M. (2009) Segmentation and customer insight in contemporary services marketing practice: why grouping customers is no longer enough, *Journal of Marketing Management*, **25** (3–4), 228–251.

Baines, P., Fill, C., and Page, K. (2011) *Marketing*, 2 edn, Oxford: Oxford University Press.

Barry, J. and Weinstein, A. (2009) Business Psychographics revisited: from segmentation theory to successful marketing practice, *Journal of Marketing Management*, **25** (3/4), 315–340

Beane, T.P. and Ennis, D.M. (1987) Market segmentation: a review, *European Journal of Marketing*, **21**, 20–42

Boejgaard, J. and Ellegaard, C. (2010) Unfolding implementation in industrial market segmentation, *Industrial Marketing Management*, **39**, 1291–1299

Bonoma, T.V. and Shapiro, B.P. (1983) *Segmenting the Industrial Market*, Lexington, MA: Lexington Books

Boyd, H.W., Walker, O.C. and Larreche, J.C. (1998) *Marketing Management: a Strategic Approach with a Global Orientation*, 3rd international edn, New York: McGraw-Hill/Irwin.

Brennan R., Canning, L. and McDowell, R., (2007) *Business to Business Marketing*, Sage

Cardozo, R.N. (1980) Situational segmentation of industrial markets, *European Journal of Marketing*, **14** (5/6), 264–276

Christensen, C.M., Anthony, S.D., Berstell, G. and Nitterhouse, D. (2007) Finding the right job for your product, *Sloan Management Review*, **48** (3), 2-11

Christopher, M. (2000) Pricing strategy, in Cranfield School of Management (eds), *Marketing Management: A Relationship Marketing Perspective*, Basingstoke: Macmillan.

Crittenden, V.L., Crittenden, W.F. and Muzyka, D.F. (2002) Segmenting the business-to-business marketplace by product attributes and the decision process, *Journal of Strategic Marketing*, **10**, 3–20

Day, M., Magnan, G.M. and Moeller, M.M. (2010) Evaluating the bases of supplier segmentation: A review and taxonomy, *Industrial Marketing Management*, **39**, 625–639

Devine, N. (2011) *The Four Buyer Types*, retrieved 4 April 2011 from www.theprintcoach.com

Dibb, S. and Simkin, L. (2001) Market segmentation: diagnosing and treating the barriers, *Industrial Marketing Management*, **30** (8) (November), 609–625

Dibb, S. and Wensley, R. (2002) Segmentation analysis for industrial markets, *European Journal of Marketing*, **36** (1/2), 231–51

Fill, C. (2009) *Marketing Communications: Interactivity, Communities and Content*, 5th edn Harlow: Pearson Education.

Freytag, P.V. and Clarke, A.H. (2001) Business to business segmentation, *Industrial Marketing Management*, **30** (6) (August), 473–486

Goller, S., Hogg, A. and Kalafatis, S.P. (2002), A new research agenda for business segmentation, *European Journal of Marketing*, **36** (1/2), 252–271

Griffith R.L. and Pol, L.G. (1994) Segmenting industrial markets, *Industrial Marketing Management*, **23**, 39–46

Hooley, G.J. and Saunders, J.A. (1993) *Competitive Positioning: The Key to Market Success*, Englewood Cliffs, NJ: Prentice Hall

Hsu, C-I., Li, H-C., Liu, S-M. and Chao, C-C. (2011) Aircraft replacement scheduling: a dynamic programming approach, *Transportation Research*, Part E 47, 41–60

Kotler, P. (1984). *Marketing Management*, international edn, Englewood Cliffs, NJ: Prentice Hall

Mitchell, V.W. and Wilson, D.F. (1998) A reappraisal of business-to-business segmentation, *Industrial Marketing Management*, **27** (5) (September), 429–445

Naudé, P. and Cheng, L. (2003) Choosing between potential friends: market segmentation in a small company, Paper presented at the 19th IMP Conference, Lugano, Switzerland, www.impgroup.org/uploads/papers/4393.pdf (accessed 26 January 2004.)

Plank, R.E. (1985) A critical review of industrial market segmentation, *Industrial Marketing Management*, **14**, 79–91

Powers, T.L. and Sterling, J.U. (2008) Segmenting business-to-business markets: a micro-macro linking methodology, *Journal of Business & Industrial Marketing*, **23** (3), 170–177

Ries, A. and Trout, J. (1972) The positioning era cometh, *Advertising Age*, 24 April, 35–38

Rogers, Everett M. (1962). *Diffusion of Innovations*. The Free Press. New York.

Shipley, D. and Jobber, D. (2001) Integrative pricing via the pricing wheel, *Industrial Marketing Management*, **30** (3) (April), 301–314

Simkin, L. (2008) Achieving market segmentation from B2B sectorisation, *Journal of Business & Industrial Marketing*, **23** (7), 464–474

Smeltzer, L.R. and Carr, A. (2002) Reverse auctions in industrial marketing and buying, *Business Horizons*, **45** (2) (March–April), 47–52

Smith, Wendell. 1956. Product Differentiation and Market Segmentation as Alternative Marketing Strategies. Journal of Marketing. July pp 3-8

Weinstein, A. (1994). *Market Segmentation*, Chicago: Probus.

Wengartner, M.H. (1987). Leasing asset lives and uncertainty: guides to decision making, *Financial Management*, **16** (2) (Summer), 5–13.

Whitely, D. (2000) *e-Commerce: Strategy, Technologies and Applications*, London: McGraw-Hill.

Wind, Y. (1978) Issues and advances in segmentation research, *Journal of Marketing Research*, **15**, 317–337.

Wind, Y. and Cardozo, R.N. (1974) Industrial market segmentation, *Industrial Marketing Management*, 3 (March), 153–166

Wykes, T. (2003) NCW News, The 4th Annual Construction Marketing Conference – 29 and 30 October; www.ncw.org.uk/news/DisplayNews.cfm?EntryNum=92 (accessed 30 January 2004.)

6 Marketing Channels

Overview

This chapter is the first of three that examine issues concerning marketing channels and the intermediaries that populate them. In this, attention is focused on understanding the principles and core concepts associated with marketing channels. In particular, consideration is given to their purpose, basic structure and key intermediaries, their characteristics and contribution to the way in which channels work.

This chapter provides foundation material in order to explore some of the more advanced ideas about channel structure, design, interaction and networks that follow in Chapter 7. The last of the three, Chapter 8, examines the way in which behaviour within marketing channels can be managed.

Aims and objectives

The aims of this chapter are to introduce and explore core concepts associated with marketing channels.

The objectives of this chapter are to enable readers to:

1 Define the nature and concept of marketing channels.

2 Examine the purpose of, and tasks associated with, marketing channels.

3 Appraise the significance of service output theory and understand how it can be used to reduce channel member uncertainty..

4 Consider ideas concerning channel flows.

5 Introduce some basic principles concerning the types and structure of marketing channels.

6 Explore the roles and main characteristics of key members of marketing channels.

A Slice of Life – User Journeys

The move towards automation of the marketing process has gathered pace in recent years. If the solution providers are to be believed, marketing automation is the (latest) panacea for businesses seeking to fully manage the customer engagement lifecycle. Unfortunately, very few companies have the scale or resources to fully manage that lifecycle. It's too complicated. There are too many links in the value chain and even if the company did want to control the entire process, there are others far better placed to deliver their specialist piece of the marketing jigsaw – the channel.

It's easy to conceive of a single step, single transaction business relationship. Buyer meets seller, agrees price, completes transaction. Easy. Except in most B2B transactions, the value chain is considerably more complex. There are multiple touch points that link a potential buyer and a willing seller. The role of marketing is therefore to unite and align the perceptions of the buyer with the many and often varied channel providers that they will encounter along the purchasing journey.

That's not as easy as it sounds. Actually, it doesn't even sound easy. Channel marketing exists as a specialist discipline specifically to recognise the differing needs and skills of the various resellers of the original product or service across the value chain. Consider 'ingredient' brands for a second – think, Gore-Tex®, or Lycra® or Kevlar® or Teflon®. The base ingredient is produced by the OEM, original equipment manufacturer. In the case of Kevlar®, for example, it's DuPont®. But the ingredient is then applied to thousands of products not by DuPont®, but by its channel. Wholesalers, distributors, fabricators, machinists, designers, retailers… they all add value to the base ingredient by moving the product through the value chain and onto the various end-users. Your customer's, customer's, customer, is my customer. And so on.

So the journey a product takes through the channel on its way to market is often significant. It's perhaps easier to appreciate the importance of channel marketing in the context of the end-user. It's one thing trying to manage a brand and ensure its values are maintained as it passes through the ever more distant hands of the channel, but at least there is a chain of command – some control over the use of the brand by the supplier channel. With end-users, there is often no direct control over the brand perceptions of the audience. That's why companies invest in their channel relationships in the first place – to ensure that the brand connects to the end-user and that it does so with its value(s) intact.

The single most important development of the social age is that people want to engage with people, not with corporate processes. However complex the channel relationships may become, they at least need to appear seamless. As customers and prospective customers embark on a search for product or service information from or about a brand, their influences and influencers are very specific to their individual needs and they are sourced from personal and social networks that give them access across the entire channel – they may just as easily connect with a wholesaler as a retailer. They are embarking on a journey of discovery and expect to encounter the brand at various ports of call along the way.

The role of the brand then, is to be active within the channel communities that the customer is likely to participate within in order to influence the networks and draw the customer towards the brand. Brands now need to learn new digital and social languages in order to remain relevant to customers who have already become fluent in those languages.

I know a reasonable amount about the language of brands, but I've had to learn a whole new digital language in the last couple of years. Haven't we all? It's a language riddled with three letter acronyms (TLAs) and a host of almost meaningless mumbo jumbo that eventually makes sense when someone explains what's going on – SEO, UCD, MMR, content aggregation, social advocacy… and, my favourite – 'user journey'. Yes, user and journey are both English words and yes, the couplet makes sense to me now in the context of digital delivery. But it didn't for a while.

'User journey' didn't make sense to me, for example, when everyone was jacking off to the sound of their own voices proclaiming themselves to be the latest 'guru' of the 'social landscape'. User journey meant very little to me when I watched Twitter users with nothing to say attract thousands of followers. And user journey meant absolutely nothing as I sifted case studies and articles of meaningless bollocks in the vain hope of enlightenment. And while I persevered with this alien new language, 'user journey' meant the sum total of naff-all until I heard from a user who had, perhaps unsurprisingly, taken a journey…

Initially, I simply received a website enquiry form. So far, so good. A prospective client outlined his need for a new brand strategy and supporting website. A Request for Proposal document was about to be signed-off and the prospect was enquiring whether I would like to submit a response to the RFP.

I said, "No". I didn't say, "No, stick your RFP up your ass", which is my usual response to large corporates expecting small agencies to have the speculative resources of large corporates. In fact I offered an uncharacteristically polite 'no' because the company simply didn't have the budget available to engage our services. So I declined the RFP, explained the typical entry-level budgets required and thanked the enquirer for considering us. That, ordinarily, would be that. And then I received this email:

"Hi Scot,

Many thanks for the reply. I was unsure of exactly where the budget may fit with you and was slightly worried that it may be light. I appreciate you clarifying the guide costs. Hopefully in the future we will be able to work together on creative campaigns.

For your own info I thought you may like to understand my Birddog journey;

1. Introduced to your brand by a colleague.

2. Regular visits to your website.

3. Discovering your blog.

4. Following you on Twitter.

5. Twitter led directly to more consumption and laughing with your blog.

6. Twitter then directly led to me buying your book. You said something like, "if you want more buy the book," and, like a sheep, I did.

7. Now I have changed jobs and have a bit of a budget you received a direct enquiry."

Well. Hold me down and feed me whipped pudding till I scream. This is a 'user journey' across traditional, digital AND social media that clearly took several years. I was suitably impressed and I said so. Actually, what I said was, "Holy shit, that's amazing!", and was then delighted to find that the journey wasn't over yet...

"Hi Scot,

I should tell you that my girlfriend has also read your AMAZING book and loves it. She mentioned it to her boss and in particular the comment about, 'I want to lick an iPhone' or words to that effect. You have another reader based on that one comment alone. It's doing the rounds now."

User journeys aren't about a single website visit. And they're not about understanding a new digital language. They're about the years of travel up to the point of contact, they're about the experience the visitor will have in the years that follow and they're about how the experience will be communicated to a wider audience on and off line. In other words, user journeys are about... brands. In the context of channel marketing, every component of the value chain has the potential to impact the perceptions of customers and the experience they have with the brand. It's called the 'value chain' for a reason. The journey continues.

Scot McKee

■ Introduction

In Chapter 1 the notion of value chains was introduced. These are an important foundation for understanding business-to-business marketing. It was suggested that organisations choose to work together in order to provide added value opportunities for end-user customers. The notion that organisations interact with each other for mutual advantage (Kotler and Keller, 2009) underpins the concept of channel marketing.

Marketing channels consist of a chain of organisations that collectively develop products and services. Each adds something of value before passing it to the next, in order that the product or service be offered in the most convenient and valued format for end-user purchase and consumption.

Marketing channels, also called distribution channels, are concerned with the interorganisational management of the processes and activities involved in moving products from manufacturers to end-user customers. The term 'interorganisational' is important because marketing channel activities are concerned with the coordination of activities that are necessary to make products readily available to end-users. This coordination of the channels, especially when there are multichannel activities (Yan *et al.* 2011) is important if profits are to be optimised for all participants.

Coordination between channel members is necessary to convert subassemblies and raw materials into final products and services that represent superior value to the end-users of each channel. Each of the various organisations electing to coordinate activities performs a different role in the chain of activities. Some act as manufacturers, some as agents and others may be distributors, dealers, value-added resellers, wholesalers or retailers. Whatever the role, it is normally specific and geared to refining and moving the product closer to the end-user.

Each organisation is a customer to the previous organisation in an industry's value chain. Some organisations work closely together, coordinating and integrating their activities, while others cooperate on a looser, often temporary, basis. In both cases however, these organisations can be observed to be operating as members of a partnership, of differing strength and dimensions, with the express intention of achieving their objectives with their partners' assistance and cooperation. So, in addition to the end-user, a further set of customers (partners) can be determined: all those who make up the marketing channel.

The distribution of products involves two main elements. The first is the management of the tangible or physical aspects of moving a product from the producer to the end-user. This must be undertaken in such a way that the customer can freely access an offering and that the final act of the buying process is as easy as possible. This is part of supply chain management and entails the logistics associated with moving products closer to end-users.

The second element concerns the management of the intangible aspects or issues of ownership, control and flows of communication between the parties responsible for making the offering accessible to the customer. The focus of this chapter is on the second of these elements, commonly referred to as channel management.

Function and Purpose of Marketing Channels

The range of skills necessary to source and assemble appropriate parts, to manufacture and distribute products to a diversity of customers, perhaps regionally, nationally or even globally and then provide suitable levels of service and support is too wide and too complex for most organisations to provide entirely by themselves. There are some specific uncertainties associated with buying and selling. For example, the risks associated with producing too much or too little for the target market, those to do with customers' buying behaviours and motivations, and those of storage, the incumbent finance and working capital costs. The uncertainty of the outcomes associated with these and other market-related activities, is usually too large for a single organisation to carry.

Marketing channels exist because they provide a means by which these uncertainties can be reduced or shared. By combining with other organisations who have different specialised skills (for example customer access, finance, transportation, storage) these uncertainties can be diminished. The added value provided by each of these organisations contributes to the superior value perceived by end-users and contributes to competitive advantage. To achieve this level of competitive advantage, organisations need to enter interorganisational exchanges to share their specialised services and the uncertainties.

Exchanges

The primary purpose of marketing channels is to enable organisations to enter into a series of exchanges that allow each party to move towards satisfying their individual, and in some circumstances collective, goals. The exchange of products and/or services is of course the most obvious element of activity. In addition, organisations must exchange information, technical, corporate or market-orientated, so that a transaction can be completed and the relationship between the parties extended. Further, in commercial transactions, there needs to be a financial exchange so that the transaction can be concluded. Finally, there is a social exchange attached to the behaviour of marketing channel members. In order for there to be either a single market exchange or long-term series of exchanges, there must be a level of trust and commitment between all parties.

Therefore, organisations combine together to reduce uncertainty by exchanging products and services which are of value to others in the channel. The degree of uncertainty, or business risk, is associated with the complexity of the various tasks to be completed. By reducing the uncertainty experienced by all members in a channel they are better positioned to concentrate on other tasks.

ViewPoint 6.1: Uncertain milk

Milk is part of the staple diet of humans around the world. In the UK, 11 billion litres of milk is produced per annum from 1.6 million cows by 13,500 dairy farmers. Processed milk is supplied to consumers via a whole host of different types of retail outlets, dominated by the large supermarkets such as Tesco, Sainsbury's, Morrisons and Asda. These retailers exert significant channel control over both the retail and trade prices. This leads to considerable uncertainty within the channel particularly from dairy farmers who invest considerable amounts in production without any real knowledge or certainty as to how much they will be paid for the milk produced.

The National Farmers Union (NFU) which represents the interests of those involved in agriculture including dairy farmers, runs a campaign for fair dairy supply contracts for the benefit of both farmers and milk buyers. Tesco announced of the 1 April 2011, that they have agreed to pay suppliers 29.78 pence per litre for milk. This agreement covers members of Tesco's Sustainable Dairy Group and is for a period of six months. This Group has been established in order to improve efficiencies and reduce costs on farmers. In effect, Tesco have taken steps to reduce the uncertainty experienced by dairy farmers. Whilst the NFU see this as a positive step, this is only one retailer amongst many and therefore uncertainty will continue to be an issue in the market as a whole.

Source: Based on www.nfuonline.com; www.tescofarming.com

Question: What roles can channel members play in reducing uncertainty in their supply chains?

■ Reducing complexity

The first aspects of complexity to be considered concern the number of transactions, and frequency of contact, with which a producer interacts with each individual end-user customer. As noted above, producers need to complete a number of tasks in order to reach and service their markets. These include pricing, transportation, negotiations, delivery, stock holding and payment. For convenience, the term exchange will be used to embrace all of these activities. For a producer to meet the needs of a market, without intermediaries, there needs to be a complete exchange with each end-user customer. This level of exchange activity, which ignores the search and processing time involved in selling to each customer, is so intense and potentially inefficient that it can become disproportionately expensive.

From Figure 6.1 it should be clear that without the use of an intermediary there are a myriad of exchanges that producers must undertake. However, if an intermediary is introduced between the producer and its end-user customers, the number of direct exchanges is drastically reduced, as demonstrated in Figure 6.2.

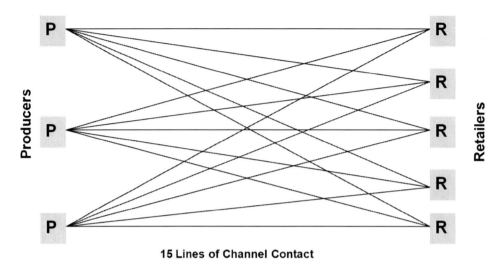

15 Lines of Channel Contact

Figure 6.1: The complexity of channel exchanges without intermediaries

10 Lines of Channel Contact

Figure 6.2:   The impact of intermediaries on channel exchanges

It is clear that the use of intermediaries redistributes and reduces the number of exchanges that producers undertake. Their contact with the market is directed to the needs of intermediaries, enabling them to focus on their core activities, production or manufacturing. In the meantime, end-user customers are better able to obtain improved individual support and service levels from channel members, than they would have received just from producers. The cost of this new level in the marketing channel is the margin that intermediaries earn for their part in the value adding process. From the end-user customers' perspective, this cost should be outweighed by the superior benefits that they derive.

This notion that the use of intermediaries reduces the number of contacts producers have with end-users, and is therefore a good thing, is not universally agreed. Mudambi and Aggarwal (2003) suggest that increasing the number of contacts that producers make with end-users can lead to greater choice. Through greater use of direct marketing and incorporating new technology using online selling, Internet-based market exchanges and B2B auction sites, breadth of market coverage can be achieved. For end-users, however, risks concerning stock availability, servicing and support increase as the number of intermediaries falls.

For producers, costs rise as more intermediaries enter the channel. However, more intermediaries enables producers, indirectly, to reach a wider array of end-user customers. Therefore, the risk is represented by the trade-off between the number of intermediaries and the breadth of the end-user market that is reached (see Figure 6.3).

In an attempt to reduce channel costs many suppliers have been cutting the number of intermediaries they use in their supply chains. Often this means moving from national warehousing systems to just a single, pan-European warehousing facility that feeds regional distribution centres. This can endanger customer service levels because end-user customers desire shorter and quicker response times and an increase in the level of service provided (Roe *et al.*, 1998).

Figure 6.3: The impact of multiple intermediaries on the number of channel exchanges

There is an assumption here that all intermediary costs are the same. This is clearly untrue and different intermediaries provide value adding services at different costs. As a result, there are many types of intermediary and there are many routes into markets. It is not surprising, therefore, that channel design and strategy decisions are further complicated by the complexity and dynamic nature of end-user customer needs. Although this is discussed in greater depth at the end of this chapter and in Chapter 8, it is worth mentioning the impact technology has had on shaping channel structures. One area of impact has been the development, in certain markets, of direct selling and the removal of intermediaries from the channel. This process is known as disintermediation. However, Internet technologies have also helped develop new types of online intermediaries, a process known as reintermediation.

Increasing Value and Competitive Advantage

The other major reason why producers utilise intermediaries is to reduce the risk that customers will reject the product or service. This is achieved by improving the overall value that customers perceive in an offering. By generating a level of superior value, relative to competing products and customer experience, producers are able to reduce the risk of purchase uncertainty.

Some producers, acting alone, might not have all the skills and core competences necessary to meet an end-users' requirements. Their skills lie with the production or manufacturing of goods and services. Intermediaries are better placed to understand, interact and deliver the value that end-user customers desire. The better the service provided by an intermediary, the greater the competitive advantage over rival intermediaries and producers. Note that competitive advantage can be considered from a channel perspective, as well as from that of an individual organisation or product. Competitive advantage can be characterised in terms of the efficiency with which the transactions are completed and the quality and value of the services provided.

Routinisation

By improving transaction efficiency, costs can be lowered and business performance improved. This is achieved by encouraging routinisation, that is, the standardisation of the transaction process. Instead of negotiating each transaction and incurring all the attendant costs, routinisation promotes cost efficiencies and the production of goods and services that are most highly valued by target markets. Distribution costs can be reduced and processes automated to regularise operations. Standardisation is encouraged by regulating order size, delivery cycles and payment frequency. This in turn promotes relationships which may evolve into relational-based transactions.

This routinisation process can be facilitated by computer-based technology such as electronic data interchange (EDI) and continuous replenishment programmes (CRP) designed to smooth out stock levels to meet customer demand yet achieve efficiency.

Specialisation

Value is also improved for customers by helping them to search for and identify sources of products that they want. Here, intermediaries can provide resources and skills that producers do not have, nor wish to develop. This specialisation adds value for end-user customers. For example, the provision of training services, frequent but small load deliveries and credit facilities can represent significant value to some retailers or OEMs.

One major dilemma concerning distribution is that manufacturers tend to want to produce large quantities of a limited variety of goods, while end-user customers only want a limited quantity of a wide variety of goods. Therefore, intermediaries sort out all the goods produced by different manufacturers and present them in quantities and formats that enable consumers to buy easily and as frequently as they wish. This is referred to as sorting and smoothing, as set out in Table 6.1.

Table 6.1: Aspects of sorting and smoothing

Aspect	Explanation
Sorting out	Grading products into different sizes, qualities or grades. For example potatoes, eggs or fruit.
Accumulation	The bringing together of different products from different producers to provide a wider category choice.
Allocation	Often referred to as breaking bulk (by wholesalers), this involves disaggregating bulk deliveries into smaller lot sizes that customers are able (and prefer) to buy.
Assorting	Assembling different collections of goods/services thought to be of value to the customer (retailers and consumers).

■ Service Outputs

Channels should be designed to meet end-user customer needs, otherwise the marketing focus is lost and a producer orientation is introduced. According to Bucklin (1966) customers seek utility from marketing channels. This utility can be observed in many forms but is essentially concerned with levels of service provided by a channel. Customers are more likely to be attracted to channels that offer higher levels of service. Bucklin argued that this channel service consists of four main elements: unit size, spatial convenience, waiting time and product variety.

■ *Unit or lot size* refers to the number of product units end-user customers are required to buy. Producers make large quantities based on mass production but marketing channels break up the production into smaller units to enable customers to consume more quickly and hold lower stocks. This process is known as breaking bulk. The more a channel breaks up the units of production into smaller and smaller unit sizes the less stock has to be held in the system, particularly by end-users, and the higher the level of service, as perceived by end-user customers. However, the higher the level of service the higher the price paid per unit.

■ *Spatial convenience* is concerned with the transportation and search costs end-user customers experience. The easier it is for customers to access products the higher the level of service output. Classic examples are shopping centres which not only provide a range of shops under a single roofed area, free of motor vehicles, they also provide parking facilities. Local convenience stores and even vending machines also provide spatial convenience and improved service output. Home shopping facilities, either by telephone or increasingly the Internet, provide new ways of furnishing 'time-poor' customers with spatial convenience. Tesco and Sainsbury's reduce the search and transportation costs for their shoppers by providing home delivery services. Customers pay for the higher utility as a trade-off against the costs associated with visiting the store.

- *Waiting or delivery time.* The time a customer waits between ordering and receiving products represents a period of inconvenience. In most circumstances customers prefer to receive their products immediately they are ordered, and the shorter the waiting time, the higher the level of service. Price is used to compensate customers for having to wait for delivery. Furniture manufacturers have traditionally presented long wait times, as they prefer to operate batch production systems. The development of self-assembly furniture (for example MFI and Ikea) has helped companies develop shorter waiting times but very often at the expense of quality.

- *Product variety.* Customers experience a higher level of utility when they are able to select from a broader or wider range of products. So, the greater the assortment of products available to customers, the higher the service output. Again price is the control mechanism and customers pay for shorter waiting times through higher prices.

By understanding the level of service outputs desired by customers, it becomes easier to segment markets, profile consumer groups and to design channels that are better able to meet customer needs. If end-user customers wish to purchase in small quantities it is necessary to build a longer channel and involve a large number of intermediaries. If breaking bulk is not important then a small number of intermediaries will suffice and price can be lowered.

Bucklin argues, as a general principle, that the more a channel has to provide in order to satisfy the level of service output expectations, the higher will be the cost and hence price that customers must pay for that level of utility. However, it is useful to consider the value of service output theory within the context of outsourcing and electronic trading formats. Bucklin developed his theory within a radically different trading environment to that which exists today. Price may still be important within market exchanges but may not be the coordinating mechanism it was once considered to be, and may now be surpassed by concepts of relative value, collaborative exchanges and competitive advantage. This aspect will be discussed further later in this chapter.

■ Channel Flows

So far reference has been made to channel activities. The term 'activities', suggests that these events are discrete and unconnected. Nothing could be further from the truth. Interorganisational coordination requires that there is flow of processes that sweep up and down the channel in order that all participa[nts] able to undertake their roles effectively and efficiently.

Channel flows engage participants according to their roles and the nature of the flow. The most obvious type of flow is information, which moves between channel members in formal and informal ways. Rosenbloom (1999) identifies five flows and Coughlan *et al.* (2001) identify eight different types of flow. Figure 6.4, shows that whatever the number, the principle holds that these flows provide a linkage, they help to bind together organisations in marketing channel.

- *Physical flow* refers to the transportation and storage of products between channel members. There are costs associated with this flow such as warehousing, and perhaps specialised protection such as refrigeration, plus the transportation costs associated with moving products to new locations. However, it is important to note that these costs are not the costs of ownership. When the legal title to products changes there are different costs associated with owning stock – for example, market value, which is treated as an asset (working capital) – which in turn impacts on profitability.

- *Negotiation flows* concern the dialogue associated with a (possible) change in ownership or how service or maintenance arrangements are to be developed. With regard to Figure 6.4, note how the dialogue is represented by a two-way arrow. The key element associated with negotiation flows is the cost of the time that the parties devote to the discussions. Any legal advice and documentation costs are also attributed to this type of flow.

- *Finance flows* refer to the credit extended to intermediaries. Most commonly this is seen in terms of the 30-, 60-, 90-day period in which customers are required, or have agreed, as part of the negotiation flow, to pay for the goods and services that they have taken into their possession. Title of ownership passes once the payment flow is completed. This 30-day period represents the time the seller agrees to finance the purchase costs of the buyer and represents a lost opportunity to use the money elsewhere.

- *Promotion flows* reflect the need to complete particular marketing communications tasks. This may be the development of awareness levels, educating current customers or persuading potential customers. The tools used for the promotion flow are primarily personal selling and direct marketing but advertising, public relations and sales promotion can also play significant roles. When considered as a whole, the promotion flow is instrumental in building and maintaining strong relationships with customers.

There are also *order flows* and the subsequent *payment flows*, both of which move from customers towards successive intermediaries back towards the producers. These one-way flows have been subject to electronic improvements. Many purchases of rebuy items and their subsequent payments have been automated to reduce costs and improve turnaround times.

...flows help identify legitimate members of the marketing channel. ...isations who participate in the negotiation and ownership flows ...selling and transfer of title) are fully constitutional members of the ...annel. Channel flows also reflect the complexity associated with ...ities and the huge number of opportunities that are emerging to use ...gies, systems and communications to improve some of these flows, ...h faster, to make them more accurate and efficient and to reduce the ...ted with these aspects of marketing channel management.

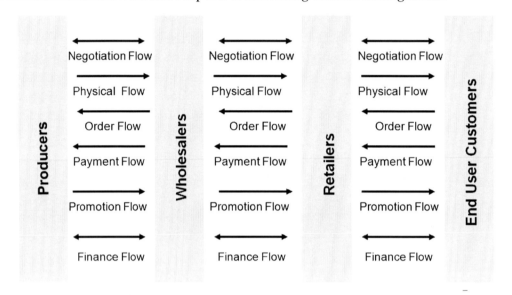

Figure 6.4: Channel flows in marketing channels

■ Types of Distribution Channel

Producers are faced with a basic decision. Should they sell direct to consumers or should they sell to another organisation that will in turn market the product to end-users? These two extremes represent the direct channel and the indirect channel respectively. Issues surrounding the nature and benefits of using an indirect channel are explored in this and subsequent channels. The decision to adopt one or the other is really a function of the uncertainty surrounding the performance of the customers, products and services, intermediaries, competitors and suppliers. See Table 6.2 for an explanation of the different types of uncertainty faced by stakeholders.

Indirect channels are selected when the degree of uncertainty concerning the delivery of end-user value exceeds acceptable levels. All organisations experience uncertainty and they use a variety of strategies, methods and techniques to contain and reduce specific risks to an acceptable level. Cooperating with organisations which have particular skills and competences is a strategic approach to reducing and sharing such uncertainty.

The structure of distribution channels varies according to whether end-users are consumers or business customers. Within each channel configuration there are several levels, each representing a different number or type of intermediary, each of whom is involved in bringing products closer to end-users. The length of a channel, therefore, is a function of the number of intermediaries involved in moving products from producers to end-users. These various configurations are presented in Figures 6.5 and 6.6. Readers should note the variety of channel members and the number of channel opportunities available. Consumer channels of type 1 (CC1) are direct-marketing channels and contain no intermediaries. All other channel types are regarded as indirect channels and contain a varying number of channel members.

Table 6.2: Stakeholder uncertainties and channel selection

Stakeholder	Type of uncertainty
Customers	In terms of their location, types and buying characteristics, their perceived value and desirable satisfaction levels.
Products/services	In terms of their attributes, availability, speed of perishability, customisation and support.
Intermediaries	In terms of their capability in terms of selling, distribution and financing, their ability to add real value.
Competitors	In terms of their channel decisions, skills and level of interaction.
Suppliers	In terms of their size, resources, level of openness and reliability.

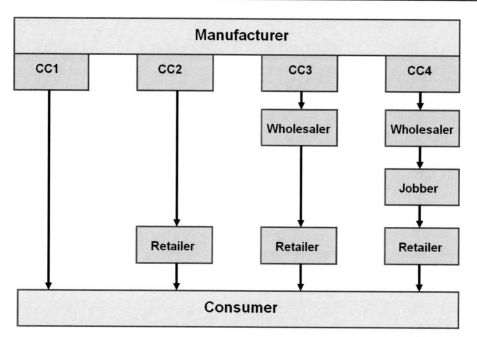

Figure 6.5: Levels of marketing channels for consumer markets

In CC1 channels there are no intermediaries, products move directly from producer to customer. For example, consumers visit farms to collect eggs or to pick their own fruit. In business markets some component manufacturers deal directly with aircraft manufacturers. For many years insurance was sold directly to consumers in this way, for example the 'Man from the Pru'. Indeed, many financial services organisations, the utilities and home improvement companies still use this direct approach.

Internet technologies have brought a new dimension to the direct channel. Through the use of eCommerce, organisations that once relied on the distribution of printed catalogues can now reach a wider audience with home shopping, for example www.avon.co.uk.

CC2-type channels are used by manufacturers to sell large quantities of product to retailers. These retailers have multiple stores through which they can distribute stock. Retailers such as large supermarket chains (Tesco, Sainsbury's and Asda Wal-Mart), car dealerships (Ford, VW and Honda) and clothing and fashion retailers (Marks and Spencer, H&M and Matalan) typify this approach.

CC3 channels are used when there are a huge number of different retail outlets necessary to reach a very large number of consumers. Shampoo, soft drinks, chewing gum and newspapers are typically distributed via wholesalers to a plethora of retailers.

CC4 channels include the use of agents. Jobbers, agents or brokers as they are sometimes called, are used by producers or even wholesalers, in order that the product sells into a variety of retail outlets. Fish, meat, fruit and other food that is to be processed is often managed in this way.

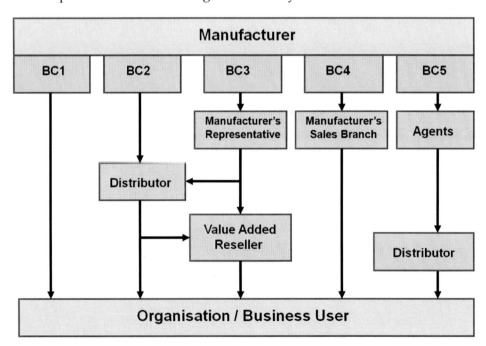

Figure 6.6: Levels of marketing channels for business customer markets

ViewPoint 6.2: Multiple channels for multiple car parts

The UK market for replacement car parts was estimated by Mintel to be £4438 million in 2009). The distribution for such products is multilayered and covers parts purchased by car dealers and independent garages and repairers (trade market) and those bought by individuals for self repairs of vehicles (consumer market). The trade market is supplied via so-called motor factors and the consumer market from petrol forecourt retailers and from retail outlets such as Halfords. Tyre and exhaust fitting centres such as Kwik-Fit and ATS Euromaster also play a significant role in both trade and consumer markets.

Main franchised car dealerships are supplied via their host franchisers with supply direct from original parts manufacturers. Motor factors are independent companies who purchase both original parts (i.e. those made for specific brand and model of car) and non-branded parts made as substitute components which are normally lower in price. The Andrew Page group is a national motor factor business which has over 50 UK distribution depots from which customers can purchase components over the counter and which offer a van delivery service to account customers.

The internet is now playing a significant role in the distribution of car parts. This allows businesses such as Andrew Page to cover a wider geographic spread and allows supply from centralised distribution centres. There are now a number of businesses supplying car components solely online which offers economies of scale and reduced stocking costs with subsequently lower and more competitive price levels.

Source: Based on Mintel (2009) *Car Aftermarket-UK*, November; www.andrewpage.com

Question: What are the advantages and disadvantages for businesses using online order and delivery systems?

In channels where the end-user is a business or organisation, level BC1 represents the same characteristics as level CC1. It is quite common for expensive industrial products to be distributed through a direct channel, if only because the negotiation flow involves a high level of interaction in order to agree the specification and order requirements and to provide the appropriate level of post-purchase technical support and service. For example, most military and high engineering contracts, such as the Italian-designed, Pendolinos-styled tilting trains bought by Virgin, were negotiated thorough direct channels (www.railway-technology.com/projects/virgin/; accessed 21 October 2010).

Direct channel marketing in the business-to-business sector has grown as new technology enables organisations to build relationships directly with each of their customers. Electronic channels represent opportunities for manufacturers to reach end-user customers but also to provide intermediaries with higher levels of service and support.

Telemarketing and printed catalogues have been instrumental in enabling the direct channel for both the consumer and business markets. Web based technologies have since brought a new dimension to the direct channel.

The office supplies, furniture and equipment sectors still use B2B printed catalogues. Their portability, ease of access, longevity and option to share among colleagues give them a real advantage over online systems. Indeed, many small companies and the self-employed prefer the convenience of next-day delivery rather than having to go to a local trade outlet. Goodwins (2007) also cites the trade tools and accessories catalogue distributed by Screwfix. Part of its success is because its A5 size enables it to fit easily into a toolbox or glove compartment.

Whilst online catalogues might lack some flexibility, they are easy to update, can be shared, allow for regular online ordering cycles and offer interactivity. However, many customers prefer a truly multichannel mix. Some prefer to visit a trade counter to see an item and then take advantage of online discounts. Others like to browse a printed catalogue and then order online for the speediest outcome and discounts.

The use of an industrial distributor enables producers to reach a variety of business buyers. Business channel 2 (BC2) is a commonly used route to reach organisational buyers, especially when a producer has many geographically dispersed customers. For example, building materials suppliers and photocopier suppliers use distributors. Similarly, when a product has a broad market appeal and is sold in small quantities, such as office stationery, furniture and equipment, distributors provide customers a level of support that the producer could not provide for all end-user businesses. Distributors hold stock and assist the ownership, negotiation, finance, payment and promotion flows. Their role in these markets can be pivotal in providing the level of service that business customers require and the breadth of market coverage that producers need to be successful.

BC3 shows that when manufacturers' representatives are used they coordinate with distributors or resellers in order to access end-user customers. Representatives are used to provide market information, business advice and selling skills. These are especially useful for smaller organisations that do not have the resources necessary to reach new markets or launch new products. Some organisations prefer to use their own sales branches in order to reach particular geographically spread clusters of customers, as shown at BC4.

The final business-to-business channel, BC5, incorporates agents and distributors. This route is frequently used by manufacturers that do not have a sales force but wish to operate in international markets. Agents are used to service and support overseas agents and provide specialist support in terms of ownership (importing), promotion and negotiation flows.

This explanation of different marketing channels is not intended to suggest that manufacturers choose a single channel for business activities. In reality, organisations employ a multichannel strategy, with growth spurred by web applications and wireless devices. There is little doubt that multichannel marketing has had an important impact on business-to-business marketing (Rosenbloom, 2007). This is because different segments prefer to use (value) different channels. A multichannel strategy is necessary in order that production efficiencies are achieved and all customer types have access to the product. It has been found that the activity levels of multichannel users are much   higher than single channel users. Valos (2009) reports that they spend more (Weinberg *et al.*, 2007), buy a greater range of products (Muller-Lankenau *et al.* (2006) and that they are more loyal (Kumar and Venkatesan, 2005) than single-channel customers. However, any idea that multichannel marketing is straightforward should be considered carefully as the channels used need to be integrated, otherwise, as Rosenbloom (2007) points out, customer loss is likely to occur.

■ Channel Roles and Membership

Membership of an organisation, or in this case a marketing channel, involves an obligation to fulfil a designated and agreed role, or roles. Within roles there are specific tasks that need to be undertaken and completed. It is important that members carry out their assigned roles, in order that all members achieve their objectives. Should a member fail to fulfil its role, either completely or partially, pressure is placed upon others to make good the shortfall. The whole channel then becomes less efficient and the added value perceived by end-user customers is threatened.

There are a number of tasks to be completed in a marketing channel. Some of the traditional ones are subject to change and evolution as technology, in particular, becomes more significant. However, the key roles are those occupied by manufacturers, wholesalers, retailers and end-user customers. The sections that follow examine the tasks that these core members undertake. Each of the main channel members is considered in the context of a traditional, uncomplicated channel. This serves as a basis for understanding fundamental tasks and roles before exploring some of the wider, structural and more strategic issues in Chapter 7.

■ Manufacturers

Manufacturers, or producers, are the source of products and services that are distributed through marketing channels. Their number and variety is immense, ranging from manufacturers of nails, milk and clothing to gas turbines, computers and space rockets. The size of these organisations also varies from sole traders to multinationals operating in many different countries and regions across the world. Despite these disparities, they have a common thread in that they must all produce goods and services that are valued by end-user customers and distributed in such a way that they are available and accessible in their target markets.

The overall role of manufacturers is to assemble parts and materials from various suppliers and to distribute these, often through intermediaries, to different market segments. To do this, manufacturers need to undertake specific roles within particular channel flows. Their participation in the physical, ownership, negotiation, finance, payment and promotion flows delineates their significance in the marketing channel. Their role is instrumental in stimulating the channel to respond to end-user customer needs.

■ Intermediaries

The term 'intermediary' refers to all those organisations that link together manufacturers and end-users. The overall role is acting as a go-between to ensure that end-users are able to access the products and services they require in quantities and locations that provide greatest utility. In Bucklin's terms, intermediaries seek to provide optimum levels of service outputs.

There are many types of intermediary but the most common are wholesalers, merchants, brokers, manufacturers' representatives, dealers, distributors, agents, retailers and value added resellers. Many of these perform similar functions but the terminology reflects market needs and historical precedent. Essentially there are two main types of intermediary, wholesalers and retailers.

■ Wholesalers

The term 'wholesalers' embraces merchants, brokers, manufacturers representatives, agents, distributors and dealers. They are (normally) independently owned and either buy, or facilitate the transfer, of products from producers and resell them to retailers, other wholesalers and end-user business customers. They perform tasks that assist producers (upstream) and they also perform tasks that assist their customers (downstream). These tasks are set out in Table 6.3.

There is a small technical difference between a wholesaler and a distributor. A wholesaler distributes products to other intermediaries but distributors sell directly to end-user customers, invariably business customers. This difference is to be noted but this text focuses on wholesalers as if they encompass distributors.

The role of wholesalers is linked to the tasks they perform in order that the channel operates efficiently. Their upstream tasks are to reduce the uncertainty producers experience. This uncertainty concerns the market for the producer's goods and the transaction activities associated with buying and selling. Of these, the provision of suitable and adequate market coverage is one of the more important tasks undertaken for producers. Jackson and d'Amico (1989) point out that the probability that wholesalers will be used increases as the geographic dispersion of customers widens, the number of industries served broadens, order frequency increases and lead times decline.

Table 6.3: Wholesaler tasks – upstream and downstream

Upstream tasks	Activities
Market uncertainty	Market coverage
	Collecting and analysing market information
Transaction uncertainty	Making sales contacts
	Relationship maintenance
	Holding stock
	Processing orders
	Providing customer support

Downstream tasks	Activities
Product uncertainty	Stock availability and delivery
	Breaking bulk
	Product quality and reliability
Service and support	Assortment
uncertainty	Extended credit
	Technical support and advice
	General service
	Customer relationship development

Associated with market coverage is the role and significance of the sales force. The uncertainty associated with maintaining a large sales force prohibits many manufacturing and producer organisations from employing their own dedicated sales forces. Experience and research show that it is more effective to leave this skilled and expensive operation to those with local knowledge and who are also better placed to develop and maintain relationships. Through good relationships it is possible to generate quality market information which can be fed back to manufacturers to influence marketing strategy and help product/service development.

Wholesalers hold stock on behalf of producers. In a sense they can be regarded as an extension to a manufacturer's production capacity in that they share the uncertainty associated with production by reducing the quantities of stock manufacturers might otherwise have to retain. This has an impact on finance through the amount of working capital each stakeholder holds.

In addition to these benefits, wholesalers contribute to the risks associated with order processing. Wholesalers buy large quantities of stock and break bulk in order to provide retailers and end-user customers with the smaller quantities they prefer to buy. Manufacturers dislike the inefficiencies associated with servicing a large number of small orders.

Wholesalers also undertake a range of downstream tasks to reduce the uncertainty experienced by retailers and end-user business customers. This uncertainty concerns both product-related issues and the mechanisms necessary to support and service each exchange. Retailers and end-user customers prefer that products are easily and quickly available. Wholesalers are better able than manufacturers to provide this function. Stock can be stored, delivered and even collected for repair and servicing quickly and regularly by wholesalers, improving the service outputs for end-user customers.

Financial uncertainty can be reduced through the use of extended credit. By allowing retailers to resell products and end-user business buyers to use the products before having to pay for them, so wholesalers help those downstream. In addition to this wholesalers hold stock which can be called off by retailers as and when it is convenient to them. This represents a further reduction in financial risk because retailers do not have to pay for holding stock until it is actually required.

Wholesalers break bulk for those lower down the channel and provide an assortment of products from an array of manufacturers that retailers and end-users prefer. By providing technical and general support the operational risks experienced by retailers can be reduced, while the perceived performance and physical risks associated with some business product purchases can be minimised.

Not all wholesalers perform all of these tasks as they vary according to industry. However, wholesalers perform a series of important roles for both upstream manufacturers and downstream retailers and end-user customers. They facilitate the movement of goods through the channel and smooth the buying processes by raising service output levels and in doing so reducing perceived risks. Wholesalers are involved with the negotiation, ownership, finance, promotion, physical, order and payment flows.

■ Retailers

Retailing is concerned with the identification of consumer demands, finding the right mix of stock and making it available to them at times and in formats that they prefer. This means that retailers enter into exchanges with consumers, unlike wholesalers who exchange with resellers and end-user business organisations. Coughlan *et al.* (2001) state that this demarcation is important because it highlights the different buying motivations and processes that both wholesalers and retailers must address in their marketing strategies and, in particular, their segmentation policies (see Table 6.4).

Retailers undertake a number of tasks for their upstream partners, namely wholesalers, manufacturers and other intermediaries. The uncertainty experienced by these upstream partners revolves around their need to have stock moved and broken down into smaller allotments. This helps their finance flows and assists the order processing flow. While wholesalers break bulk for producers, so retailers perform the same exercise for wholesalers, although the scale of each individual operation is smaller. Retailers provide wholesalers with sales contacts and sales outlets through which stock is transferred to individual consumers for consumption. It is more efficient for retailers to undertake this operation than for wholesalers.

Table 6.4 : Retailer tasks – upstream and downstream

Upstream tasks	Activities
Product uncertainty	Breaking bulk
	Sales contacts
	Storage
Market uncertainty	Collecting and analysing market information
	Promotion
	Collecting and processing orders

Downstream tasks	Activities
Demand uncertainty	Turnover/margin model
	Spatial convenience
	Waiting time
	Lot size
	Product variety
Service and support uncertainty	Stock availability and delivery
	Extended credit
	Technical support and advice
	Customer relationship development

In a similar way retailers reduce wholesalers' storage risks by taking small amounts of stock on a regular basis. This enables wholesalers to plan their own stock-holding operations more accurately. Uncertainty is shared by spreading stock, in different amounts, throughout the entire channel. Stock levels constitute a major area of uncertainty for retailers. For example, a great deal could depend on a manufacturer's or wholesaler's policy on accepting returned products. Should the policy accommodate returns then it is likely that retailers will over-order and hence over-stock (Tsay, 2002). This sharing of risk might improve downstream service levels but can result in stock being returned and the wholesaler's performance reduced.

Retailers provide a point of contact with consumers which can stimulate the order and payment flows. This also offers other upstream parties a means by which they can collect market information. Indeed this market research function has become a source of influence for many retailers who have become 'data rich'. The use of new technology, in particular databases, has enabled retailers (and manufacturers) to overcome the complexity associated with getting to know customers' preferences and needs (O'Malley and Mitussis, 2002). Through understanding these aspects of their customers, it becomes possible to develop meaningful and mutually rewarding relationships. Uncertainty about consumer demand can be reduced by a retailer's choice of level of service outputs and their positioning decision regarding the turnover/margin model that they adopt.

According to Coughlan *et al.* (2001) there are two main retail models. The established retail model works on the basis of high margins and low stock turnover. Retailers offer consumers products in small quantities but charge a higher price and hence earn a higher margin. The second, more contemporary, model has evolved on the basis that it is more efficient to generate lower margins on a high stock turnover. Under this model, retailers offer consumers the opportunity to buy large amounts of stock and they are compensated with a lower unit price. There are many variants based on these two simple constructs but what emerges is the impact on the level of service output offered to customers.

As a generalisation, the first model provides a high level of service output and is consumer-centric. The second model presents a lower level of service output and is channel-centric. There is, of course, a mixture of both models in existence, reflecting the needs of different segments. Indeed, it is not really about just higher or lower levels of service output, but about the different value that consumers and channel members now attribute to various types and combinations of service output. For example, Sweeny and Soutar (2001) propose that consumers use four primary dimensions with which to assess the value of a consumer durable good: emotional, social, quality/performance and price/value for money. This should be reflected in the retailer proposition communicated through promotion, store location and ambience, stocking levels and levels of personal service.

It is worth noting that, although the channel-centric model reflects a concentration on the efficiencies of production and distribution, consumer preferences and shopping habits have changed. Consumers are more time-poor, more affluent and better educated. As a result they value different service outputs in diverse ways. Retailers have moved to reflect this, literally, by moving out-of-town and creating huge retail stores in order to provide a wide range of stock at lower services but with a higher level of personal service and support. Consumers therefore still value spatial convenience, but that convenience is reflected in easy parking, collection of goods and, in some categories, even self-assembly. New technology allows retailers and manufacturers to offer home shopping facilities to increase the perceived value of their services by emphasising convenience

Waiting times can be reduced by retailers through over-stocking, a strategy supported by favourable manufacturer's return policies,. Hand-held scanners allowing consumers to self-scan purchases have yet to achieve widespread use but will help time-poor consumers by reducing checkout time.

The decisions retailers make about product variety also have strategic importance. A seller stocking a narrow variety but deep range of products will often be perceived by consumers as a specialist or expert retailer. In these circumstances there should be high levels of service output and customer support. For example, Jessops for photographic equipment or Clarks shoe shops. Retailers who provide a broad variety of products but little depth within each line, for example Asda Wal-Mart, will be perceived as convenient and price-orientated stores. Here low margin and high stock turnover combined with good customer service is the preferred model.

ViewPoint 6.3: RFID in practice

Radio frequency identification (RFID) is an automatic identification and data capture technology. Although not new, the technology has been developed over the past 10 years for various commercial applications. According to McFarlane *et al.*, (2003), the RFID contains three elements.

- A chip, which contains an Electronic Product Code (EPC), and antenna

- A reader which emits radio signals and receives response from tags

- Middleware that bridges RFID hardware and enterprise application.

A radio signal, received by the antenna, activates the chip, which in turn transmits a unique code identifying the object that the tag is attached to (Blau, 2003).

RFID technologies provide real-time communication with numerous objects simultaneously, from a distance, without contact or line of sight (Garcia *et al.*, 2007). As a result the system enables each product to be identified uniquely. This improves product tracking and visibility within supply chains. It can increase accuracy, efficiency and speed of processes. It can also reduce storage, handling and distribution costs and improve sales by decreasing the number of stock-outs (Li *et al.*, 2006, as cited by Sarac *et al.* (2010).

Procter & Gamble and Wal-Mart simultaneously reduced inventory levels by 70%, improved service levels from 96% to 99%. They also reduced administration costs by re-engineering their supply chains.

Some sectors, such as healthcare, retail, automotive, textile, and the luxury goods industries (Li *et al.*, 2006) have greater opportunities to gain from RFID application, than others. RFID technologies can improve the efficiency and effectiveness of healthcare operators in numerous ways. For example, Banks *et al.* (2007) refer to smarter physical flows (patients, beds, etc.), improved accuracy of information flows (patient's history, treatment records, etc.) and better stock management (medicine linens, beds, etc.). Hedgepeth (2007) states that the 'assembly process' used within the automobile industry in USA and Canada, to be one the most popular RFID applications.

Source: Sarac *et al.* (2010)

Question: To what extent should the use of RIFD technology improve service delivery in hotels?

Top-performing supermarket retailers were found to excel because they offered broader assortments of stock and have high performing own label brands, charge significantly lower everyday prices, process and feature advertising, the promotion flow that drives store traffic (Dhar *et al.* 2001).

In addition to dealing with demand uncertainty, retailers also deal with the uncertainties associated with consumer service and support. By providing credit facilities, consumer uncertainty with respect to financial risks can be overcome. The level of in-store personal service needs to reflect the overall positioning of the store and complement the balance of service outputs provided. Although more staff can lead to higher levels of service output, it also means that there is a higher cost base and this drives a need to earn higher margins. Out-of-store support can also be important in some categories such as domestic appliances, computers and financial services sectors. Here guaranteed call-out times, extended warranties and use of authorised outsourced providers all serve to reduce the pre-purchase uncertainties experienced by consumers.

Retailers perform a number of important tasks and undertake significant roles in the marketing channel. This section has presented some of the uncertainties and models and methods used to resolve them. All policies undertaken by retailers have implications right the way through a marketing channel and this highlights the importance of coordinated channel strategies and clear segmentation policies.

■ End-users

End-users are as much a part of marketing channels as the intermediaries referred to above. There are two types of end-user – individual consumers and business customers – constituting an integral part of the processes and flows that a marketing channel supports. For example, end-users buy products from retailers or purchase direct from manufacturers or wholesalers and in doing so generate payment, order processing, stock holding and ownership flows. They enable the channel to function and the various flows to be actioned. End-users stimulate the payment flow by prompting customer orders. From these orders there is a reason for stock to be made, moved, stored or presented.

Summary

Here are the key points about the B2B marketing channels, set out against the learning objectives.

1 Define the nature and concept of marketing channels.

Marketing channels, also called distribution channels, are concerned with the interorganisational management of the processes and activities involved in moving products from manufacturers to end-user customers.

Marketing channels consist of a chain of organisations that collectively develop products and services. Each adds something of value before passing it to the next, in order that the product or service be offered in the most convenient and valued format for end-user purchase and consumption.

2 Examine the purpose of, and tasks associated with, marketing channels.

Marketing channels exist because they provide a means by which uncertainties can be reduced or shared. By combining with other organisations who have different specialised skills (for example customer access, finance, transportation, storage) these uncertainties can be diminished. The added value provided by each of these organisations contributes to the superior value perceived by end-users and contributes to competitive advantage.

3 Appraise the significance of service output theory and explain how it can be used to reduce channel member uncertainty.

Channels should be designed to meet end-user customer needs as they seek utility from marketing channels. This utility can be observed in many forms but is essentially concerned with levels of service provided by a channel. Customers are more likely to be attracted to channels that offer higher levels of service. Channel service consists of four main elements: unit size, spatial convenience, waiting time and product variety.

4 Consider ideas concerning channel flows.

Interorganisational coordination requires that there is flow of processes that sweep up and down the channel in order that all participants are able to undertake their roles effectively and efficiently. Channel flows engage participants according to their roles and the nature of the flow. The main types of flows are information, physical, order, negotiation, financial, payment and promotion.

5 Introduce some basic principles concerning the types and structure of marketing channels.

Producers can decide to sell direct to end-user customers or to another organisation that will market the product to end-users. These two extremes represent the direct and the indirect channels respectively. Indirect channels are selected when the degree of uncertainty concerning the delivery of end-user value exceeds acceptable levels.

The structure of distribution channels varies according to whether end-users are consumers or business customers. Within each channel configuration there are several levels, each representing a different number or types of intermediaries, each of whom is involved in bringing products closer to end-users. The length of a channel is a function of the number of intermediaries involved in moving products from producers to end-users.

6 Explore the roles and main characteristics of key members of marketing channels.

Membership of a marketing channel involves an obligation to fulfil a designated and agreed role, or roles. Within roles there are specific tasks that need to be undertaken and completed. It is important that members carry out their assigned roles, in order that all members achieve their objectives. Should a member fail to fulfil its role, either completely or partially, pressure is placed upon others to make good the shortfall. The whole channel then becomes less efficient and the added value perceived by end-user customers is threatened.

There are a number of tasks to be completed in a marketing channel. Some of the traditional ones are subject to change and evolution as technology, in particular, becomes more significant. However, other roles include those occupied by manufacturers, wholesalers, retailers and end-user customers.

■ Discussion Questions

1 Discuss the extent to which the use of channel intermediaries reduces organisational uncertainty and complexity.

2 Explore the potential contribution of EDI to the performance and development of marketing channels.

3 Identify four different ways in which marketing channels can be configured.

4 Compare and contrast two marketing channels and evaluate the different levels and functions of the various participants.

5 Make notes in preparation for a presentation in which you explain the nature and purpose of marketing channels.

6 Explain sorting and smoothing and then determine the key characteristics of the service output concept.

References

Banks, J., Hanny, D., Pachano, M.A. and Thompson, L.G. (2007) *RFID Applied*, John Wiley & Sons, Inc

Blau, J. (2003). Supermarket tunes into wireless. Available: www.computerweekly.com/articles

Bucklin, L. (1966). *A Theory of Distribution Channel Structure*, Berkeley, CA: IBER Special Publications.

Coughlan, A.T., Anderson, E.L. and El-Ansary, A. (2001) *Marketing Channels*, 6th edn, Englewood Cliffs, NJ: Prentice Hall.

Dhar, S. K., Hoch, S.J. and Kumar, N. (2001) Effective category management depends on the role of the category, *Journal of Retailing*, **77**, 165–184.

Garcia, A., Chang, Y., Abarca, A. and Oh, C. (2007) RFID enhanced MAS for warehouse management, *International Journal of Logistics: Research and Applications* **10** (2), 97–107.

Goodwins, S. (2007) Catalogues: going by the book, 28 February, retrieved 21 October 2010 from www.b2bm.biz/Features/CATALOGUES-Going-by-the-book/

Hedgepeth, W.O. (2007) *RFID Metrics—Decision Making Tools for Today's Supply Chains*, Boca Raton, FA: CRC Press

Jackson, D.M. and d'Amico, M.F. (1989) Products and markets served by distributors and agents, *Industrial Marketing Management* **18** (1) (February), 27–33

Kotler, P., & Keller, K. (2009) *Marketing Management*, Englewood Cliffs, NJ: Prentice Hall

Kumar, V. and Venkatesan, R. (2005) Who are the multichannel shoppers and how do they perform?: correlates of multi-channel shopping behaviour, *Journal of Interactive Marketing*, 19, 2, 44–62

Li, S., Visich, J.K., Khumawala, B.M and Zhang, C. (2006) Radio frequency identification technology: applications, technical challenges and strategies, *Sensor Review* **26** (3), 193–202.

McFarlane, D., Sarma, S., Chirn, J.L., Wong, C.Y. and Ashton, K. (2003) Auto ID systems and intelligent manufacturing control, *Engineering Applications of Artificial Intelligence* **16** (4), 365–376.

Mudambi, S. and Aggarwal, R. (2003) Industrial distributors: can they survive in the new economy?, *Industrial Marketing Management* **32** (4), 317–325.

Muller-Lankenau, C., Wehmeyer, K. and Klein, S. (2006) Multichannel strategies: capturing and exploring diversity in the European retail grocery industry, *International Journal of Electronic Commerce* **10** (2), 85-122

O'Malley, L. and Mitussis, D. (2002) Relationships and technology: strategic implications, *Journal of Strategic Marketing* **10**, 225–238.

Roe, M., Weinstein, M., Bumstead, J. and Charron, H. (1998), Forging a strong European chain, *Transportation and Distribution* **39** (6) (June), 100–101.

Rosenbloom, B. (1999). *Marketing Channels: a Management View*, 6th edn, Orlando, FL: Harcourt Brace.

Rosenbloom, B. (2007) Multi channel strategy in business-to-business markets: prospects and problems, *Industrial Marketing Management* **36** (1), 4-9

Sarac, A., Absi, N. and Dauzère-Pérès, S. (2010) A literature review on the impact of RFID technologies on supply chain management, *International Journal of Production Economics*, **128** (1) (November), 77-95

Sweeny, J.C. and Soutar, G.N. (2001) Consumer perceived value: the development of a multiple item scale, *Journal of Retailing* **77**, 203–220.

Tsay, A.A. (2002). Risk sensitivity in distribution channel partnerships: implications for manufacturer return policies, *Journal of Retailing* **78**, 147–160.

Valos, M.J. (2009) Structure, people and process challenges of multichannel marketing: insights from marketers, *Journal of Database Marketing and Customer Strategy Management* **16**, 197-206

Weinberg, B.D., Parise, and Guinan, (2007) Multi-channel marketing: mindset and program development, *Business Horizons* **50** (5), 385-394

Yan, R., Guo, P., Wang, J. and Amrouche, N. (2011) Product distribution and coordination strategies in a multi-channel context, *Journal of Retailing and Consumer Services* **18**, 19–26

7 Supply Chains, Channel Structures and Networks

Overview

This chapter deals with two main elements. The first concerns the management of the logistical and physical flow of goods from producers to end user customers. This is referred to as 'supply chain management'.

The second element concerns the management of the marketing channels. These are structural configurations organisations use to add value and which enable end users to access finished goods (and services) in the most convenient way. Attention is given to conventional marketing channel structures, vertical marketing systems and network approaches to interorganisational channel structures.

Aims and objectives

The aims of this chapter are to explore ways in which organisations cooperate with one another in order to make their products and services available to end-user customers. This concerns the management of supply chains and marketing channels.

The objectives of this chapter are to enable readers to:

1 Understand ideas about organisational interdependence and independence.

2 Explain the issues associated with supply chain management.

3 Examine the design and structure of different marketing channels.

4 Consider contemporary forms of organisational networks.

5 Explore ideas concerning the use of electronic channels in B2B trading contexts.

A Slice of Life – The Chain of Events

This story has less perhaps to do with the client's work than the impact of the supply chain. It's no coincidence that the example is a company involved with supply chain management itself, but the issues surrounding the supply chain are more important than the individual business mentioned.

My client was a software company that provided solutions for global supply chain sourcing and management. For predominantly large retail chains, the ability to source and supply products from around the world is critical in maintaining profits – buy it cheaper, ship it cheaper, sell it cheaper. The successful management of the supply chain delivers competitive advantage and better margins. As large retailers expand their global empires, or simply look further afield to find newer, cheaper sources of supply for a local market, supply chain management enables the cost-effective delivery of products to markets. A penny saved here becomes millions saved there. The company provided the software for the retailers to find the suppliers, manage the transactions, deliver the products and make the savings.

Back in 1999, as the Internet was just starting to find its commercial purpose in the world, this company was one of many technology companies developing its software and its business hoping to capitalise on the seemingly insatiable appetites of the financial markets to invest in all things tech. There were 457 companies listed for IPO (independent placement offering) on the NASDAQ stock exchange in 1999. They were mainly technology companies – 'dot-coms'. Of the 457 placements, 117 companies doubled their share price on the first day of trading. Everyone wanted a part of the action. By 2001, however, IPO listings were down to just 76. The dot-com bubble had burst.

On 10 March 2000 the NASDAQ listings for leading technology companies spiked – it hit its peak, then fell dramatically. A pending court case surrounding Microsoft's alleged monopoly in the software industry is thought to have contributed to the crash. Overheated spending to ensure systems would continue to function in the new millennium – Y2K compliance – may also have contributed to the fall. Whatever the reasons, the market had risen a massive 24% in 1999 but on 10 March 2000 it dropped 10% in 6 days. Ouch.

By 2001 most of the dot-coms had gone. They had burnt their initial venture funding secured at the height of the market but didn't subsequently deliver any profit. In a deflated 'bear' market they failed to secure further funding. The technology companies that remained struggled to find investment, or indeed customers, with any appetite to support their businesses. My client was one such company.

My marketing agency business at the time was fully exposed to the technology markets. A snapshot of my business in 1999 would show record revenues and profits derived primarily from the technology sector. A typical client would be an American software company under pressure from investors to expand from the UK into Europe – in other words, dot.coms. The technology sector represented about 85–90% of my business. As the market grew, so did my expertise and reputation in this field and the business opportunities also grew.

This represented a significant opportunity for me – the client had a good software product, it was growing exponentially and required all of the marketing services I could provide. We discussed the resourcing of such an opportunity and agreed an 18-month retained contract whereby I would be paid a sickeningly large amount of cash for as little work as possible and could plan my retirement in the Bahamas thereafter. I don't mind admitting, I was pretty pleased. The contract was signed on 10 September 2001 amid much drinking, horn blowing and even hugging. All I had to do at that stage, was wait for the cash to roll in.

On the 11th of September, perhaps now better known as '9/11' The International Trade Centre Twin Towers were attacked by terrorists and collapsed. Whatever other ailments the technology market may have been dealing with, 9/11 was the landmark date for me. The towers came down, the lights went out and America metaphorically switched off the power. Everything stopped.

On the 12th September I received a phone call from the Marketing Director. The company had, that day, cut the majority of its staff in the UK and would no longer be able to meet the terms of the contract we had signed only 2 days previously. "Funding has been cut." I spluttered for a while, naturally, but it was clear that after a difficult trading environment for the previous two years, this was the final straw. Overnight the company was forced to change from global expansion to fighting for survival – the call to me was simply passing the news down the supply chain. There was no point in arguing, so I tore up the contract and wished my client the very best of luck.

In the course of the next two weeks, I lost almost every client I had for broadly the same reasons. Budgets were cut, staff made redundant, my clients were out of work. The effects of the dot com crash and the Twin Towers disaster would affect millions of people. Every business across every part of the supply chain (including the company with the software to manage it) was affected.

It was another five years before the Marketing Director was in a position to come back to me – but to his credit, he did. The company weathered the storm, dug its heels in, restructured and rebuilt its business. The return match was never as glamorous as the original opportunity. The requirement was reduced, the budgets were smaller and perhaps most disappointingly, the expectation and belief in the potential was significantly reduced. This malaise was prevalent throughout the IT supply chain – from original equipment manufacturers (OEMs) through the channel partners, the distributors and the solutions providers – the entire value chain hurt. Including me.

Nevertheless, the brand was restructured, a Creative Platform® was built and some tactical campaigns were delivered. The work was 'OK', but never really had the full commitment of the organisation to deliver on the promise. The company was growing again, but, even five years on, business nerves were still raw. Progressive steps throughout the supply chain were small and tentative – I've seen the same market reservations towards marketing activity in the recessionary years following the collapse of the Lehman Brothers bank in 2008. In the words of the R.E.M. song, 'Everybody Hurts'.

Ultimately the company was sold to (ironically) a larger American software company for many millions of dollars – but it was now almost 10 years behind the original management exit strategy, a delay attributed by the management to the rebuilding of market confidence generally and, specifically, rebuilding the supply chain. In B2B marketing the focus of activity is perpetually placed on the next scheduled campaign 'event' – lead generation, awareness building, customer satisfaction. In my experience, however, the events are all interrelated throughout the business and throughout the supply chain. Instead of looking simply at the next event, we would all do far better to consider the 'chain of events'.

Scot McKee

Introduction

Two important concepts underpin ideas relating to marketing channels. The first of these is the dichotomy between the freedom organisations seek to operate autonomously and the necessity to cooperate and combine their resources in order to work with other organisations. The need to balance the drive for independence and the need to be interdependent can often be a point of tension for organisations. Decisions regarding the selection and deselection of channel partners, the degree to which organisations can or should use direct marketing and decisions to enter into alliances, undertake new roles in established channels or to develop new channels all require judgement about the appropriate balance of interdependence.

Following a decision to be interdependent and to work with other organisations, the second underpinning concept concerns the degree to which an organisation should cooperate and coordinate activities with other organisations. At one end of a coordination spectrum, cooperation may be casual, cursory and perfunctory. At the other end, cooperation may be intense, involved and fully supportive of the other channel participants. In other words, the level of cooperation is partly a function of the type of relationship that exists in the channel. At one end there are purely market exchanges and at the other purely collaborative exchanges. Most organisations adopt a position between these two extremes.

Supply Chains

The majority of organisations have little choice but to cooperate with other organisations. Through cooperation, organisations link themselves to other organisations that have the necessary specialist skills, resources and core competences. These linkages are an external representation of the (internal) value chains that organisations use to enhance the products and services with which they are involved. Current thinking emphasises the need to integrate internal and external functions across the supply chain as there appears to be a strong link between integration and performance (Martin and Patterson, 2009).

Xinyan et al. (2010) acknowledge that the coordination among the various members of the supply chain is important and that sellers demonstrating high degrees of flexibility prefer to establish more cooperative relationships with a buyer. Indeed, they found that a supply chain system becomes more effective when there is a high level of supply chain integration among the members. In other words, it is highly probable that supply chain integration can lead to higher forms of cooperation, which can lead to higher performance outcomes.

In addition to the added value concept associated with marketing channels, there are activities associated with the management of the physical flow, namely the movement of parts, supplies and finished products, from the very first supplier in the chain to the end-user customer. These linkages are referred to as supply chains and current terminology refers to this concept as supply chain management (SCM).

Although there are many subtle differences in terminology, SCM is a more contemporary term for logistics and before that, physical distribution. Melnyk et al. (2009) agree that definitions and interpretations vary widely, with some arguing that the supply chain starts with the suppliers of raw materials (New and Payne, 1995) and others arguing that it only deals with finished goods (Christopher et al., 1998). It is interesting to note that Melnyk et al. (2009) consider SCM to be subject to severe change, that it incorporates upstream and downstream activities, and that now behavioural issues and relationships between parties in the supply chain have now become incorporated under this banner. This suggests some similarity with the behavioural and management issues considered in the marketing channels literature.

The approach adopted here is that SCM is concerned with the whole value creation chain of physical distribution activities. These start with the suppliers of the basic raw materials and parts of a product, continue through the assembly and manufacturing stages, and distribution to the eventual consumption by the end-user customer.

■ Key elements in Supply Chain Management

Integrated SCM is concerned with the business processes associated with the efficient movement of parts, raw materials, work in progress and finished goods. The goal of SCM is to improve efficiency and effectiveness with regard to the physical movement of products. In contrast to marketing channels, which are concerned with the management of customer behaviour, finished goods and the added value that interorganisational relationships can bring, SCM is essentially about the management of all the business activities necessary to get the right product, in the right place, for the right customer to access in a timely and convenient way.

To achieve this integration, all participants in a supply chain need to reconstruct their internal functional activities so that they can coordinate events and share information with their partner organisations. Change processes are an increasingly important element within the supply chain management, especially at the interface with other functions internally and with other external parties. As van Hoek *et al.* (2010) argue, managing these changes is vital if organisations are to survive.

The detailed nature of these events will be examined shortly, but it is worth establishing the overall tasks that SCM needs to accomplish. Brewer and Speh (2000) argue that SCM seeks to achieve four main goals. These are waste reduction, time compression, flexible response and unit cost reduction. These are explained in Table 7.1.

Table 7.1: SCM goals

Goal	Explanation
Waste reduction	By reducing the level of duplicated and excess stock in the chain, it becomes possible to harmonise operations between organisations to achieve new levels of uniformity and standardisation.
Time compression	Reducing the order-to-delivery cycle time improves efficiency and customer service outputs. A faster cycle indicates a smoother and more efficient operation and associated processes. Faster times mean less stock, faster cash flow and higher levels of service output.
Flexible response	By managing the order processing elements (size, time, configuration, handling) specific customer requirements can be met without causing them inconvenience and contributes to efficiency and service delivery.
Unit cost reduction	By understanding the level of service output that is required by the end-user customers it then becomes possible to minimise the costs involved in delivering to that required standard.

Source: Based on Brewer and Speh (2000).

Supply Chains, Channel Structures and Networks

7

By achieving these four goals the efficiency of a supply chain is improved and, as a result, end-user customers experience increased levels of service output.

For the purposes of this text, the primary element of SCM is regarded as logistics. The foundation stones of logistics are the activities necessary to move products through to end users and to do so in such a way that the four efficiency goals are met. By concentrating on particular supply chain activities, organisations are better placed to achieve the efficiency goals. These activities are: stock management, warehousing, fulfilment and transportation, and presented at Figure 7.1.

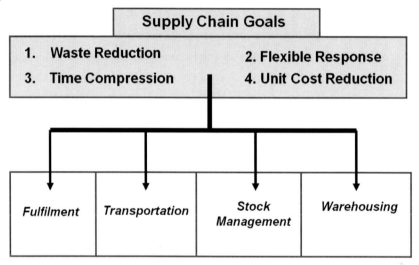

Figure 7.1: Key supply chain activities

Stock Management

Stock management is crucial to all organisations involved in the production and distribution of finished and unfinished products. The management of stock embraces storage and warehousing issues and this includes related matters of stock quality, security, insurance and value. This last item has important implications for the channel members. The value of finished stock represents on the one hand an opportunity to provide higher levels of service output but on the other a high financial inventory or working capital cost which is reflected in the profit and loss account. One important question, therefore, is how much stock should an intermediary hold?

Finished goods cost more than unfinished goods to hold in stock. If demand allows, manufacturers prefer to withhold production until the very last moment or pass finished goods to intermediaries. This could be seen as simply a matter of transferring costs to other parts of the supply chain, but this would not reflect a strong relationship in which members seek to support each other.

Two interesting theories associated with the transfer of stock and associated service outputs are postponement and speculation. Postponement is about delaying the point at which products become finished goods. So, the greater the period of time that products can remain undifferentiated and postponed within the marketing channel, the lower will be the associated costs.

Speculation is concerned with the anticipation of desired service outputs, that customers want products now and are not prepared to wait. This means creating finished goods at the earliest opportunity. Through this approach costs can be reduced through long production runs. By reducing the number of stock outs, the costs associated with customer dissatisfaction can be reduced together with the frequency with which orders are placed by intermediaries. Postponement is about having more work in progress and speculation is about more finished goods in the channel.

Paint manufacturers are happy to supply end-user customers with the popular colours of paint in huge quantities and in a variety of sized containers. But, because it is not economic to produce and to shelf-stock paint that has limited appeal, retailers will make up cans of these tones and shades, on-site and on-demand in front of the end-user customer. This is achieved using bulk quantities of specific base paints mixed to manufacturers' specifications. In this way it is possible to meet the specific requirements of customers, in-store and in this case with limited waiting time. Therefore, paint manufacturers practise both speculation, with regard to the popular colours, and postponement, with regard to the less popular tints and shades.

Warehousing

Finished and unfinished products should spend as little time waiting to be used or consumed as is possible. This waiting time is referred to as storage and in many cases storage is undertaken in warehouses.

The location of warehouses is an important strategic aspect of logistics. Indeed, the location, size, design and operating systems used in warehouses can have a considerable impact on the level of service outputs experienced by subsequent members of the supply chain. The number and location of warehouses is a function of many variables but one of these concerns the structure of the marketing channel. In channels where producers use distributors, a lower number of warehouses will be necessary as distributors take ownership and physical possession of stock. In channels where agents and manufacturers' representatives are preferred, a higher number of warehouses are required because these intermediaries do not take ownership or physical possession.

Some companies outsource their storage and warehousing activities with the benefit of lower fixed costs and improved flexibility with regard to transportation and associated activities. For example, in October 2010 the International Warehouse Logistics Association website referred to over 500 members, who offer third-party logistics and warehousing service. For more information see www.iwla.com. and www.warehouselogistics.org.

Distribution centres have developed as a complement to warehouses. The main difference between the two is that warehouses are used to store goods on a long-term basis while distribution centres hold minimal quantities for a short period of time. Distribution centres are often located near to customers (retail outlets) in order that they are better positioned to deliver low numbers of units at a high frequency.

■ Fulfilment

Once orders are received and flow upstream, it becomes necessary to pick and pack stock to make up orders. The contemporary terminology is fulfilment or materials handling and it is about locating and picking stock, packing and securing it before shipping the selected items or bundle to the next channel member.

This part of the logistics system can be critical to the overall efficiency of a supply chain. Very often specialist equipment and software systems are required to ensure that intra-warehouse stock movement is minimised while inter-warehouse movement is optimised.

For example, the Wine Society uses Maginus software to improve customer service across all channels. Part of this includes warehousing and the picking of over 1,000 products, which are sold in full or mixed cases or by the bottle. This is part of an integrated eCommerce system. See Viewpoint 7.1 for more information about the Wine Society.

The ability to fulfil an order quickly and accurately, can provide a point of differentiation for a marketing channel. Cross-docking represents an attempt at minimising fulfilment costs and time. Under this approach, instead of receiving, storing, picking, packing and despatching items for an order, supplies are received already packaged so that they are received at one door of a warehouse and are then sent out immediately from another despatch bay.

■ Transportation

Transportation is about routing and delivering selected items which are bundled as an order. Transportation is expensive so pick up and delivery points become an important part of analysis within the management of logistics. Location is important because of the need to reduce costs and yet provide members with a high frequency of low-unit-size deliveries.

Transportation involves documentation and, when goods are shipped, freight forwarders provide services such as the preparation of all necessary documentation for import/export or for meeting other transportation requirements such as safety, when moving hazardous materials.

Transportation becomes an important factor in redirecting materials and part finished goods. Through alliances and what is known as third-party logistics providers (3PL) organisations join together to provide new forms of service outputs for producers. These new members of the supply chain are referred to as contract logistics providers. They represent combinations of members from within the logistics system, such as the pairing of freight forwarders and transportation agencies, or fulfilment and transportation specialists.

ViewPoint 7.1: Getting the wine delivered as promised

The Wine Society is a co-operative organisation, specialising in supplying fine wines to its 90,000 members and turning over approximately £50 million. When the society was established in 1874, its constitution specified that service, product quality and value for money were to be its core values.

Orders can be placed by phone, web, fax, post, e-mail and physically through the shop. There are 30 telesales staff, a figure which doubles at Christmas when up to 40% of the annual turnover is handled in two months.

The Maginus Commerce Software uses a central database to control the management of all the orders, and their fulfilment, regardless of the sales channel. From a customer service perspective this gives The Wine Society a single point of maintenance for all product, pricing and other business information.

The Maginus system needs to manage different types of order, as there are over 1000 products in the main catalogue. Wine can be purchased in full or mixed cases, or even by the bottle. Staff have access to substantial amounts of product data on the system, in order to answer member queries and questions.

In addition to routine orders, the e-commerce system needs to manage promotions, themed offers, subscription schemes, *en primeur* sales, where wine is offered for sale before its been bottled, and customer reserves.

The warehouse is temperature controlled at 13° C and contains approximately 2 million bottles. Research amongst members has shown that accuracy of order is more important than speed of delivery. To ensure the accuracy of picking whilst maintaining efficiency within the warehouse, the Wine Society have a number of picking areas – fast moving goods, slow moving goods and an assembly area for customer mixed cases – the goods are then moved to a marshalling area and collated by van route. Approximately two-thirds of orders are delivered by their own vans, the rest by external carrier. Maginus controls this entire process, including revising product status to ensure, for example, that goods coming onto promotion are moved into the fast moving area.

The Wine Society claim that following the installation of the Maginus system they have been able to shorten their average delivery promise by 50%.

Source: www.maginus.com/results/case-study/the-wine-society/

Question: Think of other categories where fulfilment is critical.

■ Principles of Supply Chain Management

Having considered the foundation stones associated with logistics management it should be apparent that a primary goal within the supply chain is to move products towards end-user customers as quickly and efficiently as possible. An adequate supply of products in marketing channels is the basis for delivering acceptable service output levels. The faster and more cost-effectively a supply chain can move materials and products, the greater the potential competitive advantage.

With ever-shortening life cycles, much reduced manufacturing costs, increases in competition and better educated, more aware and demanding customers, many organisations have been forced to move from physical logistics management towards the more integrated and software-based solutions offered by supply chain management providers. Through the use of information and communications technologies such as databases, communication systems and advanced computer software, it is possible to develop cost-effective supply chain management.

Electronic data interchange (EDI) provides an important facility for sharing information between partnering organisations. EDI is the electronic transfer, using agreed standards, of structured data from one organisation's computers to another. Through EDI, organisations can integrate much of their logistics and improve efficiency and customer service. WebEDI allows companies of all sizes to interact using just a web browser, and without implementing a complex EDI infrastructure.

As stated earlier, SCM is about being faster and more efficient in providing end-user customers with the products they need. There are many ways of achieving these goals but two are very important: quick response and efficient customer response systems. Both of these approaches are founded on the same pull-based, that is to say customer driven, principles. The customers inform the supply chain about what assortment to make, what to despatch and where and when it should arrive.

■ *Quick response* (QR) systems are designed to enable manufacturers to adapt to unpredictable and volatile demand, such as that experienced in the fashion clothing industry. When consumers shop for clothes they do not know in advance what they want, what they will like and whether the size and cut will be appropriate. Their decisions are usually made at the point of purchase, that is, in the store. Benetton, an early pioneer of QR systems, were often faced with large stocks of unsold (and hence unfashionable) stock. They developed a system that enabled retailers to feed back early customer preferences based on limited amounts of demonstration stock. Only once this feedback was received did Benetton dye its wool and then produce, often through an outsourced production team, the large quantities of clothing ranges that retailers and customers preferred. This process was accomplished in a very short period and stock was delivered within a few weeks to their retail partners, at any location in the world. Benetton now use POS (point of sale) technology to inform about preferred colours and sizes but the principle to develop flexible and responsive manufacturing facilities is the hallmark of QR approaches.

- *Efficient consumer response* (ECR) systems are based on the same ideas. The concept emerged within the FMCG sector and seeks to reduce waste by predicting demand accurately, based on the premise that consumers know what they want to buy, ahead of the purchase occasion. Therefore, the decision is not about what to make, it is about how many to make and when to make them available. Storage of these items is possible, subject to perishability issues, as, unlike fashion items, they do not have a limited life or very brief fad cycles. The emphasis with ECR therefore, is not on manufacturing but on distribution and marketing communications, especially sales promotions to stimulate demand in the short term.

One particular form of ECR is continuous replenishment programmes (CRP). These operate on the basis that when a sale is made to a consumer, the stock is automatically replaced. Through use of POS equipment and scanners, retail stock is maintained at predetermined optimum levels. The principle is that CRP reduces the opportunity for stock-outs which can lead to lengthy waiting times, a fall in service output levels and consumer inconvenience. Indeed, Zhao *et al*. (2002) report work by Lee *et al*. (1997) which found that both producers and retailers can benefit through sharing information with CRP. Retailers also benefit as CRP systems are run and maintained by other intermediaries. There is little to suggest that manufacturers who operate CRP earn any more from the system than they might normally. However, as Vergin and Barr (1999) suggest, CRP might lock retailers into particular manufacturers and in doing so act as an exit barrier.

In B2B markets, just-in-time systems seek to achieve the same type of goals as CRP. Here suppliers dovetail their deliveries to the manufacturer's production schedule, and in doing so eliminate waste and reduce storage costs. As a result, the number of deliveries increases, the number of units delivered decreases and the pressure on logistics increases to maintain the cycle. Trust, commitment and an integration of software systems, or EDI, becomes necessary to enable the system to operate smoothly.

Both ECR and QR offer advantages and disadvantages. They impact on relationships and channel structures. For example, the pressure on members in QR situations can be intense and discourage the development of trust, while the variability in demand might reflect on commitment. In these situations, some manufacturers prefer to use vertical integration as a means of controlling the retail function in markets where QR predominates. By owning the retailing part of the operation it is possible to generate fast feedback about changing demand.

In addition, vertical integration to control the design function is critical to manufacturing and associated activities. Benetton never lost control over the design process and for a long time was managed directly by one of the Benetton family. Although the retail operation is largely a franchise arrangement, Benetton own a few outlets in most countries, simply to be close to the market and be able to feed back quickly any changes in consumer preferences.

In comparison, ECR approaches focus on the need for all channel participants to work and trust each other. There should be a high propensity to share information among the members and the channel structure can be more flexible and open, as long as the logistics are operated tightly.

Logistics can influence marketing decisions and reduce channel costs. The challenge for supply chain managers is to make decisions that are primarily founded on end-user demand, rather than cost reduction.

■ Marketing Channel Design

The second part of this chapter is concerned with the management of the marketing channel and associated structural decisions. These will vary with context as channels for a new product or organisation start up, will be different to the more common issue of modifying an existing structure in order to adapt to changing market conditions. Assuming a decision has been made previously to use an indirect channel, the channel design decision process requires consideration of three main factors.

1 The level of purchase convenience required by the different end-user customer segments to be served, the distribution intensity decision.

2 The number and types of intermediaries necessary to deliver products to the sales outlets, the channel configuration decision.

3 The number of different types of channels to be used, the multichannel decision.

■ Distribution Intensity

Sometimes termed *coverage*, distribution intensity refers to the number of outlets from which an end-user customer can buy a particular product. This decision, therefore, is concerned with the degree of convenience customers expect and suppliers need to provide to be competitive. One of the major implications of this is that the wider the coverage the greater the number of intermediaries and this impacts on cost, management control of the intermediaries and the consequent perceived level of service outputs. There are three levels of distribution intensity: intense, selective and exclusive.

Intense Distribution

Consumers expect some products to be available from a variety of different outlets. These products often carry little perceived risk, are capable of easy and quick substitution and require little thought or time to purchase. For example, products such chewing gum, newspapers, breakfast cereals and chocolate bars are readily available from a variety of stores. These may be supermarkets, CTNs (confectioners, tobacconists and newsagents), vending machines and convenience stores. The wide availability of the product through a large number of outlets, promotes the opportunity for high-volume sales.

Selective Distribution

By placing the offering in a limited number of outlets, a more favourable image can be generated and the producer can determine which intermediaries would be best suited to deliver the required service outputs. Customers are more involved with the purchase, and the level of perceived risk is correspondingly higher. As a result, buyers are prepared to seek out appropriate suppliers, and those that best match the overall requirements of the customer will be successful. Televisions, hi-fi equipment and clothing are suitable examples of this form of distribution.

Exclusive Distribution

Some customers may perceive a product to be of such high prestige or to be positioned so far away from the competition that just a single outlet in a particular trading area would be sufficient to meet the needs of the channel.

There is little need to make these products available from a number of different stores. Products such as cars are bought infrequently and are expected to be the subject of considerable search and consideration. For example, Mazda cars are normally only available from a single outlet in any one area. If the offering requires complex servicing arrangements or tight control then the exclusive form of distribution may be best, as it fosters closer relationships. A further reason not to make a product widely available would be the threat of price competition, which would be inconsistent with the positioning strategy these products would normally adopt.

■ Channel Configuration

Having decided about the number and types of outlets that end-user customers require to access products, the next question is about the number and types of intermediaries necessary to maintain adequate stock and levels of service in the channel. Resolving this concerns both the length and breadth of the channel, essentially the number and types of intermediaries to be involved.

Length is about the number of channel levels necessary to optimise the overall service outputs. In many industries this is determined by custom and practice, where there is an established approach to using particular types of intermediary. In other industries there is scope for flexibility and development. The more challenging decision concerns not the type (and hence length) of the channel but the numbers of each type of intermediary to be used. This horizontal or breadth dimension reflects the desired intensity at each level.

The issues of intensive, selective and exclusive distribution, mentioned earlier with regard to sales outlets, apply equally to each of the other levels in a marketing channel. However, there are certain other matters concerning the intensity of channel members at different levels.

Multiple Channels

Today it is quite common for manufacturers to use a number of marketing channels in order to reach different target markets. This is referred to as dual distribution or multichannel marketing and was introduced in the previous chapter. This can of course be the cause of some tension between channel partners but recognition of the different levels of service output required by different segments leads to the creation of multiple channels. Many FMCG brands use supermarkets, convenience stores, vending machines and distress purchase[1] outlets to distribute their products in order to maximise their distribution and optimise their sales and profits opportunities.

Decisions about channel structure and design involve all three of these elements, namely, what level of intensity is appropriate, how long channels should be and how many channels should be used in order to provide the right level of service outputs expected by end-user customers.

Generally speaking the greater the intensity of distribution desired by manufacturers (of retailers and distributors) the greater the number of intermediaries required to service them. The greater the number of intermediaries the lower influence a manufacturer has over them. This then poses an interesting problem for manufacturers. On the one hand, greater channel intensity leads to higher rewards but on the other hand, it reduces the level of influence that they have over their channel partners and it raises costs.

Retailers and distributors also face a dilemma because they want, or prefer to have, exclusivity. They want to distribute the leading brands but on the basis that they are the only stockists in a particular geographical area. This gives customers a reason to shop, or be drawn into a store. However, as the number of outlets that a brand is available from increases, so the exclusivity and reasons to shop at a particular store decreases. As markets become saturated or shop sales decrease, pressure is applied upstream in terms of lower wholesale prices in order to drive

---

1 A 'distress purchase' is made by people when they have little choice in the decision about where and when to make the purchase. Many pharmacy products are distress purchases because of pain or sickness – and the immediate need to get relief. Further examples are funerals, petrol and, often, corner shops for immediate food supplies such as a loaf of bread or pint of milk.

higher margins. Stores (and distributors) then drive end-user customers to products and brands where there is a higher margin.

This signals an important issue for manufacturers when selecting new members or when reconfiguring marketing channels. First and foremost, channel decisions should be based on a channel's perspective and what is in the best interests of channel partners. Adopting this principle helps avoid dysfunctional conflict (see Chapter 8) and sub-optimal channel performance.

■ Channel Structure

So far marketing channels have been considered in terms of different types of intermediaries who are brought together because of a shared need to cooperate and combine resources. However, the assumption that these organisations remain independent is not necessarily correct. The structure of marketing channels reflects other factors, of which the desire to control or influence other organisations is particularly strong.

While the design of a channel should be based on end-user customer requirements, the structural pattern that any channel assumes is partly a result of the relationships between the individual organisations that compose the channel. Channels are dynamic, so the structure should be flexible in order that it can respond to a changing environment.

There is, of course, no single optimal channel structure and the design varies according to the manufacturers' perception of the needs of the markets they serve. However, it is useful to look at some of the more common approaches ranging from those where there is little overt influence over the performance of others by a single channel member to those where there is total control and direction of channel activities.

■ A Spectrum of Influence in Channel Structures

Traditionally, organisations group together, to reduce uncertainty. Through cooperation each is in a better position to achieve its objectives. By working together members can concentrate upon those activities that they do best. This may be retailing or manufacturing, but, whatever it is, the objectives of each organisation are best served by allowing others to perform alternative, specialist functions for them. This principle underpins the growth in outsourcing experienced in recent years. The degree of influence that one organisation has over another varies considerably. In Figure 7.2 the spectrum of influence is represented in terms of the different channel structures that have emerged.

Opportunity networks

At one end of the spectrum are opportunity networks (Achrol, 1997). These are loose alliances of independent organisations that often come together to provide a one-off solution for a customer. Once the task is completed, the alliance might disband. The network is based on interorganisational relationships that promote close cooperation and win–win situations for all involved. They work together as a response to fast-changing market conditions. No one organisation is dominant or able to assert undue influence on others. Opportunity networks are a recent development and are a response to turbulent and unpredictable market conditions. Network configuration is discussed in greater depth later in this chapter.

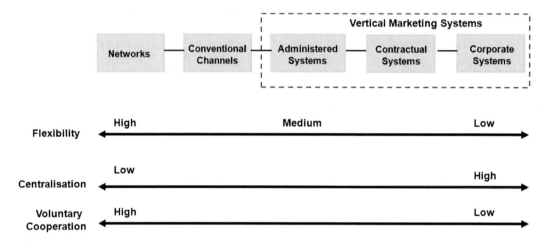

Figure 7.2: A spectrum of marketing channel structures

Conventional Channels

These channels are characterised by the temporary, often loosely aligned, partnerships with a range of organisations. Organisations in this alignment retain their independence and autonomy. Bipolar relationships typify these structures, as decisions are often self-orientated and reflect the needs of just the two members.

As a consequence of this self-interest, the level of influence that any member has over the others in the channel is minimal, except where access to an important raw material or product can be affected. This framework allows offerings to move through the entire system or through parts of it. There is no single controlling organisation and the framework is viewed as a set of independent organisations working in free association with one another. Market coverage is free of any overt influence.

Attempts to secure coverage usually result in a loss of control in the marketing channel. Furthermore, the level of loyalty is low, which is indicative of the instability that exists in these configurations as organisations are able to enter and exit with relative freedom.

ViewPoint 7.2: Volvo Trucks use conventional channels

The Volvo Truck Corporation is the second largest manufacturer of heavy duty trucks in the world. Products also include buses and coaches. Their vehicles are sold and serviced in over 140 countries across the globe. Group headquarters are in Gothenburg, Sweden. Manufacturing is undertaken at eight wholly-owned facilities and nine factories which are owned by local interests. These operations are spread around Sweden, Belgium, Brazil and the USA. Sales of vehicles to large fleets, international groups and governments are managed by centralised sales operations.

Other sales and service is provided via a network of over 2300 dealerships and workshops. These are mainly based around a franchised network. Franchises are independently owned businesses but operate exclusively under the Volvo brand umbrella. Many of these consist of regionally dispersed groups covering specific geographic territories.

In addition to sales and service facilities, these dealerships offer a range of support service activities including vehicle breakdown recovery, trailer maintenance, truck rental, sales of parts, and tyre services. The largest companies in the distribution channel cover the whole of the Volvo product portfolio of trucks, buses and coaches.

This approach to distribution is typical of the commercial vehicle industry as a whole.

Source: Based on Keynote (2009); www.volvotrucks.com

Question: Are there any alternatives for a company such as Volvo Trucks to distribute their products?

■ Vertical Marketing Systems

The following three types of channel structure are characterised by the influence that one organisation is able to exert over other organisations in the channel. These are known as vertical marketing systems (VMS) and the three forms are administered, contractual and corporate. These are explained in Table 7.2.

Table 7.2: Three forms of vertical marketing system

Form of VMS	Explanation
Administered	A loose alignment of organisations who voluntarily choose to work together. One organisation assumes responsibility for the channel activities, the channel leader or captain. High risk and high levels of flexibility.
Contractual	A contract is used to specify roles, expectations and responsibilities. The organisation issuing the contract largely determines the trading strategies and formats. Medium risk and flexibility.
Corporate	One organisation owns and hence influences all the other organisations in the channel. Risk is low and so is flexibility.

VMSs attempt to trade off distribution intensity against the lack of influence or control – more control means less coverage. They have evolved since the mid-1970s and consist of vertically aligned and coordinated sets of marketing partners. They function as a system, centrally driven by an organisation that is able to assert itself through a collaborative partnership in an attempt to satisfy end-user customer needs.

The tighter cooperation and interdependence of members is formally recognised and a planned approach ensures that a greater degree of stability is achieved. The entry and exit of partners to the system is controlled to meet the needs of the channel and not any one member. The coupling between members is tight and the level of connectedness is similarly strong.

Administered systems

Administered systems are similar to conventional channels in that members work together and are tied by the attraction of potential rewards. The main difference between the two is that with administered systems one organisation is able to exert influence over others. These organisations have influence due to their size and power which might, for example, be developed through their access to particular resources, size of market share, breadth and depth of product range, research and development skills or corporate reputation. These organisations are sometimes referred to as the channel leader or channel captain.

Organisations work together to fulfil strategies developed by a limited number of channel partners. These strategies are administered through informal 'voluntary' collaborative agreements, led by the channel leader. It is important to recognise that members of this system retain their own authority and that each member's commitment to the system is largely motivated by self-interest.

Contractual Systems

When voluntary agreements fail to produce the required level of channel performance, channel members develop a more formal arrangement. This is rooted within a contract, which brings legally binding terms and conditions to the roles and expectations of all involved in the channel system. These contractual partnerships consist of a written agreement between a dominant member and the other members of the channel, setting out members' rights and obligations. There are three kinds of contractual arrangement.

- *Wholesaler-sponsored chains*. These consist of independent retailers who, under the organisation of a wholesaler, agree to work together to obtain discounts and other advantages in purchasing, distribution and promotion, in order to compete against large chain organisations, for example, Mace.

- *Retailer-sponsored chains*. Similar to the wholesaler chains, independent retailers join together to jointly own the wholesale operation. The sponsored chain approach allows small and medium-sized organisations to compete against the purchasing power of many retail and wholesale multiples. Spar and VG are examples of retailer cooperatives.

- *Franchise*. There are three forms of franchise:
  1 Manufacturer-sponsored retailer systems, for example, Ford.
  2 Manufacturer-sponsored wholesaler systems, for example, Coca-Cola.
  3 Service-sponsored retailer systems, for example, McDonald's.

Franchise arrangements are a fast-growing form of retailing. Under franchise arrangements the right to distribute a particular product or service is agreed between two parties. There are two main approaches to franchising. The first is a product franchise, where the channel's dominant organisation authorises particular organisations to distribute their offering. In other words, organisations are selected into a channel and each is permitted to use the trade name and promotional materials (which are deemed to be of value to the customer) of the dominant organisation. Various German kitchen appliance and furniture manufacturers use this form of authorisation to allow particular UK retailers (independent kitchen design-and-fit organisations) to distribute their offerings. The second form of franchise can be referred to as a business franchise. Under this format not only is the product permitted to be used by the franchisee but the whole trading approach must be utilised. McDonald's restaurants are an example of the latter, with franchisees having to adopt the entire established trading style.

Corporate Systems

A corporate vertical marketing system (CVMS) is a discrete grouping of organisations that are owned, and hence controlled, by one dominant member. This structural arrangement provides for the greatest influence in comparison to the previous two forms of VMS. These structures often emerge when there are few alternatives. Uncertainty is reduced to a minimum and the influence of the dominant organisation is maximised, often in an attempt to achieve economies of scale.

Corporate systems are achieved through either backward or forward vertical integration. Organisations can choose to integrate upstream (backward) to control their sources of supply (their inputs), or they can move downstream (forward) and seek to control the distribution of their offerings, or both. However, the inherent lack of flexibility associated with corporate systems has led many organisations to move away from this structure.

Traditionally, breweries owned not only the brewing and production facilities, but also the public houses and restaurants and hotels through which beer was distributed.

■ Networks

Much of this chapter depicts marketing channel structures as a vertical alignment of organisations, one which is linear and essentially bipolar. That is, interorganisational relationships are regarded as one-to-one or dyadic in nature, as if to exclude the impact and influence that other organisations bring to a relationship. One of the difficulties of this approach is that organisations are viewed out of the true context in which they operate. It is better to consider the whole system of affiliations, because the relationship of any two organisations is contingent upon the direct and indirect relationships of all the organisations (Andersson, 1992). A network of relationships therefore provides the context within which exchange behaviour occurs.

Organisations are embedded not just in a set of exclusive buyer–seller relationships, but in a variety of associations with different organisations. These can be intertwined, resulting in various networks of relationships. Each organisation (and individual) is a member of a rich mosaic of networks, embedded in them to different degrees depending upon levels of dependence and of access to the resources of other members (Halinen and Törnroos, 1998). There appears to be growing recognition that networks of interacting organisations are a more satisfactory interpretation of management practice than the relatively rigid distribution channels approach so widely accepted in the 1970s and 1980s.

Networks hold together partly through 'an elaborate pattern of interdependence and reciprocity' (Achrol, 1997: 59). The position an organisation occupies in a network is important. It is determined by the functions performed, their importance, the strength of relationships with other organisations and the identity of the organisations with which there are direct and indirect relationships (Mattsson, 1989). The position of an organisation, and the degree to which it is connected to others, partly determines the extent to which it can mobilise resources and achieve designated goals. As Achrol states, the strength and duration of a relationship is partly dependent upon 'the network of relationships that collectively define and administer the norms by which dyadic relationships are conducted'. He goes on to quote Macneil (1978: 57) who suggested that the more relational an exchange becomes the more it takes on the properties of 'a minisociety with a vast array of norms beyond those centered on the exchange and its immediate processes'. Network approaches provide a dynamic interpretation of the relationships that organisations have with one another.

The ability of an organisation to manage the networks in which it operates has been termed 'network competence' (Ritter and Gemünden, 2003). They distinguish between the skills and competences necessary to manage single dyadic relationships and those that are necessary to manage a portfolio or network of relationships. Although their research is embryonic (at the time of writing) they conclude that there appears to be a strong link between an organisation's network competence and the degree to which its technology and systems are involved (interwoven) with other interdependent organisations. They go further to claim that there is a significant link between this type of competence and new product development and innovation success.

Value Networks

Particular forms of marketing channels and business strategies are emerging based on the principles of voluntary, flexible, cooperative relationships in which members share specific core competences. Businesses are shedding their involvement in activities that are no longer regarded as core. So, activities such as order processing, finance, IT, manufacturing and logistics are being outsourced to trading partners who have the necessary core competences. These activities are processed by many different organisations as if they were one organisation. Thus, value networks can be regarded as virtual organisations, comprising constellations of networked companies.

Value networks are characterised by the collaborative, and often relatively temporary, structures that are assembled by organisations, each with specialist skills. The extent to which a network is capable of creating superior value is largely determined by the core capabilities and competences of the members (Kothandaraman and Wilson, 2001). The nature of the organisational relationships in a network shapes its value. The network forms in response to a customer's problem or market opportunity. Once the solution to the problem is identified and implemented the network might, but not necessarily, disband. Some members remain within these networks because they have a common and consistent role to play. However, some members might have only a temporary role, dependent upon the nature of their core capability. It is the flexibility and close relationships between members that separate networks from all other channel structures.

Based largely on Porter's (1985) value chain ideas, previously channel structures were seen to consist of individual organisations who are each regarded as individual value creators. In the network interpretation, value is vested in the collaborative group of organisations, the network itself. Reference has already been made to this idea in terms of an industry value chain. However, one of the major differences concerns the nature and duration of the structure. In industry value chains, the participants are invariably the same and work together over the long term. In value networks (VNs) membership can vary according to the task, and membership requires deep levels of integration, co-ordination and connectedness. A distinguishing characteristic of value networks is the level of electronic integration between partners. Just as individual value chains can be linked up so can value networks, into what IBM refer to as ecosystems. Whereas value networks deliver component solutions for end-user customers, ecosystems consist of networks of collaborating, system-to-system connected organisations, all geared to deliver total solutions for end-user customers.

ViewPoint 7.3: Business ecologies bring IBM partners together

In 2009, the Object Management Group (ONG) set up the Business Ecology Initiative (BEI) with IBM as the founding sponsor. The BEI is a non-profit member-led organisation which promotes 'effective, adaptive, sustainable and secure practices within organisations and among them'.

The adoption of a business ecology requires the formation of cross-functional teams consisting of both business and IT professionals, from a range of organisations, and not just on the supply side. Processes revolve around the use of technology to lead business change. The BEI publishes white papers and press releases, holds an annual case study awards programme and industry conferences.

Communities of Practice (CoPs) are made up of practitioners, service providers and technology companies, and are used to promote business value and business technology strategies to large corporations, government bodies and other businesses. Other CoPs are active in the areas of cyber security, event processing and resource sustainability.

IBM view the Business Ecology Initiative as a support for their drive for improved business/IT alignment, which they regard as key elements for long-term client success. BEI participants include businesses from a number of market sectors – professional services (Accenture, Price Waterhouse Coopers), financial services (HSBC, Bank of America), automotives (Ford Motor Company), computing, (IBM, Hewlett Packard), airlines (Lufthansa, United Airlines) and government agencies (Department of Homeland Security, Department of Justice, US Army).

Source: Based on www.business-ecology.org; www.ibm.com; www.omg.org

Question: Can the Business Ecology model be applied in any kind of business?

To enable the flow of information within value networks and to provide superior value, IBM argue that four technology enablers, or tools, need to be in place:

■ *Enterprise resource planning* tools seek to provide an electronic platform that connects all VN members so that there is system to system connection. An enterprise resource planning system is a packaged business software system that allows a company to automate and integrate the majority of its business processes, to share common data and practices across the entire enterprise, and to produce and access information in a real-time environment (*source*: www.sap.info, February 2003). Suppliers include Oracle and SAP.

■ *Supply chain management* tools manage the information flows, forecast demand, and facilitate timely, collaborative planning. Suppliers include Ariba, JDA, Oracle and SAP. A good source of information and articles, both academic and commercial, can be found at ITtoolbox.com (supplychain.ittoolbox.com/).

- *Customer relationship management* tools attempt to help organisations improve their understanding of customers' characteristics, values and behaviour in order to better meet their needs and retain their loyalty. These systems have been subject to criticism following a failure to deliver against expectations.

- *Exchanges*, which have evolved from simple online transactions between two parties, via third-party market creation tools, to consortiums which 'seek to exchange huge virtual markets, attempt to smooth out demand and lead to fewer inventories'. (Lichtenthal and Eliaz, 2003: 8).

A further structural approach is based on the notion of business ecologies. These consist of much larger communities of organisations (than virtual networks) all supporting a particular standard or system but not necessarily contracted in a formal way to the core or focus organisation. The key feature in ecologies is that they all support a dominant platform or leading technology (Kraemer and Dedrick, 2002). For example, ecologies have developed around the IBM mainframe, Cisco's Internet networking systems, and the Microsoft Windows operating system. Organisations such as Dell, IBM, Microsoft and Cisco have adopted the ecology approach, partly because it enables them to achieve and sustain leadership status in their respective markets. See Table 7.3.

There is room for ideas about traditional marketing channels, value networks and ecologies. Conventional thoughts about marketing channels delivering added value may be appropriate for stable market conditions, such as those experienced in FMCG markets. Contemporary thoughts about flexible, nimble and responsive networks are more appropriate for fast changing, dynamic market conditions, such as those experienced in high technology and fashion clothing markets. Competitive advantage in value networks lies in managing the complexity of relationships that make up the network where organisations compete through the alliances and partnerships that focal organisations create around themselves (Christopher *et al.*, 2002) and by shedding non-core work and concentrating on core competences.

Table 7.3: Virtual organisations and business ecologies

Structure	Explanation
Value networks	Independent organisations who work for a central or focus company to whom they are formally connected. Very often they are designated subcontractors or out-sourced business partners. The have a generally fixed role to play in providing a part of the focus organisation's activities. Value is vested in the collaboration of all network partners.
Business ecologies	Independent organisations, only some of whom, a minority, have any formal relationship with the focus organisation. The essential aspect is that these organisations all support a central and dominant technological standard.

■ Electronic Channels

Rosenbloom (2004) regards marketing channels to be a network of independent organisations that work together interdependently for purposes of trade, and as Kotler and Keller (2009) put it, mutual advantage. Digitisation has enabled new channels to be opened, others closed, effectively, and the term multichannel become quite common. Valos (2009) reports that marketers use multichannel approaches to increase customer numbers, cross-sell and enhance service quality. In addition he observes, multichannel customers spend more money than single-channel customers.

Despite this, Sharma and Mehrotra (2007) indicate that organisations find it difficult to achieve the optimal mix of channel types.

Web applications and mobile technologies offer B2B organisations the opportunity to adopt a direct marketing strategy with end-user customers. However, it has also enabled organisations a new way of working with their channel partners. Through the use of intranets more information can be shared, much more quickly, and this richer information can be used to develop stronger market entry barriers and competitive advantages. In essence, the use of new technologies with intermediaries can assist the development of stronger relationships. It is that important.

The Internet offers producers and manufacturers the opportunity to communicate and enter into exchanges with end-user customers, without the use of intermediaries. In comparison to conventional channels, Internet channels offer B2B enterprises the opportunity to reach new market segments, to cut costs and to not only conduct business transactions more quickly and efficiently but also to undertake business in new and innovative ways.

Apart from basic enterprise-resource-planning systems, research by Constantine *et al.* (2009) found that investment in formal IT systems does not appear to improve supply chain performance, or at least, by not as much as some managers expect. Organisations using low technology such as spreadsheets were nearly three times as likely to be inventory leaders and twice as likely to be cost leaders, compared to companies using formal IT systems extensively.

■ Structural Impact

For some organisations the Internet is the only channel open to them, but these organisations were invariably set up expressly to deal with particular markets on a direct basis. The most obvious impact of a strategy that introduces Internet-based channels into an established organisation is to remove some or all of the established distribution intermediaries. However, this need not always be the case as current channel members may have their role enhanced or it may be left unchanged. Very rarely will an established organisation abandon all of its established marketing channel partners and move all their business activities online. The safer and more obvious route is gradually to adopt a mixed channel structure.

The introduction of an Internet channel enables established organisations to adapt their segmentation policies, to develop incrementally their eCommerce offerings or to use the direct channel to reach particular segments. Established intermediaries are then used to service other segments which cannot be reached effectively through the Internet or they are forced to adopt new roles.

The use of extranets enables organisations to pursue multi-channel strategies, especially when there are low levels of competition (Dou and Chou, 2002). End-user customers may interact directly with the producer but extranets, for example, enable intermediaries to be kept informed of the direct business in their domain and be in a better position to service and support the client once the initial exchange is completed.

The decision to retain intermediaries is primarily a function of the value that they bring to particular markets, customers and producers. Should a channel member or horizontal level of intermediaries fail to add sufficient value to the marketing and supply chain processes then they will be bypassed. This process is referred to as disintermediation and there is much evidence of this process in both B2C and B2B markets.

Just as existing intermediaries may be removed through the introduction of direct Internet channels, so might new ones emerge as innovative roles and facilities are identified to add fresh forms of value. The process whereby new online channel members evolve is referred to as reintermediation and the members themselves are referred to as cybermediaries. These organisations seek to supply downstream services by providing search information for end-user buyers and upstream services in terms of market coverage and wider accessibility for producers.

There are many types of cybermediaries including those that provide cross-market evaluation or comparator services, online communities, portals and e-marketplaces plus directories and financial services. In the B2B market, one of the more significant types of cybermediary brings buyers and sellers together. These organisations are known as 'infomediaries' and they add value by becoming a single point of contact, often in fragmented and diverse markets.

7

Supply Chains, Channel Structures and Networks

Summary

Here are the key points about supply chains and channel structures, set out against the learning objectives.

1 Understand ideas about organisational interdependence and independence.

Most organisations need to decide on the balance between operating autonomously and the necessity to cooperate and combine their resources in order to work with other organisations. The need to balance the drive for independence and the need to be interdependent can often be a point of tension for organisations. Decisions regarding the selection and de-selection of channel partners, the degree to which organisations can or should use direct marketing and decisions to enter into alliances, undertake new roles in established channels or to develop new channels all require judgement about the appropriate balance of interdependence.

2 Explain the issues associated with supply chain management.

Organisations involved with the distribution of physical goods and materials have to manage the physical flow or movement of parts, supplies and finished products. This flow will encompass the very first supplier in the chain right the way through to the end-user customer. This flow is referred to as a supply chain, and its governance as supply chain management (SCM).

There are four core activities associated with SCM, these are: stock management, ware-housing, fulfilment and transportation.

3 Examine the design and structure of different marketing channels.

The length and breadth of a channel concerns the number and types of intermediaries to be involved. Length is about the number of channel levels necessary to optimise the overall service outputs. In many industries this is determined by custom and practice, where there is an established approach to using particular types of intermediary. In other industries there is scope for flexibility and development. The more challenging decision concerns not the type (and hence length) of the channel but the numbers of each type of intermediary to be used. This horizontal or breadth dimension reflects the desired intensity at each level.

The structural pattern that any channel assumes is partly a result of the relationships between the individual organisations that compose the channel. Channels are dynamic, so the structure should be flexible in order that it can respond to a changing environment. Several channel structures can be identified, conventional channels, vertical marketing systems, and networks, including value networks and ecologies.

4 Consider contemporary forms of organisational networks.

Organisations are embedded not just in a set of exclusive buyer–seller relationships, but in a variety of associations with different organisations. These can be intertwined, resulting in various networks of relationships. Such networks therefore provide a more realistic context within which exchange behaviour can be considered.

Value networks are characterised by the collaborative, and often relatively temporary, structures that are assembled by organisations, each with specialist skills. Business ecologies are much larger communities of organisations (than virtual networks) all supporting a particular standard or system but not necessarily contracted in a formal way to the core or focus organisation. The key feature in ecologies is that they all support a dominant platform or leading technology.

5 Explore ideas concerning the use of electronic channels in B2B trading contexts.

Web applications and mobile technologies offer B2B organisations the opportunity to adopt a direct marketing strategy with end-user customers. It also enables organisations a new way of working with their channel partners.

Through the use of intranets more information can be shared, much more quickly, and this richer information can be used to develop stronger market entry barriers and competitive advantages. In essence, the use of new technologies with intermediaries can assist the development of stronger relationships.

■ Discussion Questions

1 Explain why some organisations decide to retain a large degree of autonomy while others willingly become interdependent with some other organisations.

2 Briefly discuss the purpose and role of supply chains and identify how they differ from marketing channels.

3 Describe the main functions associated with logistics management and, using the Internet, identify an example of each listing and their stated core activities.

4 Vertical marketing systems are no longer suitable marketing channels for organisations in the twenty-first century. Critically appraise this statement.

5 Consider the contribution of network theory to our understanding of marketing channels.

6 Explain some of the advantages offered by electronic marketing channels, and consider the nature and variety of new trading formats that have emerged.

References

Achrol, R.S. (1997). Changes in the theory of interorganisational relations in marketing: toward a network paradigm, *Journal of the Academy of Marketing Science*, **25** (1), 56–71

Andersson, P. (1992). Analysing distribution channel dynamics: loose and tight coupling in distribution networks, *European Journal of Marketing*, **26** (2), 47–68

Brewer, P.C. and Speh, T.W. (2000) Using the balanced scorecard to measure supply chain performance, *Journal of Business Logistics*, **21** (1) (Spring), 75–95

Christopher, M., Magrill, L. and Wills, G. (1998) Educational development for marketing logistics, *International Journal of Physical Distribution and Logistics Management*, **28** (4), 234–241

Christopher, M., Payne, A. and Ballantyne, D. (2002) *Relationship Marketing: Creating Stakeholder Value*, Oxford: Butterworth-Heinemann

Constantine, B., Ruwadi and B., Wine, J. (2009) Management practices that drive supply chain success, *McKinsey Quarterly*, 2 retrieved 12 January 2011 from: www.mckinseyquarterly.com/Operations/Supply_Chain_Logistics/ Management_practices_that_drive_supply_chain_success_2250

Dou, W. and Chou, D.C. (2002) A structural analysis of business digital markets, *Industrial Marketing Management*, **31** (2) (February), 165–76

Halinen, A. and Törnroos J.Å. (1998) The role of embeddedness in the evolution of business networks, *Scandinavian Journal of Management*, **14** (3), 187–205

Hoek, van R., Johnson, M., Godsell, *J., and* Birtwistle, A. (2010) Changing chains: three case studies of the change management needed to reconfigure European supply chains, *International Journal of Logistics Management,* **21** (2), 230-250

Keynote (2009) Commercial Vehicles, January.

Kothandaraman, P. and Wilson, D. (2001) The future of competition: value creating networks, *Industrial Marketing Management*, **30** (4) (May), 379–388

Kotler, P. and Keller, K. (2009) *Marketing management,* Englewood Cliffs, NJ: Prentice Hall

Kraemer, K.L. and Dedrick, J. (2002) Strategic use of the Internet and e-commerce: Cisco Systems, *Journal of Strategic Information Systems*, **11**, 5–29.

Lee, H., Padmanabhan, V. and Whang, S. (1997) Information distortion in a supply chain: the bullwhip effect, *Management Science*, **43**, 546–558.

Lichtenthal, J.D. and Eliaz, S. (2003). Internet integration in business marketing tactics, *Industrial Marketing Management*, **32** (1), 3–13

Macneil, I.R. (1978). Contracts: adjustment of long-term economic relations under classical, neoclassical and relational contract law, *Northwestern University Law Review*, 72 (January–February), 854–905

Martin, P. R .and Patterson, J.W. (2009) On measuring company performance within a supply chain, *International Journal of Production Research*, **47** (9) (May), 2449–2460

Mattsson, L.-G. (1989). Development of firms in networks: positions and investments. *Advances in International Marketing*, **3**, 121–139

Melnyk, S.A., Lummus, R.R., Vokurka, R.J., Burns, L.J. and Sandor, J. (2009) Mapping the future of supply chain management: a Delphi study, *International Journal of Production Research*, **47** (16) (August), 4629-4653

New, S.J. and Payne, P. (1995) Research frameworks in logistics: three models, seven dinners and a survey, *International Journal of Physical Distribution and Logistics Management*, **25** (10), 60–77

Porter, M.E. (1985) The generic value chain in M.E. Porter, *Competitive Advantage: Creating and Sustaining Superior Performance*, New York: Free Press.

Ritter, T. and Gemünden, H.G. (2003) Network competence: its impact on innovation success and its antecedents, *Journal of Business Research*, **56** (9) (September) 745–55

Rosenbloom, B. (2004) *Marketing channels: A management view*. Mason, OH: South Western

Sharma, A. and Mehrotra, A. (2007) Choosing an optimal channel mix in multi-channel environments, *Industrial Marketing Management*, **36** (1), 21–28.

Valos, M. (2009) Structure, people and process challenges of multichannel marketing: Insights from marketers, *Database Marketing & Customer Strategy Management*, **16** (3), 197–206

Vergin, R.C. and Barr, K. (1999) Building competitiveness in grocery supply through continuous replenishment planning: insights from the field, *Industrial Marketing Management*, **28** (2), 145–153

Xinyan, Z., Huang, G.Q., Humphreys, P.K and Botta-Genoulaz, V. (2010) Simultaneous configuration of platform products and manufacturing supply chains: comparative investigation into impacts of different supply chain coordination schemes, *Production Planning & Control*, **21** (6) (September), 609-627.

Zhao, X., Xie, J. and Zhang, W.J. (2002) The impact of sharing and ordering co-ordination on supply chain performance, *Supply Chain Management: An International Journal*, **17** (1), 24–40

8 Managing B2B Relationships

Overview

Following the exploration of the nature and characteristics of marketing channels, it is necessary to consider some of the managerial issues, processes and systems associated with maintaining and developing collaborative relationships. First, the nature, dispersion and use of power in relationships is examined, then time is spent looking at channel conflict and ways in which it can be minimised, recognising that some conflict can be constructive. Following a consideration of two important concepts, trust and commitment, which are considered to be a foundation of successful B2B relationships, the chapter concludes with a brief overview of the role of technology in managing relationships with a focus on CRM systems.

Chapter aims and objectives

The aims of this chapter are to consider some of the behavioural concepts associated with the management of interorganisational relationships in business marketing.

The objectives of this chapter are to enable readers to:

1 Explore the concept of power and appreciate its significance in B2B relationships.

2 Examine the various sources of channel power and consider the different influence strategies that organisations can use.

3 Introduce basic principles concerning channel conflict and examine ways in which tensions between organisations can be managed.

4 Appreciate the dimensions and significance of trust and commitment in relationships as a means for building cooperation and channel collaboration.

5 Explain the impact of technology on channel relationships.

6 Consider the extent to which CRM systems can assist the management of B2B relationships.

A Slice of Life – Believing in the Relationship

The intricacies of business relationships can be (and are) infinitely complex. They can be dissected, investigated and managed ad nauseam. The closer you care to look, the more complex they become. Larger companies dedicate entire workforces to the sole task of looking after the clients. And so they should because, 'the customer is king', almost always. The majority of business relationships however, particularly in the SME market (small/medium enterprises), will fall simply into one of two categories – direct or indirect relationships.

The labels may change, the categories can be subdivided, but essentially, your business will have a direct one-to-one relationship with a paying customer, or the relationship will be indirect – remote contact with a prospective customer through a third party. But however complex or simple a structure we try to put in place to manage customer relationships, it all comes down to one thing – do you like the brand enough to work with it? More specifically, do you like the people who represent the brand. No matter what the commercial imperative, sooner or later, for a business to deal with a business, people have to deal with people. In my old age, I've elected to sort those relationship issues out early...

Having received a brief for a European corporate 'Awareness Campaign' for a reasonably large telecoms company, the day arrived to reveal to the customer how we would approach the project. I duly presented the accumulated wisdom of my many years of awareness campaigning to Sir and a considerable flock of subordinates, (including a slightly sallow, moist and inexplicably flaking representative from a media agency...). The client expressed his "disappointment" that I hadn't addressed their need for a "value proposition". He worked his way around the room gathering opinion from his team who all said, "Baaaa... oooh yes Sir, you're so right..."

I felt like a gunslinger walking into the saloon where the conversation had stopped and the piano player had taken a dive behind the bar. The safety catch was off. I now had a choice. I could back out the door slowly and hope I made it to my horse before my mouth started firing random abuse, or I could slug it out. Sometimes I wish I could just, you know, 'not'. But there we are...

The red mist welled up and all I can really remember is that I didn't jab my finger in anyone's face. I saw an interview with Bill Clinton once where he said that in heated debate, it was essential not to point fingers as the gesture was overly aggressive. Clinton used his thumb which, apparently, is politically correct. So there I was, purple faced, neck vein bulging, spraying spittle across a good metre and a half of conference table as I ranted uncontrollably and all I could think of was, "It's OK Scot, it doesn't matter what names you're calling him, you're not pointing, you're using your thumb. All is well."

All was in fact very far indeed from 'well'. It was unacceptable in my opinion that a two billion dollar company should ask a number of small agencies for their unpaid responses to their brief and then move the goalposts from 'awareness' to 'value proposition'. I was particularly incandescent because this was at least the second time this particular client (I use the term loosely) had shape-shifted mid-stroke. 18 months earlier the brief had been for a (expressly and specifically) "radical and creative brand strategy." That's what I delivered. It turned out that my proposal was "too radical…" and, "too creative…" The agency appointed was, "safe, with a process". Safe it may well have been, but the client had seemingly spent 18 months producing a brand strategy with a worthless proposition and decided that the best time to be disappointed at my lack of telepathy skills was after I had presented the requested brand awareness campaign. Tisk.

At some undefined point, my spleen was fully vented and a stunned silence reigned. (There was still a wild howling in my ears of course, but for the most part, the room was quiet.) I packed up my things, and, with the surprising absence of 'any further questions', I left.

He called me the following day. I'm still not sure why. Apparently, "it's important to follow these things up." Well, no, it isn't. Everything had been said. It turns out he still thought he was right and just wanted another fight. I nearly gave it to him too. But as the red mist rose, I caught myself, took a deep breath and simply said, "Look, you're worth nothing to me. You've been worth nothing for years and you'll never be worth anything. You're a drain on my resources and my energy. I can apply both to considerably better commercial advantage elsewhere. The conversation's over. Goodbye." And I hung up.

It's possible I was wrong. It's possible that the work I presented didn't answer the brief. It's even possible that it just wasn't good enough. But that's not the point. The point, is that everyone has to believe in the business relationship from the very beginning. The potential for conflict in business has enriched every lawyer you have ever met. The relative perceptions of power, conflict and cooperation are based wholly on the belief in the relationship. Sometimes businesses attempt to maintain unacceptable business relationships for profit despite the inevitable discord. Personally, I think there is a base level of belief from which cooperation should be established at the outset. So you have to believe. Because no one else will. Least of all the client. Believe it, live it and hang up on any mutthafuggah who isn't prepared to die for the cause.

Scot McKee

■ Introduction

The management of interorganisational relationships is complicated by a number of different issues. Two of these involve the nature and distribution of power and the degree of conflict that exists between organisations and especially those in marketing channels. These two topics are interrelated because the use or misuse of power can be a source of conflict (Welch and Wilkinson, 2002). In order to manage these interrelated concepts and help ensure all participating organisations achieve their performance objectives, it is important to develop suitable forms of cooperation.

Cooperation can be achieved in two main ways. One way is to exercise authority through the use of the power that one organisation may have over others. Another way is to establish trust and a spirit of collaboration between organisations. Through trust it is possible to develop a sense of commitment so that all organisations attempt to support one another.

■ The Concept of Power

As already established, organisations seek to achieve their objectives by working with other organisations in an interdependent manner. To work effectively and efficiently the interdependence, specialisation and expertise of individual organisations should be encouraged (Rosenbloom, 1978). However, interdependence is rarely distributed in a uniform and equitable way. Therefore, the inequality of organisational interdependence becomes a major source of power. This asymmetric distribution means that no single organisation can have absolute power (Stern and Gorman, 1969) but does provide some organisations the opportunity to exploit others. The relationship therefore between members of a marketing channel will be shaped by them. A supplier, distributor or retailer with high market power, is in a more advantageous position to drive financial benefits from another party (Mottner and Smith, 2009).

Power concerns the ability to get another (individual or organisation) to do what they/it would not normally have done. In a channel context, power is obtained through the possession and control of resources that are valued by another member. As Belaya and Hanf (2009) declare, power represents a major element of channel management.

Channel and interorganisational relationships can be regarded as a reflection of the balance of power that exists between organisations. Emerson (1962) referred to power as a function of dependency. The more dependent X is on Y, the greater power Y has over X. As all members of a channel are interdependent then all members have a degree of power. It is therefore imperative that the power wielded by constituent members is utilised to further the development of the collective membership of a marketing channel (or network) and the achievement of its objectives and goals. If used otherwise, power may lead to negative consequences for the member and in turn for the channel.

Dependency is concerned with two main elements, the value that one organisation derives from interacting with another and the number of alternative sources of equivalent value that an organisation has. Such dependency is encapsulated in social exchange theory (see Chapter 6). According to Stern and El-Ansary (1992), there are two main constructs associated with this theory: comparison level (CL) and comparison level of alternatives (CLalt). The former concerns the expected performance levels of channel members based on experience. The latter is based on the expected performance of the best alternative organisation to a current channel member. As this is true for all channel members, there is a certain level of dependence upon each other. This means that each channel member can affect, by its own actions, the performance of others. It is this ability to influence the performance of others that is seen by advocates of social exchange theory as a source of power.

■ Sources of Power

In what is regarded as a classic study, French and Raven (1959) determined five bases for power: rewards, coercion, expertise, legitimate and reference bases.

- *Rewards* are one of the more common sources of power. They are based on the belief that one organisation intends, and is able, to reward another with a resource (source of value) that the other desires if agreed actions are accomplished. For example, a manufacturer might grant a wholesaler particular discounts dependent upon the volume of products bought during an agreed period. A value added reseller might be included on a high-profile manufacturer's list of preferred distributors, should it achieve the necessary standards of performance.

- *Coercion* is the other side of the 'reward-based' coin, where negative measures, or punishments may be administered. These sanctions may take the form of reduced margins, changes to delivery cycles, withdrawal of product range privileges or perhaps alterations to geographic or territorial areas the organisation is entitled to serve. One of the difficulties associated with the use of coercive power is that it is perceived as an attack, which often provokes self-defence and a counterattack. For example, should a retailer feel threatened by a manufacturer then a range of responses might include, delisting, reduced stocking, moving orders to a competitor or even competing directly by developing their own manufacturing facilities or developing competitive eCommerce facilities to enter new markets.

- *Expert* power is based on the perception that one organisation considers another to possess particular knowledge and expertise that they do not possess but require if they are to fulfil their obligations. This makes them dependent upon the flow of (expert) information from the source organisation. Interestingly, the expert power exercised by leading pharmaceutical manufacturers is derived from the dependency of the pharmacies and general practitioners (GPs) on them and not so much on the dependency of the wholesalers. Franchise systems are based on the expertise owned by the franchisor. Problems can arise through the transfer of expertise, over time, which, if not controlled through government licensing arrangements, may enable other recipient organisations to operate independently of the expert organisation.

- *Legitimate* power exists when one party recognises the authority of another to manage a relationship. This is similar to a manager recognising the authority of an executive director. Legitimacy is provided either through the judicial system (for example trademarks and contracts) or through the norms and social values established within particular markets and industries. At the heart of this source of power is the notion of consent, that one organisation acknowledges the right of another to assert themselves in a particular way. However, the use of legitimate power is relatively uncommon in conventional channels and it is only in contractual and corporate vertical marketing systems (for example franchisors) where legitimate power can be exercised.

- *Referent* power works on the basis of association and identification – 'being in the same boat' as Rosenbloom refers to it. If members of a network are able to share and empathise with the problems of their 'channel partners' then a channel-wide solution to a common problem may well result in increased understanding, collaboration and trust. Referent power is about public acknowledgement in order to gain increased value. Therefore, a retailer may find it beneficial, that is of increased value, to be able to carry particular prestigious brands as the association will enhance the perception end-user customers will have of them. Similarly, some manufacturers may benefit from distribution through association with particular retailers. Chu and Chu (1994) refer to this as 'renting a reputation'.

These power bases need to be considered as a collective group, not as separate sources. This means that there is a level of reinforcement between different types of power. Thus, reward power may be used to support expert power or legitimate power may be used in combination with referent power. Equally, it is likely that there may be conflict between certain types, especially when coercion is used. This may negate any expertise or referent power that might have been established.

Power is not distributed symmetrically and no one organisation is totally dependent upon another. Therefore, power needs to be understood as an imbalance between organisations which are, to varying extents, dependent upon each other.

Managing B2B Relationships

ViewPoint 8.1: Powerful burgers

Relationships between organisations are often influenced by the perception of power vested in one of the parties. To what extent might the British Airports Authority hold power over the airlines that use their airports? Virgin Atlantic withheld landing fees from BAA in December 2009 when Heathrow shut down due to heavy snow which was not cleared by BAA for several days.

It is said that Tesco and Sainsbury's exert power over their suppliers to drive down prices, sometimes to uneconomic levels.

Franchise holders exert power over their franchisees, often through the terms of the contract. For example, potential MacDonald's franchisees must have significant business experience, pass a number of investigative interviews and be able to invest a minimum $300,000, none of which can be borrowed. Ongoing costs involve a payment of 4% of gross monthly sales, as a royalty, in addition to other expenses such as rent as MacDonald's normally own the franchisee property , the cost of stock and utilities.

Not all franchise opportunities are as restrictive as MacDonald's but there is inevitably a trade-off between the costs of buying into a concept and how much control or power the franchise holder has over the business they maintain. The British Franchise Association maintains a code of ethics aimed at ensuring fair and good business practice in the franchise sector.

Source: Based on www.articlesbase.com; www.macdonalds.co.uk; www.thebfa.org

Question: Do franchise holders such as MacDonald's exert too much control?

■ Using Power for Influence

By recognising and understanding the bases of power, the levels of cooperation and the form of the relationships between members, the nature of communication, its pattern, its frequency and its style can be adjusted to complement the prevailing conditions. Furthermore, such an understanding can be useful to help shape the power relationships of the future and to enhance corporate/marketing strategies. Once the current and anticipated power bases are determined, influence strategies can assist the shaping process. Of the power propositions provided by French and Raven (1959), reward and coercion seem more apt for use within channels where market exchange-based transactions predominate. Legitimate and expert power might be better applied in channels with a high level of relational exchanges.

Organisations seek to influence interorganisational relationships through a variety of communication strategies. Coughlan *et al.* (2001) claim the most common ones are, promise, threat, legal, request, information exchange and recommendation strategies, as set out at Table 8.1.

Table 8.1: Influence strategies

Strategy	Message	Power source
Promise strategy	If you do what we wish we will reward you	Reward
Threat strategy	If you do not do what we wish we will punish you	Coercion
Legalistic strategy	You agreed, so you should do what we wish	Legitimacy
Request strategy	Please do what we wish	Referent, reward, coercion
Information exchange strategy	We are not going to tell you what we wish (very subtle, often oblique)	Expertise, reward
Recommendation strategy	If you do what we wish you will be rewarded (e.g. more profitable)	Expertise, reward

Source: Based on Coughlan *et al*. (2001).

What this suggests is that, for some segments, where customers use online communications as an integral part of the buying process, there has been a swing in the balance of power, away from retailers to manufacturers, from down- to upstream sites. Therefore, manufacturers need to be aware of this source of influence over their end-user groups and develop information channels accordingly.

The use of power within marketing channels can be effective in helping to achieve a number of outcomes. Among these are activities associated with the provision of information, operations and channel developmental linkages and channel development through training and the selection of new members.

■ Channel Conflict

It is inevitable that there will be some level of conflict between channel members, if only because channels are open social systems (Katz and Kahn, 1978). The degree of conflict will also vary from channel to channel and from organisation to organisation but, despite this, conflict has always been considered to be widely prevalent in dyadic relationships (Hunt and Nevin, 1974). In B2B markets, interorganisational conflict can be observed between vertically aligned channel members and also between organisations that operate across channels horizontally. Conflict occurs in established offline channels, in online channels and in multichannel situations. In many cases, the development of multichannel distribution systems has given rise to increased levels of conflict, not only between organisations but also between channels within a single organisation (Webb and Hogan, 2002).

As mentioned earlier, interorganisational cooperation is important because of the varying degrees to which members are interdependent. Enabling the continuity of the interdependent conditions is crucial if channel and organisational goals are to be achieved. It is assumed that conflict impairs channel performance but some research, cited by Duarte and Davies (2003) suggests that the reverse is true and that conflict can improve channel performance (Rosson and Ford, 1980; Assael, 1969). This supports the view that conflict can be functional as well as dysfunctional in its impact on channel members.

Duarte and Davies argue that performance effectiveness, such as meeting sales targets, is not affected by conflict. They contend that conflict is triggered by a failure (of a dependent channel member) to reach performance threshold levels. In other words, managers should be concerned more with efficiency than performance effectiveness when managing conflict. This research was only concerned with UK car dealership channels and may therefore only be relevant to business-to-business relationships where there is a high level of dependency.

So, if conflict is a result of a breakdown in the levels of cooperation between channel partners (Shipley and Egan, 1992) and may well affect channel performance, management has a prime responsibility to manage conflict. Invariably, managers attend to conflict when it breaks out but management should also seek to prevent conflict occurring and hence be proactive in reducing tension and creating cooperation and dialogue. Therefore, the task of conflict management is to manage relationships such that the frequency, intensity and duration of interorganisational conflict is minimised.

■ The Nature of Conflict

Technically, the word 'conflict' has its roots in the word 'collision' and the idea of two moving parts colliding and causing conflict is well founded. A more relevant interpretation is that conflict concerns an incompatibility of ideas, purpose, understanding and aims. By finding new, shared solutions to an incompatibility of ideas or purpose, improved levels of understanding may arise which in turn can lead to improved cooperation and enhanced performance. There are a number of definitions of channel-based conflict but perhaps one of the more typical and straightforward was offered by Gaski who states that it is 'the perception on the part of a channel member that its goal attainment is being impeded by another, with stress or tension the result' (Gaski, 1984: 11).

Negative, or dysfunctional, conflict is normally associated with hostility, disagreement, friction and contention. As mentioned earlier, dysfunctional conflict is often assumed to have a negative impact on channel performance, although there is little empirical evidence to support this. Indeed, this negative view is countered by those who regard conflict as capable of having positive outcomes (Anderson and Narus, 1990; Morgan and Hunt, 1994). They suggest that positive or functional conflict can be healthy as it may encourage change and development, often by generating a new, more efficient allocation of resources. Rosenbloom (1978) argues that conflict is more likely to be constructive, or functional, when there are moderate levels of conflict present and dysfunctional when there are either very high or very low levels of conflict.

Rose and Shoham (2002) identify a further means of categorising conflict, namely task and emotional conflict. Using the work of Amason (1996), Jehn (1994) and Menon *et al.*, (1996) they identify task conflict to be incompatibilities and disagreements between organisations about respective responsibilities. It is based on judgements about the most appropriate way to achieve shared goals. On the other hand, emotional conflict is concerned with interpersonal incompatibilities and friction between members of each participating group.

■ Competition or Conflict

Conflict should not be confused with competition and competitive behaviour. Conflict is behaviour that is opponent-centred, it is personal and direct. In a channel or B2B context this means that upstream or downstream members attempt to block, or are perceived to be blocking or impeding another member from achieving their goals.

On the other hand, competition is behaviour that is object-centred, it is impersonal and indirect. In a channel or B2B context, this means that members of different channels attempt to attain goals controlled by others such as customers or those who control or regulate performance. Channel competition is about members striving, with others, to overcome their environment, whereas channel conflict is about members struggling with one another (Coughlan *et al.*, 2001).

■ Dimensions of Conflict

Conflict is far from being a one-dimensional concept. Organisations do not experience either uniform levels of conflict or no conflict at all. In reality, conflict is a complex, dynamic (Rosenberg and Stern, 1970) and multidimensional concept. Conflict is complex because it is thought to occur at a number of levels, ranging from the latent, through perceived, affective, manifest and aftermath states (Pondy, 1967).

It should be understood that movement through these stages is not necessarily sequential and does not have to incorporate all stages all of the time. In addition to these different levels of conflict there are major variations in the intensity and frequency of conflict and there are varying degrees of importance attached to different conflict issues, hence the multidimensional aspect. These levels or states have been accepted and used by many authors, partly because they have a general validity (Duarte and Davies, 2003) based upon our understanding of the attitude construct. However, they have never been proved empirically and to that extent remain a useful but hypothetical construct.

Electronic information management and trading systems have made many manufacturers concerned about channel conflict. The development and implementation of these systems can bring them into direct competition with existing channels. Difficulties lie not just externally but also internally. Internal conflicts arising from the development of multi-channels can be observed, involving competition either for finite internal resources, or for the same customers (Webb and Hogan, 2002). Inevitably intermediaries become confused and frustrated in their own attempts to secure their own goals, and conflict emerges.

As with conflict which originates offline, the intensity, frequency and duration will depend on many factors, including the nature of each organisation and the industry in which it operates. Manufacturers who introduce online facilities yet do not closely control their offline distribution channels risk damaging channel relationships and revenue streams. However, organisations that do control their own channels and introduce online facilities without a clear strategy, are at risk of cannibalising their revenues by taking customers out of existing channels and decreasing the profitability of the established channels.

■ Reasons for Conflict

The reasons why conflict emerges clearly need to be appreciated, as identification of the appropriate cause can lead to marketing management strategies that prevent, remedy or at least seek to repair any damage. Tension can arise between organisations for any number of reasons but some of the more common reasons are: deviance from agreed roles and responsibilities, disagreements about resources or the decisions other members make, differences in the way organisations perceive the actions of others and poor interorganisational communications.

All of these reasons can be distilled into three main factors (Stern and Heskett, 1969). These concern differences relating to:

- Competing or incompatible goals
- Domains
- Perceptions of reality.

Underpinning all of them is inadequate communication.

■ Competing Goals

This is a common form of conflict and typically occurs when one upstream member changes strategy so that its goals become difficult for other downstream members to support. For example, a manufacturer may decide that it wants to reach new market sectors but current dealers might resist this strategy as it is not in their interest to supply other (new) channels with the same products. Indeed, if implemented, it might give rise to increased channel competition and then impact on dealer revenues and profits.

Another example of competing goals can be seen when retailers try to increase performance by lowering their stock levels. Conflict is likely as the manufacturer's goal is to increase the level of stock in the channel, while intermediaries prefer to be able to pull down stock on demand and, hence, avoid working capital costs.

Alternatively, a departmental manager in a retail organisation may not be too concerned which product offerings in a particular category help the department achieve its volume and margin contributions. However, the manufacturer of an individual brand will be most concerned if its brand is not included in the retailer's portfolio of category brands. The two have different goals, yet the same product focus.

ViewPoint 8.2: Presentation raises sports brands' tensions

The UK market for sports goods was estimated to be worth £5.585 million in 2010 (Mintel 2010). This market consists of products bought for both participation in the actual sport and general leisure/fashion wear. Manufacturers include global brands such Nike, Adidas, Puma, Reebok.

The distribution channels for these kinds of brands present a number of tensions and potential points for conflict. The main forms of conflict centre on their relationship with retailers and the resellers' preferred presentation and eagerness to discount prices.

For premium brands Adidas and Nike these issues represent significant problems. They are reliant on a high street retail presence for sales volume, but in marketing terms, these retailers adopt competitive discount policies and display goods in ways that conflict with the standards expected by the brands themselves.

Both Adidas and Nike maintain their own high street stores in major retail centres where displays and pricing vary significantly from the discount stores which are based almost side by side. The branded stores base their proposition on a premium shopping experience and target customers who are seeking a higher level of customer service and are prepared to pay for it. The potential for conflict is further extended via the branded manufacturers own retail discount outlets, located in out of town retail parks as well as the growth in sales online.

Distinguishing between the participation and fashion elements of the market also represents complexity and points of conflict in the distribution channels. High street fashion retailers such as Next market sports brands alongside their fashion ranges. The sector as a whole is also subject to supermarket own brand challenges.

Source: Mintel (2010); www.adidas.com; www.nike.com

Question: How does channel conflict benefit the consumer?

Managing B2B Relationships

8

■ Domain Differences

A channel domain refers to an area, field or sphere of function. According to Stern *et al.* (1996) it has four main elements: population, territory, member roles and issues concerning technology and marketing. So, disputes can arise because one channel member perceives another member operating outside of the previously designated (agreed) area, perhaps geographically, or in terms of its role.

For example, a wholesaler and a manufacturer may disagree about margins, training, marketing policies or, more commonly, territorial issues. McGrath and Hardy (1986) see conflict emanating from manufacturers' policies, such as sales order policies. The tighter and more constricting they are, the greater the likelihood that conflict will erupt than if the policies are flexible and can be adjusted to meet the needs of both parties.

So, wholesalers who start to sell direct to end-user consumers, or retailers who begin to sell to other retailers, are blatantly adopting a new role and this may infringe upon another member's role and prevent or impede them from achieving their objectives. A more common example exists when a manufacturer decides to sell through a dealer's competitors, to the extent of even breaking an exclusivity arrangement. The reverse of this intra-channel type of conflict is when a manufacturer perceives an intermediary selling another (competing) manufacturer's products at the expense of its own range of products.

Another cause of domain-based conflict concerns the emergence of multiple channels. An intermediary might feel threatened by increased competition and reduced financial performance opportunities.

Disagreements about pricing, sales areas or sales order processing, for example, are sensitive issues that can also lead to channel conflict. Once agreement has been made about policy terms or operational formats, any changes should be negotiated and managed in a cooperative and considered way. Indeed, some channels often stipulate the way in which changes to key domain-based issues should be managed.

Perceptions of Reality

Through the process of selective perception any number of members may react to the same stimulus in completely different and conflicting ways. The objectives of each of the channel members are different, however well bonded they are to the objectives of the distribution system. It is also likely that each member perceives different ways of achieving the overall goals, all of which are recipes for conflict. As each member organisation perceives the world differently, their perception of others and their actions may lead to tensions and disagreements. So, an action taken by member X with one intention might be perceived differently by member Y. Any action that Y takes as a result of this perception may result in conflict. Perceptions about a product attribute, its applications and appropriate segments can all give rise to perceptually based conflict.

Apart from poor or incomplete communication, the main reason for this tendency to have differing perspectives on information or actions may arise because, in the absence of a strong cooperative relationship, different channel members are focused on different business elements (Coughlan *et al.*, 2001). A manufacturer might be focused on products and processes, whereas a dealer may be concentrating on customers and how to meet their needs. Cultural differences in perception and focus may arise amongst channel members. What may be an appropriate behaviour in one culture may simply be different from that in another, or may not be understood. This can obviously be a problem for internationally-based organisations.

Managing Interorganisational Conflict

Conflict cannot be eradicated but it can be managed. Through the provision of adequate proactive strategies, the frequency, intensity and duration of conflict can be reduced even if it cannot be totally prevented. Although the management of interorganisational conflict is a continuous activity, it can be considered in two contexts.

The first concerns the management of conflict at the early stages of development, from latent through to felt stages. Here the management goal is to diffuse levels of incompatibility, in terms of its intensity and frequency, with a view to preventing any escalation. The task is to manage or contain any disagreement.

The second context concerns the management of conflict when it breaks out or reaches the manifest stage. The task now is to resolve or bring to an end the conflict or cause of disagreement, so that relationships between all parties can be restored to a point of equilibrium that enables exchanges to continue and relationships to develop constructively. These two aspects of containment and resolution are considered and depicted at Figure 8.1.

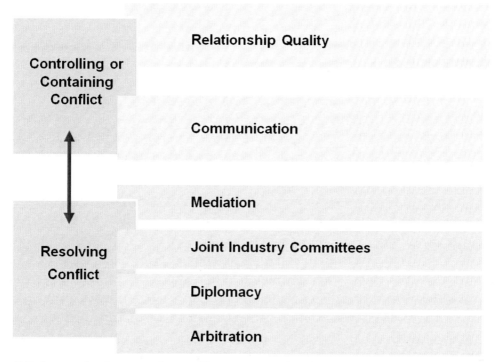

Figure 8.1: Approaches to managing conflict

■ Context One – controlling or containing conflict

There are a number of methods that can be used, but at the root of them all are two overriding factors, the quality of the relationship between organisations and the quality of the (marketing) communications used to bind participating organisations together.

Relationship quality

It is clear that one of the founding principles for successful performance in the business-to-business sector is the development of flourishing interorganisational relationships. These relationships concern not only buyers and sellers in and across marketing channels but also all other organisations that participate or contribute to active networks and supply chains.

As outlined in Chapter 4, the key to the formation and maintenance of interorganisational relationships is the development of trust and commitment (Morgan and Hunt, 1994). These important concepts are explored in more depth later in this chapter. One of the ways trust between organisations can be developed is an awareness by all parties of the need to consider how others in the network of relationships will react to a particular strategy, policy change or initiative – by gauging the reaction and needs of others in advance so that areas of incompatibility can be minimised and opportunities for conflict to emerge, reduced.

The importance and significance of the roles played by boundary spanning staff in the development of interorganisational relationships cannot be underestimated. Larson (1992) reports that conflict and uncertainty is reduced through the use of suitable personal relationship management staff. As a result, interorganisational trust improves.

Communication

The second important element to be considered when controlling levels of conflict is interorganisational communications. Marketing communication is examined in greater depth in subsequent chapters but, for now, note that conflict management is based upon a willingness of all organisations to share appropriate information. What is deemed by one organisation as an appropriate strategy may in fact be a source of potential conflict if communication is ineffective. Effective interorganisational communication requires that there be a dialogue between all members. Two-way communication rather than a one-way, monologic transmission can improve understanding and, more importantly, reduce or minimise misunderstanding and incorrect perceptions of the message content and source.

This notion of two-way communication underpins a fundamental construct within interorganisational communication, namely the propensity or willingness of organisations to share information with one another. Although some information has always been exchanged, access and openness to competitively sensitive information has often been withheld. Relational exchanges are based on an open exchange of information and therefore parties should be willing to share information that will enable the channel to attain its goals. Where such a propensity does not exist information may become withheld, distorted or used as part of a power imbalance in the marketing channel or network. This is regarded as information deviance, from which conflict is likely to develop.

Communication between organisations can be formal or informal. Formal communication is characterised by the use of technology such as electronic data interchange (EDI). Interorganisational cooperation might improve because of the impact of EDI on channel formalisation and because it can reduce task uncertainty (Nakayama, 2003). As if to confirm the obvious, Downing (2010) found that organisations using web and non-web-based EDI systems experienced superior performance outcomes, compared to those who do not use electronic systems across their supply chains. However, one of the prime reasons why companies expressly avoid web-based systems is the perceived risk associated with these forms of IT.

On the other hand, sharing sensitive information may affect the distribution of power and influence negotiations between suppliers and retailers. For example, suppliers might be in a better bargaining position regarding the amount of promotional support retailers will receive, if EDI supplies them with point of sale and stock information. What Nakayama points out is that risks and benefits associated with the use of EDI are not always shared equally between all members of a marketing channel.

Communication between organisations can be improved and the incidence of conflict reduced by an exchange of people. This may involve a single senior manager or a number of managerial staff being deployed to either a similar position or to the operational level at their customers' sites. Through direct experience of the other party's environment and a constant flow of information, conflict can be managed and contained without causing widespread damage.

Informal communications consist of a variety of soft methods and techniques. Some of these are conferences, seminars, memos, emails, telephone conversations and corridor meetings and are used in parallel with more formal communication methods. By improving the quality and frequency of communication, by regularising activities and even establishing ways of behaving or institutionalising, conflict containment can become a matter for all parties in a network, with relationships conditioned by the communication and interaction.

■ Context Two – resolving conflict

In order to resolve conflict that has broken out between organisations, a number of approaches have been proposed. Many of these approaches have the potential to contain conflict as well as resolve conflict that has reached damaging proportions.

Rosenberg and Stern (1970) suggested the use of a joint industry committee or group, composed of elected members from the industry. The group would be able to provide a forum for the views of the organisations in conflict to be heard. Larger industry forums can establish various subcommittees entrusted with responsibility for particular aspects of the industry's affairs. Trade associations such as the Engineering Employers' Federation, the Freight Transport Association and the Cementitious Slag Makers Association provide this mechanism and by forming voluntary rules and procedures, enable constituent organisations to work to agreed behaviour patterns. Therefore, trade associations provide a means by which conflict can be contained and also resolved.

The same principle of cooperation enables manufacturers to meet groups of industry-wide dealers to discuss problems and complaints; to review proposed pricing strategies; to consider advertising and marketing communications campaigns; to hear ways in which dealers perceive the actions of manufacturers; as well as providing a means for putting forward new ideas and advancing channel-wide performance.

The use of diplomacy can also be used to resolve and contain conflict. By appointing an individual or a customer centre that has responsibility for a particular dealer or set of retailers, and empowering them with decision making capability, it becomes possible to resolve conflict before it becomes a potent force. Although diplomacy might have a defensive orientation, it can be localised and prevent conflict from spreading to other intermediaries.

An alternative approach to these internally driven mechanisms is the introduction of an external agent. These can provide objectivity and a fresh perspective to any disagreement. Arbitration is an externally based facility that is capable of providing a fast and confidential means of resolving conflict. It is less expensive than legal action and can be officiated by people who understand the industry or context within which the conflict has occurred. With arbitration, the third party makes the final decision, and the organisations in conflict are bound by that decision.

In contrast to arbitration, mediation requires a third party to be involved but their role is to encourage dialogue to enable the parties to reach their own agreement. Encouragement can be in the form of floating possible solutions, suggesting solutions, establishing the facts and once a solution is agreed ensuring that it is implemented correctly.

Finally, to conclude this section on conflict management there are a number of overall strategies that can be employed to deal with conflict and interorganisational disagreements; these are set out in Table 8.2.

The strategies depicted range from selfishness (and to some degree stubbornness) and refusal to work with other organisations, through compromise and cooperativeness to seeking entirely to accommodate the views of other parties, to the extent that one's own position may be jeopardised. The selection and deployment of these strategies is a function of the prevailing corporate culture, attitude towards risk and the sense of power that exists within coalitions.

Table 8.2: Conflict resolution strategies

Strategy	Explanation
Accommodation	Modify expectations to incorporate requirements of others
Argument	A considered attempt to convince others of the correctness of your position
Avoidance	Removal from the point of conflict
Compromise	Meet the requirements of others half way
Cooperation	Mutual reconciliation through cooperation
Instrumentality	Agree minimal requirements to secure short-term agreement
Self-seeking	Seek agreement on own terms or refuse further cooperation

In some ways, these two contexts ignore the importance of what has been learned. A third context, therefore, concerned with understanding the nature of the conflict event, and how it was resolved, should be added. Chang and Gotcher (2010) refer to this as 'conflict-coordination learning' and identify three dimensions: information exchange, joint interpretation and coordination, and relationship-specific knowledge memory.

Information exchange refers to the process where channel members listen, respect and understand partner opinions. This means that participants each become a source and a recipient of knowledge (Selnes and Sallis, 2003), enacting the response model of communication (Fill, 2011).

Joint interpretation and coordination refers to the process that allows channel members to analyse, interpret, and understand the causes of conflict and build on the resolutions achieved. This leads to an improved understanding of the position of their channel partners.

Relationship-specific knowledge memory builds on the work of Ballantyne (2004) and refers to the way channel members adjust their activities and routines to complement partner needs and goals. By having a standard procedure to follow when handling conflict, partners can learn from experience about how best to deal with conflict.

Chang and Gotcher (2010) go on to classify CCL into four stages: defensive, compliance, managerial, and strategic. These are set out in Table 8.3.

Table 8.3: Four stages of conflict-coordination learning (Based on Chang and Gotcher, 2010)

CCL Stage	Explanation
Defensive	Channel members deny conflict responsibilities and defend against different ideas and opinions held by others. CCL does not occur.
Compliance	Channel members are willing to listen and accept others' ideas and opinions. During conflict compliance processes, CCL information exchange occurs.
Managerial	Channel members embed conflict issues into their management processes. Channel members know the expectations of other members, what their specific responsibilities are, and how their actions will be executed. Through joint interpretation and conflict coordination, channel members are aware of potential conflict areas, and reduce conflict situations before they escalate.
Strategic	Channel members integrate the conflict issue into their business strategies. Channel members memorise (procedurally and declaratively) relationship-specific knowledge and accomplish collective sets of tasks through which joint transaction value can be created.

■ Building Relationships

There are a number of factors that contribute to the development of strong relationships and reduced levels of conflict but linking them all are ideas concerning trust and commitment. At one time, power was regarded as the best means to manage a marketing channel and avoid conflict. As the relationship marketing approach has gathered momentum, so trust and commitment have become the focus for conflict resolution and avoidance.

■ Trust

The interdependence of organisations and indeed of most strong and longer running buyer–seller relationships, is founded on a degree of trust between parties. Trust is the confidence that one party has in the other's reliability and integrity. In a B2B context, trust is the confidence that one organisation has interacting with another organisation with respect to their reliability, integrity and predictability regarding desirable outcomes. A lack of trust can lead to uncertainty and from that position, conflict and dissatisfaction.

Trust brings feelings of security, can reduce uncertainty and create a supportive climate. It follows that honesty and benevolence are an integral part of the trust concept and an important part of the relationships that evolve between organisations. Honesty is concerned with the belief that a partner stands by their word, fulfils their role, meets their obligations and is sincere. Benevolence is about the belief that one partner is interested in the welfare of the other and will not take unexpected actions (opportunistic behaviour) that might be to the detriment of the partner (Geyskens and Steenkamp, 1995). Interestingly, Svensson

(2001) refers to the establishment of a trust chain running through a marketing channel.

A further perspective on trust concerns the demarcation made by Shankar *et al.* (2002) and others regarding offline and online trust. Although it is recognised that there are many similarities, online trust is different because the focus is not so much about people, such as sales representatives and customer support staff, as about trust with respect to technology, whether it be a website, an eCommerce channel, email or a kiosk. The linkage between offline and online trust is also important and the interaction between the two, especially in multichannel systems must not be overlooked.

■ Commitment

Commitment is associated with a partner's consistency, competence, honesty, fairness and willingness to make sacrifices, take responsibility, be helpful and benevolent. The level of commitment determines acquiescence and hence the partner's propensity to exit the relationship.

Commitment can be interpreted as the desire to continue and maintain a valued relationship. Therefore, a strong relationship requires that trust be established between channel members. Once trust is formed the opportunity arises for relationship commitment and it is through this cooperation that a major outcome might be end user satisfaction.

In Chapter 4, relationship marketing was discussed, with the work of Morgan and Hunt (1994) being given particular prominence. However, in terms of interorganisational conflict the development of trust is important in limiting the development of conflict in the first place. If conflict should emerge, the presence of trust should determine that any conflict will be functional and should go some way towards reducing the intensity and duration of any incompatibility or tension. If there is a high degree of commitment then the fact that both parties value the relationship will go a long way to preventing the issue giving rise to conflict emerging in the first place.

■ Cooperation

There is general agreement that effective supply (and marketing) chain management requires trust and communication (Tan, 2000; Grieco, 1989). As already identified, Morgan and Hunt propose that building a relationship based on trust and commitment can give rise to a number of benefits. Some of these include developing a set of shared values, reducing costs when the relationship finishes and increasing profitability as a greater number of end-user customers are retained because of the inherent value and satisfaction they experience. Cooperation arises from a relationship driven by high levels of both trust and commitment (Morgan and Hunt, 1994).

Mohr *et al.* (1999) refer to cooperation as the extent to which organisations voluntarily undertake similar or complementary actions to achieve mutual or singular outcomes with expected reciprocation over time. Therefore, in view of prevailing uncertainties before collaborative relationships are reached, organisations need to calculate the appropriate level of cooperation they judge to be necessary. Harris and Dibben (1999) suggest that the criteria necessary for cooperation between parties is a reflection of the factors set out in Table 8.4.

Table 8.4: Factors influencing level of cooperation

Factor	Cooperative element
Utility	A perception of the potential economic value associated with remaining in the relationship.
Importance	A perception of the non-economic value associated with remaining in the relationship.
Competence	A perception of the potential social/economic loss of remaining in the relationship.
Self-competence	An individual's perception of their own ability within the relationship.
Risk	A perception of the professional ability of another (organisation).

These are useful because they focus attention on the importance of perception in the maintenance and management of interorganisational relationships. However, they do not provide sufficient managerial precision to direct these important decisions. Southam (2002) suggests that in an eCommerce channel, margins, brand strength, customer involvement, intensity of competition and whether customer value is added through the Internet or at the retailers' location shapes decisions about between whom, where and when cooperation should occur. In addition there are certain intra-organisational factors that will shape a channel strategy, namely a range of resources such as finance, technological and human factors, let alone the organisational structure, culture, fulfilment and marketing capabilities amongst others.

■ The Impact of Technology on Business Relationships

The development of electronic and web based technologies has helped to transform the nature of channel management and related issues. eCommerce has evolved and developed so much that through automation, standardisation and improved communications, greater efficiencies and increased quantities of targeted information have helped all members of marketing channels.

The impact of electronic trading facilities and formats on the structural dimensions of channels has already been noted. However, new technology has also had a major impact on the relationships between organisations. One view of web-based auctions is that they have the potential to destroy previously established buyer–seller relationships. It is thought that they can lead suppliers to distrust buyers who move to reverse auction formats because price is perceived as the dominant issue and there is little apparent scope to develop relationships. However, as Yap and Haruvy (2008) found, the type and frequency of bidding in these auctions appears to be a function of the relationship after the auction. So, suppliers forced to make severe price concessions were found to be less willing to help build relationships with the buyers once the auction was completed.

The counterview is that web-based auctions present an opportunity to develop new relationships with channel members. However, web auctions might reduce channel length and width (Sashi and O'Leary, 2002). These researchers postulate that where auction intermediaries are formed by groups of suppliers or buyers there are occasions where competition may be weakened because certain organisations are excluded. The dominant exchange therefore might succeed to a more powerful position than in offline situations and price collusion and market manipulation becomes a threat.

With supply chain auctions still required regardless of the method of buying, organisations need to be sure that their portfolio of relationships takes account of the buying opportunities afforded by the Internet and that these are offset against situations where strategic purchase items are held within a collaborative relationship. This view was developed by Skjott-Larsen *et al.* (2003). They formulated a procurement portfolio based on a firm's different forms of supplier relationships and various types of Internet-driven electronic marketplaces (IEMPs).

The outcome is that the Internet should be used in certain purchasing situations according to the significance of different types of purchase items so that some strategically orientated purchases may be maintained through strong relationships between partnerships and alliances.

■ eCommerce and Conflict

Many of the current disputes between organisations concern the introduction of an online sales channel. These online channels may be designed by a manufacturer (upstream) to complement current offline distributor arrangements. Alternatively they may be used to augment their direct sales force (external and internal conflict possibilities). Alternatively, a distributor (downstream), against the wishes of the upstream partner, may decide to offer a manufacturer's brand through their own online channels.

In order to build a successful online channel, care should be taken not to enrage current intermediaries, indeed every effort should be made to find an online channel solution that will help build trust and commitment. Of the many channel strategies open to manufacturers, some are incompatible with established offline

8

Managing B2B Relationships

channel approaches and openly invite tension and conflict. There are a number of strategies that manufacturers can employ when developing eCommerce facilities, although not all of them are appropriate as they often generate mistrust and conflict.

- *An independent strategy* refers to manufacturers who develop an online channel and either bypass their established offline intermediaries or enter into direct online competition with them. This invariably leads to conflict and if the product has no significant or unique features, dealers will substitute the manufacturer's brand and take their business elsewhere. The inertia strategy concerns those manufacturers who either do not provide a website or fail to provide suitable content, referral sites or online purchasing facilities. Retailers perceive this as a failure to provide competitive parity so inevitably retailer frustration and subsequent conflict results in retailers delisting these manufacturers.

- *The lead generator strategy* provides customers with information about the location of its retailers. If the information is unbiased and covers all authorised outlets, this model can be perceived positively by retailers. However, this positive view arises because the manufacturer site merely becomes a traffic generator. Retailers are free to cross-sell different brands to these leads as the manufacturer loses control over their own brand and those who expressed interest.

- *The participatory strategy* requires that once customers have selected their products at the manufacturer's site they then select a retailer and, through a co-branded site with the retailer, complete the purchase. This can be successful as all parties are involved and rewarded when transactions are completed. The win–win strategy enables manufacturers to retain brand control and avoid conflict with channel partners. Selling directly to end-user customers online, the manufacturer helps the end-user customer to select the brand they want and choose the channel partner they prefer for post-purchase service and support. Through this arrangement, channel partners are involved, not excluded, and are rewarded through profit and volume for their contribution to the customer experience.

At a tactical level there are a number of other reasons that can generate conflict within a B2B eCommerce context. Standifer and Wall (2003) found that there are two main issues which give rise to conflict. These are technical and socially induced causes of conflict. Technical problems concern difficulties with incompatible systems interfaces, system crashes, for example when placing orders or problems concerning product identification codes not being read and matched by the 'other' system. Social problems tended to centre on either internal interpersonal conflicts, such as the unwillingness of one person to assist another with the system, or socio-technical interactions demonstrated by a reluctance or refusal to change codes or processes to be compatible with the design of the system.

These authors found that such disagreements did not always escalate into conflict. However, when it did become difficult, high costs, problem reoccurrence, uncertainty and a lack of cooperation appeared to be the most frequent catalysts, as they termed them.

■ Customer Relationship Management Systems

From the early days of electronic data interchange (EDI) through to advanced eBusiness systems and solutions, organisations have sought to use IT to improve their internal and external transactions. Databases, communications networks, office and business applications have all contributed to increasing sophistication in this area. Such systems have had a significant impact not only on transactional efficiency but also on interorganisational relationships. For example, as Borders *et al.* (2001) observe, systems such as enterprise resource planning (ERP) and customer relationship management (CRM) bolt onto the upstream and downstream sides of the value chain.

ViewPoint 8.3: All sorts use all types of new technologies

New digital tools are being utilised by major firms to enhance their customer relationship management capabilities. Motorola report that new tools ranging from salesforce automation and CRM, search marketing measurement and the emergence of social network channels provide the basis for measuring return on investment from marketing campaigns. Earlier sales and marketing methods were described as cumbersome, making them unattractive for users as well as being considered expensive.

The US broadcaster NBC Universal has been utilising software from the 'Salesforce' system that delivers a central hub which allows all business units to access information. NBC reported that four weeks after installation they had achieved 75% user adoption. The new systems are providing a source of competitive advantage.

Communications business Verizon utilises a 'Computing as a Service' system which uses technology developed by SAP to provide employees with access to data from PCs and hand-held devices.

Groupon the daily deals web business has developed an 'Echosign' electronic signature application which significantly reduces the time involved in processing contracts via more traditional routes of scanning and mailing. Harris Products, a metal working specialist, has used a SAP system which involves a database of past and present customers to simplify feedback processes and facilitate more detailed statistical analysis.

Source: Taylor (2011); www.warc.com/news

Question: In what ways can CRM systems provide a basis for competitive advantage?

8

Managing B2B Relationships

Regarded as a front-end application, early CRM applications were designed for supplier organisations to enable them to manage their end-user customers. CRM applications were originally developed as sales force support systems (mainly sales force automation) and have subsequently evolved as a more sophisticated means of managing direct customers.

The aim of CRM systems is to provide all employees who interact with customers, either directly or indirectly, access to real-time customer information. To avoid fragmentation, a complete history of each customer's needs is made available to all staff who interact with customers. This is necessary in order to answer two types of questions. First, there are questions prompted by customers about orders, quotations or products, and second, questions prompted by internal managers concerning, for example, strategy, segmentation, relationship potential, sales forecasts and sales force management.

CRM applications typically consist of call management, lead management, customer record, sales support and payment systems. They are representative of a common perception of customer relationships which, although multifaceted, have the potential to achieve only a limited impact. Whether concentrating on loyalty schemes, cleansing the content of relational databases or even improving performance in customer contact centres, the perspective is anything but the overall management of customers.

Ideally, CRM systems should be incorporated as part of an overall strategic approach (Wightman, 2000). However, such systems are invariably treated as add-on applications that are expected to resolve customer interface difficulties. Unsurprisingly, many clients have voiced their dissatisfaction with CRM as many of the promises and expectations have not been fulfilled. Even in 2008 it is estimated that 70% of CRM projects have failed to deliver against their objectives (Gartner Group, 2008). Perhaps this apparent failure is not unexpected, if as Rapp et al. (2010: 1235) find, that durable customer relationships are best maintained using a "combination of customer-centric technology, human, and business resources along with a relationship-focused strategy".

O'Malley and Mitussis (2002) refer to the failure of CRM systems in terms of internal political squabbling and associated issues about who owns particular systems and data. Where an organisation has not established a customer-orientated culture nor begun to implement enterprise-wide systems and procedures, it is probable that access to certain data might be impeded or at least made problematic. From this, they claim, it is not surprising that conflict may arise between functional managers and information systems managers.

One of the latest developments in this area concerns social CRM. This is used to track incoming social media messages and then measure the impact or effectiveness of various social media postings. These can then be tracked through the sales cycle and a measure of return on the social media activity determined. Whether social CRM has any longevity has yet to be determined. However, the observation by Burdge, as cited by Matthews (2010), that traditional CRM is about data and that social CRM is about dialogue, might trivialise the transformational process, but it does serve to express the essence of the direction in which this aspect of CRM is headed.

Summary

To consolidate your understanding of the principles of managing business relationships, here is a summary of the main points set against the learning objectives.

1 Explore the concept of power and appreciate its significance in B2B relationships.

Power concerns the ability to get another (individual or organisation) to do what they/ it would not normally have done. In a channel context, power is obtained through the possession and control of resources that are valued by another member. Channel and interorganisational relationships can be regarded as a reflection of the balance of power that exists between organisations. However, the use of relative power positions based on access to and control of resources is no longer regarded as the preferred and pervasive marketing management tool.

2 Examine the various sources of channel power and consider the different influence strategies that organisations can use.

French and Raven (1959) determined five bases for power: rewards, coercion, expertise, legitimate and reference bases. Promise, threat, legalistic, request, information exchange and recommendation are the key strategies used to influence other organisations.

3 Introduce basic principles concerning channel conflict and examine ways in which tensions between organisations can be managed.

Conflict is to be expected whenever organisations seek to cooperate with one another, it is endemic. Conflict can be generated through competing or incompatible goals, domains, and perceptions of reality. Underpinning all of them is inadequate communication.

Conflict can be managed when it breaks out, through resolution and through learning about the event and the position and perceptions of the other participants.

4 Appreciate the dimensions and significance of trust and commitment in relationships as a means for building cooperation and channel collaboration.

As the relationship marketing approach has gathered momentum, so trust and commitment have become the focus for conflict resolution and avoidance, displacing power as the main management approach. Developing trust can lead to enhanced levels of commitment, which in turn improves cooperation and, theoretically, output and performance. Therefore, a strong relationship requires that trust be established between channel members.

Cooperation and collaborative behaviours arise from a relationship driven by high levels of both trust and commitment.

5 Explain the impact of technology on channel relationships.

The Internet and development of digital and web-based applications have had a major impact on B2B marketing and in the development of interorganisational relationships. Ecommerce should be used in certain purchasing situations according to the significance of different types of purchase items so that some strategically orientated purchases may be maintained through strong relationships between partnerships and alliances.

6 Consider the extent to which CRM systems can assist the management of B2B relationships.

The development of electronic trading formats once threatened established channel relationships but these digital facilities should be regarded as complementary tools. CRM systems have generally failed to deliver against promises but the emergence of social CRM might prove successful.

■ Discussion Questions

1 Evaluate social exchange theory as a means of explaining dependency and power.

2 Identify the five bases of power cited by French and Raven and then write brief notes explaining how three of them work.

3 What are the main reasons for interorganisational conflict within marketing channels? How can the impact of these different types of conflict be reduced?

4 Explain how an understanding of relationships and communication might help resolve conflict.

5 Identify four ways in which a technology has a positive influence on the management of channel relationships.

6 Identify and explain the four stages of CCL as proposed by Chang and Gotcher (2010).

References

Amason, A.C. (1996). Distinguishing the effects of functional and dysfunctional conflict on strategic decision making: resolving a paradox for top management teams, *Academy of Management Journal*, **39** (1), 123–148

Anderson, J.C. and Narus, J.A. (1990) A model of distributor firm and manufacturer firm working partnerships, *Journal of Marketing*, **54** (January), 42–58

Assael, H. (1969). Constructive role of interorganisational conflict, *Administrative Science Quarterly*, **14** (December), 573–582

Ballantyne, D. (2004). Dialogue and its role in the development of relationship specific knowledge, *Journal of Business and Industrial Marketing*, **192** (2), 114-123.

Belaya, V. and Hanf, J.F. (2009) The two sides of power in business-to-business relationships: implications for supply chain management, *Marketing Review*, **9** (4), 361–381

Borders, A.L., Johnston, W.J. and Rigdon, E.E. (2001) Electronic commerce and network perspectives in industrial marketing management, *Industrial Marketing Management*, **30** (2) (February), 199–205

Chang, K-H., and Gotcher, D.F (2010) Conflict-coordination learning in marketing channel relationships: The distributor view, *Industrial Marketing Management*, **39** (2) (February), 287–297

Chu, W. and Chu, W. (1994) Signalling quality by selling through a reputable retailer: an example of renting the reputation of another agent, *Marketing Science*, **13** (Spring), 177–89

Coughlan, A.T., Anderson, Stern, L. and El-Ansary, A. (2001) *Marketing Channels*, 6th edn, Englewood Cliffs, NJ: Prentice Hall.

Downing, C. (2010) Is web based supply chain integration good for your company? *Communications of the ACM*, **53** (5) (May) 134–137

Duarte, M. and Davies, G. (2003) Testing the conflict-performance assumption in business-to-business relationships, *Industrial Marketing Management*, **32** (2) (February), 91–93

Emerson, R. (1962). Power-dependence relations, *American Sociological Review*, **27** (February), 32–33

Fill, C. (2011) *Essentials of Marketing Communications*, Harlow: FT/Prentice Hall

French, J.R. and Raven, B. (1959) The bases of social power, in D. Cartwright (ed.), *Studies in Social Power*, Ann Arbor: University of Michigan

Gartner Group (2008) CRM success is in strategy and implementation, not software, (available at http://www.gartner.com)

Gaski, J.F. (1984). The theory of power and conflict in channels of distribution, *Journal of Marketing*, **48** (Summer), 9–29

Geyskens, I. and Steenkamp J.-B. (1995) *An Investigation into the Joint Effects of Trust and Interdependence on Relationship Commitment*, Proceedings of the European Marketing Academy Conference, 1995

Grieco, Jr, P.L. (1989) Why supplier certification? And will it work?, *Production and Inventory Management Review and APIC News*, **9** (5), 38–42.

Harris, S. and Dibben, M.R. (1999) Trust and co-operation in business relationship development: exploring the influence of national values, *Journal of Marketing Management*, **15** (July), 463–483

Hunt, S.B. and Nevin, J.R. (1974) Power in channel of distribution: sources and consequences, *Journal of Marketing Research*, **11**, 186–193

Jehn, K.A. (1994) Enhancing effectiveness: an investigation of advantages and disadvantages of value based intra group conflict, *International Journal of Conflict Management*, **5** (3), 223–238

Katz, D. and Kahn, R.L. (1978) *The Social Psychology of Organizations*, 2nd edn, New York: John Wiley.

Larson, A. (1992). Network dyads in entrepreneurial settings: a study of governance of exchange relationships, *Administrative Science Quarterly*, **37**, 76–104

Matthews, B. (2010) Listen and learn, *B2B Marketing*, **7** (10) (November/December), 28–29

McGrath, A. and Hardy, K. (1986) A strategic paradigm for predicting manufacturer–reseller conflict, *European Journal of Marketing*, **23** (2), 94–108

Menon, A., Bharadwaj, S. and Howell, R. (1996) The quality and effectiveness of marketing strategy, *Journal of the Academy of Marketing Science*, Springer Netherlands, **24** (4), 299–313

Mintel (2010) *Sports Goods Retailing*, May.

Mohr, J., Fisher, R., Nevin, J. (1999) Communicating for better channel relationships, *Journal of Marketing Management*, **8** (2) (Summer), 39–45

Morgan, R.M. and Hunt, S.D. (1994) The commitment-trust theory of relationship marketing, *Journal of Marketing*, **58** (July), 20–38

Mottner, S. and Smith, S. (2009) Wal-Mart: Supplier performance and market power, *Journal of Business Research*, **62** (5), (May) 535–541

Nakayama, M. (2003) An assessment of EDI use and other channel communications on trading behaviour and trading partner knowledge, *Information and Management*, **40** (6) (July), 563–581

O'Malley, L. and Mitussis, D. (2002) Relationships and technology: strategic implications, *Journal of Strategic Marketing*, **10 (3)**, (September), 225–238

Pondy, L.R. (1967) Organisational conflict: conflict and models, *Administrative Science Quarterly*, **12** (September), 296–320

Rapp, A., Trainor, K.J. and Agnihotri, R. (2010) Performance implications of customer-linking capabilities: Examining the complementary role of customer orientation and CRM technology, *Journal of Business Research*, **63** (11) (November) 1229-1236

Rose, G.M. and Shoham, A. (2002) Interorganisational task and emotional conflict with international channels of distribution, *Journal of Business Research*, **57** (9) (September), 942–950

Rosenberg, L.J. and Stern, L.W. (1970) Toward the analysis of conflict in distribution channels: a descriptive model, *Journal of Marketing*, **34** (4) (October), 40–46

Rosenbloom, B. (1978). Motivating independent distribution channel members *Industrial Marketing Management*, **7** (November), 275-281

Rosson, P. and Ford, D. (1980) Stake, conflict and performance in export marketing channels, *Management International Review*, **20** (4), 31–37

Sashi, C.M. and O'Leary, B. (2002) The role of Internet auctions in the expansion of B2B markets, *Industrial Marketing Management*, **31** (2) (February), 103–110

Selnes, F. and Sallis, J. (2003) Promoting relationship learning, *Journal of Marketing*, **67** (3), 80–95

Shankar,V., Urban, G.L. and Sultan, F. (2002). Online trust: a stakeholder perspective, concepts, implications and future directions, *Journal of Strategic Information Systems*, **11** (3/4), (December), 325–344

Shipley, D. and Egan, C. (1992) Power, conflict and co-operation in brewer–tenant distribution channels *International Journal of Service Industry Management*, **3** (4), 44–62

Skjott-Larsen, T., Kotazab, H. and Grieger, M. (2003) Electronic marketplaces and supply chain relationships, *Industrial Marketing Management*, **32** (3) (April), 199–210.

Southam, A.G. (2002) 'Understanding channel conflict', available at www.reshare.com, accessed December 2007

Standifer, R.L. and Wall, Jnr., J.A. (2003). Managing conflict in B2B e-commerce, *Business Horizons*, March–April, 65–70

Stern, L.W. and El-Ansary, A. (1992) *Marketing Channels*, 4th edn, Englewood Cliffs, NJ: Prentice Hall.

Stern, L.W., El-Ansary, A.I. and Coughlan, A.T. (1996) *Marketing Channels*, 5th edn, Englewood Cliffs, NJ: Prentice Hall.

Stern, L.W. and Gorman, R.H. (1969) Conflict in Distribution Channels: An exploration, in *Distribution Channels: Behavioral Dimensions*, L.W. Stern ed., Boston: Houghton Mifflin

Stern, L.W. and Heskett, J.L. (1969) Conflict management in interorganisational relations: a conceptual framework, in L.W. Stern (ed.) *Distribution Channels: Behavioural Dimensions*, Boston, MA: Houghton Mifflin, pp. 288–305.

Svensson, G. (2001). Extending trust and mutual trust in business relationships towards a synchronized trust chain in marketing channels, *Management Decision*, **39** (6), 431–40.

Tan, K.C. (2000). A framework of supply chain management literature, *European Journal of Purchasing and Supply Management*, **7** (1) (March), 39–48

Taylor, P. (2011) Sales moves from art to science, *Financial Times*, 15 March,

Webb, K.L. and Hogan, J.E. (2002) Hybrid channel conflict: causes and effects on channel performance, *Journal of Business and Industrial Marketing*, **17** (5), 338–356

Welch, C. and Wilkinson, I. (2002). Network perspectives on interfirm conflict; reassessing a critical case in international business, *Journal of Business Research*, available online

Wightman, T. (2000) e-CRM: the critical dot.com discipline, *Admap* (April) 46–48.

Yap, S.D. and Haruvy, E. (2008) Bidding behaviour in industrial online reverse auctions, *Journal of Marketing Research*, **XLV**, (October) 550–561

9 Principles of Business Marketing Communications

Overview

The main aim of this chapter, and the next, is to develop an understanding of the principles and characteristics of marketing communications. From an exploration of its role and tasks, the chapter considers some of the strategic issues and explores marketing communications strategy from a business audience perspective. A framework for the development of marketing communication plans follows.

B2B branding and integrated marketing communications are explored before examining marketing channel-based communications. If channels are to operate successfully and inter-firm relationships are to be developed for the benefit of all channel members, then sound trade channel communications are crucial. The chapter concludes with an examination of relationship-based marketing communication, and in particular, the nature, role and dynamics associated with client/agency based relationships.

Aims and objectives

The aim of this chapter is to explore issues concerning the role and characteristics of business marketing communications.

The objectives of this chapter are to enable readers to:

1 Explain the role and tasks of business-to-business marketing communications.

2 Examine the nature of strategy and planning in business marketing communications.

3 Consider issues related to business-to-business branding.

4 Explain the core ideas and characteristics associated with integrated marketing communications.

5 Consider the nature of channel-based marketing communications.

6 Explore ways in which marketing communications might be used to develop business relationships.

A Slice of Life – Evolution or Revolution?

There are few better places to look for good examples of good marketing and brand communications than where they didn't exist previously. That's almost impossible to achieve of course, because every business starts to communicate in some form or other from the day of its incorporation. Some businesses, however, are better at it than others. Some are in fact required to be better at it than others. Service companies without a tangible 'product' to sell, for example, focus on their message very quickly. Companies in saturated or highly competitive marketplaces inevitably seek a point of differentiation in order to stand out from the crowd.

The trick is to recognise and accept, early in the development of any kind of business, that no one except those with a vested interest in the business really gives a shit about communications. Armed with that salutary thought, the requirement for a coherent brand strategy and a sustainable barrage of communications that constantly assault the ambivalent prospective customer base, becomes more obvious. Unfortunately, I spend more time listening to clients saying, "I wish we'd started this years ago," than I hear them say, "The very first thing I need to do is sort out is my marketing."

I worked with a recruitment company that had been slow to adopt marketing practices, but was nevertheless a success long before my involvement. The company had grown quickly to achieve annual revenues of over £50m and it had done so with almost no marketing investment at all. It was succeeding in a hugely competitive environment - recruitment was (and is) one of the industries everyone treats as a 'necessary evil'.

Recognising that to maintain continued and sustainable growth, the company needed to communicate more effectively, it approached me to help create a brand and communications strategy. I succeeded with the former, and probably failed with the latter.

Taking a company through the steps to releasing the brand is always formative. You never really 'create' a brand strategy – the brand is always there, the trick is to articulate it in a way that positively influences people's perceptions of it. Even the simplest tools can become the strongest assets. Helping the company to identify who it was talking to, what to say, why it was important and what made it different sounds easy, but never is. When it's done, however, those assets provide the building blocks for all further communications – now, and long into the future.

In the case of this brand, and indeed any brand, the requirement was threefold. Firstly, the company needed to understand what their customers wanted – which was predominantly the functional service of, 'find me a job,' or, 'find me a candidate for a job'. The customer didn't want a new best friend from the recruitment company. The second revelation was that while the company delivered the same services that other recruitment companies provided, the customer experience was very different – and something that could be capitalised on.

The brand strategy was unanimously agreed and adopted by the board. They got it. They liked it. They believed in it. They even started using it - in conversation, in proposals, in presentations. But the transition from strategy to communications proved harder. The creative concept was to be built around 'being different' – providing familiar recruitment services, but with a better customer experience. The distinction was not to be found in criticising other recruiters, but in delivering something different. Apple, for example, succeeded not by criticising others, but by delivering everything 'differently' – the operating system, the software, the product, the user experience. Apple wasn't specifically competing with Microsoft or any other provider, Apple was just being Apple. It was 'different', and importantly, people liked it. This recruitment brand needed to do the same. Recruitment, but different.

Unfortunately, that proved too difficult. With the brand strategy in place (what people 'think' about us), the second stage for communications was to produce the Creative Platform® (what we 'look' like). I had visions of the new brand revolutionising the recruitment market. If I tell you that the creative execution of this vision involved a Nordic looking cartoon character with a beard and strange messages on his sweater and an animated goat, maybe that'll give you a clue to the direction for communications that I favoured. As the work evolved through client consultation however, it became safer and safer until the final creative work consisted of little more than a few black and white images of corporate-types in suits looking eminently employable for the camera. It was, you know... fine. But hardly 'different' in the way that it needed to be to set the recruitment world on fire.

The third stage of planning focuses on the channels for communication. My strategy was to use what were at the time emerging digital channels. Twitter and Facebook, for example, were proven media, but little used as B2B marketing channels. That made them the perfect channels for recruitment communications in my mind. None of the competitors had ventured into the space at the time and so the opportunity was enormous.

Unfortunately, the board was considerably more cautious. For a company advocating change, they were finding it hard to live up to the brand. Their view of communications was to do little more than they had always done, which was almost nothing. So the new Creative Platform® was applied to the company website and I think a poster may have been produced, and that was it. What became clear during our planning discussions was that when you have been spending nothing on marketing for a long time, spending anything at all suddenly seems like a lot. Without committed investment in the communication of the brand however, it can never really develop. How can the perceptions of audiences be influenced if the brand is never presented in the places where the audience is active?

It's worth noting that everyone was delighted with the new brand strategy, the Creative Platform and the new communications plan (however minimalist). The company was undoubtedly better armed and better prepared for the next stage of its development as a result of the work undertaken. The Chief Executive pointed out to me at the time that the company needed a brand that suited its relatively conservative market of public sector clients. It's not how I would have delivered a new recruitment brand had I been given a free rein, but who's to say who's right and who's wrong? The company never made the 'take your breath away' assault on the recruitment market that I wanted them to, but it protected and improved its market position which precisely fulfilled the company's objective. That is the final thing to remember when planning and developing any brand strategy and supporting marketing communications activity – to stay on track, make sure the strategy and planning meets the needs of the company. My brand is not your brand.

Scot McKee

■ Introduction

Effective communication is critically important for all organisations. One of the reasons for this is the necessity to inform customers of their products and services but another, and perhaps even more important reason, is to establish and maintain suitable relationships with a wide array of stakeholders. Communication enables organisations to join up and to facilitate the development and maintenance of active, positive relationships with a range of stakeholders. To assist this linkage, organisations use a mix of communication tools, media and messages, and these are examined in Chapter 10.

Many organisations focus on the needs of distributors and channel intermediaries. As determined earlier, organisations in the channel work together to satisfy their individual and collective objectives. The degree of conflict and cooperation in the channel network depends on a number of factors, but some of the most important factors are the form and quality of the communications between member organisations. This means that marketing communications must address the specific communication needs of members of the distribution network and those other stakeholders who impact on or influence trade channel performance.

■ Defining Marketing Communications

The conventional perspective on marketing communications is that it is an umbrella term embracing activities designed to convey information and persuade customers to purchase products and services. The focus of marketing communications has traditionally been product-orientated, and corporate communications have either encompassed all of an organisation's product and company image-based communications (van Riel, 1995) or just those communications associated with the organisation's image and reputation. This separation of communication activities reflects a silo or compartmentalised approach to communication. It is inward looking and considers the communication of information as one-way and hierarchical. Furthermore, it fails to encompass the variety of touch points customers, organisations and their staff have with other organisations and their products and services.

Business-to-business marketing communications are concerned with the way in which an organisation communicates with other organisations with regard to its products, services and its own desired corporate identity and associated reputation. Communication in this context is not about static, one-way information but about the meanings that are both intended (by the source organisation) and derived, as a result of interpretation, by the audiences (other organisations) in the communication process. Marketing communications are about participation and involvement and not exclusion or distance. Therefore, marketing communications should not be primarily about products, instruction and communication instruments, but rather concerned with audiences, involvement and meanings.

In order for marketing communications to work, they must be based on an understanding of the context and environment of the target audience, not that of the source organisation. This enables the development and presentation of relevant and timely messages, plus evaluation and reaction to responses received. The communication process should be symmetrical, such that both the audience and the originating organisation are willing and able to adjust their position, according to the messages received. The basis should not be power or price, indeed marketing communications should be an audience-centred activity.

Marketing communications is an audience-centred activity which attempts to encourage engagement between participants and provoke conversations.

The first key point is that marketing communications should be audience-centred. Traditionally marketing communications has been used to convey product-related information to largely customer audiences. Today, marketing communications needs to connect with a range of stakeholders all of whom have a variety of relationships with the organisation. Marketing communications should seek to provide added-value opportunities for the target audience, based on their needs and that means that marketing communications should be an audience-centred activity. To be successful, marketing communications should be grounded in the behaviour and information-processing needs and style of the target audience; an outside-in approach.

This definition involves the word 'engagement', or level of captivation that a communication episode can fashion between people and between people and machines. Captivation refers to a moment when audiences perceive messages that are relevant, meaningful, are of interest and which arouse curiosity. Engagement may last seconds, such as at the sight of a beautiful person, the impact of a stunning ad, or the emotion a film or video might bring to an individual. Conversely engagement may be protracted over hours, days, weeks, months or years, depending on the context and the level of enjoyment or loyalty felt towards the event, object or person. In either case engagement should lead to interaction and conversations with others.

In this sense marketing communications need to be interesting, relevant and both interactive and participatory, both of which are necessary to drive and sustain brand affinity or loyalty. Whatever the duration, engagement concerns the communication of messages that are understood, are rich in information or emotional content and which have meaning for the participants. In turn these messages provoke people to talk about their experiences. These conversations may be conducted through face-to-face, ear-to-ear or various electronic formats.

■ The Role of Marketing Communications

Organisations communicate with a variety of audiences in order to pursue their marketing and business objectives. Marketing communications can be used to engage business audiences with messages designed to encourage individual members of target audiences to respond to the focus organisation (or product/brand). This response can be immediate through, for example, purchase behaviour, through the website, or it can be deferred as information is assimilated and considered for future use. Even if the information is discarded at a later date, the communication will have attracted attention and consideration.

The reason to use marketing communications will vary according to the prevailing situation or context but the essential goal is to provoke an audience response. This might be geared to developing brand values and the positive thoughts an individual might have about a business brand. This is grounded in a 'thinking and feeling orientation', a combination of both cognitive thoughts and emotional feelings about a brand.

Another type of response might be one that stimulates the audience to act in particular ways. Referred to as a behavioural or sometimes brand response, the goal is to 'encourage particular behaviours'. For example, these might include sampling a piece of cheese in a supermarket, encouraging visits to a web site, placing orders and paying for goods and services, sharing information with a friend or peers, registering on a network, opening letters, signing a petition or telephoning a number. See Figure 9.1 for a list of the factors that can drive engagement opportunities.

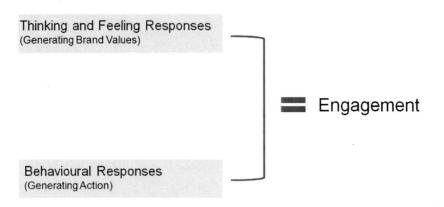

Figure 9.1: Factors that drive engagement opportunities

Apart from generating cash flows, the underlying purpose of these responses can be considered to be a strategic function of developing relationships with particular audiences and or from (re)positioning brands. For example, Truphone began business delivering downloadable voice over Internet protocol (VoIP) solutions for high international call costs for smartphones. Now it has rebranded as Tru, and been repositioned as the first global mobile network with a clear B2B division (Anon, 2011).

Engagement therefore can be considered to be a function of two forms of response. The quality of engagement cannot be determined but it can be argued that marketing communications should be based on driving a particular type of response that captivates an individual. For example, some brands focus on developing and building a brand and associated values in its early years. However, later in life the strategy might switch to market penetration and growing volume (customers, products, services used). This requires a behavioural strategy with communications that are complementary.

From this it can be concluded that the primary role of marketing communication is to engage audiences. Engagement acts as a bridge or mechanism through which brands and organisations link with target audiences and through which the goals of both parties can be achieved: mutual value. Engagement is much more than just getting an individual's attention, as suggested by Mitchell (2011). Attention is normally a prerequisite to engagement and is not just about cognitive information processing.

Engagement suggests that understanding and meaning has been conveyed effectively. The greater the frequency of information exchange the more likely collaborative relationships will develop. So, the role of marketing communications is to engage audiences.

ViewPoint 9.1: Stanley engage the trade

Stanley Tools manufacture and distribute tools and equipment for professional trades-men. For a long time they have been synonymous with measuring tapes and knives.

The rise of the Do-it-Yourself (DIY) sector following a spate of popular home improve-ment television programmes, led Stanley to shift their strategy from one that focused on professional tradesmen, where it was the Number 1 rated brand, to the consumer. Although the sector rose 76% in value in the period 1996 – 2006, DIY gave way to Do-it-For You (DFY). The implication for Stanley was that they needed to re-establish their position as the Number 1 supplier for professional tradesmen.

To achieve this a three-stage programme was developed. First Stanley created a new range of tools and equipment called Stanley 'FatMax XL', only available through profes-sional trade channels. The next stage was to use Stanley's 'Discovery Team' to research and understand the market. This was important as they found that advocacy was really important in the market. They also uncovered the criticality of key influencers or opinion formers. These are certain on-site tradesmen whose opinion is sought by others. This is because they are often the best performing and technically expert. If they rate a piece of equipment or a tool then it is likely that others would follow.

The third stage was the design and implementation of a communication strategy. The research indicated that an engagement strategy that emphasised behaviour rather than the brand values approach, one that was previously employed by Stanley through conventional media such as TV, print and online, would be more effective. The cam-paign was called 'Judgement Day' echoing the judgement a key influencer could make. The aim was to demonstrate though individual experience the quality of the FatMax XL range. This was achieved by visiting major building sites and professional trades events (e.g. InterBuild) and inviting the key influencers to trial the FatMax XL range, against competitor products. Using a boxing ring to stage the event, 'contestants' had to take on challenges such as how long it would take to hammer a six-inch nail into a piece of wood, using a Stanley hammer. Winners received tool belts of Stanley prod-ucts and were encourage to talk about their experiences and become advocates.

In addition to the on-site events, trade buyers were invited to meetings and open dis-cussions at Stanley's head office. Public relations was used to reach journalists. This was important as it provided credibility and reassured advocates of their role.

The overall impact of the programme exceeded expectations and enabled Stanley to achieve the majority of their objectives, including an ROI of 69% and a return to growth after a period of decline.

Source: Turland *et al*. (2009); Reiter, (2009)

Question: Why do you think Stanley used a behavioural rather than a brand value approach to engagement?

■ The Tasks of Marketing Communication

Bowersox and Morash (1989) demonstrated that communication plays an important part in the process through which information flows as it can help accomplish one or more key tasks:

First, marketing communications can act as a differentiator, particularly in markets where there is little to separate competing products and brands. Office stationery products, such as water coolers, filing trays and folders, are largely similar: it is the communications surrounding the products that create various brand images, enabling customers to make purchasing decisions. In these cases it is the images created by marketing communications that enable people to differentiate one business brand from another and position them so that a buyer's purchasing confidence and positive attitudes are developed.

Second, communications can also be used to reinforce experiences and beliefs. This may take the form of reminding people of a need they might have or reminding them of the benefits of past transactions with a view to convincing them that they should enter into a similar exchange. In addition, it is possible to provide reassurance or comfort either immediately prior to an exchange or, more commonly, post-purchase. This is important as it helps to retain current customers and improve profitability, an approach to business that is much more cost-effective than constantly striving to lure new customers. Brands are often refreshed, in order that they maintain currency among the target audience and remain competitive.

The third task identified was that communication can inform and make potential customers aware of an organisation's offering. Generally, no purchase can be made without prior awareness. Sometimes buyers and their DMUs need to be educated, shown how to use a product or service or advised about why a product might be helpful. The fourth and final task is to use communication to persuade current and potential customers of the desirability of either trialling a product, buying a product or entering into a relationship.

Therefore, communication can build images about a brand, that is **D**ifferentiate it, **R**einforce memories and understanding, **I**nform and make audiences aware of its presence and finally **P**ersuade an individual to buy and consume a product or service. To put it another way: DRIP (Fill, 2002). See Table 9.1 for an example.

The notion of value can be addressed in a different way. All organisations have the opportunity to develop their communications to a point where the value of their messages represents a competitive advantage. This value can be seen in the consistency, timing, volume or expression of the message. Heinonen and Strandvik (2005) argue that there are four elements that constitute communication value. These are the message content, how the information is presented, where the communication occurs and its timing. In other words, the all-important context within which a communication event occurs.

Table 9.1: DRIP elements of marketing communications

DRIP element	Examples
Differentiate	Xerox used the campaign 'Ready for real business' to reposition it as more than just a copier company.
Reinforce	Opta used communications to reinforce their core values as the business launched a single new identity and positioned itself for the future.
Inform	Servcorp used a campaign to show its markets how its virtual office space and solutions can help their businesses.
Persuade	TNT Post use direct mail and social media to encourage major corporates to try their services

ViewPoint 9.2: Client cooperation helps Xerox move forward

For many people, the word Xerox means copiers. Unfortunately this perception does not fit reality. Today, Xerox are a $22 billion leading global enterprise, offering a range of back office solutions which incorporate business processes and document management. The key benefit is that Xerox enable their clients to concentrate on their core business activities.

It was important therefore to change the way stakeholders, and customers in particular, understand the modern-day Xerox. 'Ready for real business' was the title of Xerox's campaign to reposition itself and change these outdated perceptions. This was achieved using an appeal based primarily on information, but through humour sought to generate an emotional response.

To demonstrate how other major companies had benefited from Xerox's business services, the campaign depicted some of the characters and mascots that are used to identify their customers. For example, the Procter & Gamble character Mr Clean and the Marriott Hotel bellboy, were shown struggling to do the back office tasks without the Xerox service.

Targeted at decision makers the campaign used television, print, web and airport advertising, plus interactive billboards that use motion-sensing and touch-screen technologies. At the centre of the activity was the RealBusiness.com microsite. This is the virtual headquarters for a fictional organisation Real Business International. Each of the five floors in the modern five-storey-office building features a different Xerox service. These range from finance and accounting and IT outsourcing to document management, customer care, and human resource support. The brand characters featured offline are found online, providing continuity and recall.

Source: Bonfanti (2010); http://news.xerox.com/pr/xerox/

Question: Using the DRIP framework, which tasks can be identified in Xerox's Real-Business campaign?

■ Strategy and Planning MCs

Traditionally, marketing communications strategy has been considered to encompass a combination of activities in the communications mix. This approach is understandable but suffers from a fundamental flaw. It is based upon an internal, production orientation, one which focuses on and around the resource base. This contradicts the audience-centred perspective and is not the essence of a sound marketing communications strategy.

Adopting an audience perspective from which to build a B2B marketing communications strategy necessitates efforts to understand the buying behaviour, characteristics and the information needs of the different target audiences. As stated previously, organisational purchase decisions are characterised by group buying centres and can involve a large number of people, all fulfilling different roles in the process and receptive to different marketing communication messages. It is also important to remember that audiences are normally attentive to messages that either have a product or company focus. As a result of understanding the broad nature of the target audience and the way we want them to position the offering in their minds, it is possible to identify three main marketing communication strategies by bringing these elements together:

■ Pull-positioning strategies – these are intended to influence end-user customers (consumers and business)

■ Push-positioning strategies – these are intended to influence marketing (trade) channel buyers

■ Profile-positioning strategies – these are intended to influence a wide range of stakeholders, not just customers and intermediaries.

These are referred to as the 3Ps of marketing communications strategy. Push and pull relate to the direction of the communication flow, relative to the marketing channel: pushing communications down through the marketing channel or pulling consumers/buyers into the channel via retailers, as a result of receiving the communications. They do not relate to the intensity of communication and only refer to the overall approach.

Profile refers to the presentation of the organisation as a whole and therefore the identity is said to be 'profiled' to various other target stakeholder audiences, which may well include consumers, trade buyers, business-to-business customers and a range of other influential stakeholders. Normally, profile strategies do not contain or make reference to specific products or services that the organisation offers. In many large organisations, profile strategies are managed by a corporate communication team and are not the direct concern of the marketing team. However, in many small and medium sized enterprises where resources for communications are tight, a profile strategy is often implemented instead of a product orientated campaign.

The demarcation of the pull/profile and push/profile strategies may be blurred, especially where the name of a company is the name of its primary (only) products, as is often the case with many retail brands. For example, messages about SAP and CAP Gemini products and services are very often designed to convey meaning about the functional capabilities and their quality and prices. However, they often reflect on the organisation itself, especially when its advertising shows members of staff doing their work and often providing customer service.

Within an overall strategy, individual approaches should be formulated to address the needs of a particular case. So, for example, the launch of a new office air-conditioning system will involve:

1 **A push-positioning strategy** to make distributors aware, educated, trained, motivated and stocked. The objectives would be to gain acceptance of the new system and to position it as an important source of new income streams for all distributors. Direct mail and personal selling, supported by trade sales promotions, web-based information plus service and support information, will be the main promotional approaches.

2 **A pull-positioning strategy** to develop awareness about the system will then be needed. Sometimes a limited amount of trade print advertising will be used, accompanied by appropriate public relations work. This might include blogging, use of social networks and social media, in order to generate awareness and even third-party credibility. Use of email and direct marketing are often used to generate particular system (brand) associations and to position the brand in the minds of target buyers. Messages may be functional or expressive but they will endeavour to convey meanings, which encapsulate a brand promise. This may be accompanied, or followed, by the use of incentives to encourage presentations, demonstrations or a short trial of the product. To support the brand, third-party reference sites will need to be established plus product specification details, normally by way of both hardcopy sales literature and a website.

Planning B2B Marketing Communication Activities

Planning is not the same as strategy, although the two terms are often used interchangeably. Marketing communications strategy is about the choice of audience and positioning that is what is to be communicated. Planning is usually about the formalisation, articulation and implementation of the strategy. This process is necessary to ensure that activities are coordinated, coherent and can be delegated and implemented within available resource constraints. Planning has an internal orientation. Marketing communications strategy has an external orientation, concerned as it is with the timing of, and approach to communication with customers and stakeholders. It must be formulated, in the context of overall business and marketing strategies, in order to encourage dialogue with selected stakeholders.

Figure 9.2 : The marketing communications planning framework (MCPF) (Fill, 2009)

So, a marketing communications plan is concerned with the development and managerial processes involved in the articulation of an organisation's marketing communication strategy. There is little doubt that planning and strategy are interlinked but it is useful to consider strategy as something that is audience and externally centred and planning which is resource and internally orientated.

The marketing communications planning framework (MCPF) set out at Figure 9.2 brings together various marketing communications activities into a logical sequence of events. Working hierarchically, the rationale for promotional decisions is built upon information generated at previous levels in the framework. It also provides a checklist of activities that need to be considered.

The MCPF represents a way of understanding the different promotional components, appreciating the way in which they relate to one another and a means of writing coherent plans in order to communicate effectively with other organisations.

The MCPF embodies a sequence of decisions that marketing managers undertake when preparing, implementing and evaluating communication strategies and plans. It should not be taken to mean that this sequence represents an immutable reality; indeed, many marketing decisions are made outside any recognisable framework. However, as a means of understanding the different components, appreciating the way in which they relate to one another and bringing together various aspects for work, the MCPF can be useful.

The process of marketing communications, however, is not linear, as depicted in this framework, but integrative and interdependent. It requires a perspective that enables messages to be developed from an understanding of the real dynamics and characteristics of a relationship. To that extent, this approach recognises the value of stakeholder theory and the need to build partnerships with buyers and other organisations networked with the organisation.

The degree to which these plans are developed varies across organisations and some rely on their agencies to undertake this work for them. However, there can be major benefits from in-house planning, for example by involving and discussing issues internally and developing a sense of ownership. Many small and medium-sized organisations can benefit from developing their own promotional plans and avoid the costs associated with agencies undertaking this work on their behalf.

As a final comment on marketing communications strategy, it is necessary to recognise that different internal audiences and coalitions often have conflicting proposals. In other words there is a political element to be considered and there may also be a strong overriding culture that not only directs the communication strategy but may also hinder innovation or the development of alternative methods of communication.

■ Is it about Campaigns or Activities?

In order that marketing communications campaigns be successful, good working relationships between all the parties involved with the campaign are necessary. These include strong managerial leadership, consultation and agreement between all the parties involved and a clear schedule and prioritisation of activities. The development of a marketing communications plan facilitates this process and enables the strategy to be articulated in such a way that the goals can be achieved in a timely, efficient and effective manner.

Traditionally agencies develop specific communication campaigns for clients. These are normally six weeks in duration, but can be longer (or shorter) according to the tasks. The campaign format provides a focus for the use of specific resources, enables measurement and is the way marketing communications has been undertaken in the modern era. This is changing because of two elements, purchase behaviour and digital media.

First, many B2B purchases do not stimulate high involvement and so campaigns, with its one off mindset, are not likely to induce sufficient engagement, even if the timing is right. Second, the media landscape has evolved into a digital array of social media, mobile and search which work more effectively outside a campaign format. In its place 'ongoing activities' have emerged as a more contemporary approach to B2B communications. Ongoing activity provides a presence, an arena in which a brand is available and buyers know where to find particular suppliers (and brands), when they are ready. See the Goodman example at ViewPoint 9.3.

Timing becomes focused on the buyer's needs, not the anticipation of a supplier. However, campaigns are not dead and continue to play a significant role, especially when launching a brand, repositioning or dealing with particular issues. So as Blyth (2010) suggests, it is probably better to recognise the influence of traditional campaign work and associated media, and to use this in an integrated, or coordinated, format with ongoing activities with online marketing.

ViewPoint 9.3: Ongoing property activities

Goodman is one of the world's largest property developers. It owns, develops and manages industrial property and business space across 16 countries. These exchanges are characterised by high value yet volume activity, suggesting that timing is always going to be a difficult issue.

For a long time Goodman used campaigns to communicate with their various audiences. These might typically involve open days in which prospective clients would be invited to view the offices or space. However, such a campaign might coincide with a buyer being on holiday or not in the market and ready to buy at that point.

Unsurprisingly these campaigns did not generate sufficient return and have now been abandoned in favour of ongoing activities. These include a regularly updated website, emails to provide updates on events at specific locations, and public relations to generate media coverage. As a result, the brand is present all times and ready for when a buyer does need to enter the market.

Source: Based on Blyth (2010)

Question: In which industry contexts do you believe activities are more appropriate than campaigns?

■ B2B Branding

Branding is a method commonly used in B2C markets to identify and add value to products and services in order to provide differentiation, assist positioning and drive competitive advantage. The benefits that can accrue from branding have been articulated by many authors (Aaker, 1996 and Keller, 1998) and from an industrial marketing perspective (Shipley and Howard, 1993). Generally these distil into three main dimensions: functional and product use benefits, emotional and self-expressive benefits. These are set out in Table 9.2.

Brands consist of two main types of attribute: intrinsic and extrinsic (Riezebos, 2002). Intrinsic attributes are the properties of an offering, which if modified in some way would alter the offering itself. By way of contrast, the extrinsic attributes of a brand are those elements that if modified would not have any influence on the performance of the offering, in other words do not influence the intrinsic attributes. For example, the intrinsic attribute of a special lubricant used in a manufacturing process may be the constituent oils and its overall viscosity. The extrinsic attributes may be the name of the supplier or type of oil, the wording on, or the colours of, the containers in which the oil is delivered.

Table 9.2: Benefits derived from branding

Brand benefit	B2B example
Functional advantages	Product performance and high quality associations.
	Superior service and support associations.
	Specific application and/or location advantages.
Emotional advantages	Improved confidence and trust through a reduction in perceived risk.
Self-expressive advantages	Buyer-related personal and professional satisfaction.

It has been alleged that B2B markets have been slow to develop brands and that B2B product-based branding is a relatively underdeveloped area (Mudambi, 2002). Indeed, Roper and Davies (2010) remark on the scarcity of true business brands, and cite Kochan, (1996) who found that in an analysis of an Interbrand list of the top 100 worldwide brands only Reuters and Boeing could be considered to be pure business-to-business brands. Whatever the position, research organisation Millward Brown (2009) believe that branding in a B2B context is very often corporate branding rather than product branding, and more importantly, that branding can influence business purchasing decisions.

This underdeveloped use of branding may stem from the nature of organisational decision making processes and associated group activities. Whatever the root cause, Mudambi states from her review of the literature and research, that branding is not of equal significance to all organisational buyers, nor is it important in all B2B buying situations. Indeed Bendixen *et al.* (2004) and Zablah *et al.* (2010) find that delivery, price and services are consistently more important to buyers than a brand name.

In contrast, work by Shipley and Howard (1993), and Michell *et al.* (2001) suggests that brand strategies are used widely by industrial organisations, as product and corporate branding can be crucial contributors to successful performance. A partnership might develop whereby the brand, among other things, reassures a buyer who supports the brand by paying the brand's price premium. As a result, brands can not only provide solutions on a continuous basis for certain customers but they may also become integral to a long-term relationship. Lindgreen *et al.*, (2010) observe that organisational buyers make decisions using emotional benefits and self-expressive benefits (such as personal and professional satisfaction), in addition to the functional elements. Indeed, work by Roper and Davies (2010) provides timely empirical evidence that B2B brands can have a demonstrable personality and that "industrial brands can benefit from the concept of brand image and personality" (p. 584).

To develop brands, three elements need to be managed. These are the symbolic devices, communication and behaviour. Together these might be considered to be the branding mix. In corporate reputation management these elements are referred to as the 'identity mix'.

■ All organisations use symbolism to signal who they are and what they stand for. Logos, company names, straplines, colours, architecture, design, work-wear, delivery vehicles are all symbols.

■ Communication can be considered in terms of management communication (internal and external), organisation communication (public relations) and marketing communications. These need to be integrated around a central theme or strategic platform.

■ The behaviour of employees and managers, not only with one another but with external stakeholders, is often overlooked in the branding and reputation management process. One of the key tasks is to align the values that employees have with those of the organisation, and this requires training, communication and attention by management.

To build corporate brands, organisations must develop modern, integrated communication programmes with all of their key stakeholder groups. Stakeholders demand transparency, accountability and instant, often online, access to news, developments, research and networks. This means that inconsistent or misleading information must be avoided. As if to reinforce this, a survey reported by Gray (2000) found that CEOs rated the reputation of their organisations as more important than that of their products. However, the leading contributors to the strength of a corporate brand are seen to be their products and services, followed by a strong management team, internal communications, public relations, social accountability, change management and the personal reputation of the CEO.

Mudambi suggests that there are three types, or clusters, of B2B customers based upon the way they each perceive the importance of branding in the organisational purchase decision process. The highly tangible, brand receptive and low-interest clusters reflect differing attitudes towards B2B brands. From this base, marketing communications can be developed more sympathetically and effectively. Note the link between segmentation and communications:

■ The highly tangible cluster require messages that stress quantifiable and objective benefits of the product and company.

■ The brand receptive cluster require messages that emphasise the support of a well-established and highly reputable manufacturer, the emotional and self-expressive benefits should be stressed.

■ The low-interest cluster are more likely to respond to brand-based communications that highlight the importance of the purchase decision and which are supported with processes and procedures that assist the ordering systems. Communications need to stimulate interest in the product and associated purchase decision, perhaps by using testimonials and mini-cases highlighting customers who have experienced similar purchase situations.

It is accepted by Mudambi that the research and data from which these clusters have been derived is not totally reliable, nor is the information based on anything other than judgement and experience. However, it is a useful step forward because Mudambi demonstrates that B2B branding opportunities are currently under-exploited.

ViewPoint 9.4: Strategic branding for Apollo

Apollo Aerospace Components operate in the aerospace and defence industry. They provide a range of aerospace components and services, including hardware, machinery and a tailored outsourcing service.

The industry had evolved in recent years experiencing some consolidation in the supply chains and an attempt to be leaner. A more global outlook had developed and associated with this was the emergence of some major industry players, who drove down costs. This made it difficult for Apollo Aerospace to compete.

A new strategy was developed, based on delivering high levels of customer service, supported by a strong technological/knowledge-based ethos. This strategy was to be targeted at specific industry sectors.

This strategy was about repositioning and needed to be communicated. As a result the identity mix was reviewed and new symbolic devices including a change of company name, (from Apollo Hitech), a new logo and strapline were introduced. In addition to the standard promotional materials and updates to the website, the company used email and face-to-face customer presentations, to explain the new strategy, and introduce new senior management. This last move was designed to underline the company's intention to reposition and to engage employees in the new strategy.

Source: Based on Crabtree (2010); www.apollohitech.com/

Question: How would you advise Apollo with regard to engaging employees in the new strategy and repositioning?

■ Internal Branding

Employees interact with customers, and other stakeholders. They deliver the functional aspects of an organisation's offering and they also deliver the emotional dimensions, particularly in service environments. Through interaction with these two elements, long-term relationships between sellers and buyers can develop. Employees therefore constitute an integral part of a brand. Scholars and practitioners such as Rach (2010) rightly emphasise the need to integrate internal audiences in brand development.

This process, whereby employees are encouraged to communicate with stakeholders so that organisations ensure that what is promised is realised by customers, is referred to as 'living the brand'. Welch and Jackson (2007) consider some of the issues associated with internal communication. They suggest that internal corporate communication refers to communication between an organisation's strategic managers and its internal stakeholders, with the purpose of promoting *commitment* to the organisation, a sense of *belonging* (to the organisation), *awareness* of its changing environment and *understanding* of its evolving goals (p. 86).

The success of many corporate and service brands is founded on the strength of the internal dimension. The greater the degree to which staff believe and uphold the values, mission and vision of an organisation the more likely reputation and performance goals will be achieved. Slowly, more energy is being put into the internal aspect of B2B marketing activities.

■ Integrated Marketing Communications

Integrated marketing communications (IMC) first emerged as part of the marketing communications vocabulary in the early 1990's. Promoted by Schultz (1993) and Kitchen (1993) IMC was considered to be the pinnacle of marketing communications best practice.

At this early stage, integration was about orchestrating the marketing communications mix. Indeed Duncan and Everett (1993) recall that this new, largely media oriented approach, has over the years been referred to variously as *orchestration*, *whole egg* and *seamless communication*. Since this time many authors have expanded upon ideas concerning IMC, including Duncan (2002) and Gronroos (2004) who have provided valuable insights into this dimension. Jaffray (2010) considers integration in terms of teams coming together to work around platforms, with a platform being a construct around which other things can be built on. Indeed the use of platforms or a strategically themed approach enables a broader and deeper understanding and application of IMC.

IMC can be considered to be a thematic approach to the strategic development of an organisation's communications. Whether at the corporate or product/service level, IMC requires that organisations coordinate their various strategies, resources and messages in order that they engage coherently and meaningfully with target audiences. The main purpose is to develop relationships with, provoke conversations among, and enable audiences to perceive brands in a positive and consistent way, which is of value.

This perspective serves to link IMC with business-level strategies and the importance of coherence within an organisation's use of resources and messages. Implicit is the underpinning notion that IMC is necessary for the development of effective relationships and that not all relationships need be collaborative and fully relational, as so often assumed to be in many contemporary interpretations. IMC is not just a managerially driven activity. It is also something that audiences do, as a result of how they perceive and experience brands.

■ Why the Interest in IMC?

One of the reasons offered for the development of IMC was that it was a reaction to the structural issues prevailing in the communications industry. For example, communications expertise was siloed into advertising, media or public relations specialists. Clients realised that their communication goals can (and should) be achieved more efficiently and effectively if the expertise was available at a single place. Indeed, clients expect and demand integrated communications, but although agencies have often promised IMC services, reality suggests otherwise. Hence there is a problem.

The explosion of interest in IMC has resulted from a variety of drivers. Generally they can be grouped into three main categories: those drivers (or opportunities) that are market-based, those that arise from changing communications, and those that are driven from opportunities arising from within the organisation itself. These are set out in Table 9.3.

Table 9.3: Drivers for IMC (Fill, 2009)

Organisational Drivers for IMC
Increasing profits through improved efficiency
Increasing need for greater levels of accountability
Rapid move towards cross-border marketing and the need for changing structures and communications
Coordinated brand development and competitive advantage
Opportunities to utilise management time more productively
Provide direction and purpose for employees

Market-based drivers for IMC
Greater levels of audience communications literacy
Media cost inflation
Media and audience fragmentation
Stakeholders' need for increasing amounts and diversity of information
Greater amounts of message clutter
Competitor activity and low levels of brand differentiation
Move towards relationship marketing from transaction-based marketing
Development of networks, collaboration and alliances

Communication-based drivers for IMC
Technological advances (Internet, databases, segmentation techniques)
Increased message effectiveness through consistency and reinforcement of core messages
More effective triggers for brand and message recall
More consistent and less confusing brand images
Need to build brand reputations and to provide clear identity cues

The opportunities offered through IMC are considerable and it is somewhat surprising that so few organisations have been either willing or able to embrace the approach. One of the main organisational drivers for IMC is the need to become increasingly efficient. Driving down the cost base enables managers to improve profits and levels of productivity. By seeking synergistic advantages through its communications and associated activities and by expecting managers to be able to account for the way in which they consume marketing communication resources, so integrated marketing communications becomes increasingly attractive. At the same time, organisation structures are changing more frequently and the need to integrate across functional areas reflects the efficiency drive.

From a market perspective, the predominant driver is the developing interest in relationship marketing and the creation of mutual value. By adopting a position designed to enhance trust and commitment, an organisation's external communications need to be consistent and coordinated, if only to avoid information overload and misunderstanding.

From a communication perspective, the key driver is to provide a series of triggers by which buyers can understand a brand's values and a means by which they can use certain messages to influence their activities within the relationships they wish to develop. By differentiating the marketing communications, often by providing clarity and simplicity, advantages can be attained.

An integrated approach should attempt to provide a uniform or consistent set of messages. These should be relatively easy to interpret and to assign meaning. This enables target audiences to think about and perceive brands within a relational context and so encourage particular behaviours. Those organisations that try to practice IMC understand that buyers refer to and receive messages about brands and companies from a wide range of information sources. Harnessing this knowledge is a fundamental step towards enhancing marketing communications.

The advantages and disadvantages associated with IMC are set out in Table 9.4. General opinion suggests that the advantages far outweigh the disadvantages and that increasing numbers of organisations are seeking to improve their IMC resource. As stated earlier, database technology and the Internet have provided great impetus for organisations to review their communications and to implement moves to install a more integrated communication strategy.

Table 9.4: The advantages and disadvantages of IMC (Fill, 2009)

Advantages of IMC

- Provides opportunities to cut communication costs and/or reassign budgets
- Has the potential to produce synergistic and more effective communications
- Can deliver competitive advantage through clearer positioning
- Encourages coordinated brand development with internal and external participants
- Provides for increased employee participation and motivation
- Has the potential to cause management to review its communication strategy
- Requires a change in culture and fosters a customer focus
- Provides a benchmark for the development of communication activities
- Can lead to a cut in the number of agencies supporting a brand

Disadvantages of IMC

- Encourages centralisation and formal/bureaucratic procedures
- Can require increased management time seeking agreement from all involved parties
- Suggests uniformity and single message
- Tendency to standardisation might negate or dilute creative opportunities
- Global brands restricted in terms of local adaptation
- Normally requires cultural change from employees and encourages resistance
- Has the potential to severely damage a brand's reputation if incorrectly managed
- Can lead to mediocrity as no single agency network has access to all sources of communications

■ What should be integrated?

The notion that some aspects of marketing communications should be integrated has received widespread and popular support over the past decade. Indeed, most agencies see integration in terms of media synergy (Easterbrook, 2010), which in part restricts its development and potential. However, defining what integration actually means and what should be integrated is far from universally agreed, especially as there is an absence of any empirical evidence or definitive research in the area (Cornelissen, 2003). While the origins of IMC might be found in the prevailing structural conditions and the needs of particular industry participants, an understanding of what elements should be integrated in order to achieve IMC needs to be established.

The problem with answering this question is that unless there is an agreement about what IMC is then identifying appropriate elements is far from easy, practical or in anyone's best interests. At one level the harmonisation of the elements of the marketing communications mix represents the key integration factors but as these represent a resource-driven view then perhaps a more strategic (audience-centred) perspective, one driven by the market and the strategic objectives of the organisation might be more realistic. Between these two extremes it is possible to identify messages, media, employees (especially in service-based environments), communication planning processes, client/agency relationships and operations, and the elements of the marketing mix all of which all need to be involved and be a part of the integration process.

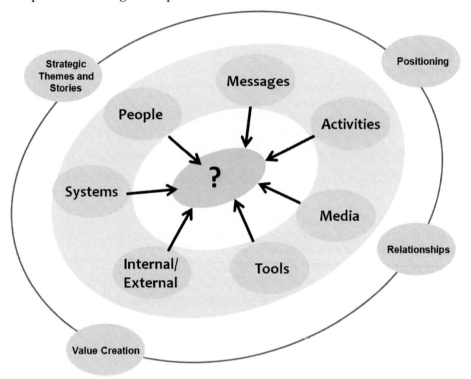

Figure 9.3: Elements to be integrated

The development of IMC is not a universally agreed concept. Scholars such as Cornelissen (2003) point out the lack of an agreed definition, that there is no theoretical base or underpinning empirical research. Luck and Moffatt (2009) observe that IMC is considered mostly as a simple integration of the traditional tools of the marketing communication mix and is invariably contexualised within the product and goods category, ignoring services, other sectors and internal markets. Practitioners such as Devon and Maker (2010) consider the word 'integration' as obsolete as it can be considered to work when there is a unifying thought driving the whole business, not just marketing.

Finne and Gronroos (2009) offer a Relationship Communication Model as a new perspective on integrated marketing communication. The core difference being that this adopts a customer (outside-in) perspective on what integrating messages whereas the most common view is on outgoing messages, an inside-out view. Ewing (2009: 113) agrees that IMC should be about how audiences integrate and attribute meaning to messages, highlighting the need for more research into IMC implementation. He considers five areas for IMC measurement and requests more research to "delineate firm-specific aspects relating to IMC. What are the best practices?"

It should be clear therefore that IMC is far from an agreed concept and that it is evolving. Indeed, rather than attempt to adopt an integrated campaign perspective, marketers can adopt a more strategically thematic approach, one that stresses continuity. For example, many B2B marketers realise the communicative power of live events. However, rather than just video an event and make it available on a website, a strategic approach can help leverage the content. So, a communication strategy designed, for example, to position a brand around innovation, can enable pre-event communications to be based on innovation. This would stress what the event will do and the sort of content to be covered and this can be done both offline, and online through FaceBook and LinkedIn groups. Webcasts, online surveys and forums can be used to increase interest and raise expectations.

During the event, Twitter and the use of live screening for those not able to attend are popular. For those attending the event, activities that promote interest and involvement without diminishing the quality of the content and overall experience are considered worthwhile. Event-based discussion groups, big screen projections of visitor behaviour and even photography (Matthews, 2010) can assist the cause.

Post-event communications should be based around editing the digital content, repackaging it into bite-sized portions and making it available on the web site. Matthews suggests this might include editing the keynote speeches, videos of significant interviews and running online workshops with headline speakers or event organisers. Throughout this content the innovation theme should be repeated and emphasised.

■ Channel-based Marketing Communications

Mohr and Nevin (1990) suggest that successful channel marketing is mainly a result of the interaction between the channel structure and the communications used between the members. Figure 9.4 depicts the relationships between communication strategies and structure. Thus, by examining the constituent elements and moulding the variables to meet the channel conditions, it may be possible to enhance the performance/success of the network.

■ Communication facets

Communication strategy within a channel results from a combination of four facets of communication. These are frequency, direction, modality and content.

Frequency

The amount of contact between members of a network should be assessed. Too much information (too frequent, aggregate volume or pure repetition), can overload members and have a dysfunctional effect. Too little information can undermine the opportunities for favourable performance outcomes by failing to provide necessary operational information, motivation and support. As a consequence, it is important to identify the current volume of information being provided and for management to make a judgement about the desired levels of communication.

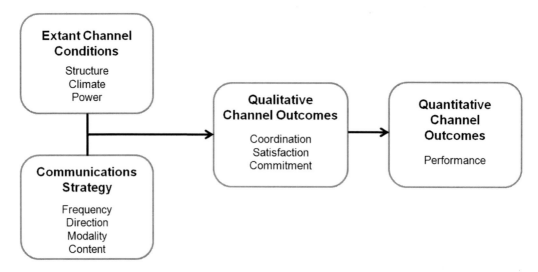

Figure 9.4: A model of communication for marketing channels. (Mohr and Nevin 1990) , used with permission

Direction

This refers to the horizontal and vertical movement of communication within a network. Each network consists of members who are dependent upon others, but the level of dependency will vary – hence the dispersion of power is unequal.

Communications can be unidirectional in that they flow in one direction only. This may be from a source of power to subordinate members (for example, from a major IT systems provider such as Cisco, to small and medium-sized distributors or resellers). Communications can also be bidirectional, that is, to and from equally powerful organisations. The relative power positions of manufacturer/producer and reseller need to be established and understood prior to the crea tion of any communication plan. Many small and medium-sized organisations suffer from unidirectional messages where larger more powerful organisational customers ignore incoming communications and fail to respond appropriately to their marketing channel partners.

Modality

Modality refers to the method used to transmit information. Mohr and Nevin (1990) agree that there is a wide variety of interpretations of the methods used to convey information. They use modality in the sense that communications can be either formal and regulated, such as meetings and written reports, or informal and spontaneous, such as corridor conversations and word-of-mouth communications, often carried out away from an organisation's formal structures and environment.

Content

This refers to what is said. Frazier and Summers (1984) distinguish between direct and indirect influence strategies. Direct strategies are designed to change behaviour by specific request (recommendations, promises and appeals to legal obligations). Indirect strategies attempt to change a receiver's beliefs and attitudes about the desirability of the intended behaviour. This may take the form of an information exchange, where the source uses discussions about general business issues to influence the attitudes of the receiver.

■ Channel structures

Communication facets can be seen in the light of three particular channel conditions: structure, climate and power.

Channel structure

Channel structure, according to Stern and El-Ansary (1988), can be distinguished by the nature of the exchange relationship. These are relational and discrete relationships. Relational exchanges have a long-term perspective and high interdependence, and involve joint decision making. Discrete or market exchanges are by contrast ad hoc and hence have a short-term orientation where interdependence is low (see Chapter 1).

Channel climate

Anderson *et al.* (1987) used measures of trust and goal compatibility in defining organisational climate. This in turn can be interpreted as the degree of mutual supportiveness that exists between channel members.

Power

Dwyer and Walker (1981) showed that power conditions within a channel can be symmetrical (with power balanced between members), or asymmetrical (with a power imbalance).

■ Channel Communication Strategies

Two specific forms of communication strategy can be identified. The first is a combination referred to as a 'collaborative communication strategy' and includes higher frequency, more bidirectional flows, informal modes and indirect content. This combination is likely to occur in channel conditions of relational structures, supportive climates or symmetrical power. The second combination is referred to as an 'autonomous communication strategy' and includes lower frequency, more unidirectional communication, formal modes and direct content. This combination is likely to occur in channel conditions of market structures, unsupportive climates and asymmetrical power. See Table 9.5.

Table 9.5: Features of channel communication strategies

	Collaborative Communication Strategy	Autonomous Communication Strategy
Communication Feature		
Frequency	Higher	Lower
Direction	Two-way	One-Way
Formality	Informal	Formal
Content	Indirect	Direct
Channel Context		
Relationship orientation	High	Low
Channel climate	Supportive	Unsupportive
Balance of channel power	Symmetric	Asymmetric

Based on Mohr and Nevin (1990)

Communication strategy should, therefore, be built upon the characteristics of the situation facing each organisation in any particular network. Not all networks share the same conditions, nor do they all possess the same degree of closeness or relational expectations. By considering the nature of the channel conditions and then developing communication strategies that complement them, the performance of the focus organisation and other members can be considerably improved, and conflict and tension substantially reduced. Where channel conditions match communication strategy, the outcomes are likely to be enhanced (Mohr and Nevin, 1990). Likewise, when the communication strategy fails to match the channel conditions, the outcomes are unlikely to be enhanced.

■ **Timing of the flows**

Message flows can be either simultaneous or serial.

■ Where simultaneous flows occur, messages are distributed to all members so that the information is received at approximately the same time. Business seminars and dealer meetings, together with direct mail promotional activities and the use of integrated IT systems between levels (overnight ordering procedures), are examples of this type of flow.

■ Serial flows involve the transmission of messages so that they are received by a preselected number of network members who then transmit the message to others at lower levels within the network. Serial flows may lead to problems concerning the management of the network, such as those concerning stock levels and production.

■ **Permanence of the flows**

The degree of permanence that a message has is determined by the technology used in the communication process. Essentially, the more a message can be recalled without physical distortion of the content, the more permanent the flow. This would indicate that the use of machines to record the message content would have an advantage over person-to-person messages transmitted at a sales meeting. Permanence can be improved by recording the meeting with a tape recorder or by putting the conversation on paper and using handouts and sales literature.

Therefore, the nature and form of the cooperation and the interorganisational relationships that develop from the exchanges influence the nature of the marketing communication activities used. The degree of cooperation between organisations will vary and part of the role of marketing communications is to develop and support the relationships that exist between partner organisations.

In this sector, organisations buy products and services and they use processes and procedures that can involve a large number of people. Fuller details about these characteristics can be found in Chapter 3. What is central, however, is the decision making unit and the complexities associated with the variety of people and processes involved in making organisational purchase decisions and the implications for suppliers in terms of the length of time and nature of the communication mix necessary to reduce the levels of risk inherent in these situations.

■ Relationship Marketing and Communications

From a relationship perspective, marketing communications can perform different yet significant roles as relationships evolve. Some of these are set out in Table 9.6.

Table 9.6: The different relationship roles of marketing communications

Relationship stage	Role of marketing communications
Acquisition	Differentiation to establish position.
	Information about organisational credentials and product features.
	Persuasion to stimulate behavioural action.
Development	Differentiation and information provision predominate as organisations become increasingly open and reveal more about themselves.
	Increasing levels of trust emerge as the boundaries of the relationship become established.
Retention	The provision of knowledge and sharing of information becomes regularised and a common part of the relationship. Reinforcement messages, based on both reminding and reinforcing, are used to provide trust and commitment in order to support valued relationships.
Decline	Discrete relationships resort to persuasion in order to extract remaining value from the relationship.

Building on the ideas about market and collaborative exchanges in Chapter 4 it is possible to discern a spectrum of marketing communications activities. Market exchanges have a product and price orientation where buyers are not interested in a long term relationships. In these circumstances communications should be based around mass media, be impersonal and monologic. In contrast, communications where collaborative relationships have been established should be personal, direct, and interactive/dialogic. See Figure 9.5.

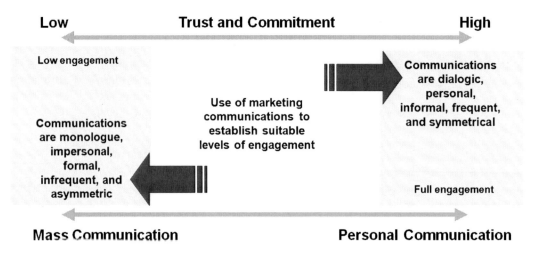

Figure 9.5: Characteristics of relationship-based communications

A relatively new and interesting perspective on marketing channels concerns the quality of the communications and the success that might be attributed to the communication behaviours of relationship partners in a network.

Mohr and Sohi (1995) considered whether communication quality might be a function of the propensity of members to share information. The inclination among members to share information could be assumed to be positive in channels and networks where members show high levels of trust and commitment. Frequency of communication flows, the level of bidirectional communications in a network and the level of communication formality are assumed to be the main elements of the propensity to share information.

Another aspect considered by the researchers was the degree to which information might be withheld or distorted (deviance). Information deviance might be high when there is an absence of rules (norms) determining what information needs to be communicated. Informality may lead to vagueness or inattentiveness and higher levels of deviance.

The research sought to determine whether any (or all) of the three factors indicated that there was a link between the variables and the quality of information perceived by channel members. The results suggested that in the sample sector (computer dealers) the only significant variable was the frequency of information. The higher the frequency of communications received by channel members, the higher the perception of the quality of the communications. Issues concerning information overload and irritance are discounted.

Satisfaction levels appear to be correlated with higher levels of bidirectional communications. So, frequency impacts on perceived quality (and hence satisfaction) and the degree of bidirectional communications is significant in determining levels of satisfaction with the communications in a channel (network) environment.

Summary

Here are the key points about the B2B marketing communications strategy, set out against the learning objectives.

1 Explain the role and tasks of business-to-business marketing communications.

Business-to-business marketing communications are concerned with the way in which an organisation communicates with its business customers, other organisations, with regard to its products and services. These communications should be audience-centred and designed to engage audiences and increasingly, to provoke brand-based conversations.

The tasks of marketing communications can be to provide a point of differentiation, reinforce memories and understanding, inform and make audiences aware of a brand's presence and finally persuade a buyer to buy and consume a product or service.

2 Examine the nature of strategy and planning in business marketing communications.

Marketing communications strategy is about two main elements, audiences and positioning. Three core strategies can be identified, pull-positioning, push-positioning and profile-positioning, based on the audiences the communications are intended to influence.

Planning is usually about the formalisation, articulation and implementation of the strategy. The marketing communications planning framework (MCPF) brings together various marketing communications activities into a logical sequence of events.

3 Consider issues related to business-to-business branding.

Brands offer advantages to both business customers and brand owners. Branding in business markets is not as common as in consumer markets, as many buyers claim to refer to delivery, price and services. However, business brands can be integral to long-term business relationships, which are important in business markets. Brands can benefit from the concept of brand image and personality.

4 Explain the core ideas and characteristics associated with integrated marketing communications.

IMC requires that organisations coordinate their various strategies, resources and messages in order that it engage coherently and meaningfully with target audiences. The main purpose is to develop relationships with and provoke conversations among audiences that are of mutual value.

5 Consider the nature of channel-based marketing communications.

Marketing communications have an important role to play in marketing channels. Communication strategy should be built upon the combination of four facets of communication with the prevailing channel conditions. In addition to this, channel-based communications can be developed by understanding the inclination or propensity of members to share information.

6 Explore ways in which marketing communications might be used to develop relationships.

Theoretically, relationship-orientated communications can be adapted to where a buyer might be in terms of the relationship life cycle. However, in practical terms it is not easy to pinpoint where a customer might be in the cycle and the communications recommended might be too generic.

Understanding the type of relationship a business customer might perceive to have with a supplier might lead to the use of a more appropriate mix of communications.

■ Discussion Questions

1 Explain each of the four aspects of the DRIP framework and find examples of B2B marketing communications that illustrate each of these elements.

2 Write brief notes explaining the differences between marketing communications strategy and planning. Without referring to the text, attempt to draw the marketing communications planning framework.

3 Explain the three brand clusters identified by Mudambi and discuss the potential for branding in B2B marketing.

4 Discuss the view that integrated marketing communications does not add significant value to a well researched and implemented campaign.

5 Critically appraise the Mohr and Nevin model of channel-based marketing communications.

6 How might marketing communications be used most effectively to reflect the prevailing relationship between a buyer and seller?

References

Aaker, D.A. (1996). *Building Strong Brands*, New York: Free Press.

Anderson, E., Lodish, L. and Weitz, B. (1987) Resource allocation behaviour in conventional channels, *Journal of Marketing Research*, (February), 85–97

Anon (2011) Brand makeover: Tru, *B2B Marketing*, 10 May 2011, retrieved 31 May 2011 from www.b2bmarketing.net/knowledgebank/branding/features/brand-makeover-tru

Bendixen, M., Bukasa, K.A. and Abratt, R. (2004) Brand equity in the business-to-business market, *Industrial Marketing Management*, **33**, 371–380

Blyth, A. (2010) Of the campaign, *B2B Marketing*, **7** (10) (November/December), 23-24

Bonfanti, P. (2010) Xerox means real business, *B2B Marketing*, October, p.10

Bowersox, D. and Morash, E. (1989) The integration of marketing flows in channels of distribution. *European Journal of Marketing*, **23**, 2

Cornelissen, J.P. (2003) Change, continuity and progress: the concept of integrated marketing communications and marketing communications practice, *Journal of Strategic Marketing*, **11**, (December) 217-234

Crabtree, J. (2010) Brand Makeover: Apollo Aerospace Components, *B2B Marketing*, **7** (10), (November/December) 20

Devon, J. and Maker, S. (2010) Integration is Dead, *Campaign: What next in Integration?* 3 December, p. 21

Duncan (2002) *IMC: Using Advertising and Promotion to Build Brands*, (International edition) New York: McGraw Hill

Duncan, T. and Everett, S. (1993) Client perceptions of integrated marketing communications, *Journal of Advertising Research*, **3** (3), 30–39

Dwyer, R. and Walker, O.C. (1981) Bargaining in an asymmetrical power structure, *Journal of Marketing*, **45** (Winter), 104–115

Easterbrook, J. (2010) Reclaim the word, *Campaign: What next in Integration?* 3 December, p.25

Ewing, M. T. (2009) Integrated marketing communications measurement and evaluation, *Journal of Marketing Communications*, **15** (2–3) (April–July), 103–117

Fill, C. (2002) *Marketing Communications, Contexts, Strategies and Applications*, 3rd edn, Hemel Hempstead: FT/Prentice Hall

Fill, C. (2009) *Marketing Communications: Interactivity, Communities and Content*, 5th edn, Harlow: FT/Prentice Hall

Finne, A. and Gronroos, C. (2009) Rethinking marketing communication: From integrated marketing communication to relationship communication, *Journal of Marketing Communications*, **15** (2–3) (April–July), 179–195

Frazier, G.L. and Summers, J.O. (1984) Interfirm influence strategies and their application within distribution channels, *Journal of Marketing*, **48** (Summer), 43–55.

Gray, R. (2000). The chief encounter, *PR Week*, 8 September, 13–16

Gronroos, C. (2004) The relationship marketing process: communication, interaction, dialogue, value. *Journal of Business and Industrial Marketing*, **19** (2), 99–113

Gundlach, G.T. and Murphy, P.E. (1993) Ethical and legal foundations of relational market exchanges, *Journal of Marketing*, **57** (4) (October), 35–46

Heinonen, K. and Strandvik, T. (2005). Communication as an element of service value. *International Journal of Service Industry Management*, **16** (2), 186-198.

Jaffray, R. (2010) Not rocket science, *Campaign: What Next in Integration?* 3 December, p. 19

Keller, K.L. (1998). *Strategic Brand Management: Building, Measuring and Managing Brand Equity*, Upper Saddle River, NY: Prentice Hall.

Kitchen, P.J. (1993) Marketing communications renaissance, *International Journal of Advertising*, **12** (4), 367-386.

Kitchen, P., Brignell, J., Li, T. and Spickett Jones, G. (2004) The emergence of IMC: a theoretical perspective, *Journal of Advertising Research*, **44**, (March) 19-30

Kochan, N. (1996), *The World's Greatest Brands*, Basingstoke: Macmillan Press.

Lindgreen, A. Beverland, M.B. and Farrelly, F. (2010) From strategy to tactics: Building, implementing, and managing brand equity in business markets, *Industrial Marketing Management* **39**, 1223–1225

Luck, E. and Moffatt, J. (2009) IMC: Has anything really changed? A new perspective on an old definition, *Journal of Marketing Communications*, **15** (5) (December) 311–325

Marshall, B. (2010) Invite, interact and engage, *B2B Marketing*, **9** (7) (October) 28–29

Matthews, B. (2010) Listen and learn, *B2B Marketing*, **7** (10) (November/December), 28–29

Michell, P., King, J. and Reast, J. (2001) Brand values related to industrial products, *Industrial Marketing Management*, **30** (5) (July) 415–425

Millward Brown (2009) What role does the brand play in business-to-business markets? *Knowledge Points*, retrieved 22 November 2009 from www.millwardbrown.com/

Mitchell, A. (2011) Want consumers' attention? First, stop trying to grab it, *Marketing*, **19** January, 24-25

Mohr, J. and Nevin, J.R. (1990) Communication strategies in marketing channels, *Journal of Marketing*, (October), 36–51

Mohr, J. and Sohi, R.S. (1995) Communication flows in distribution channels: impact on assessments of communication quality and satisfaction, *Journal of Retailing*, **71** (4), 393–416

Mudambi, S. (2002) Branding importance in business-to-business markets: three buyer clusters, *Industrial Marketing Management*, **31** (6) (September) 525–33

Prince, M. and Davies, M. (2002) Co-branding partners: what do they see in each other?, *Business Horizons*, September–October, 51–55

Rach, M. (2010) Brand on the run, *B2B Marketing*, **7** (10) (November/December) p38

Reiter, (2009) Profile David Osbourne – Head of Marketing, Stanley Tools, retrieved 10 March 2011 from www.b2bm.base01.co.uk/features

Riezebos, R. (2002). *Brand Management*, Harlow: Pearson Education.

Roper, S. and Davies, G. (2010) Business to business branding: external and internal satisfiers and the role of training quality, *European Journal of Marketing*, **44** (5), 567-590

Shipley, D. and Howard, P. (1993) Brand-naming industrial products, *Industrial Marketing Management*, **22** (1) (February), 59–66

Schultz, D. (1993) *Integrated Marketing Communications: Putting It Together and Making It Work*, Lincolnwood, IL: NTC Business Books.

Stern, L. and El-Ansary, A.I. (1988) *Marketing Channels*, Englewood Cliffs, NJ: Prentice Hall

Turland C., Power, J., Holmes, T., Aston, A., Nealon, D. and Sutton, N. (2009) Stanley Tools - Stanley 'Judgement Day': the case for turning communications inside out, *Institute of Practitioners in Advertising, IPA Effectiveness Awards*. Retrieved 10 March 201, from www.warc.com.

van Riel, C.B.M. (1995). *Principles of Corporate Communication*, Hemel Hempstead: Prentice-Hall

Welch, M. and Jackson, P.R. (2007) Rethinking internal communication: a stakeholder approach, *Corporate Communications: an International Journal*, **12** (2), 177-198

Zablah, A.R., Brown, B.P. and Donthu, N. (2010) The relative importance of brands in modified rebuy purchase situations, *International Journal of Research in Marketing* **27** (3) (September) 248-260

10 The Business Marketing Communications Mix

Overview

Digital technologies have had a profound impact on the way in which organisations communicate with each other. However, this is not to suggest that the influence of the traditional offline communication tools has waned, indeed it can be argued that marketing communications have been augmented by the application of new technologies.

In this chapter each of the three elements that make up the marketing communications mix is considered; tools, media and messages. Consideration is given to the key characteristics and effectiveness of each of the primary tools used in B2B marketing communications. The chapter then examines each of the main media from a communication perspective and concludes by considering the type of messages used to reach business audiences.

Aims and objectives

The aims of this chapter are to explore the main characteristics of each of the elements of the marketing communications mix and to determine their contribution to business-to-business marketing communications.

The objectives of this chapter are to enable readers to:

1 Introduce the elements that make up the marketing communications mix.

2 Examine the characteristics of each of the primary tools of the marketing communications mix.

3 Comment on the use of secondary tools in B2B marketing.

4 Consider the range and forms of media used in business marketing.

5 Explain the way in which digital media can be used in B2B marketing.

6 Explore how messages and content can be used in business marketing.

7 Describe the principles of demand generation.

A Slice of Life – The Importance of Pants

The Internet has changed the marketing communications mix. We have progressed, at speed, from a relatively straightforward model using the '5 tools' to something more complex. The last time I looked, it includes countless media, including social media and various digital applications, plus, of course, an array of different ways of messaging. Our communications have changed.

It is no longer acceptable to apply the traditional methods and models of marketing exclusively to a world that no longer engages with communications in the traditional way. The introduction of social media and the advancement of new digital channels means the audience has shifted – from the offline world to an online one. The audience now expects to engage with its own online network(s) long before it ever engages directly with the brand. Sources of information have shifted – from communications supplied by the corporate entity, to 'friends', 'followers', 'likes', 'diggs', 'contacts', 'bloggers'. The shift affects every area of the marketing communications mix.

Print advertising circulations have fallen as the customer elects not to read newspapers or magazines, preferring 'news' from blogs, RSS feeds and social network channels. Direct mail has been reduced to almost zero, data companies now sell 'insight' not mailing lists. Even email is 'old'. Personal selling has less to do with the territory offered to a salesperson and more to do with the brand's ability to maintain a viable and compelling YouTube broadcast channel. Advertising and public relations professions are still attempting to redefine their respective roles in the new digital economy. Marketers, and specifically B2B marketers, have been slow to accept and make changes to the marketing mix. In other words, we haven't been listening to our customers – and that can be fatal. The impression is that the changes in the market have come quickly. They haven't. We may have been slow to respond, but the writing's been on the wall for years...

I was invited to a meeting with the Chief Executive and Financial Director of a medium-sized IT support and technical staffing company in London way back in 2006. I was there to help Sir and the bean counter articulate their marketing needs better than simply telling me they wanted, "more leads". The company offered broadly commoditised services and showed little appetite to invest in a brand strategy that might identify an area of competitive differentiation. To the company's credit, however, a 'creative' solution was briefed as the requirement. They hoped that a creative interpretation of their service delivery would generate the required leads. I agreed that a creative approach would help, but I was concerned that the company's prescriptive reliance on a traditional communications channel, namely direct mail, would restrict the opportunity to fully engage a wider audience and attract the large response the company was hoping for.

The audience of mid/senior-level IT Managers within medium to large corporates across all vertical markets, was agreed. The messages were also agreed. In broad terms, the company wanted to communicate that they gave clients greater 'control' over their IT and technical staffing. Greater 'support' would be offered to help customers achieve their objectives. The 'flexibility' to scale services up and down would provide customers with a more cost-effective solution. It wasn't really much to work with, but it was something. Of more immediate concern was the client's predilection towards direct mail. "We want more leads, which means more mailers..."

We discussed multiple online tools and mixed delivery channels but even a dedicated landing page for the campaign was an uphill struggle. They eventually relented, but insisted that they would build and control the online elements of the promotion – they were, after all, IT experts.

A lead-generation, direct marketing campaign was therefore specified and agreed. It consisted of little more than a series of 3 printed mailers supported by equivalent emailers and a promotional microsite that would act as the call to action destination for data capture. The final words from the CEO were, "Whatever happens, get me leads – a lot of leads." And that's where the trouble started.

With little to work on from a product/service perspective, the creative team randomly explored whatever they liked. Unsurprisingly, they ended up with an underwear concept. In my experience, whenever a creative team is light on brand insight for inspiration, it's almost inevitable that the outcome will be underwear related, or worse.

In this instance it was a good underwear concept, albeit slightly tenuous. Comparisons to the client's technical services were made with the functionality of pants. We had big baggy pants 'for endurance'. Bridget Jones pants 'for sanity, not vanity', 'comfort is everything', 'stretching to fit...'

In order to achieve the agreed objective of, 'get me leads', we added a promotional aspect. Recipients of the mailers and emails could click through to the landing page, register their interest and select a free pair of pants to the size and style of their choosing – thong, Superman Y-Fronts, Bridget Jones, etc. It created a bit of fun out of what would otherwise have been a fairly dull message. And it worked.

The campaign ran across traditional media using the client's prospect database of around 6000 contacts and responses started to hit the landing page immediately. In the first week, around 800 people registered their interest and claimed their free pants. An 11% response rate was very good for services which historically received 0.5% response. The client was very pleased. I was very pleased. Everyone was very pleased.

Unfortunately, even in 2006, the potential for online communities and online networking to accelerate the distribution of and response to popular content, was becoming apparent. Word was spreading. Responses to the landing page were increasing, rapidly. We had our first B2B 'viral'. That was quite an achievement for IT services back in 2006.

The client, however, took a dimmer view of the 'success' of the campaign. In the second week, responses had climbed from 800 to over 30,000 and showed no signs of abating. Considering the database of prospects was only 6000, questions were being asked about the relevance of the additional 24,000 contacts. I suppose the clues were in the response forms – Name: Sizzlin' Sophie. Title: Pole Dancer...

The client had failed to appreciate the potential power and speed of digital distribution. They assumed that by taking responsibility for the online element of the campaign, the requirement would be 'functional'. In fact, distribution now encompassed almost every element of the marketing mix and digital communication became pivotal to the whole campaign. The client asked me what to do. Responses were still climbing and the potential promotional redemption cost was giving the CEO cause to change his own underwear.

I told him to catch the wave because it was unlikely to ever pass his way again. Send out press releases, call the magazines and TV stations. Post notices on the company website. Extend the campaign. Report the success to the core database. Leverage the awareness and interest. Build the campaign creative into sales presentations. Free pants for everyone! Become 'famous' for something, rather than infamous for nothing. That was my plan at least. In the event, the client pulled the plug on the whole campaign. The responses went unanswered. Sizzlin' Sophie was left dancing without pants, probably not for the first time.

The brand had the opportunity to capitalise on emerging digital communications across the marketing mix but decided instead to play it safe. It still resides in the comfort of its own obscurity.

Scot McKee

■ Introduction

The strategic marketing communications process involves the implementation and deployment of the marketing communications mix. This is the bundle of communication tools, media and messages used to reach, engage and interact with audiences and which supports the marketing communications strategy determined earlier.

- ■ **Tools:** There are five principal marketing communications **tools**: advertising, sales promotion, public relations, direct marketing and personal selling (see Figure 10.1). These tools are used in different combinations to achieve a variety of tasks. In B2B marketing there is a greater emphasis on personal selling and direct marketing than the other tools. Indeed, the significance of direct-response media in direct marketing should not be underestimated.

- **Media:** There is a huge variety of media available, all used to convey messages to and from audiences. These range from trade magazines and newspapers to billboards, websites and social media. Each has particular characteristics that enable it to reach distinctive audiences.

- **Content or Messages:** Organisations need to determine how they are to influence audiences and this requires determining what to say. Two key formats are used, messages that primarily carry information, and messages that are primarily emotional or transformational. All messages are a blend of both as it is the balance that is critical.

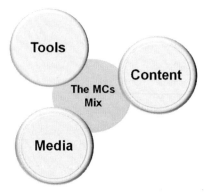

Figure 10.1: The marketing communications mix

The characteristics and issues of each of the main elements are now considered. Prominence is given to those that are particular use in B2B marketing contexts, but it should be appreciated that space limits the extent to which each of these can be explored. More information can be found at www.fillassociates.co.uk.

■ Advertising and B2B communications

Advertising is a non-personal form of mass communication, paid for by an identifiable sponsor. It offers a high degree of control for those responsible for the design and delivery of advertising messages. However, the ability of advertising to persuade target audiences to think or behave in a particular way is suspect. Furthermore, the effect on sales is extremely hard to measure. Advertising suffers from low credibility, in that audiences are less likely to believe messages delivered through advertising than those received through some of the other tools.

In the B2B market, advertising is not considered to be a primary tool. There are several reasons for this, including the potentially high cost of production and media placement relative to the number of prospective buyers, so that the cost per contact can be prohibitive. Further, the audience often needs rational, detailed information and advertising is not the most suitable means of delivering this.

Perhaps the most important roles of advertising in a B2B context are to inform and remind, whereas differentiation and persuasion are delivered through other tools of the mix, namely public relations, direct marketing and personal selling. Apart from an increasing use of online advertising, used to drive website traffic and develop name awareness, the most important form is print advertising in trade journals and newspapers.

The online environment and increasingly the mobile arena, are environments where the prime objective of business customers is to seek information. So, the use of banner advertisements, pop-ups, microsites and superstitials or interstitials, has a supportive rather than a lead communication role. B2B advertisers prefer to emphasise the informational aspect rather than the emotional, particularly when purchase decisions evoke high involvement and central route processing. At present, the prime objective of organisational customers appears to be to seek information and, until this changes in the B2B context, the emotional and entertainment aspect of advertising messages will continue to have a lower significance and online advertising a low profile in the communication mix.

New forms of advertising such as online video are becoming increasingly popular. Used to drive website traffic and engage audiences without the attendant face-to-face costs, business marketers can use video to achieve a variety of goals. For example, to demonstrate products, provide cases studies, deliver conference and corporate events to remote audiences, as well as provide news and develop reputation. Cisco and Apple make extensive use of online video.

■ Trade Promotions and B2B communications

Sales promotion seeks to offer buyers additional value, as an inducement to generate action, often to make an immediate sale. In B2B marketing these inducements, normally referred to as trade promotions, are targeted at three main audiences; intermediaries, end-user customers and the sales force.

Sales promotion is used for one of two main reasons: as a means to accelerate sales or to generate a change in attitude. Essentially, these are achieved by either rewarding current customers or encouraging prospective customers. The acceleration represents the shortened period of time in which a transaction is completed, relative to the time that would have elapsed had there not been a promotion. This action does not mean that an extra sale has been achieved. Indeed, B2B promotions are often aimed at moving buyers along the buying process rather than making a complete transaction. Therefore, gifts, free merchandise or premiums are used in the hope of generating reciprocal action. For example, they are used at trade shows to attract buyers to a stand, are left at the end of sales visits as a way of triggering name recall and as a form of residual value, and they are used as an insert in a piece of direct mail to stimulate interest and to provoke further action, such as an appointment.

The Business Marketing Communications Mix

10

Trade promotion is an important tool for organisations supplying low unit value products and where there is a high purchase frequency. Product differentiation within the grocery and office stationery markets, for example, is difficult to achieve and, in these circumstances, provides a point of added value. Conversely, trade promotions can be of limited value in high technology markets and where the unit value is high and purchase frequency low. In such circumstances buyers are able to discern many technical and service attributes that provide differentiation and added value, thus negating the use of sales promotion techniques.

The main type of sales promotion used to motivate intermediaries is an allowance. Allowances can take many forms but some of the more common ones are buying, count and recount, buy-back allowances, merchandising and promotional allowances. Allowances are a means of achieving a short-term increase in sales. In the grocery sector they can be used defensively to protect valuable shelf space from aggressive competitors. By offering to work with resellers and providing them with extra incentives, manufacturers attempt to guard territory gained to date. The main types of allowances are set out in Table 10.1.

Table 10.1: The main types of B2B trade promotion and allowances

Type	Explanation
Buying allowance	Reward for specific orders between certain dates, a reseller will be entitled to a refund or allowance of x% off the regular price.
	Used to encourage new stores to try the manufacturer's products or to stimulate repeat usage (restocking).
Count and recount allowance	Reward for each case shifted into the reseller's store from storage, during a specified period of time.
	Used to prevent stock outs and encourage resellers to move stock into the store and clear the way for a new or modified product to be introduced.
Buy-back allowance	Reward for purchases after the termination of a count and recount scheme. Normally limited to the number of units exchanged under the scheme.
	Used to encourage stores to replenish their stocks with the manufacturer's product and not that of a competitor.
Merchandising allowance	Reward of extra free units delivered to a reseller once their order reaches a specific size.
	Used to open up new distributors and dealerships.
Promotional allowance	Reward against purchases or a contribution to the cost of an advertisement or campaign in return for promoting a manufacturer's products.
	Used to encourage stocking, lock out competitors and to create shelf space for new products.
Gifts and premiums	Used to provoke reciprocal actions and to provide a longer lasting internal advertisement for the organisation or as an incentive to take further action (e.g. visit an exhibition stand or make an appointment).

The use of trade promotions is an often understated aspect of marketing communications. However, trade promotions, retrospective and volume discounts and incentives are common and generally effective. Manufacturers use competitions and sweepstakes to motivate the sales forces of its distributors, as well as technical and customer support staff in retail organisations and as an inducement to encourage other businesses to place orders and business with them.

Public Relations and B2B communications

Public relations is about establishing and maintaining relationships with various stakeholders and with enhancing the reputation of the organisation. The increasing use of public relations, and in particular publicity, is a reflection of the high credibility attached to messages conveyed through this form of communication.

Publicity involves the dissemination of messages through third-party media, such as magazines, newspapers or the Web. There is no charge for the media space or time but there are costs incurred in the production of the material. There is a wide range of other tools used by public relations, such as event management, public affairs, sponsorship, lobbying, and issues management. It is difficult to control a message once it is placed in the media, but the endorsement offered by a third party can be very influential and have a far greater impact on the target audience than any of the other tools in the marketing communications mix.

ViewPoint 10.1: Reducing late payments with PR

BACS is the organisation that runs the system used to clear and settle automated payments. It is run by 15 of the leading banks and building societies in Europe.

A recent campaign sought to increase market penetration and increase the number of companies using the automated payment system. To achieve this it was important for BACS to be perceived as the authority and legitimate body for SMEs, so positioning was important.

BACS undertake regular research regarding SMEs owners' experiences relating to late payment. The results of this research are then utilised as part of a public relations programme. This provides opportunities for BACS to provide best practise advice, shape perceptions of credibility and contributes to a core part of BACS corporate identity.

In line with this proven approach, BACS launched a 13-month campaign in April 2009, utilising print and online as the primary media. This time the campaign not only featured SMEs but also targeted opinion formers such as media commentators, journalists and business advisors. Press releases highlighted the results of previous research and developed new angles and issues of interest. A series of seven separate campaign releases were developed, all supported by detailed information on a dedicated website www.paymedirect.co.uk.

Quotes from influential associations and experts were distributed in conjunction with materials designed to grab attention about late payment and engage journalists, consumers and SME owners.

The results of this campaign exceeded expectations and delivered a significant increase in the volume and quality of positive media coverage. It also helped BACS develop their reputation.

Source: Rust (2010); BACS (2010); www.bacs.co.uk/Bacs/Press/PressReleases

The degree of trust and confidence generated by public relations makes this tool important because it can reduce buyers' perceived risk. However, while credibility may be high, the amount of control that management is able to bring to the transmission of the public relations message is very low. For example, a press release may have been carefully prepared in-house, but as soon as it is passed to the editor of a magazine or newspaper, a possible opinion-former, all control is lost. The release may be destroyed (highly probable), printed as it stands (highly unlikely) or changed to fit the available space in the media vehicle (almost certain, if it is decided to use the material). This means that any changes to the copy have probably not been agreed with management, so the context and style of the original message may be lost or corrupted.

Table 10.2: Main types of public relations

Type	Explanation
Media Relations	
Press releases	Press releases are a written report concerning a change in the organisation, which is sent (or posted on a website) to various media houses for inclusion in their media vehicles as an item of news.
Press conferences	Press conferences are used when a major event has occurred and where a press release cannot convey the appropriate tone or detail required by the organisation.
Interviews	Interviews with representatives of an organisation enable news and the organisation's view of an issue or event to be conveyed.
Events	Product, corporate or community activities designed to improve goodwill and understanding.
Lobbying	Helps ensure that the views of the organisation are heard in order that legislation and regulations can be shaped appropriately, limiting any potential damage that new legislation might bring.
Corporate advertising	One of the means by which stakeholders can identify and understand the essence of an organisation. This is achieved by presenting the personality of the organisation to a wide range of stakeholders, instead of portraying particular functions or products.

Sponsorship	This is used to develop awareness in the target market and to enable them to make associations between the event (or sponsee) and the sponsor. Through such sponsorship activities it is intended that levels of credibility will be increased.
Crisis management	The increasing occurrence of crises throughout the world has prompted many organisations to review the manner in which they anticipate managing such events, should they be implicated. It is generally assumed that those organisations that take the care to plan in anticipation of disaster will experience more favourable outcomes than those that fail to plan.
Investor relations	Relationships with the money markets and financial stakeholders, are a vitally important part of an organisation's communication activities. The ability to maintain confidence in an organisation during periods of economic buoyancy and downturn can be crucial in delivering consistent shareholder value.

■ Direct Marketing and B2B Communications

Use of direct marketing signifies an attempt to actively remove channel intermediaries, reduce costs and improve the quality and speed of service for individual customers. The significance of B2B direct marketing is that it can be used to complement personal selling activities and in doing so reduce costs and improve overall performance. By removing the face-to-face aspect of personal selling and replacing it with either self managed web support, an email communication, a telephone conversation or a direct mail letter, many facets of the traditional sales persons' tasks can be removed, freeing them to concentrate on their key skills, and potentially reduce costs. What is more, the personalisation associated with direct marketing messages is compatible with a relationship marketing strategy.

Direct marketing seeks to target individual customers with the intention of delivering personalised messages and building a relationship with them based on their responses. In contrast to conventional approaches, direct marketing attempts to build a one-to-one relationship, a partnership with each customer, by communicating with customers on a direct and personal basis. Direct marketing is generally regarded as the second most important tool of the communication mix for most B2B organisations, after personal selling.

There are a growing number of direct marketing methods but essentially there are three main approaches; direct mail, telemarketing and web-supported.

■ Direct Mail

Direct mail refers to personally addressed promotional materials delivered through the postal system. It can be personalised and targeted with great accuracy, and the results precisely measured. Direct mail has been an important part of the

B2B communication mix for some time, especially as it can be coordinated to support personal selling by building awareness, enhancing image and establishing credibility. The generation of enquiries and leads, together with the purposeful building of personal relationships with customers, are the most important factors contributing to the growth of direct mail. However, the intention to build loyalty is not always reflected in the statistics. This is because direct mail is often used for customer acquisition, not retention. Direct mail can be expensive, and should therefore be used selectively and for purposes other than creating awareness.

Telemarketing

Telemarketing can be used in both an inbound and outbound manner. When used outbound the goal is to generate leads, make appointments, close sales and to collect information about the market and particular customers. When used for inbound calls the role is to collect orders, provide support and information for both customers and the sales force and to coordinate sales activities.

Telemarketing is also used within an international context as despite the use of digital channels, some buyers still prefer to have a face-to-face conversation at some point in their journey. International campaigns are often handled centrally by an agency and then leads are followed up by localised sales force teams. This approach stresses the need for close integration between the telemarketing team (multilingual) and the local sales teams (Weekes, 2010).

By using telemarketing as a sales order processing system to collect routine low value orders, the sales force is freed up to concentrate on other more profitable activities. In particular, the use of an inside telemarketing department is seen as a compatible sales channel to the field sales force. A telemarketing team can accomplish many tasks. These include:

- Searching for and qualifying new customers, so saving the field force from cold calling;
- Service existing customer accounts and prepare the field force should they be required to attend to the client personally;
- Seek repeat orders from marginal or geographically remote customers, particularly if they are low unit value consumable items; and finally,
- Provide a link between network members that serves to maintain the relationship, especially through periods of difficulty and instability.

Many organisations prefer to place orders through telesales teams, or directly through a web site, as it does not involve the time costs associated with personal sales calls. The routine of such orders gives greater efficiency for all concerned with the relational exchange and reduces costs. The complementary use of direct marketing and personal selling is explored further in Chapter 11.

■ Web Enabled

Many of the tasks accomplished through telemarketing and direct mail have been overtaken or superseded by the use of the Internet and web-enabled services. Questions can be answered, information shared, orders placed and tracked and complaints registered, all with great speed and accuracy. The Web enables greater user convenience, as it is they who control the time and speed of their enquiries and search for technical information. This convenience is tempered by the design and navigability of the website.

Websites represent a great opportunity to realign communications from a company-controlled perspective to one that is audience centred. Websites can be used to engage buyers directly, reshape the channel mix, reach employees in order to build brand values, and provide a hub for all other communication activities. These include social media which is looked at later in this chapter.

■ Personal Selling and B2B Communications

Personal selling is the most important and most expensive tool of the communication mix used by organisations operating in the B2B market. It is an interpersonal communication tool which involves face-to-face activities undertaken by individuals, often representing an organisation, in order to differentiate, inform, persuade or remind an individual or group to take appropriate action, as required by the sponsor's representative. A salesperson engages in communication on a one-to-one (or one-to-group) basis where feedback is often instantaneous.

Personal selling is very important when building relationships with members of buying centres. It can be used to demonstrate, explain and answer questions concerning product-related technical issues. In support of the personal selling effort (and trade shows), trade promotions, trade advertising, direct marketing and public relations all play important roles. Increasingly, online and mobile technologies provide not only new direct routes to customers and intermediaries but also vibrant new communications media in which interactivity is common.

In support of personal selling there are three allied activities. These are trade shows, field marketing and video conferencing. Of these, consideration is given to exhibitions and trade shows whilst Chapter 11 explores personal selling in greater detail. Further information on these elements and the marketing communication mix can be found at www.fillassociates.co.uk.

■ Trade Shows

According to Boukersi (2000) industrial fairs, or trade shows, tend to be smaller, more specialised and of shorter duration than consumer-orientated exhibitions. There are many reasons to use trade shows, but the primary reasons are not 'to make sales' or 'because the competition is there' but because they provide opportunities to meet potential and established customers and to create and sustain a series of relational exchanges. Li (2007) cited by Geigenmüller (2010) stresses that the impact of trade shows can have on the development of valuable long-term buyer–seller relationships.

The main aims, therefore, are to develop closer relationships with customers, to build upon or develop the corporate identity and to gather up-to-date market intelligence (Shipley and Wong, 1993). In addition, these events can be more about managing conflict rather than generating sales (Blythe, 2002). This implies that trade shows should not be used as isolated events, but that they should be integrated into a series of campaign activities. These activities can serve to develop and sustain buyer relationships. The reasons for attending exhibitions are set out in Table 10.3.

Table 10.3: Reasons exhibitors choose to attend trade shows

To meet existing customers and develop relationships
To get leads and meet prospective new customers and develop relationships
To meet lapsed customers
To provide market research opportunities and to collect marketing data
To take orders/make sales

One of the main drawbacks associated with trade shows is the vast and disproportionate amount of management time that can be tied up with their planning and implementation.

The costs associated with exhibitions, if controlled properly, can mean that this is an effective and efficient means of communicating with customers although the quality of the audience can vary considerably.

As a form of marketing communications, trade shows enable products to be presented, and brands built. They can be an effective means of demonstrating products and developing industry-wide credibility in a relatively short period of time. Attendance at exhibitions may also be regarded from a political dimension. For example, non-attendance may be seized as an opportunity by attendees to suggest weaknesses (Kerin and Cron, 1987).

In the B2B sector new products and services are often introduced at exhibitions, especially if public relations activities and events can be spun off the launch. In other words, exhibitions are not independent of the other parts of the communication mix. If used effectively they can be part of a coordinated communications campaign. Advertising prior, during and after a trade show can be dovetailed with public relations, sponsorship and personal selling. Sales promotions can also be incorporated through competitions among customers prior to the show to raise awareness, generate interest and to suggest customer involvement. Competitions during a show can be focused on the sales force to motivate and stimulate commercial activity and among visitors to generate interest in the stand, raise brand name attention and encourage focus on particular products (new, revised or revolutionary) and generate sales leads and enquiries. Increasingly social media can be used to launch and develop B2B products.

Above all else, exhibitions are an important way of building relationships and providing corporate visibility. Positive relationships with customers, competitors and suppliers are often reinforced through face-to-face dialogue that happens both formally in the exhibition hall and informally through the variety of social activities that surround and support these events.

■ Business-to-Business Media

The second element of the communications mix is the media. Of the many available media, six main *classes* can be identified. These are broadcast, print, outdoor, digital, in-store and 'other' media classes. Within each of these classes there are particular media *types*. For example, within the broadcast class there are television and radio, and within the print class there are newspapers and magazines. Within each type of medium there are a huge number of different media *vehicles* that can be selected to carry an advertiser's message. For example, in print, there are business-orientated magazines such as *The Economist* and there are also an expanding number of specialist magazines such as the *Timber Trades Journal* and *ThirdSector*. Therefore, there are three ways of categorising the media: classes, types and vehicles.

Another, perhaps broader, interpretation of the media is to consider them in terms of their purpose. Traditionally a medium is considered to be a channel that is rented by an advertiser in order that their message be communicated. However, some messages about a brand are conveyed by people in word of mouth communications. This can be referred to as 'earned' media. McKinsey (2010) supplement this with 'hijacked' media, when groups or individuals spread negative information about a brand, and use the example of two Domino's employees who were filmed contaminating food, and the video ended up on YouTube. A third type of media embraces the media elements that are owned by an organisation. For example, websites, signage on a company's owned transport vehicles, buildings and equipment and products, workwear, and logos on written communications. McKinsey supplement this with sold media, where brands host space on their website to other brands in order to drive traffic and appear objective. This trilogy is referred to as POEM; Paid, Owned, Earned Media and is useful because it broadens our perspective of media beyond the paid-for-only approach.

Organisations use a variety of media in order to deliver their messages to a number of target audiences. As a general rule business marketers use print rather than broadcast media, simply because of the informational nature of the messages they wish to convey and the (small) size and (large) geographic dispersion of their audiences. While choosing a single medium is reasonably straightforward, combining media and attempting to generate synergistic effects is far from easy.

One of the key tasks is to decide which combination of vehicles should be selected to carry the message to the target audience. First, it is necessary to consider the campaign goals and then use the main characteristics of each media type in order that media planning decisions can be based on some logic and rationale. The fundamental characteristics concern the costs, delivery and audience profile associated with a communication. Each media vehicle has a discrete set of characteristics that will also influence the way in which messages are transmitted, received and meaning assigned.

Broadcast media is usually associated with consumer marketing activities but can be used to reach a general business audience. Both Hewlett Packard and IBM have made extensive use of television and radio to launch campaigns and build corporate reputation. The use of outdoor posters on specific road and rail sites and at airports can be effective in reaching elusive buyers. In addition, small and medium-sized organisations can create general levels of awareness and reach buyers who are difficult to reach by other methods.

As mentioned above, print media is an important part of B2B communications. It enables reasonably detailed information to be conveyed to buyers and designers. Trade journals, business magazines and industry-based directories are common media. Online video is used by 69% of IT buyers when researching technical solutions. Web-based materials can also be downloaded and printed.

Sales support literature is used extensively to follow up leads and to bolster the personal selling effort. Used early in the buying process, it can be an important means of clarifying features and benefits, and also differentiate an organisation as customers compare, contrast and draw up their shortlists of prospective suppliers. There are a number of different forms of sales support literature, each of which should be used to achieve specific goals.

Product brochures and catalogues not only provide detailed information but serve to add value to the communication process as they can be left after a sales visit. Normally these brochures contain information about standard ranges of products and equipment and can be used to prompt orders. These communication devices can be an integral part of a transactional relationship.

Corporate-based brochures, which reflect on the supplier organisation and its overall capability, are more likely to be of use in situations where the customer has a specific problem and is looking for a partner or collaborator in a particular project. In addition to the overall technical capability of the supplier, its credibility is presented, often through the use of testimonials and third-party references. This can be supported through the use of technical data sheets, independent test reports and case histories. This approach is best used where the relationship between the organisations is more relational and hence collaborative.

A great deal of this information is now available at company websites where the prime advantages are that the information is instantly accessible and can be updated regularly.

ViewPoint 10.2: OKI generate leads

OKI Printing Solutions are pioneers in innovative print technologies and have won many awards for their range of high performance machines. OKI is a global business-to-business brand and is number two in Europe in the A3 colour segment, in terms of both value and shipped units. The EMEA group employs 1200 people in 21 production sites and sales offices and is represented in 60 countries throughout the region.

To launch their new MC860 A3 printer a centralised, integrated campaign was developed. The target was managing directors, IT managers, office managers, PAs, financial directors, finance managers, operations directors and facilities managers associated with SMEs.

The overall aim of the campaign was to generate leads for use by both OKI and their channel partners across the region. In particular, the goals were to reach A4 customers who are looking to replace their existing printer, and A3 customers who are looking to replace their existing printer.

At the core of the activity was an incentive for visitors to respond to an invitation to by entering a competition. This invitation was visible on all media used in the campaign to drive traffic to individual country microsites.

Using the theme, 'A4 Price, A3 Output', the imagery showed how materials looked better when printed in A3, a features and benefits approach. In addition to print advertising, the campaign used web-based direct marketing, banners, SEO, PPC and sales support materials.

One of the challenges faced by the in-house team was to ensure that not only did all OKI operating companies buy into the campaign idea, but also that the concept would penetrate a range of marketing channels.

Source: www.b2bmarketingawards.co,uk; www.b2bmarketing.net/node/12386; www.oki.co.uk/press-centre/printer-reviews/; www.binfo.co.uk

Question: To what extent is lead generation a 'behaviour only' form of engagement?

■ Digital Media and B2B Marketing Communications

In addition to the various traditional tools used online, as mentioned previously, the Internet is a medium that allows for interactivity, and is possibly the purest form of marketing communications dialogue outside personal selling. Electronic communication is two-way and very fast, allowing businesses and individuals to find information and enter exchange transactions in such a way that some traditional communication practices and exchanges are being reconfigured.

The Web combines many of the strengths of other media. For example, it bundles together, text (print), audio (radio), visual (television) and semiotics/display (outdoor). The Web is therefore a hybrid of various media and enables advertising, trade promotions, public relations, direct marketing and personal selling activities. However, there are an increasing range of methods that are especially useful in B2B marketing communications, of these attention here is given to the use of company websites, search, email and social media communications.

■ Websites

When commercial websites were first developed the trend was to design them as online brochures. This static and passive approach changed as the opportunities afforded by Web 2.0 and interactivity became recognised and technically within reach of a wider range of organisations. As a result, rich media content emerged, eCommerce sites flourished and bidirectional communications became established. Website design and the ability to enter into interactive communications, now permits organisations to develop customised content and personal solutions for those customers who provide specific, individually orientated information.

A customer-orientated approach to the design of a website should improve its performance. For example, the ease with which a site is accessible and navigable will not only be a positive factor for site visitors but will also reduce their search time and associated costs. However, knowledgeable and experienced buyers may not find these attributes of particular relevance.

Website attractiveness is a function of many elements but one important one concerns the degree of interactivity and engagement that a site visitor experiences. The development of multimedia facilities that enable sound, music, graphics, text and video can help customers focus on relevant parts of a website's presentation. This in turn can reduce search costs and improve levels of interactivity.

According to Usunier *et al.* (2010) there is "empirical evidence that confirms that B2B website design and content influence business buying and selling behavior, negotiation strategies, pricing practices, and performance in a B2B context."

The content discovered on a website should be relevant, stimulating and contain something new to the visitor. In terms of the range of content, Karayanni (2000) argues that the content of B2B websites should emphasise the identity and reputation of the company and also assist customer-related information exchange. The company-related information helps reduce buyer risk while the exchange encourages customer participation in the communication flow and hence increases buyer control. Both of these elements were found to be significant drivers of web-based sales (Karayanni and Baltas, 2003).

■ Search Engine Marketing

Websites need visitors and the higher the number of visitors the more effective the website is likely to be. The majority of people arrive at sites following a search using particular key words and phrases to search for products and services and the information they need. They do this through search engines and the results of each search are displayed in rank order. It is understandable therefore, that those ranked highest in the results lists are visited more often than those in lower positions.

Therefore, from a marketing perspective it is important to undertake marketing activities to attain the highest possible ranking position, and this is referred to as search engine marketing (SEM). There are two main search engine marketing techniques; search engine optimisation (SEO) and pay-per-click (PPC) with the latter outweighing the former quite substantially (Jarboe, 2005).

- **Search engine optimisation** (SEO) is a process used to get a high ranking position on major search engines and directories. To achieve top-ranking positions, or least a first page listing, it is necessary to design web pages and create links with other quality web sites, so that search engines can match closely a searcher's key words/phrases with the content of registered web pages.

- **Pay-per-click** (PPC) is similar to display advertising found in offline print formats. Ads are displayed when particular search terms are entered into the search engine. These ads appear on the right-hand side of the results page and are often referred to as sponsored links. Instead of paying upfront for an ad to be displayed, payment is only required once the link is clicked, and the searcher is taken through to the company's web page.

■ Email Marketing

There are two key characteristics associated with business email marketing. First, it can be directed at clearly defined target groups and individuals. Second, email messages can be personalised and refined to meet the needs of individual buyers. In this sense email is the antithesis of broadcast communications, which are scattered among a mass audience and lack any sense of individualisation, let alone provide an opportunity for recipients to respond. In addition, email can be used with varying levels of frequency and intensity, which is important when building awareness, reinforcing messages or when attempting to persuade someone into a trial or purchase.

Email was used originally as a standalone means of reaching prospects and customers. However, it is now understood that in order to optimise the use of email it is necessary to build a tailored one-to-one email channel in order to deliver personalised content, and ensure that email activity is coordinated within an overall strategic approach.

Organisations need to manage two key dimensions of email communications; outbound and inbound email. Outbound email concerns messages sent by a company often as a part of a direct marketing campaign, designed to persuade recipients to visit a website, to take a trial or make a purchase. The inbound dimension concerns the management of email communications received from customers and other stakeholders. These may have been stimulated either by an individual's use of the website, exposure to a news item about the product or organisation, or through product experience, which often entails a complaint.

Managing inbound email represents a huge opportunity not only to build email lists for use in outbound campaigns, but also to provide high levels of customer service interaction and satisfaction. If undertaken properly and promptly this can help to build trust and reputation, which in turn can stimulate word-of-mouth communication, all essential aspects of marketing communication. Activity-triggered email that incorporates the interests of the target audience and which follow up on audience behaviour are deemed to be more successful and good practice, if only because of the higher conversion rates and return on investment.

However, Brennan (2010) notes that the reputation and use of email has fallen considerably in recent years, based on usage, unscribe and opt out rates. In contrast to this view Econsultancy reports that the UK email industry increased in value by 15% in 2009, worth £336 million. Rather than see social media as a threat, the integration of social media into email appears to be the way forward for many organisations (IAB, 2010).

The short-term problem facing B2B marketers is the sheer volume of emails and the information overload it causes. 'Priority Inbox' from Google is an attempt to filter and prioritise email messages but perhaps the longer-term challenge concerns the use of social networks as the main form of contact messaging.

■ Mobile

Mobile marketing is developing rapidly and is not a consumer-only facility. Whilst it only accounts for 1% of overall digital spend (Weekes, 2010), this area is expected to grow quickly as technological developments and smartphone penetration accelerates.

Whilst websites need to be tailored for mobile access, it is location based services that add value. Through the use of apps product demonstrations, personalised information, and access to rich content and systems that enable them to do their work more effectively, mobile is perceived to be good for customer acquisition as well as developing relationships.

■ Social Media

Although similar, the terms 'social media' and 'social networks' do not mean the same, yet are often used interchangeably, and mistakenly. Kaplan and Haenlein (2009: 61) define social media as "a group of Internet based applications that build on the ideological and technological foundations of Web 2.0 and that allow the creation and exchange of user generated content". In other words social media refers to a broad range of web-based applications, and social networking sites are one of the many applications that are available. Others include weblogs, content communities (e.g. YouTube), collaborative projects (eg Wikipedia), podcasts and virtual social worlds (e.g. Second Life).

The use of social media in B2B marketing is growing according to research published by Baseone (2011). It is a virtual world populated by buyers who effectively invite brands into their networks. Brands therefore have a different role to play as they can no longer legitimately lead and assert themselves on buyers. This is because buyers willingly share information among themselves. Word-of-mouth communications becomes even more critical due to the amplification effect that these buyer interactions can have.

However, the most influential channels are the 'traditional online' channels, email web searches and supplier websites, not social media (Baseone, 2011).

Dimensions of Social Media

There are a range of social media applications, of which these are the more prominent.

- **Social networks**, for example, MySpace, YouTube and Facebook, and for professional and business use, LinkedIn, are about people using the Internet to share lifestyle and experiences. The participants in these networks not only share information and experiences, but they can also use the interactive capacity to build new relationships. The content is user-generated which means users own, control and develop content according to their needs, not those of a third party.

- **Blogs** (Web logs) are personal online diaries. A large proportion of blogs concern organisations and public issues, and they are virtually free. Blogging represents a simple, straightforward way of creating a web presence.

  Business-related or corporate blogs represent huge potential as a form of marketing communications for organisations. This is because blogs reflect the attitudes of the author, and these attitudes can influence others. Organisations can set up external corporate blogs to communicate with customers, channel partners and other stakeholders. The other form of corporate blog is the internal blog. Here the focus is on enabling employees to write about and discuss corporate policies, issues and developments.

- **Microblogging** or nanoblogging as it is sometimes referred to, is a short format version of blogging. It is a form of eWoM (electronic word of mouth) and uses web social communication services (Jansen *et al.*, 2009) of which Twitter is probably the best known. A microblog, or tweet, consists of a short comment, a post of 140 characters, which is shared with a network of followers. This makes production and consumption relatively easy in comparison to blogs.

  Microblogging offers huge potential to marketers and now ads on Twitter are permitted. These are an integral part of conversations, and are referred to as 'promoted tweets'. The messages, limited to 140 characters, appear at the top of the search results when a user has searched for that word (Steele, 2010).

- **Podcasting** is a process whereby audio content is delivered over the Internet to iPods, MP3 players and computers, on demand. A podcast is a collection of files located at a feed address, which people can subscribe to by submitting the address to an aggregator. When new content becomes available it is automatically downloaded using an aggregator or feed reader which recognises feed formats such as RSS (see below).

  Podcast material is prerecorded and time-shifted so that material can be listened to at a user's convenience, that is, on demand. Listeners can take the material they have chosen to listen to, and play it at times and locations that are convenient to them. They can listen to the content as many times as they wish simply because the audio files can be retained.

  Podcasting is relatively inexpensive and simple to execute. It opens up publishing to a host of new people, organisations as well as individuals, and it represents a new media channel for audio content. Users have control over what they listen to, when they listen to it and how many times they listen to the content.

- **RSS** stands for 'really simple syndication' and refers to the distribution of news content on the Web. Rather than trawl all relevant web pages to find new content and updates, RSS allows for specific content to be brought together and made available to an individual without their always having to return to numerous sites. Just checking the RSS feed to see whether something new has been posted online can save huge amounts of time.

  From a marketing perspective RSS feeds act as a media channel delivering a variety of information about news stories, events, headlines, project updates and even corporate information, often as press releases. This information is delivered quickly and efficiently to audiences who have signed up and effectively given express permission to be sent the information.

- **Online communities** are groups of people who come together freely to share a common interest. They interact, share information, develop knowledge and understanding and build relationships. Four main types of community can be identified, defined by their purpose, position, interest and profession (Durlacher, 1999). Their individual contributions to the community can add value to others involved with the community. These communities can be setup, hosted and run by an organisation (a corporate community) or they can be driven by users, who meet independently of any corporate body.

  From a business marketing perspective online communities offer organisations opportunities to listen to and develop customer insight. Corporate driven communities offer opportunities to test ideas, prototypes and explore ways in which an company's value proposition can be improved.

ViewPoint 10.3 A stroke of genius at Maginus

Maginus had developed multichannel commerce software designed to help retailers and other intermediaries such as wholesalers, sell through a range of channels, to improve customer service and control costs. Some of these solutions are developed on Microsoft Dynamics AX and so faced competition from other Microsoft distributors. Another problem was that market awareness of Maginus was relatively low.

The solution was found in an avatar, a multichannel guru called My Genius, a play on Magnius and a way of affirming the leadership status the company desired. This served as a peripheral cue, an emotional bond for customers, in a market that was primarily product and price led.

My Genius appeared on a variety of marketing materials including print ads, trade show stands, direct mail, his own website, microsites, newsletters, guides, ebooks and other owned media properties such the offices. Used in direct mail and viral campaigns, My Genius was also used as a 3D model sent to selected number of customers and prospects.

Online campaigns are now geared to driving responses to the My Genius website. Linked to Livechat, video via YouTube and opportunities to upload photographs, the My Genius concept has engaged employees as well as the market and provided the point of differentiation the campaign set out to achieve.

Source: Anon (2010)

Question: Following this example, does it mean that all B2B websites should move to an emotional approach to engagement?

■ Content or Messages

The third element of the marketing communications mix concerns the message, or content, that is conveyed to, received from and shared among audiences. It is therefore important to understand what organisations intend to say, how they say it, and how they expect audiences to respond. However, in an age of interaction, individuals also create and share content with others. In both cases, it is important that the presentation of the content is appropriate for the target audience so that they can engage, assign meaning and respond appropriately.

Messages should reflect a balance between the need for information and the need for pleasure or enjoyment in the consumption of a message. At a broad level, messages can be considered to be product-oriented and rational or customer-oriented and based on feelings and emotions. All messages contain some information and some transformational (emotional) content. It is the balance between the two that needs to be managed, according to the task and context.

10

The Business Marketing Communications Mix

Messages where there is high involvement require an emphasis on the information content, in particular the key attributes and the associated benefits. This style is often factual and product oriented. Where there is low involvement, the message should contain a high proportion of emotional content and seek to develop brand values through imagery and associations. In business marketing the factual and product-oriented approach can be observed more often.

Messages should be developed that enable recipients to not only respond to the source but to also encourage them to talk to others through conversation, both offline or online. For example, through forums, discussion boards, communities and corporate blogging. Viral marketing, the passing on and sharing of content with others, has potential within B2B marketing, although it is not yet used as extensively as in consumer markets.

Digital media provides excellent opportunities to deliver rational, product-based information. On the other hand, traditional media are generally considered to be much better at developing brand values. The former have a dominant cognitive orientation and the latter an emotional one. There are other differences, but the predominant message is that these types of media are, to a large extent, complementary, suggesting that they should be used together, not independently of each other.

The credibility of the source of a message is considered important. High source credibility can occur when the source is perceived to be expert or knowledgeable, objective and trustworthy. B2B branding can help develop an organisation's credibility although perception of the individual people representing an organisation is a critical factor. The use of spokespersons is common in consumer markets and four main ones can be identified: the expert, the celebrity, the chief executive officer and the consumer. In business markets, experts and the CEO are the most frequently used spokespersons.

- *The expert* can be recognised quickly because they are often dressed in white coats and round glasses, or dress and act like 'mad professors'. Through the use of symbolism, stereotypes and identification, these characters (and indeed others) can be established very quickly in the minds of receivers and a frame of reference generated that does not question the authenticity or credibility of the message being transmitted.

- *CEOs* often relish the opportunity to sell their own products and there have been some notable business people who have 'fronted' their organisation. For example, Steve Jobs actively promotes the launch of new products. Tyrell, as reported by Marshall (2010) refers to three categories or types of CEO. There are evangelists such as Richard Branson and Stelios who often started and still own a company. They are not the most receptive to changing the way the present their companies. Second, there are the strategists who are brought in to a company to make changes and redirect the organisation. The third group Tyrell refers to are generals. These individuals see the brand as bigger than they are and who use inspiration to drive an internal focus.

ViewPoint 10.4: Sharing content through Cisco Webex

Cisco Webex is a well established and well regarded online meeting facility. Webex enables people to communicate with anyone, anywhere in the world and to share documents, make presentations, demonstrate products and services, and run secure web meetings from a desktop. In short, Webex facilitates online collaboration.

However, to strengthen market appeal outside of North America, especially in EMEA (Europe, Middel East and Africa), it was important to reach new users. Rather than perpetuate the perception that Webex is a meeting tool, thought was given to encouraging its use as an everyday tool to share ideas all day, not just in formal meetings.

The agency behind the Cisco product identified young new workers, those aged between 22 and 32, who have always been immersed with technology. It is common nature for them to share music, gossip, files and they invariably use an iPhone, Blackberry or a laptop.

In order to reach this group of young influencers, Webex had to be positioned in such a way that it became a natural addition to their daily multichannel working life. To accomplish this it was important to be contemporary and avoid words such as 'work', 'meetings' and 'collaboration', and use 'conversations', 'ideas', and 'sharing' instead. With competitors using propositions about reducing meeting travel time and costs, and being kind to the environment, none of them were talking about sharing or ideas or trying to engage with the younger audience profile.

So, to help make associations with the 'sharing ideas' concept, a Webex ball was developed. The invitation to "share an idea" became "pass the ball". Webex used a multiphoto technique to convey ideas about communication between people separated by buildings, regions or countries. This flexible and visually striking approach is suitable for working in any medium from flash banners to cross-track Underground posters.

The £500k campaign was rooted in the website, which became a central point for storing all ideas, which everyone could rate. At the London launch event, a 7ft video ball booth was set up at Victoria Station. People were invited to share their ideas via video. These were then posted on the website and were supplemented by online contributions. The event was supported by promotional staff who handed out branded stress balls, plus outdoor and poster activities. The campaign also included online banners, a viral "Don't drop the Ball" game and a viral email in which people were encouraged to pass a ball around the world and track its progress.

In Germany, traffic to Webex's own site increased by 65% during the campaign and search hits increased by 60%. In the UK, these figures were 40% and 70% and in France, the figures were 100% and 15% respectively.

Source: www.b2bm.biz/Features, www.b2bmarketingawards.co.uk,

Question: How else might the Webex idea be conveyed?

■ Message Appeals

The main choice of presentation style, therefore, concerns the degree of factual information transmitted in a message, an Information-based appeal, against the level of imagery thought necessary to make sufficient impact for the message to command attention and then be processed, an emotional (or transformational) appeal.

There are numerous presentational techniques associated with each of these approaches, but the following are some of the more commonly used appeals.

- **Informational appeals** often use a factual, slice of life, demonstration or comparative approach.
- **Emotional appeals** often use fear, humour, animation, sex, music, fantasy and surrealism.

The majority of B2B content is product-orientated and use factual and demonstration appeals. Traditionally the focus is on product/service attributes, their characteristics and performance qualities. Third-party endorsers, testimonials and recognition by statutory bodies and regulators are used to provide credibility, reduce risk and uncertainty and enhance visibility. However, content has evolved as digital media developed.

■ User-Generated Content

An increasing number of messages are developed and communicated by ordinary individuals, just like you and me. Not only are these used to communicate with organisations of all types and sizes but they are also shared with peers, family, friends and others in communities such as social networks and specialist interest online communities (e.g. supply chain software portals). This is referred to as user-generated content (UGC) and in B2B terms can be seen in action at YouTube, Twitter and LinkedIn.

What is interesting is that although people understand the rules and norms associated with communicating across peer groups and social networks, B2B marketers have yet to fully embrace this approach. However, it appears that there are an increasing number of B2B organisations using UGC as an integral part of their content.

One of the more common forms of UGC is corporate blogging. This involves individuals, posting information about topics of corporate interest. Some organisations such as IBM openly encourage their employees to engage in blogging activities. They recognise that a large majority of employees have personal social network accounts and want them to utilise these by talking about the company. Other, rather unenlightened organisations prevent their employees from using MySpace/Facebook when at work, and so miss the opportunity to be associated with shared content through social media.

Social networks thrive on the shared views, opinions and beliefs, often brand-related, of networked friends. YouTube and LinkedIn user groups in particular, provide opportunities for individuals to share video and contacts and developments respectively, Users post their content and respond to the work of others, often by rating the quality or entertainment value of content posted by others.

Table 10.4: Comparison of content

Websites/Internet	Traditional media
Good at providing rational, product-based information	Better at conveying emotional brand values
More efficient as costs do not increase in proportion to the size of the target audience	Costs are related to usage
Better at prompting customer action	Less effective for calling to action except point-of-purchase and telemarketing
Effective for short-term, product-oriented brand action goals and long-term corporate identity objectives	Normally associated with building long-term values
Increasingly good at generating awareness and attention (e.g. seeding online video)	Strong builders of awareness
Measures of communication effectiveness weak and/or in the process of development Measures of website use very high	Established methodologies, some misleading or superficial (mass media); direct marketing techniques are superior
Dominant orientation – cognition	Dominant orientation – emotion

Digital content can be reworked and represented extending its value. For example, a white paper can be reused to develop tweets, podcasts, articles, webinars, and blogs.

■ Demand Generation

So far in this chapter the elements of the marketing communications mix have been considered. To bring these elements together the chapter closes with a consideration of a popular concept used by B2B practitioners, and referred to as demand generation.

Finding contacts and converting them into customers is a well-established marketing process. It involves gathering contact names, filtering them to find those that offer the greatest potential, and then handing over the hot leads or prospects for the sales force to close. Through the use of technology contemporary demand generation systems have been designed to interpret this process. This involves gathering the names of potential customers using email and web contacts, filtering them to determine the better prospects, developing relationships to the point that the leads are qualified and viable before they are passed over to the sales department.

It is quite common for organisations to use a range of computer-based applications in order to improve the efficiency and effectiveness of their marketing activities. So, the use of marketing databases and systems to generate direct mail, place advertising, manage call centres, track performance, manage email programmes is widespread. Indeed, the use of lead management systems, scoring tools, campaign managers, and marketing resource management software are equally familiar. Demand generation systems bring all of these functions into a single system.

However, there is one major difference between demand generation, and systems such as customer relationship management or marketing automation programmes. This is that the latter seek to manage the entire customer lifecycle, whereas demand generation only deals with lead management, those activities that precede a customer's first purchase.

However, demand generation is not about buying a list of email addresses. As with all marketing activities it is important to provide the right information, at the right time, and to deliver it through the right media. If this is accomplished then the percentage of all those interested who become engaged prospects and who become clients is likely to increase. This can be understood in terms of a demand funnel, as depicted in Figure 10.2.

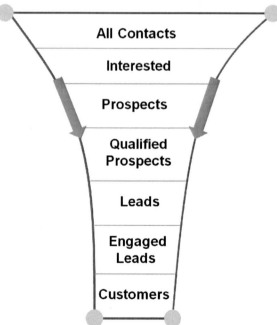

Figure 10.2: The B2B demand generation funnel

The mix of tools, media and content used within demand generation will not be the same for all products and services, for all target groups and not necessarily the same when the need is to develop relationships with customers.

Summary

Here are the key points about the B2B related marketing communications mix, set out against the learning objectives.

1 Introduce the elements that make up the marketing communications mix.

The marketing communications mix is a particular configuration of communication tools, media and messages used to reach, engage and interact with audiences and which supports the marketing communications strategy.

2 Examine the characteristics of each of the primary tools of the marketing communications mix.

There are five primary tools that make up the B2B marketing communications mix. These are advertising, trade promotions, public relations, direct marketing and personal selling. Each tool is capable of achieving particular goals and their use is therefore geared to the campaign goals and context.

3 Comment on the use of secondary tools in B2B marketing.

A significant secondary tool in the B2B Marketing armoury is the trade show. These enable organisations to meet current and prospective customers, and to develop relationships with them that have a long-run mutual benefit. The focus is not on sales.

4 Consider the range and forms of media used in business marketing

Organisations use a variety of media in order to deliver their messages to a number of target audiences. As a general rule, business marketers use print rather than broadcast media, simply because of the informational nature of the messages they wish to convey and the size and geographic dispersion of their audiences. Digital media is becoming an increasingly significant part of the media mix for many businesses.

Of the many available media, six main classes can be identified. These are broadcast, print, outdoor, digital, in-store and 'other' media classes. Within each of these classes there are particular media types, and within each type of medium there are a huge number of different media vehicles that can be selected to carry an advertiser's message.

5 Explain the way in which digital media can be used in B2B marketing

Digital media is an important element in B2B marketing communications. The development of websites as a rich source of information for buyers, is alone a significant factor. In addition search, email, and social media are critical aspects of most progressive B2B campaigns.

6 Explore how messages and content can be used in business marketing.

The content of marketing communications messages should reflect a balance between the need for information and the need for pleasure or enjoyment in the consumption of a message. All messages contain some information and some transformational (emotional) content. It is the balance between the two that needs to be managed, according to the task and context.

User-generated content refers to messages developed by audiences as well as organisations. Readily observed in online communities, blogs and viral marketing, UGC reflects the trend towards buyers sharing information.

7 Describe the principles of demand generation.

Demand generation refers to the process whereby digital technologies are used to gather the names of everyone expressing a general interest, filter them to determine strong and weak prospects, develop relationships to the point that leads are qualified and hence viable, before passing them to the sales department.

■ Discussion Questions

1 Using examples to illustrate your points, compare and contrast the roles of trade promotions and public relations.

2 Consider whether organisations should stop using direct mail and telemarketing and move everything to a website.

3 Find details on the Internet of a trade show and examine the information provided about the visitor profile. Why might organisations wish to attend this show as an exhibitor and as a visitor?

4 Using an organisation (or product range) with which you are familiar, examine the different media used to reach organisational buyers and consider the effectiveness of this media mix. How might you improve it?

5 Critically evaluate the use of social media in B2B marketing communications.

6 To what extent might the marketing communication mix be enhanced when a deliberate attempt is made to promote word-of-mouth communication?

References

Anon (2010) B2B marketing awards; *B2B Marketing Supplement*, **7** (10) (November/ December), 20

BACS (2010) BACS payment schemes, *B2B Marketing Awards*, p.10

Baseone, (2011) *Buyersphere Report*, 2011, Retrieved 19 April 2011 from www.baseone.co.uk

Blythe, J. (2002). Using trade fairs in key account management, *Industrial Marketing Management*, **31** (7) (October), 627–635

Boukersi, L. (2000). The role of trade fairs and exhibitions in international marketing communications, in S. Moyne (ed.), *The Handbook of International Marketing Communications*, London: Blackwell, pp. 117–135.

Brennan, J. (2010) Good email = good customers, *B2B Marketing*, **7** (10) (November/ December), 41

Durlacher (1999) UK on-line community, *Durlacher Quarterly Internet Report*, Q3, 7–11, London

Geigenmüller, A. (2010) The role of virtual trade fairs in relationship value creation, *Journal of Business and Industrial Marketing*, **25** (4), 284–292

IAB (2010) UK email marketing enjoys 15% increase, *WARC News*, retrieved 3 November 2010 from www.warc.com/News

Jansen, B.J., Zhang, M., Sobel, K. and Chowdury, A. (2009) Twitter Power: Tweets as Electronic Word of Mouth, *Journal of the American Society for Information science and Technology*, **60** (11), 2169–2188

Jarboe, G. (2005) Why does search engine marketing look like a penny-farthing bicycle? *Internet Search Engine Database*, 11 January. Retrieved 27 July 2007, from www.isedb.com/news/article/1086/

Kaplan, A.M. and Haelein, M. (2010) Users of the world unite! The challenges and opportunities of social media, *Business Horizons*, **53**, 59–68

Karayanni, D.A. (2000). An integrated model of communication strategies for business network alliances, antecedent conditions and business performance, using the Internet as the mediating communication means, PhD thesis, Athens University of Economics and Business

Karayanni, D.A. and Baltas, G.A. (2003) Web site characteristics and business performance: some evidence from international business-to-business organisations, *Marketing Intelligence and Planning*, **21** (2), 105–114

Kerin, R.A. and Cron, W.L. (1987) Assessing trade show functions and performance: an exploratory study, *Journal of Marketing*, **51** (3) (July), 87–94

Li, L.Y. (2007), Marketing resources and performance of exhibitor firms in trade shows: a contingent resource perspective, *Industrial Marketing Management*, **36**, 360-370

Marshall, M-L (2010) Is high profile high risk? *B2B Marketing*, **7** (9) (October) 12-13

McKinsey, (2010) Marketers must keep pace with media evolution, retrieved 11 September 2010 from www.warc.com/News/PrintNewsItem.asp?NID=27478

Rust, W.A. (2010) Bacs late payment campaign, *B2B Marketing*, retrieved 14 March 2010 from www.b2bmarketing.net/knowledgebank/branding/case-studies/case-study-bacs-late-payment-campaign-ware-anthony-rust-bacs-pay

Shipley, D. and Wong, K.S. (1993) Exhibiting strategy and implementation, *International Journal of Advertising*, **12** (2), 117–130

Steele, F. and Ahmed, M. (2010) Twitter unveils advert Tweets in bid for profits, *Times Online*, 13 April, Retrieved 8 September 2011 from http://business.timesonline.co.uk/tol/business/industry_sectors/media/article7095914.ece

Usunier, J-C., Roulin, N. and Ivens, B.S. (2010) Cultural, national and industry-level differences in B2B web site design and content, *International Journal of Electronic Commerce*, **14** (2), (Winter), 41–87.

Weekes, C. (2010) Ringing all over the world, *B2B Marketing*, **7** (10), (November/December) 32

Wells, G. (2010) How to ...develop an effective content marketing programme, *B2B Marketing*, **7** (10), (November/December) 36

11 Personal Selling and Key Account Management

Overview

The importance of personal selling in the B2B communications mix should not be underestimated. Although all the tools can play a significant part in an organisation's overall marketing communications activities, personal selling, delivered through a sales force, has traditionally been the most potent. Personal contact and selling can be critical for the development of meaningful collaborative relationships between customers and suppliers.

In this final chapter, consideration is given to the role and characteristics of personal selling. However, the main thrust is centred on the impact of selling on interorganisational relationships and how the other communication tools can be blended to provide cost and communication effectiveness. In addition, issues concerning the management and organisation of the sales force are explored before concluding with an examination of key account management.

Aims and objectives

The main aims of this chapter are to consider the key characteristics of personal selling and to examine how this communication tool can best be used to influence the nature and shape of relationships between organisations and individual buyers and sellers.

The objectives of this chapter are to enable readers to:

1 Consider the role and tasks of personal selling.

2 Examine the characteristics of personal selling and determine when it should be a major part of the mix.

3 Evaluate the contribution sales force activities can and should make to the development of interorganisational relationships.

4 Appraise the effective mix of the communication tools for selling through multiple channels.

5 Appreciate the broad ways in which sales managers can manage the sales force.

6 Determine the role and key characteristics of key account management.

A Slice of Life – The Origin of Business

The sales function is always, always, always at the forefront of the business. Businesses are there to sell things and salespeople do the selling. Contrary to what you may have heard, products very rarely 'sell themselves', they have to be sold – even online businesses have learnt the hard way that they need to have 'real people' available to close sales. But it would be wrong to suppose that it is just the salespeople who sell. Everyone associated to a brand including the brand itself and indeed its customers are capable of selling the products or services. The less obvious sales activities are 'indirect'. That leaves the sales and marketing teams slugging it out on the frontline for direct sales. And they do slug it out, but at some point, the sales and marketing functions have to work together – because the personal selling model is rarely, if ever, fully scalable.

The trigger is usually when the sales team simply can't sell any more by themselves. There are only so many hours in the day and sales people are expensive. When a company can no longer achieve continued growth by selling 'one to one', their thoughts inevitably turn to selling 'one to many'. In other words, they need marketing support. The obvious support comes in the form of marketing communications activity – campaign development and lead generation activities for example – but an important and often over-looked area of support is where marketing expertise helps make the sales activity more effective by positioning the brand and shaping the story it tells.

A large technology client recently set me just such a challenge. In an uncharacteristically frank briefing meeting, it was revealed that the sales team was struggling with its ability to articulate a complex technical message in a way that would attract sufficient sales growth. In a nutshell, the customers weren't listening. The marketing team was used to providing tactical campaign support, but had yet to deliver a simple, compelling story that customers would relate to and engage with. So that became my challenge.

The category was 'business intelligence' and data analytics. It's a bit dry. And a bit complex. Sandal-wearing maths professor territory. In essence, the company provided software that could analyse vast quantities of operational data from a business to provide management insight and decision making intelligence. Across every aspect of a large operation and across all market sectors, my client would use complex algorithms based on past and present data, to predict the future. Creepy, but cool. Management teams within customer organisations could use the results of the data analysis to make quicker and better decisions. Who in business wouldn't want that decision making capability? Who could resist a crystal ball to see into the future of the organisation and make changes to affect outcomes? Almost no one actually. My client was hugely successful – an established, multi-billion dollar, global company. It already had a lot of customers. To maintain growth, however, it needed to penetrate deeper into the customer organisations and every time it tried, it had to re-sell a deeply technical, complex story that no one had time for. It was a slow and painful process for the sales team and they wanted to make it easier and faster. And who'd blame them?

The solution came through an extensive process of consultation with the sales and marketing teams that, ultimately, was distilled into the understanding that decision making is not academic, or business analytical, or mathematical. It's rooted in the real commercial world of taking action. The software made a difference to decision making because it helped businesses to adapt to a changing world. It was a relatively small step at this point, to lead the client from the unfamiliar territory of building a Creative Platform® using a brand narrative, towards the more familiar and comfortable concept of business evolution – businesses had to adapt to a new environment just to survive and that called for a different way of thinking. But did we need to fundamentally change the way businesses thought about the nature of business? No – because it has already been done for us. By Charles Darwin. The concept was simply to apply Darwin to business. By doing so we would give the audience a framework they already understood to differentiate the company, and we would give the sales team a familiar story they could re-tell easily – evolution, business evolution.

Imagine how the human race might have evolved if it had been able to make better, faster decisions. The implications for business are the same. An ongoing series of small decisions, in the right place, at the right time, ensure businesses adapt to their changing environment, and through being better adapted to their environment, create a stronger species of business. My client's software turned chance, intuition and decisions into 'natural selection' for the 'survival of the fittest'. We didn't even need to mention the consequences of NOT using the software (or a competitor's software). The alternative to survival, is extinction. It was implicit.

The company applied Darwin's idea of evolution through natural selection to businesses, allowing businesses to grow and adapt to their changing environment by introducing the software that made the differences in the evolutionary process evident, giving people the ability to make better decisions faster and the confidence to change into a more profitable business. Very nice. With the story agreed, we just needed a device to help the sales team remember the story and find a way of starting to tell it without the whole thing becoming a little trite. The solution came in the form of a coin. We managed to find a commemorative coin from The Royal Mint denoting Darwin's image and the evolution of an ape on one of the coin's faces.

Every sales person would be supplied with one of the special coins to carry around and, whenever possible, use the coin to introduce the 'What do you do?' discussion. Instead of an answer that began with, "Let me just fire up my laptop and bore you to death with algorithms…", the sales person could reach into a pocket and toss the coin to the customer and the conversation could start with a story – "See this coin? That's what we do. I don't just mean we make money; if you look carefully you'll see it commemorates Charles Darwin. We apply Darwin to making money. Your business has to evolve, it needs to adapt to the changing environment. We use complex software to reveal what's actually going on in this evolutionary process. How one thing affects another. And that allows you to make better decisions, faster. We accelerate the evolution of your business…"

You can provide the sales team with whatever tools you like to promote sales and they may use them or they may not. But give them a good story to tell and the battle is more than half won.

Scot McKee

■ Introduction

Personal selling is different to the other communication tools and methods mainly because these messages represent dyadic communication. This means that there are two persons involved in the communication process. Feedback and evaluation of transmitted messages is possible, more or less instantaneously, so that these messages can be tailored to be much more personal than any of the other methods of communication.

Since personal selling brings buyers and sellers into close proximity it is possible to induce a change in behaviour. This occurs because information can be provided quickly and with conviction, in the context of the buyer's environment. In addition to product demonstration, information is provided in the setting of the transaction and can be used to overcome objections and encourage buyers to place orders.

Given that the costs associated with personal selling are high, it is vital that sales staff are used effectively. To that end, many organisations seek methods to decrease the time that the sales force spends on administration, travel and office work and to maximise the time spent in front of customers, where they can use their specific selling skills.

Organisations adopt a mixture of personal selling activities, often based on the proven methods appropriate to their type of business. Indeed, there is evidence that the activities undertaken by a sales force are strongly related to the overall marketing strategies that an organisation seeks to implement (Cross *et al.*, 2001). It is normally assumed that the sales force seek out, negotiate, collect and bring into the organisation orders from customers wishing to make purchases. This aspect of personal selling can be typified in four ways:

- *Order takers* are salespersons to whom customers are drawn at the place of supply. Reception clerks at hotels and ticket desk personnel at theatres and cinemas typify this role.

- *Order getters* operate away from the organisation and attempt to gain orders largely through the use of demonstration and persuasion.

- *Order collectors* aattempt to gather orders over the telephone, through email or a combination involving the Web. The growth of telesales operations as a sales support programme is designed to save the time of both the buyer and seller. Telesales are used to gather repeat and low-value orders, reduce costs, speed transaction time, improve cash flow and free valuable sales personnel to seek new customers and build relationships with current ones.

- *Order supporters* are all those who support salespeople in that they are involved with the order once it has been secured, or with the act of ordering, usually by supplying information. Order processing or financial advice services typify this role.

These types of personal selling are to some degree superficial as they all represent people who have a customer-facing role and who are expected to engage in customer interaction. It is the depth of customer contact that provides the real measure of customer interaction.

Personal selling cannot work effectively in isolation from the other elements in the mix. For example, members of the sales force are literally representative of the organisation for which they work so, in one sense, they provide constant visibility for it. Stakeholders perceive them and shape their perception of the organisation they represent partly on, for example, the way in which they dress, speak and handle questions, the type of car they drive and the level of courtesy they display to support staff.

■ The Role and Tasks of Personal Selling

It is generally agreed that personal selling is most effective at the later stages of the buying process, rather than at the earlier stage of awareness building. It follows that each organisation should determine the precise role the sales force is to play within their communication mix. Personal selling is the most expensive element of the communications mix, so the use of a sales force should be a very carefully considered element of an organisation's promotional activities. In terms of the DRIP framework (see Chapter 9), personal selling may fulfil different tasks. Where the relationship between organisations is new or basically discrete in nature, information and persuasion will tend to be the predominant roles. Where the relationship is established and more collaborative, information and reinforcement will be the more prominent roles.

In B2B markets it is often assumed that sales personnel operate at the boundary of the organisation. They provide the link between the needs of their own organisation and the needs of their customers and in this sense they perform an important representational role. This linkage is absolutely vital, for a number of reasons that will be discussed shortly, for without personal selling, communication with other organisations would occur through impersonal, electronic or print media, probably to the detriment of relationships. However, the notion that there is a boundary between organisations who operate within a close network or within a collaborative relationship is both tenuous and contradictory. Boundaries may exist where market exchanges predominate but in situations where trust, commitment and reciprocity are fundamental, it is unlikely that a boundary could, or should, be identified.

When these factors are brought together, the salesperson is not only expected to act as a manager of customers (Wilson, 1993) but increasingly also as a person responsible for, among many other elements, the development of customer relationships (Marshall *et al.*, 1999). Strong personal interaction with clients, based upon a collaborative or transactional (problem–solution) perspective to buyer needs, can provide a source of sustainable competitive advantage for organisations.

Salespersons do more than get or take orders and organisations should decide which tasks it expects its representatives to undertake. The list in Table 11.1 is an adaptation of the work by Guenzi (2002). These tasks provide direction and purpose, and also help to establish the criteria by which the performance of members of the sales force can be evaluated.

Table 11.1: Tasks of personal selling. Based on Guenzi (2002).

Activity	Explanation
Market research	The analysis and forecasting of market trends and related activities. The identification of sales opportunities,
Inbound information	Reporting information to the organisation about the market, customers and associated stakeholders.
Outbound information	Reporting organisational information to customers and associated stakeholders about products and organisational issues.
Prospecting	Finding and using leads to generate new customers.
Marketing & sales team coordination	Developing strong internal links with sales support teams, the marketing department and other agencies.
Selling	Leading prospects (and established customers) to a successful close.
Customer relationship	Developing mutually satisfying relationships with customers.
Sales service	Pre-sales support to encourage buyer engagement and trust prior to any transaction. Post-sales support to provide reassurance and formative collaborative gestures.

Personal selling is often referred to as interpersonal communication and from this perspective Reid *et al.* (2002) determined three major sales behaviours, namely, getting, giving and using information.

- *Getting information* refers to sales behaviours aimed at information acquisition, e.g. gathering information about customers, markets and competitors.

- *Giving information* refers to the dissemination of information to customers and other stakeholders. For example, sales presentations and seminar meetings designed to provide information about products and an organisation's capabilities and reputation.

- *Using information* refers to the sales person's use of information to help solve a customer's problem. Associated with this is the process of gaining buyer commitment through the generation of information (Thayer, 1968, cited by Reid *et al.* 2002).

These last authors suggest that the *using information* dynamic appears to be constant across all types of purchase situations. However, as the complexity of a purchase situation increases so the amount of giving information behaviours decline, and getting information behaviours increase. This finding supports the need for a salesperson to be able to recognise particular situations in the buying process and to then adapt their behaviour to meet buyer's contextual needs.

However, salespeople undertake numerous tasks in association with communication activities. Guenzi (2002) determined that some sales activities are generic simply because they are performed by most salespeople across a large number of industries. These generic activities are selling, customer relationship management and communicating with customers. Other activities such as market analysis, pre-sales services and the transfer of information about competitors to the organisation, are industry specific. Interestingly he found that information-gathering activities are more likely to be undertaken by organisations operating in consumer markets than in B2B, possibly a reflection of the strength of the market orientation in both arenas.

The roles and tasks of the sales force have been changing because the environment in which organisations operate is shifting dramatically. These changes, in particular those associated with the development and implementation of new technologies, have had repercussions on the activities of the sales force and are discussed later in this chapter.

■ Characteristics of Personal Selling

There are a number of characteristics, seen as strengths and weaknesses, associated with this communication tool. It is interesting to note that some of the strengths can in turn be seen as weaknesses, particularly when management control over the communication process is not as effective as it might be.

■ Strengths

Dyadic communications allow for interaction, which, unlike the other communication tools, provide for fast, direct feedback. In comparison with the mass media, personal selling allows for the receiver to focus attention on the salesperson, with a reduced likelihood of distraction or noise.

There is a greater level of participation in the decision process by the vendor than in the other tools. When this is combined with the power to tailor messages in response to the feedback provided by the buyer, the sales process has a huge potential to solve customer problems.

■ Weaknesses

One of the major disadvantages of personal selling is the cost. As reach is limited, costs per personal contact are normally high. Costs include salaries, commission, employment costs, expenses including travel, accommodation and subsistence. This means that management must find alternative ways of communicating particular messages and improve the amount of time that sales personnel spend with prospects and customers. Reach and frequency through personal selling is always going to be low, regardless of the level of funds available.

The amount of control that can be exercised over the delivery of messages through the sales force can be low. This is because each salesperson has the freedom to adapt messages to meet changing circumstances as negotiations proceed. In practice, however, the professionalism and training that members of the sales force often receive and the increasing accent on measuring levels of customer satisfaction, mean that the degree of control over the message can be regarded, in most circumstances, as very good, although it can never, for example, be as high as that of advertising.

The potential disadvantage of message inconsistency can lead to confusion (perhaps a misunderstanding with regard to a product specification), the ramifications of which can be enormous in terms of the cost and time spent by a variety of individuals from both parties to the contract. The quality of the relationship can, therefore, be jeopardised through poor and inconsistent communications.

■ Personal Selling and the Communication Mix

In view of the role, advantages and disadvantages of personal selling, when should it be a major part of the communications mix? The following is not an exhaustive list, but is presented as a means of considering some of the important issues: complexity, network factors, buyer significance and communication effectiveness.

Complexity

Personal selling is very important when there is a medium to high level of relationship complexity. Such complexity may be associated with either the physical characteristics of the product, such as computer software design, or with the environment in which the negotiations are taking place. For example, decisions related to the installation of products designed to automate an assembly line may well be a sensitive issue. This may be due to management's attitude towards the operators currently undertaking the work that the automation is expected to replace. Any complexity needs to be understood by buyer and seller in order that the right product is offered in the appropriate context for the buyer. This may mean that the buyer is required to customise the offering or provide assistance in terms of testing, installing or supporting the product.

When the complexity of the offering is high, advertising and public relations cannot always convey benefits in the same way as personal selling. Personal selling allows the product to be demonstrated so that buyers can see and, if necessary, touch and taste it for themselves. Personal selling also allows explanations to be made about particular points of concern to the buyer or about the environment in which the buyer wishes to use the product.

Buyer significance

The significance of the product to the buyers in the target market is a very important factor in the decision on whether to use personal selling. Significance can be measured as a form of risk, which is associated with benefits and costs.

The absolute cost to the buyer will vary among organisations. The significance of the purchase of an extra photocopier for a major multinational organisation may be low, but for a new start-up organisation or for an established organisation experiencing a dramatic turnaround, an extra photocopying machine may be highly significant and subject to high levels of resistance by a number of different internal stakeholders.

The timing of a product's introduction may well be crucial to the success of a wider plan or programme of activities. Only through personal selling can delivery be dovetailed into a client's schedule.

Communication effectiveness

There may be a number of ways to satisfy the communication objectives of a campaign, other than by using personal selling. Each of the other communication tools has strengths and weaknesses; consequently, differing mixes provide different benefits.

One of the main reasons for using personal selling occurs when advertising alone, or any other tool or medium, provides insufficient communication. The main reason for this inadequacy surfaces when advertising media cannot provide buyers with the information they require to make their decision. For example, a fleet car buyer may well observe and read various magazine and newspaper advertisements, often as a consumer. The decision to buy on behalf of their organisation, however, requires information and data upon which a more rational decision can be made. This rationality and experience, through face-to-face negotiations, visits, road reports and test drives, balances the former, more emotional, elements that shaped their earlier thoughts.

The decision to buy capital assets normally evokes high involvement. Therefore, manufacturers tend to provide a wealth of factual information in various formats, from which prospective buyers seek further information, experience and reassurance, usually via a salesperson, that is, a personal point of contact.

Personal selling provides a number of characteristics that make it more effective than the other elements of the B2B promotional mix. As discussed, the complexity of many products requires salespeople to be able to discuss with clients their specific needs; in other words, to be able to talk in the customer's own language, to offer source credibility through expertise and, hopefully, trustworthiness, and build a relationship that corresponds with the psychographic profile of each member of the DMU. In this case, mass communications would be inappropriate.

There are two further factors that influence the decision to use personal selling as part of the communications mix. When the customer base is small and dispersed across a wide geographic area it makes economic sense to use salespersons, because advertising in this situation is inadequate, ineffective and inefficient.

■ Channel factors

If the communication strategy combines a larger amount of push, rather than pull, activities then personal selling is required to provide the necessary communications for the other members of a network. Following on from this is the question of what information needs to be exchanged between members, in what form and with what timing. Handling objections, answering questions and overcoming misconceptions are also necessary information exchange skills.

When the number of members in a network is limited, the use of a sales force is advisable, as advertising is inefficient in these circumstances. Furthermore, the opportunity to build a close collaborative relationship with channel members may enable the development of a sustainable competitive advantage. Cravens (1987) suggested that the factors in Table 11.2 are important and determine when the sales force is a significant element of the communications mix.

Although personal selling may be the most persuasive single tool, combining it with advertising (or other tools) often results in a more potent form of communication. Their strengths serve to complement each other. Advertising is more effective at the initial stages of the response hierarchy, but the later stages of inducing trial and closing the order are the strong points of personal selling.

Table 11.2: When personal selling is a major element of the communications mix

	Advertising relatively important	Personal selling relatively important
Number of customers	Large	Small
Buyers' information needs	Low	High
Size and importance of purchase	Small	Large
Post-purchase service required	Little	A lot
Product complexity	Low	High
Distribution strategy	Pull	Push
Pricing policy	Set	Negotiate
Resources available for promotion	Many	Few

Source: Based on Cravens (1987).

ViewPoint 11.1: Eventful selling

Corporate entertainment has long been an important element in the communication mix used by B2B companies. Following the recession, when the industry was savaged, organisations have been reviving their entertainment-based communications, partly in anticipation of the Olympic Games in London and the 2014 World Cup in Brazil.

Today the smart approach is to integrate corporate hospitality with events, social media, and the latest technology in order to provoke two-way communications and so extend their reach, longevity and effectiveness of the investment. For Investec, a specialist bank and asset management company, events are a central part of the marketing strategy, which includes sponsorship of international rugby series and the Epsom Derby. Their hospitality is focused around the events they sponsor because the entertainment is conducted in a branded environment, which adds to the occasion.

Deloitte, the accountancy and consultancy firm, have involved themselves in the London Olympics by providing services associated with the planning, scheduling and development of the event. It is reported that Deloitte will have provided over one million hours of consultancy time to the event's organising committee. In return the consulting company will have their name displayed around the Olympic Park and provide hospitality during the Games. Perhaps even more importantly, they will be able to use the ultimate credential and testimonial in order to attract and retain clients. Their association and contribution to the Games will be evidence of their proven expertise to organise and manage the most complex projects.

Source: Whiteling (2011); Twentyman (2011); Downie (2011); Archer (2011)

Question: From a hospitality perspective, does it matter if an event fails to live up to expectations?

To illustrate the potency of this combination, Levitt (1967) reported that organisations that invest in advertising to raise awareness are more likely to create a favourable reception for their salespeople than those organisations that do not undertake such activities. However, those that had invested were also expected to have a better trained sales force. Morrill (1970) found that selling costs were as much as 12% lower if the customer had been made aware of the salesperson's organisation prior to the call. Swinyard and Ray (1977) determined that, even if a purchase was not made for reasons other than product quality, further use of advertising increased the probability of a future sale. All these findings suggest that, by combining advertising with personal selling, costs can be reduced, reach extended and the probability of a sale considerably improved.

Personal selling is a major tool of the B2B mix and a significant part of marketing management (Anderson, 1996) in business markets. One of the reasons for this is the responsibility sales people have to manage customer relationships.

■ Personal Selling and Managing Relationships

One view of personal selling is that the sales force is responsible for selling, installing and upgrading customer equipment. Another is that they are responsible for developing, selling and protecting accounts. The interesting point from both views is that responsibilities, or rather objectives, are extended, vertically upstream, into offer design, or vertically downstream, into the development and maintenance of long-term customer relationships. It is the last point that is becoming increasingly important. In the B2B sector the sales activity mix is becoming more orientated to the need to build and sustain the relationships that organisations have, or want, with their major customers.

Many authors consider the development, organisation and completion of a sale in a market exchange-based transaction to be the key part of the personal selling role. The focus of activity is on closing the sale and is very much transaction-orientated. Sales personnel provide a source of information for buyers so that they can make the right purchase decisions. In that sense they provide a good level of credibility, but they are also perceived, understandably, as biased. The degree of expertise held by the salesperson may be high, but the perception of trustworthiness will vary, especially during the formative period of the relationship, unless other transactions with the selling organisation have been satisfactory.

Once a number of transactions have been completed and product and service quality established, the perception of trustworthiness may improve. Indeed, a more relational perspective can start to emerge based around customer needs concerning the sales process, the quality of the overall buyer–seller interaction and the wider network implications and expectations of the participants.

Research indicates that for salespeople to be successful within a relational context there are three particular characteristics that can influence outcomes.

These are a customer/selling orientation (Saxe and Weitz, 1982; Kelly, 1992), adaptability (Morgan and Stoltman, 1990) and a service orientation (Cronin and Taylor, 1992) (see Table 11.3).

Keillor *et al.* (2000) found the customer/selling orientation to be significantly related to salesperson performance, which has implications for sales training, although these authors did not find any significant relationship with the other two variables.

Table 11.3: Categories associated with developing relational sales activities

Category	Explanation
Customer orientation	By discovering customer needs and working to satisfy them by supplying products and services that will provide customers with benefits, a long-term approach is adopted and short-term sales may be forsaken for longer-term goals.
Adaptability in the sales process	A salesperson's ability to adapt their sales approach in order to maintain a dialogue and continued interaction with the client. Adaptability should be seen as superior to both self- and task-orientated approaches. Listening, probing, questioning and detecting a variety of client clues are all signs of an adaptable approach.
Service orientation	This refers to the perception a buyer has of a salesperson's enthusiasm to engage in both selling and non-selling tasks, throughout the buyer–seller relationship. Service quality is an antecedent to customer satisfaction, which in turn has a positive impact on purchase intentions (Cronin and Taylor, 1992).

The behaviours most associated with relational selling have been identified as the intensity of the interaction, the mutual disclosure of information and cooperative intentions (Guenzi, 2002). There is also some general agreement that these behaviours do not necessarily impact on sales performance but do influence the quality of the relationship and the inherent trust between partner organisations. Indeed, trust, a concept examined in Chapter 8, appears to increase as the selling task adopts a deeper relationship orientation (Wilson, 1995). Customer perception of the levels of trust (in a salesperson and the organisation represented) and expertise constitute two crucial sales attributes. When these attributes are positive it is more likely that long-term interorganisational relationships will develop (Liu and Leach, 2001). Not surprisingly, sales training programmes should, according to Guenzi, be designed to highlight the importance of developing and maintaining customer trust and emphasise the benefits of adaptive relational behaviours.

Sales managers are broadly seen to be responsible for the management and achievement of the sales goals set for a particular salesperson, team and/or regions. They are, as Mehta *et al.* (2002: 430) put it: 'trainers, motivators, coaches, evaluators and counsellors for their sales people'. They perform many other roles but one, that appears to be identified as significant yet understated, concerns marketing channels. Initial work by these researchers indicates that many sales managers are increasingly acting as channel managers and take on the task of managing customer relationships across an increasing number of channels. They point out the implications of this development in terms of the range and type of training that sales managers need in view of the strategic significance of channel strategy and customer relationships.

◼ Multichannel Selling

As discussed earlier in this book, many organisations have restructured their sales operations, partly in an attempt to reduce costs and partly to meet the future channel needs of their customers. With the huge variety of sales channels that are available there is also an increased complexity. These channels include the electronic and direct marketing channels at one end of the spectrum and at the other, multi-functional, global, personal sales teams (Ingram *et al.*, 2002).

The restructuring of sales channels has often taken the form of introducing multiple sales channels, where the simple objective is to use less expensive channels to complete those selling tasks that do not require personal, face-to-face contact and which are typified by transaction-orientated relationships. In contrast, collaborative relationships tend to be better supported by personal, face-to-face selling efforts.

This principle can be best observed within a simple matrix, based on the dimensions of potential account attractiveness and strength of relationship. *Account Potential* refers to the opportunities a buying organisation represents to the supplier while the *Strength of Relationship* maps the extent to which two organisations are experienced and actively engaged in transactions with each other (see Figure 11.1).

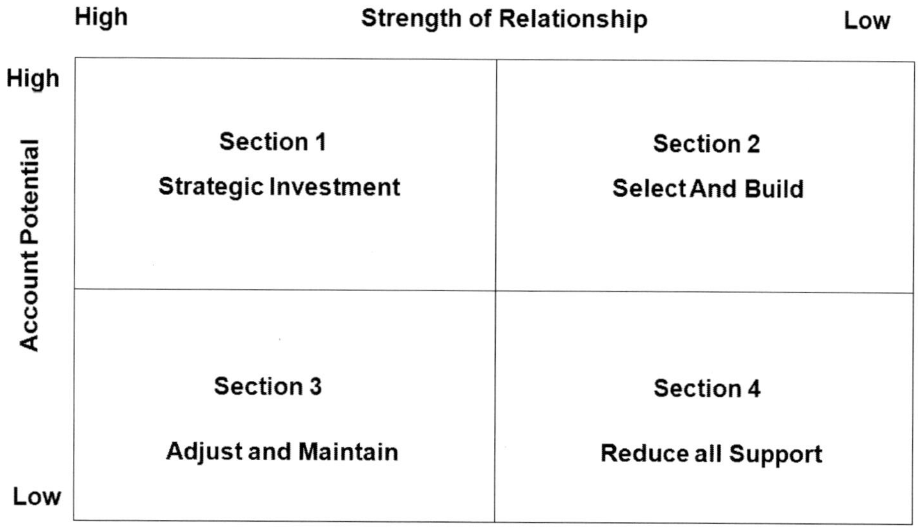

	Strength of Relationship	
High		**Low**
Section 1 **Strategic Investment**		**Section 2** **Select And Build**
Section 3 **Adjust and Maintain**		**Section 4** **Reduce all Support**

Account Potential — High / Low

Figure 11.1: Account investment matrix

Personal Selling and Key Account Management

For reasons of clarity, these scales are presented as either high or low, strong or weak. However, they should be considered as a continuum, and with the use of some relatively simple evaluative criteria, accounts can be positioned on the matrix and strategies formulated to move them to different positions, which in turn necessitates the use of different sales channel mixes.

Using the approach originally proposed by Cravens *et al.* (1991), appropriate sales channels are superimposed on the matrix in order that optimum efficiency in selling effort and costs be managed (Figure 11.2). Accounts in Section 1 vary in attractiveness, as some will be assigned key account status. The others will be very important and will require a high level of selling effort, which has to be delivered by the field sales force.

ViewPoint 11.2: Kern weighs up the audience

Kern Precision Sales (KPS) provide pharmacists, scientists, and engineers, amongst others, with scales and weighing instruments that are capable of measuring to seven decimal points. The market is product-driven, strongly orientated to price and nearly all the messages are informational. There is no real branding so the market for these particular tools and devices can be characterised as a commodity.

The task facing KPS was to stand out in the market and break free from the vicious cycle of product/price competition which inevitably leads to low margins and unprofitable activities. To achieve this much-needed differentiation and generate good quality leads, an eight week campaign was developed. Understanding the nature of the audience was important because the communication needed to resonate with targeted end users, purchasing buyers and distributors and intermediaries. One of the elements that characterised them all was that they were all regarded as intelligent and inquisitive individuals, some of whom might be referred to as slightly geeky.

As result of this insight a direct mail campaign was developed. A feather was attached to the letterhead to attract attention and all of the pack's contents, such as the paper, compliments slip and even the ink, had their weight listed. The core of the campaign was founded on a 'guess the weight' incentive. The challenge for recipients was to guess the weight of a range of low mass objects. Email messages containing details about the competition drove people to a website. Here they could make their guesses and then watch experiments, solutions to weighing challenges and of course see the results of the competition. Not only did the campaign serve to develop interest in KPS, it also helped them to stand out on a more emotional basis. The response rate to the campaign was 24%, 167 quality leads were generated and four new intermediaries were signed up, with a predicted £200,000 revenue for next year.

Source: Kern (2010); www.b2bmarketing.net/knowledgebank/; www.warc.com/Content

Question: To what extent do you think KPS can legitimately sustain an emotional approach, when the audience are driven by the need for data and rational information?

	High Strength of Relationship Low	
High	**Key Account Management** **Field Force Selling**	**Field Force Selling** **Telemarketing / Call Centre** **Web Site** **EMail**
Account Potential	**Directed Field Force Selling** **Telemarketing / Call Centre** **Web Site** **Email**	**Direct Mail** **Telemarketing** **Email**
Low		

Figure 11.2: Multichannel mix

Accounts in Section 2 are essentially prospects because of their weak competitive position but high attractiveness. Selling effort should be proportional to the value of the prospects: high effort for good prospects and low for the others. All the main sales channels should be used, commencing with direct mail to identify prospects, telesales for qualification purposes, field sales force selling directed at the strong prospects and telesales for the others. As the relationship becomes stronger, so field selling takes over from telesales. If the relationship weakens then the account may be discontinued and selling redirected to other prospects.

Table 11.4: Core business capabilities

Category	Explanation
Product development management	Developing and maintaining suitable products and services to meet customer needs and provide customer value.
Supply chain management	The acquisition and transformation of resources (inputs) into valued customer offerings, throughout the supply chain.
Customer relationship management	Creating, sustaining and developing customer relationships for mutual benefit.

Source: Based on Srivastava *et al.* (1999).

In order to decide on an appropriate sales strategy, the nature of the desired communication needs to be examined. Are there to be salespersons negotiating individually, or as a team with a single buyer or buying team? Is a sales team required in order to sell to buying teams or will conference and seminar selling achieve the desired goals? What is the degree of importance of the portfolio of accounts, and how should the organisations be contacted?

The primary, and traditional, sales channel is the field sales force. These are people who are fully employed by the organisation and are referred to as the direct sales force. Salespersons, like any other unit of resource, should be deployed in

318

a way that provides maximum benefit to the organisation. Sales organisation effectiveness results from the performance of salespeople, organisational factors and various environmental factors (Baldauf et al., 2002).

Grant and Cravens (1999) suggest that the effectiveness of the sales organisation (or unit) is determined as a result of two main antecedents – the sales manager and the sales force itself. To this should be added the context in which the sales organisation operates. The content of these antecedents is shown at Figure 11.3.

Figure 11.3: Antecedents of sales organisational effectiveness. Based on Grant and Cravens (1999)

The performance of salespeople is a measure of both their work- or task-related, behaviours and the results of their activities and inputs. Therefore, a sales management control strategy should refer to the degree to which sales managers actively manage the inputs as well as reward against targeted outcomes (sales, market share and so on).

From this it is possible to identify two main sales management approaches, behaviour-based and outcome-based control systems (Baldauf et al., 2002). Essentially, control through behaviour-based systems is based on managing the inputs or processes to a salesperson and rewarding with a high fixed salary and low commission. Conversely, control through outcome-based approaches is characterised by a focus on results, little managerial supervision and direction, and high levels of commission as an incentive to perform.

Many organisations use a hybrid approach but research by Baldauf et al. indicates that sales managers appear to utilise a 'coaching rather than command and control management styles' (p. 591). The emphasis appears to be on the long term

Business Marketing

11

and the value of developing relationships. The performance of salespeople is therefore enhanced by sales management strategies that are based on generating positive behaviour. However, results from previous work undertaken by Piercy *et al.* (1998) supported many previous findings that salespeople with high levels of behaviour performance also exhibit high levels of outcome performance. This implies that sales managers should spend a greater amount of their time selecting, training and developing salespeople rather than just selecting, directing and measuring results.

From this brief overview of sales management responsibilities it can be concluded that managers are responsible for five broad activities associated with salespeople:

- Selection and recruitment
- Training and coaching
- Deployment
- Motivation and supervision
- Evaluation, control and reward.

■ Key Account Management

The increasing complexity of both markets and products, combined with the trends towards purchasing centralisation and industrial concentration, mean that a small number of major accounts have become essential for the survival of many organisations. The growth in the significance of key account management (KAM) is expected to continue and one of the results will be the change in expectations of buyers and sellers, in particular the demand for higher levels of expertise, integration and professionalism of sales forces.

It has long been recognised that particular customer accounts represent an important, often large proportion of turnover. Such accounts have been referred to variously as national accounts, house accounts, major accounts and key accounts. Millman and Wilson (1995) argue that the first three are orientated towards sales, tend to the short term and are often only driven by sales management needs. However, Ojasalo (2001) sees little difference in the terminology KAM, national account marketing (NAM) and strategic account management (SAM).

Key accounts may be of different sizes in comparison with the focus organisation, but what delineates them from other types of 'account' is that they are strategically important and attract dedicated resources (Richards and Jones, 2009). Key accounts are customers who, in a business-to-business market, are willing to enter into relational exchanges and who are of strategic importance to the focus organisation.

There are two primary aspects of this definition. The first is that both parties perceive relational exchanges as a necessary component and that the relationship is long term. The second aspect refers to the strategic issue. The key account is strategically important because it might offer opportunities for entry to new markets, represent access to other key organisations or resources, or provide symbolic value in terms of influence, power and stature.

The importance of the long-term relationship as a prime element of key account identification raises questions about how they are developed, what resources are required to manage and sustain them, and what long-term success and effectiveness results from identifying them. Essentially this comes down to, who in the organisation should be responsible for these key accounts? Generally there are three main responses: to assign sales executives, to create a key account division or to create a key account sales force (see Table 11.5).

■ Key Account Managers

Abratt and Kelly (2002) report Napolitano's (1997) work which found that, to be successful, a KAM programme requires the selection of the right key account manager. This person should possess particularly strong interpersonal and relationship skills and be capable of managing larger, significant and often complex customers. Key account managers act as a conduit between organisations, through which high value information flows, in both directions. They must be prepared and able to deal with organisations where buying decisions can be protracted and delayed (Sharma, 1997).

Table 11.5: Three ways of managing key accounts

Category	Explanation
Assigning sales executives	Common in smaller organisations that do not have large resources. Normally undertaken by senior executives who have the flexibility and can provide the responsive service often required. They can make decisions about stock, price, distribution and levels of customisation.
	There is a tendency for key accounts to receive a disproportionate level of attention, as the executives responsible for these major customers lose sight of their own organisation's marketing strategy.
Creating a key account division	The main advantage of this is that it offers close integration of production, finance, marketing and sales. The main disadvantage is that resources are duplicated and the organisation can become very inefficient. It is also a high-risk strategy, as the entire division is dependent upon a few customers.
Creating a key account sales force	This is adopted by organisations who want to differentiate through service and they use their most experienced and able salespersons and provide them with a career channel.
	Administratively, this structure is inefficient as there is a level of duplication similar to that found in the customer-type structure discussed earlier. Furthermore, commission payable on these accounts is often a source of discontent, both for those within the key account sales force and those aspiring to join the select group.

Benedapudi and Leone (2002) agree that the key account manager is vitally important to the success of a KAM relationship but they also consider the relationship differences between the organisations as distinct from the interpersonal relationships between the customer firm's contact person and the supply side firm's key account manager, or contact employee as they refer to them. These relationships will vary in strength and there are differing consequences for the KAM relationship should the contact person leave the supply-side organisation.

Among the key success factors, Abratt and Kelly report that, in addition to selecting the right key account manager, the selection of the right key account customers is also important for establishing KAM programmes. Not all large and high volume customers are suitable for KAM programmes. Segmentation and customer prioritisation according to needs and an organisation's ability to provide consistent value should be used to highlight those for whom KAM would not be helpful.

In addition, particular sales behaviours are required at this level of operation. As the majority of key account managers are drawn internally from the sales force (Hannah, 1998, cited by Abratt and Kelly) it is necessary to ensure that they have the correct skills mix. It is also important to take a customer's perspective on what makes a successful KAM programme. Pardo (1997) is cited as claiming that the degree of impact a product has on the customer's business activity will determine the level of attention offered to the supplier's programme. Also, the level of buying decision centralisation will impact on the effectiveness of the KAM programme.

Abratt and Kelly found six factors were of particular importance when establishing a KAM programme. These are the 'suitability of the key account manager, knowledge and understanding of the key account customer's business, commitment to the KAM partnership, delivering value, the importance of trust and the proper implementation and understanding of the KAM concept' (p. 475).

One final point can be made concerning key account managers. The inference is that one multi-talented individual is the sole point of contact between the supplier and customer. This is not the case as there are usually a number of levels of interaction between the two organisations. Indeed, there could be 'an entire team dedicated to providing services and support to the key account' (Ojasalo, 2001:109). Therefore, it is more appropriate to suggest that the key account manager should assume responsibility for all points of contact within the customer organisation.

■ Key Account Relationship Cycles

A number of researchers have attempted to gain a greater understanding of KAM by considering the development cycles through which relationships move. Millman and Wilson (1995) offer the work of Ford (1980), Dwyer *et al.* (1987) and Wotruba (1991) as examples of such development cycles.

Millman and Wilson have attempted to build upon the work of the others and have formulated a model which incorporates their own research as well as that established in the literature. McDonald (2000) has since elaborated on their framework providing further insight and explanation.

The cycle develops with the **exploratory KAM** level where the main task is to identify those accounts that have key account potential, and those that do not, in order that resources can be allocated efficiently. Both organisations are considering each other; the buyer in terms of the supplier's offer in terms of its ability to match their own requirements and the seller in terms of the buyer providing sufficient volume, value and financial suitability.

The next level is **basic KAM**, where both organisations enter into a transactional period, essentially testing each other as potential long-term partners. Some relationships may stabilise at this level while others may develop as a result of the seller seeking and gaining tentative agreement with prospective accounts about whether they would become 'preferred accounts'.

At the **cooperative KAM** level, more people from both organisations are involved in communications. At the basic KAM level both parties understand each other and the selling company has established their credentials with the buying organisation, through experience. At this next level, opportunities to add value to the relationship are considered. This could be encouraged by increasing the range of products and services transacted. As a result more people are involved in the relationship.

At the **interdependent KAM** level, both organisations recognise the importance of the other to their operations, with the supplier either first-choice or only supplier. Retraction from the relationship is now problematic as 'inertia and strategic suitability', as McDonald phrases it, holds the partners together.

When the two organisations view the relationship as consisting of one entity where they create synergistic value in the marketplace **integrated KAM** is achieved. Joint problem solving and the sharing of sensitive information are strong characteristics of the relationship and withdrawal by either party can be traumatic at a personal level for the participants involved, let alone at the organisational level.

The final level is **disintegrating KAM**. This can occur at any time due to a variety of reasons, ranging from company takeover to the introduction of new technology. The relationship may return to another lower level and new terms of business are established. The termination, or readjustment, of the relationship need not be seen as a negative factor as both parties may decide that the relationship holds no further value.

McDonald develops Millman and Wilson's model by moving away from a purely sequential framework. He suggests that organisations may stabilise or enter the model at any level, indeed he states that organisations might readjust to a lower level. The time between phases will vary according to the nature and circumstances of the parties involved. The labels provided by McDonald reflect the relationship status of both parties rather than of the selling company (for example 'prospective') or buying company (for example 'preferred supplier'). While the Millman and Wilson and McDonald interpretations of the KAM relationship cycle, provide insight they are both primarily dyadic perspectives. They neglect to consider the influence of significant others, in particular those other network member organisations who provide context and interaction in particular networks and who do influence the actions of organisations and those key individuals who are strategic decision makers.

ViewPoint 11.3: Thriving in the wind with KAM at Vestas

The increasing interest and adoption of wind power across the globe has led plant manufacturing companies such as Vestas to reappraise their use of resources. Apart from technical and production issues, Vestas see the need to support not only new customers but large international organisations as well. In anticipation that considerably larger customers will account for a growing share of demand, Vestas have introduced key account management (KAM). This is intended to improve the services provided to the largest customers by offering them direct and swift access to the company through a dedicated key account manager.

At the beginning, Vestas was organised to service small, local customers. However, the customer portfolio has changed and the company now collaborates with large utility companies, each with international operations. Not only does KAM enable a more professional approach to customer relations, and retention, it also improves Vestas' competitive strength in an increasingly competitive market. When Vestas won its largest order to date in 2010, a 1500 MW from Energias de Portugal Renováveis (EDPR), one of the world's leading utility companies dedicated to renewable energy, KAM was an integral part of the success.

Part of the overall strategy at Vestas is to position the company as a quality supplier who delivers a 'green bond'. This means that any investment in a Vestas wind power plant provides customers with 'Business Case Certainty', a promise of excellence and performance. To enable this to materialise KAM has an important role developing dialogue and deepening relationships with major customers.

In 2010 Vestas launched 'Wind Summits', a new concept for traditional customer visits. Customers are given an in-depth view of Vestas' different competencies and product offerings and an opportunity to enter into detailed discussions and negotiations with Vestas' experts in a large number of areas pre-selected by the customer.

Source: Vestas Annual Report retrieved 27 May 2011 from www.vestas.com/en/annual-report-2010/management-report/management-focus/customers.aspx

Question: What criteria would you use to determine whether a Vestas customer should be supported by Key Account Management?

■ Some Final Aspects of KAM

In mature and competitive markets, where there is little differentiation between the products, service may be the only source of sustainable competitive advantage. Key account management allows senior sales executives to build a strong relationship with each of their customers and so provide a very high level of service and strong point of differentiation.

This approach enables an organisation to select its most experienced and able salespersons and, in doing so, provide a career channel for those executives who prefer to stay in sales rather than move into management. Administratively, this structure is inefficient as there is a level of duplication similar to that found in the customer-type structure discussed earlier. Furthermore, commission payable on these accounts is often a source of discontent, both for those within the key account sales force and those aspiring to join the select group.

The development and management of key accounts is complex and evolving. Key account relationships are rarely static and should be rooted within corporate strategy, if only because of the implications for resources, which customers seek as a result of partnering in this way (Spencer, 1999). Key accounts are concerned with the development and maintenance of important relationships. Richards and Jones (2009: 312) introduce the concept 'relationship effectiveness' as "a measure of the relational aspects of a buyer–seller union." Its antecedents are considered to be commitment, information sharing, trust, cooperation and conflict resolution, thereby reinforcing Morgan and Hunt's (1994) KMV model.

Summary

Here are the key points about personal selling and KAM, set out against the learning objectives.

1 Consider the role and tasks of personal selling.

Personal selling is often referred to as interpersonal communication and from this perspective three major sales behaviours have been identified. These are getting, giving and using information. Personal selling can be used to engage groups and individuals and achieves this largely through the provision of rational, logical information, designed to provoke changes to behaviour. The primary task of this tool is persuade people to behave in particular ways and the secondary task is to provide information.

2 Examine the characteristics of personal selling and determine when it should be a major part of the mix.

Dyadic communications allow for interaction, which provides for fast, direct feedback and allows for the receiver to focus attention on the salesperson, with a reduced likelihood of distraction or noise. Messages can be personalised and tailored in response to feedback.

Costs per personal contact are normally high and reach and frequency is low, regardless of the level of funds available. Control and message inconsistency are further issues associated with personal selling.

Personal selling should be part of the communications mix when buyer information needs are high, where the purchase is important and the product technically complex, of high value and where there is no fixed price and negotiation is expected.

3 Evaluate the contribution sales force activities can and should make to the development of interorganisational relationships.

As the number of transactions with buyers increase, so the relationship changes from a market to a collaborative exchange. Indeed, a more relational perspective develops one which indicates that the development and maintenance of interorganisational relationships is of primary importance for the sales force to undertake.

4 Appraise the effective mix of the communication tools for selling through multiple channels.

A company's sales accounts can be categorised within a simple matrix, where the dimensions of potential account attractiveness and strength of relationship form the two axes. By understanding the different value that customers represent, so marketing communication resources, including personal selling, can be allocated accordingly. This matrix approach can reduce costs and improve levels of customer satisfaction and strengthen key relationships.

5 Appreciate the broad ways in which sales managers can manage the sales force.

The performance of salespeople is a measure of both their task-related behaviours and the results of their activities and inputs. Therefore, a sales management control strategy should refer to the degree to which sales managers actively manage the inputs as well as reward against targeted outcomes (sales, market share and ROI).

Sales management control can be affected through behaviour-based systems, based on managing the inputs or processes to a salesperson and rewarding with a high fixed salary and low commission. Conversely, control through outcome-based approaches is characterised by a focus on results, little managerial supervision and direction, and high levels of commission as an incentive to perform.

6 Determine the role and key characteristics of key account management.

Key accounts are customers who, in a business-to-business market, are willing to enter into relational exchanges, who are of strategic importance to the focus organisation and which attract dedicated resources.

These accounts are so important that a Key Account Manager is normally appointed to manage and develop the relationship. To support them some companies assign sales executives, create a key account division or create a key account sales force.

■ Discussion Questions

1 Describe the role of personal selling and highlight its main strengths and weaknesses.

2 Make a list of those factors that need to be considered when determining the size and role of personal selling in the promotional mix.

3 Explain the three methods used to determine the optimal size of the sales force.

4 Evaluate the way in which direct marketing might be best used to assist personal selling activities.

5 Suggest four ways in which technology could be used by a sales force to improve its performance.

6 Appraise the role of the key account manager and evaluate the extent to which they are just sales people responsible for very important accounts.

References

Abratt, R. and Kelly, P.M. (2002) Perceptions of a successful key account management program, *Industrial Marketing Management*, **31** (5) (August), 467–476

Anderson, R.E. (1996) Personal selling and sales management in the new millennium, *Journal of Personal Selling and Sales Management*, **14** (4) (Fall), 17–32

Archer, P. (2011) At the crossroads of innovation, *Raconteuron*, 10 March 2011, p.1

Baldauf, A., Cravens, D.W. and Grant, K. (2002) Consequences of sales management control in field sales organisations: a cross-national perspective, *International Business Review*, **11** (5) (October), 577–609

Benedapudi, N. and Leone, R.P. (2002) Managing business-to-business customer relationships following key contact employee turnover in a vendor firm, *Journal of Marketing*, **66** (April), 83–101.

Cravens, D.W. (1987) *Strategic Marketing*, Homewood, IL: Irwin.

Cravens, D.W., Ingram, T.N. and La Forge, R.W. (1991). Evaluating multiple channel strategies, *Journal of Business and Industrial Marketing*, **6** (3/4), 37–48

Cronin, J. and Taylor, S. (1992). Measuring service quality: a reexamination and extension, *Journal of Marketing*, **56** (July), 55–68

Cross, J., Hartley, S.W., Rudelius, W. and Vassey, M.J. (2001).Sales force activities and marketing strategies in industrial firms: relationships and implications, *Journal of Personal Selling and Sales Management*, **21** (3) (Summer), 199–206.

Downie, I. (2011) Why events make business sense, *Raconteuron*, 10 March 2011, p.3

Dwyer, F.R., Schurr, P.H. and Oh, S. (1987) Developing buyer–seller relationships, *Journal of Marketing*, **51**, 11–27

Ford, I.D. (1980). The development of buyer–seller relationships in industrial markets, *European Journal of Marketing*, **14** (5/6), 339–353

Grant, K. and Cravens, D.W. (1999) Examining the antecedents of sales organisation effectiveness: an Australian study, *European Journal of Marketing*, **33** (9/10), 945–957

Guenzi, P. (2002). Sales force activities and customer trust, *Journal of Marketing Management*, **18**, 749–778

Hannah, G. (1998). From transactions to relationships – challenges for the national account manager, *Journal of Marketing and Sales* (SA), **4** (1), 30–33

Ingram, T.N., LaForge, R.W. and Leigh, T.W. (2002) Selling in the new millennium, *Industrial Marketing Management*, **32** (7) (October), 559–567

Keillor, B., Parker, R.S. and Pettijohn, C.E. (2000) Relationship orientated characteristics and individual salesperson performance, *Journal of Business and Industrial Marketing*, **15** (1), 7–22.

Kelly, S. (1992). Developing customer orientation among service employees, *Journal of the Academy of Marketing Sciences*, **20** (1), 27–36

Kern (2010) Kern Precision Weighing, B2B Marketing Awards, The Winners, *B2B Marketing Awards 2010*, p. 4

Levitt, T. (1967) Communications and industrial selling, *Journal of Marketing*, **31** (April), 15–21

Liu, A.H. and Leach, M.P. (2001) Developing loyal customers with a value adding sales force: examining customer satisfaction and the perceived credibility of consultative salespeople, *Journal of Personal Selling and Sales Management*, **21** (2) (Spring), 147–156.

Marshall, G.W., Moncrief, W.C. and Lassk, F.G. (1999) The current state of sales force activities, *Industrial Marketing Management*, **28**, 87–98

McDonald, M. (2000) Key account management – a domain review, *Marketing Review*, **1**, 15–34.

Mehta, R., Dubinsky, A.J. and Anderson, R.E. (2002) Marketing channel management and the sales manager, *Industrial Marketing Management*, **31** (5) (August), 429–439

Millman, T. and Wilson, K. (1995) From key account selling to key account management, *Journal of Marketing Practice: Applied Marketing Science*, **1** (1), 9–21

Morgan, R. M. and Hunt, S. D. (1994). The Commitment-Trust Theory of Relationship Marketing, *Journal of Marketing*, 20-38

Morgan, A.J. and Inks, S.A. (2001) Technology and the sales force: increasing acceptance of sales force automation, *Industrial Marketing Management*, **30** (5) (July), 463–472.

Morgan, F. and Stoltman, J. (1990) Adaptive selling insights from social cognition, *Journal of Personal Selling and Sales Management*, Fall, 43–54.

Morrill, J.E. (1970). Industrial advertising pays off, *Harvard Business Review*, (March/April), 159–69.

Napolitano, L. (1997). Customer–supplier partnering: a strategy whose time has come, *Journal of Selling and Sales Management*, **17** (4), 1–8

Ojasalo, J. (2001). Key account management at company and individual levels in business-to-business relationships, *Journal of Business and Industrial Marketing*, **16** (3), 199–220.

Pardo, C. (1997). Key account management in the business-to-business field: the key accounts point-of-view, *Journal of Selling and Sales Management*, **17** (4), 17–26.

Piercy, N.F., Cravens, D.W. and Morgan, N.A. (1998) Salesforce performance and behaviour-based management processes in business-to-business sales organisations, *European Journal of Marketing*, **32** (1/2), 79–100

Reid, A., Pullins, E.B. and Plank, R.E. (2002) The impact of purchase situation on salesperson communication behaviors in business markets, *Industrial Marketing Management*, **31** (3), 205–213

Richards, K.A. and Jones, E. (2009) Key account management: adding elements of account fit to an integrative theoretical framework, *Journal of Personal Selling & Sales Management*, **XXIX** (4) (Fall), 305–320.

Saxe, R. and Weitz, B. (1982) The SOCO scale: a measure of the customer orientation of salespeople, *Journal of Marketing Research*, **19** (August), 343–351

Sharma, A. (1997). Who prefers key account management program? An investigation of business buying behaviour and buying firm characteristics, *Journal of Personal Selling and Sales Management*, **17** (4), 27–39.

Spencer, R. (1999) Key accounts: effectively managing strategic complexity, *Journal of Business & Industrial Marketing*, **14** (4), 291–310

Srivastava, R.K., Shervani, T.A. and Fahey, L. (1999) Marketing, business process and shareholder value: an organizationally embedded view of marketing activities and the discipline of marketing, *Journal of Marketing*, **63**, 168–179

Swinyard, W.R. and Ray, M.L. (1977) Advertising–selling interactions: an attribution theory experiment, *Journal of Marketing Research*, **14** (November), 509–516

Thayer, L. (1968). *Communication and communication systems*, Homewood, IL: Irwin.

Twentyman, J. (2011) Driving forward with high-profile sport sponsorship, *Raconteuron*, 10 March 2011, p. 11

Whiteling, I. (2011) People connect in marketing mix, *Raconteuron*, 10 March 2011, p. 4

Wilson, D.T. (1995). An integrated model of buyer–seller relationship, *Journal of the Academy of Marketing Science*, **23** (4), 335–345

Wilson, K. (1993). Managing the industrial sales force of the 1990s, *Journal of Marketing Management*, **9**, 123–139

Wotruba, T.R. (1991). The evolution of personal selling, *Journal of Personal Selling and Sales Management*, **11** (3), 1–12

Index

accountability in government purchases 13
acquisition of customers 102
advertising 20, 276
alliances 106
  eMarket 108
  types of integration 107
Apollo Aerospace Components 255
arbitration 224
attributes, tangible and intangible 34
audience in marketing communications 242

B2B marketing 5
  characteristics 18
BACS campaign 279
blogging 291
  corporate 296
Bombardier Aerospace 51
branding 252–255
  internal 255
brands
  and conflict in distribution channels 219
  communication strategy 3
  corporate 254
  in B2B markets 253
Broadstock Office Furniture 35
brochures and catalogues 286
BT 141
business channels 3
business ecologies 201
Business Ecology Initiative 200
business marketing communications 238–271
business markets
  and consumer markets 5
  buying processes 7
  characteristics 6
  demand in 6
  goods 16
  international aspects 8
  relationships 8
buyclasses 68, 69
buyer behaviour, business and consumer 64
buyers in high-technology markets 55
'Buyersphere' report 78
buying behaviour of organisations 63
buying centre 7, 66
buying processes in business 7
buying stages 68
buyphases 68, 71

campaigns 251
channel conflict 215

channel domain 219
channel exchanges 156
channel flows 160
  in marketing channels 162
channels of business 3
  communication strategies 263–264
  outputs 159
channel structures and technology 157
channel systems, formal arrangements 196
Cisco 123
Cisco Webex 295
collaborative exchanges 92
commitment in relationships 227
communication
  and managing conflict 222
  effectiveness 310–313
  in marketing channels 262–263
communications, relationship-based 266–267
conflict
  and competition 217
  in channels 215
  management of 221–223
  nature of 216–237
  reasons for 218–237
  resolution strategies 225–237
  resolving 223–237
contacts, converting to customers 297
content in marketing communications mix 293
continuous replenishment programmes 189
convenience, customer access 159
cooperation 227
corporate entertainment 312–315
costs, reducing by routinisation 158
coverage 190
custom-built products 37
customer acquisition 102
customer relationship life cycle 101
customer relationship management systems 231–237
customer's needs and perception of value 22

decision-making process 68
  cuts both ways 63
  organisational and consumer 65
decision making unit (DMU) 7, 66
delivery time 160
demand generation 297
dependency in relationships 211
DHL, a service business 40
digital media and marketing 287–293
digital technology and buying behaviour 79

direct mail 281
direct marketing 281
disintermediation 157
distress purchase 192
distribution channels 162
distribution intensity 190
distributors 10
domain 219
DRIP elements 247

earned media 285
EC directives and government buying 14
eCommerce 124, 229–232
  and conflict 229
  strategies for development 230–231
efficient consumer response (ECR) systems 189
electronic channels 202
electronic data interchange (EDI)
  and channel formalisation 223
  and routinisation 158
  in supply chain management 188
email marketing 289
eMarket alliances 108
end-users in marketing channel 174
engagement in marketing communications 244
eProcurement 83
equipment goods 16
evaluation in buying process 73
exchange behaviour
  and relationships 98
  market and collaborative 92
  relationships 26
extranets 203

flows, timing 264–265
franchises 197
  and power in relationships 214
Fujitsu 138
fulfilment in supply chain 186

goals and conflict in channels 218
government procurement 71
government v. commercial purchasing 12
governments
  budgets and impact on purchasing 13
  in B2B markets 11
group purchasing 15

high-technology markets, buyer types 55
hijacked media 285

idea generation 49
industrial network analysis 100
influence strategies 215
information processing 42
input goods 16

inside-out pricing 140
institutional markets 15
integrated marketing communications 256
  advantages and disadvantages 258–259
  alternative concepts 260–261
  drivers 257
interactional theory 100
intermediaries in channels 156, 168
Internet channels 203
Internet-driven electronic marketplaces 229
interorganisational behaviour, study of 94
IT systems and supply chain performance 202

just-in-time systems 189

Kern Precision Sales 316
key account management 319–324
  in practice 323
  relationship cycles 321
key account managers 320

lean supply 82
leasing 143
life cycle
  customer relationship 101
  product 44
  technology adoption 54
living the brand 255
loyalty 104

Maginus 293
maintenance, repair and operating materials
    (MRO items) 17
manufacturers, role in channels 167
marketing channels 149–177
  and manufacturers 167
  business customer market 164
  configuration 191
  consumer markets 163
  definition 153
  design 190
  electronic 202
  end-users 174
  function and purpose 154
  intermediaries 168
  retailers 170
  roles and members 167
  structure 193–197
  wholesalers 168
marketing communications 242
  and relationships 265–266
  channel-based 261–262
  planning 249, 250
  role 243
  strategy 248
  tasks 246

marketing communications mix 272–301
  impact of Internet 273
  integration 256
marketing management approach 18
marketing mix 18
marketing plans 118
market segmentation 120–134
  and current market conditions 124
  B2B markets 122
  barriers to 133
  by buyer characteristics 127
  by market characteristics 126
  decision making unit 128
  methods 123
  models 123
media
  earned and hijacked 285
  in communications mix 285
mediation 224
mental stimulus processing 42
message
  appeals 296
  credibility of source 294
  in marketing communications mix 293
microblogging 291
mobile marketing 290
mobile technologies 202
multichannel selling 315–319
My Genius campaign 293

national account marketing 319
Nectar Business 103
networks 198–203
  and value chains 199
new product development 47
new service development 52
not-for-profit organisations 15

O2 campaign 79
Object Management Group 200
OKI Printing Solutions 287
Olympic Delivery Authority 5
online auctions 84
online communities 292
organisational buying behaviour 63, 60–87
  influences on 76
  perceived risk 81
organisational decision-making, types of risk 80
organisational interdependence and power 211
organisational marketing 9
organisations, types of 9
original equipment manufacturers (OEMs) 10
outside-in pricing 140

pants, importance of 273
partnerships 106

people processing 41
perceived value 21
personality depth/breadth 99
personal selling 283, 305–319
  and customer relationships 313–315
  and the communications mix 309–312
  channel factors 311–314
  characteristics 308
  cost 309
  roles 306
  tasks 307
place, in B2B markets 19
podcast 292
political objectives and buying decisions 13
Porter's value chain 23
positioning 135–139
  strategies for B2B markets 136
  tactics 137
possession processing 41
power
  in relationships 211–216
  sources of 212–213
pricing 139–144
  approaches to 140
  in business markets 19, 139–144
  methods 142
  strategies 141
principal marketing communications tools 275
product, importance of perception 135
product life cycle 44
  management 46
  stages 45
  technological applications 46
  varying strategies 47
products
  attributes 34
  catalogue and custom-built 37
  development of new 47
  in B2B markets 19
  launch 52
  lines 36
  reasons for failure 50
products and services 32, 31–59
product/service innovation stages 53
product–service spectrum 43
product specification 72
product strategy 36
promotion, in B2B markets 20
public contracts 71
public relations 279
  types 280
purchase order specification 72
purchasing journey 150

quick response (QR) systems 188

radio frequency identification (RFID) 173
raw materials 16
rebuy 70
reintermediation 157
relationship communication model 260–261
relationship marketing 21, 88, 98
relationships 25, 208–237
  and marketing communications 265–266
  and value 96
  background 93
  building 226–237
  business and personal 90
  close or remote 105
  different types 104
  dimensions of intensity 101
  impact of technology 228–231
  in B2B markets 8, 25
  influence on buying decisions 77
  liking the people you work with 209
  supplier/buyer 82
retailers 11, 170
retail models 172
retention of customers 103
routinisation 158
RSS feeds 292

sales management responsibilities 319
sales organisation effectiveness 318
SAP Business Objects 67
search engine marketing 289
segmentation
  see market segmentation
selling 303
  multichannel 315–319
semi-manufactured parts 16
service-dominant logic (SDL) group 96
service outputs 159
service processes 41
services 39
  as after-sale product support 53
  development of new 52
  Hewlett-Packard's 'PC Tune Up' 53
  Motorola's 'Total Network Care' 53
social exchange theory 98
social media 290
  applications 291
social networks 290
social penetration theory 99
sorting and smoothing 159
spatial convenience 159
Standard Industrial Classification codes 127
Stanley Tools 245
stock management in supply chain 184
strategic account management (SAM) 319
supplier
  multiple or single sources 73
  selection 73

supply chain management 179
  goals 183
  principles 188
supply chains 25, 182–190
  goals 184
  integration 182
supply goods 17

target market selection 130
technology adoption life cycle 54
technology and channel structures 157
telemarketing 282
test market 50
trade associations and conflict resolution 224
trade journals 286
trade promotions 277
trade shows 283
transactional marketing 91
transportation in supply chain 186
trust 108
  elements of institutional 109
  in relationships 226
  key factors 110
  managing conflict 222
Twitter 291

Unilever 17
used apple policy 47
user-generated content (UGC) 296
user journey 151

value
  and competitive advantage 158
  and relationships 96
  perception of 22
value added resellers 10
value chain 23
  and marketing channels 153
value creation strategies 97
value generation processes 24
value networks 199
  technology enablers 200
vertical marketing systems (VMS) 195–199
  corporate 197
Vestas, KAM example 323
viral marketing 275

warehousing, in supply chain 185
web applications 202
web-based sales 83, 229
websites
  and B2B communications 283
  design 288
wholesalers 168
Wine Society 187

Xerox 24, 247